Screening Culture, *Viewing Politics*

Screening Culture, *Viewing Politics*

An Ethnography of Television, Womanhood, and Nation

in Postcolonial India ■ *Purnima Mankekar*

Duke University Press Durham and London 1999

© 1999 Duke University Press
All rights reserved
Printed in the United States of America on acid-free paper ∞
Typeset in Scala by Tseng Information Systems, Inc.
Library of Congress Cataloging-in-Publication Data appear
on the last printed page of this book.

3rd printing, 2004

For Kamla Mankekar

Contents

Acknowledgments   *ix*

Chapter 1 *Culture Wars*   *1*

Part I *Fields of Power: The National Television Family*

Chapter 2 *National Television and the "Viewing Family"*   *45*

Chapter 3 *"Women-Oriented" Narratives and the New Indian Woman*   *104*

Part II *Engendering Communities*

Chapter 4 *Mediating Modernities: The* Ramayan *and the Creation of Community and Nation*   *165*

Chapter 5 *Television Tales, National Narratives, and a Woman's Rage: Multiple Interpretations of Draupadi's "Disrobing"*   *224*

Part III *Technologies of Violence*

Chapter 6 *"Air Force Women Don't Cry": Militaristic Nationalism and Representations of Gender*   *259*

Chapter 7 *Popular Narrative, the Politics of Location, and Memory*   *289*

Epilogue: *Sky Wars*   *335*

Notes   *359*

Bibliography   *395*

Index   *417*

Acknowledgments

This book has drawn sustenance from a large body of well-wishers, advisers, colleagues, and friends. Lorna A. Rhodes has combined all these roles. As this project developed, so did our relationship: from being a trusted adviser, she is now a trusted colleague and friend. I also thank Ann Anagnost, Susan Jeffords, Charles F. Keyes, and Edgar V. Winans for their guidance and support. Other mentors nourished this project in valuable ways. Ella Taylor introduced me to the promise of cultural studies and encouraged me in my work on television and the constitution of subjectivities. In the early stages of the conceptualization of this project, Val Daniel put the ball in my court and encouraged me to run with it; he taught me the value of ethnography, and for this I will always be grateful.

Fieldwork for this book was funded by a Fulbright-Hays Dissertation Fellowship (1990 1991) and an American Institute for Indian Studies Doctoral Dissertation Award (1992). One of the joys of this project has been the opportunity to forge long-lasting relationships with the "women viewers" I got to know in Vikas Nagar and Basti. My relationships with them were not always smooth or uncomplicated, but they taught me more than I can describe about representation, narrative, and the everyday struggles of women. This book owes more to them than to anybody else.

Excerpts of this manuscript have appeared in different incarnations and sites. Portions of chapter 1 appeared in "National Texts and Gendered Lives: An Ethnography of Television Viewers in a North Indian City," *American Ethnologist* 20(3) (1993): 543–563. Thoughtful comments from Donald Brenneis and two anonymous reviewers enabled me to sharpen my analysis in that essay and also in the rest of this work. A shorter version of chapter 5 appeared as "Television Tales and a Woman's Rage: A Nationalist Recasting of Draupadi's 'Disrobing,'" *Public Culture* 5 (1993): 469–492. I thank two anonymous reviewers and Carol Appadurai Breckenridge for their comments and am especially grateful to Lila

Abu-Lughod for her detailed suggestions for revisions and, most of all, for her encouragement. Portions of chapter 2 were presented at a panel titled "Space and the Field in Cultural Studies" at Crossroads in Cultural Studies, Tampere University, Finland, July 1–4, 1996; and at a panel co-organized by Ralph Litzinger and myself titled "Identity, Community, and the Local in Transnational Cultural Production" at the Ninety-fourth Annual Meeting of the American Anthropological Association, Washington, D.C., November 18, 1995, where I benefited from the comments of Orin Starn and Ken Surin. Excerpts from chapter 3 were presented at the Department of Anthropology, University of Minnesota, on May 20, 1998; the Screen Studies Conference, Glasgow, U.K., June 28–30, 1996; a conference titled "Mass Media and Representations of Women" held at the International Institute of Asian Studies, Leiden, Netherlands, November 6–8, 1995; and the Department of Anthropology, University of California, Berkeley, on October 30, 1995. At these forums I benefited from comments from my audiences, in particular from Ien Ang, Ann Gray, Donald Moore, Shoma Munshi, Sherry Ortner, Gloria Raheja, and Patricia Uberoi. A brief version of chapter 6 was presented at a MacArthur Workshop on Gender at the University of Minnesota, May 2–3, 1997; the Feminist Studies Colloquium, Stanford University, in May 1996; a panel coorganized by Akhil Gupta and myself titled "The Gender of the State" at the Annual South Asia Conference, Madison, Wisconsin, October 21, 1995; and the Gender and Society Workshop, University of Chicago, October 19, 1995. I am appreciative of comments from my audiences there, in particular, from Jane Collier, Malathi de Alwis, Karen Brown-Thompson, Lisa Disch, Norma Fields, Estelle Freedman, Joan Fujimura, Roshni Rustomji-Kerns, Arvind Rajagopal, and Parama Roy. I am especially grateful to Donald Moore, Mei Zhan, and Saba Mahmood for their thorough reading of chapter 1. Chapter 4 has benefited from the careful readings and thoughtful suggestions of Linda Hess and Saba Mahmood. I thank George Collier and Sylvia Yanagisako for their comments on different parts of the manuscript.

I take this opportunity to thank my editor at Duke University Press, Ken Wissoker, for his encouragement, guidance, and many kindnesses, and reviewers at Duke Press and the University of California Press. Cari Costanzo and Kathy Chetkovich helped copyedit my revisions of this manuscript. I gratefully acknowledge the help of staff in the libraries at India International Centre, New Delhi, and Goa University, Panaji. Susan

McMahon at the South Asia Library, University of California, Berkeley, helped me locate materials at a critical moment in the production of the book. I am especially thankful to my mother, Kamla Mankekar, for taking time off from her hectic schedule to procure photographs and permissions from television producers.

This project has been shaped by the influence and support of various members of my family. Even as he instilled in me a love of learning, my late father, Dinkar Rao Mankekar, taught me that the pursuit of knowledge is worthwhile only if it can be channeled toward struggles for social justice. His absence has been intensely felt, but his stubborn idealism will always inspire me. My brother Ajit Mankekar has never allowed his ambivalence toward my choice of career to overcome his love for me. He has not been unquestioning in his support—and for this I am thankful: his skepticism of my objectives compelled me to stay honest to my commitments. Other members of my family—Aruna Bhargava, Harsh Bhargava, Akash Bhargava, Gauri and Amit Gangolli, Lucia Mankekar, Aaron Mankekar, and Nina Mankekar—have given me sound advice, affection, and support. My parents-in-law, Jwala and Meena Gupta, and sister-in-law Anita Aggarwal and her family have always been generous in their love and in their emotional and material support. My aunt Kamala N. Mankikar and cousins Ahalya Katrak and Vijaya Bhatt sustained me with unstinting love and wonderful Mangalorean food during my fieldwork in Bombay.

Colleagues and friends in Delhi and Bombay participated in this project in various ways. Neera Desai, Sujata Patel, and Vibhuti Patel generously provided several key insights into nationalist constructions of gender. Urvashi Butalia and Uma Chakravarti provided friendship and sound advice at all stages in the writing of this book: I am particularly grateful to Uma for driving across the city on a frigid December morning in 1994 to give me detailed comments on chapter 3. Conversations with Kavita Choudhry, Anita Dighe, Razia Ismail, the late Akshay Kumar Jain, Ravindra K. Jain, P. C. Joshi, Azra Kidwai, Prabha Krishnan, C. S. Lakshmi, Iqbal Masud, and Patricia Uberoi enabled me to problematize the politics of Doordarshan's representations of Indian Womanhood. I also profited from discussions with Urvashi Butalia, Zoya Hassan, Neerja Jayal, Indivar Kamtekar, and Michael Watts on questions of agency and resistance. Radha Namboodri of Doordarshan-Bombay helped me overcome numerous logistical and practical fieldwork problems, and S. Venkataraman provided me with research and secretarial assistance. Swarna Rajagopal was a wonderful companion and guide in Bombay: her support ranged from helping me set up appointments with elusive film industry people to participating in endless discussions on representations of gender in Doordarshan serials. The company of Gautam Bhatia, Ritu Bhatia, Amrita Cheema, Nirmala George, Sujata Hemmady, Raje Mehta, C. Rajamohan, and Ritu Walia always makes "coming home" all the more pleasurable.

Other friends nurtured this project in various ways. Kathie Friedman Kasaba and Resat Kasaba always provided me with a home in Seattle. I also thank Anil and Pama Deolalikar for their hospitality and friendship. In California, Tara, K. P., and Ammu Mohanan provided intellectual, emotional, and culinary support. I will always be thankful to Aditya Behl, Lawrence Cohn, Jim Ferguson, Ruth Frankenberg, Beth Gerstein, Inderpal Grewal, Sharon Holland, Ralph Litzinger, Saba Mahmood, Liisa Malkki, Lata Mani, Donald Moore, and Parama Roy for their affection and their guidance. Julia Jaroch; Ethiraj Venkatapathy; Poornima, Arun, Ashvin, and Vikram Kumar; and Suruchi and Ravi Oswal are always generous in their love, hospitality, and good humor, all of which nurtured me during periods of exhaustion and frustration.

At Stanford, George Collier, Jane Collier, Carol Delaney, Paulla Ebron, Akhil Gupta, Miyako Inoue, Renato Rosaldo, and Sylvia Yanagisako have been unstinting in their support. All of these colleagues, together with Alice Bach, Joel Beinin, Rudy Busto, Gordon Chang, Estelle Freedman, Claire Fox, Sharon Holland, Terry Karl, Suvir Kaul, David Palumbo-Liu, and Lora Romero, provided an intellectual and political community that sustained me during a very difficult period. Ellen Christensen and Beth Bashore have helped and supported me at several crucial junctures in my career at Stanford. I am especially grateful to Cari Costanzo for her meticulous preparation of the index.

I continue to learn a great deal from all my students; in particular I have benefited from the stimulation, challenges, and feedback provided by Falu Bakrania, Robin Balliger, Tom Boellstorff, Victoria Bomberry, Shelly Cadora, Peter Chavannes, Rozita Dimova, Mimi Ito, Vivek Narayan, Samir Pandya, Amisha Patel, Aly Remtulla, Victoria Sanford, Becky Schweig, Aradhana Sharma, and Miriam Ticktin. Cari Costanzo, Aly Remtulla, Alejandro Rubio, Betsey Rubio, and Aradhana Sharma provided invaluable research assistance. Monica de Hart de Galicia, Samir Pandya, Aly Remtulla, Aradhana Sharma, and Miriam Ticktin have been very special allies, and have left me awestruck with their resilience and political savvy.

Parts of this book were revised in Durham, North Carolina, while I was a Mellon postdoctoral fellow at the Department of Cultural Anthropology. Ralph Litzinger and Charlie Piot made it possible for me to be at Duke and provided me with a safe haven. I learned a great deal about the power of fantasy from conversations with Anne Allison. With their hospitality and generosity, Anne Allison, Mahadev Apte, Donna Daniels, Kathy Ewing, Bruce Lawrence, Ralph Litzinger, William O'Barr, Charlie Piot, and Naomi Quinn made me feel welcome at Duke. Anne Allison, Cathy Davidson, Donna Daniels, Anjoo Fellner, Vivek Fellner, Ernestine Friedl, Carol Linden, Ralph Litzinger, Cynthia Rivera, and Ken Wissoker made my stay in Durham especially enjoyable.

I cannot begin to acknowledge the role of my partner, Akhil Gupta, in making this book happen. He has always been selfless and generous in his emotional, intellectual, and material support. He has been a colleague in all senses of the word, and his mark is on every page that follows. His quirky sense of humor and unstinting faith in me have enabled me to take on every challenge that has come my way. His courage, integrity, and generosity continue to inspire me. This book is dedicated to my mother, Kamla Mankekar, who has taught me more about feminism than anybody else. Her passion for women's struggles for justice, together with her courageous commitment to fighting for dignity and independence in her own life, will always sustain me. She has supported me in more ways than I can enumerate: from providing me with a home in New Delhi and helping me negotiate the practical, emotional, and political hurdles of fieldwork, to participating in discussions about the serials analyzed in this study and reading and discussing almost everything I write. Readers will sense that her presence suffuses this book.

Chapter 1 *Culture Wars*

In 1990 the monsoon was whimsical, full of still days and sultry nights. One afternoon, as my family and I set out from my mother's home in New Delhi, I sensed tension in the air. When we reached the main road at the edge of our neighborhood, we noticed an enormous crowd of people. We drew closer and saw that these were students with angry, resolute faces. The prime minister had been attempting to introduce legislation, known as the Mandal Commission Bill, to set aside quotas in educational institutions and government offices for people belonging to "backward" (lower) castes.¹ The young people thronging the streets were from two colleges near our neighborhood; they were protesting the Mandal Commission Bill. As someone who had grown up in New Delhi, I could map most of the educational institutions (and neighborhoods, bazaars, and cinema houses) in the city onto a fairly predictable grid of class. I knew that these two colleges were attended primarily by lower-middle-class students; the chances were very high that they were also upper caste. From their perspective, the Mandal Commission Bill appeared to snatch from them their very lifelines, their meager chances for upward mobility: no wonder they were so angry, so desperate.

Our car was soon surrounded by the students. A young man tapped on the windshield and I rolled down my window, full of foreboding but curious. Never one to panic, my husband asked the students why they had gathered. Never one to be intimidated by anyone, least of all someone a fraction her age, my mother demanded to know what was going on. "Someone just burnt himself," the young man cried. At a busy intersection less than a mile from us, another student, whose name we later learned was Rajiv Goswami, had poured kerosene over his body and set fire to himself in protest against the Mandal Commission Bill. The students had just found out; they were marching in solidarity and in rage.

"You won't be able to go any further," someone else in the crowd shouted, "You should turn back and go home." Stunned, we did.

Rajiv Goswami's attempted suicide unleashed a spate of violence that rocked north India. Upper-caste, (primarily) lower-middle-class students in cities and small towns throughout the area took to the streets in protest. Millions of Indians watched in horror as young upper-caste school and college students, all members of lower-middle-class families struggling to achieve upward mobility, committed suicide. The predominantly upper-caste print media sensationalized their suicides, portraying these young men and women as martyrs.

Media portrayals of the agitations against the Mandal Commission proposals foregrounded the middle- and lower-class (rather than upper-caste) positions of the protesters: in this manner, dominant discourses about "middle-class anxieties" displaced the presence of inequities resulting from caste differences. As lower-caste communities garnered their forces in support of the proposed bill, the Supreme Court stepped in to impose a stay order deferring all legislative actions until the violence in the nation's towns and cities had subsided.

The tension surrounding the Mandal Commission Bill had barely died down when Hindu nationalist campaigns to "liberate" a temple in Ayodhya reached a climax. Defying all historical evidence, Hindu nationalists alleged that this temple was the original birthplace of Lord Ram, and had been "desecrated" by the sixteenth-century Moghul emperor Babar, who built the Babri Mosque on its remains. Hindu nationalists portrayed the "liberation" of the temple as an attempt to avenge the "humiliations" of centuries of Islamic rule: reclaiming this temple became symbolic of a cultural cleansing that would permit "India" to recuperate its supposedly pristine Hindu heritage. In this campaign, which erupted in waves of Hindu-Muslim violence throughout the land, the Indian nation was represented as a Hindu nation (Hindu *rashtra*) whose "original" (read: Hindu) inhabitants would finally be able to assert their "pride" in their "national (i.e., Hindu) culture."

The Hindu nationalist coalition had been consolidating itself for several years, but in 1990 things came to a head. L. K. Advani, the leader of the Hindu nationalist Bharatiya Janata Party (BJP), launched a ritual procession through some of the holiest of Hindu sites to garner support for his cause. According to press reports, he was welcomed by mammoth crowds wherever he went; in some places he was greeted by men and women bearing urns of blood, their own blood, which they offered as tokens of their dedication to the cause of the Hindu Indian nation. In a few months, towns and villages across the nation reverberated with Hindu-Muslim riots. Some of these places had never witnessed communal violence before, not even during the apocalyptic Partition riots of 1947.

What a year it was; a crazy time to start fieldwork, and that, too, on television. I was never able to write fieldnotes about the afternoon I tried to leave my neighborhood and was stopped by the students. But I remember it as vividly as if it had happened yesterday. Even at the time, it felt like a harbinger of things to come, like the beginning of a war. What did my research have to do with any of this? I had planned to study the role of television in the reconstitution of postcolonial "Indian Womanhood." There were times when the fear of violence and restrictions of curfew made it difficult for me to conduct my research. Suddenly, notions of womanhood, community, belonging, nationhood, and culture were no longer abstract or "merely academic" concepts: they had become sites of violent, sometimes bloody, contestation. As I started to trace the role of television in these battles, my project acquired a new urgency. It was quite a year; a fitting time to start fieldwork on television.

What did television have to do with the battles erupting around me? The developments described above shaped and emblematized the late 1980s and early 1990s, the sociohistorical conjuncture in which this study is situated, and signaled the coalescing of battles for the hegemonic control of popular consciousness around issues relating to social justice, nationhood, and identity. The riots surrounding the Mandal Commission Bill highlighted the anxieties and aspirations of poorer upper castes for upward mobility into the middle class and the struggle of lower castes to survive in an increasingly competitive, acquisitive society with limited educational and job opportunities. Opposition to the bill reinforced the consolidation of the upper castes and middle classes as an assertive historical bloc. At the same time, the broadening base of popular support received by the predominantly upper-caste, middle-class Hindu nationalist elite reflected the hegemonic success of their supremacist ideologies. The campaigns to reclaim the Ram Temple reflected the manner in which the very notion of the nation had been communalized.[2]

As an Indian woman and a feminist who had returned "home" to do fieldwork, I was struck by the subject positions assumed by women in this reconfiguration of discourses of social justice, identity, and culture. Photographs, video reports, and my observations of the Mandal Commission protests and Hindu nationalist campaigns for the destruction of the Babri Mosque revealed the conspicuous presence of middle- and lower-middle-class Hindu women. When lower-middle-class and upper-caste men and women formed "parents' groups" to protest the Mandal Commission, women were at the forefront of these efforts. Similarly, women were actively involved in the organization and mobilization for the "liberation" of the Ram Temple. In fact, some of the most visible and vocal spokespersons of Hindu right-wing organizations were women.[3] Women were also actively involved at the grassroots in women's wings of the Bharatiya Janata Party and the militant Durga Vahinis. Indeed, when I now look back at the first few months of my fieldwork, two images stand out in my memory. During the protests against the Mandal Commission Bill, a metropolitan newspaper published an unforgettable photograph: a lower-middle-class and upper-caste woman in her late forties wearing a shabby, rumpled salwar-kameez stands with her hands on her hips staring up disdainfully, defiantly, at a policeman striding purposefully toward her with a baton in his hand. Upper-caste women's positions as parents, anxious about the future of their children, combined with their claims as citizens, concerned about the future of the nation, elided their privileges as members of the upper castes. In a video report of an effort by Hindu right-wing groups to destroy the Babri Mosque, the camera scanned the faces of a number of middle-class Hindu women of different ages. The expression on all their faces was similar: a combination of rage and an excitement bordering on frenzied rapture.

In the pages that follow, I do not intend to explain the processes by which some women were motivated to participate in conservative politics (see Tharu and Niranjana 1996). Nor do I mean to attribute these women's interpellation by reactionary, often exclusionary, discourses of identity and nationhood solely to television: the mobilization of lower-middle-class women into right-wing politics is complex and worthy of a separate study (see Sarkar and Butalia 1995). The point of the foregoing discussion is to suggest the historical and political contexts that underlie this study: the tale I want to tell is about the role of a popular mass medium—state-run television, Doordarshan—in the ideological construction of nation, womanhood, identity, and citizenship. This is a story about the role of television in the culture wars fought to define the Indian nation.

A comparatively new phenomenon, Doordarshan unleashed sweeping and far-reaching cultural changes in a relatively short time. Yet, despite its increasing cultural and political significance, until very recently it has been ignored in anthropological analyses of contemporary Indian culture and politics.[4] In part, this is a reflection of the relative absence of research on mass media in anthropology and the neglect, in Euro-American cultural studies, of mass media in "non-Western" contexts.[5] As a full-length, ethnographic study of television in a non-Western context, this book is an attempt to address those gaps in both anthropology and cultural studies. (Other ethnographic studies of television in non-Western contexts include Abu-Lughod 1993, 1997; Ginsburg 1993; and Rajagopal [forthcoming].) I aim not just to introduce a "comparativist" perspective to the cultural studies of mass media but to expand, perhaps revise, some of our fundamental assumptions about mass media, cultural politics, and subjectivity.

TELEVISION IN POSTCOLONIAL INDIA

State-run television, or Doordarshan as it is officially and popularly known, was first introduced in 1959 as part of the larger nationalist project of building a modern nation.[6] But it was not until the early 1980s that it acquired much political and cultural significance. In 1982 low-power transmitters began relaying the "National Programme," a two-hour sequence of news and entertainment programs produced in metropolitan centers, to viewers all over the country. The explicit objective of the National Programme was to forge a modern, national culture through the televisual dissemination of discourses of development and national integration. Entertainment serials were introduced for the first time in 1984. Although nationalist messages were woven into their narratives, the serials illustrated a crucial shift from overtly didactic programs to entertainment. The mid-1980s and early 1990s witnessed a dramatic expansion of television to different parts of India, with the number of transmitters increasing from 26 in 1982 to 523 in 1991.

With the introduction of entertainment serials, the state intensified its efforts to deploy Doordarshan in the task of creating a pan-Indian national culture (Krishnan 1990: 103). Entertainment serials (e.g., *Hum Log, Buniyaad, Ramayan, Mahabharat,* and *Udaan*) were phenomenally successful in creating mass audiences. The tremendous popularity of entertainment serials on Doordarshan can be measured from the fact that the number of television sets purchased increased from 5 million in 1985 to 35 million in 1990. By 1992, more than 80 percent of the Indian population had access to television (obviously, actual viewership was determined by the availability of power). The core of Doordarshan's target audience was the urban middle class: more than 75 percent of Indians who lived in cities or small towns watched television regularly for at least four hours a week. The serials, sponsored by private corporations and advertising agencies, also helped facilitate a critical shift from a capital goods to a consumer economy by creating and encouraging consumerist desires. With its political, cultural, and economic impact, Doordarshan thus became centrally engaged in contemporary battles over the meaning of nationhood, belonging, and cultural citizenship. Indian popular culture, and indeed, "Indian culture," would never be the same again.[7]

Extensive survey data are available on the manner in which Indian viewers responded to Doordarshan. For example, the 1992 National Readership Survey (NRS IV), drawn from a sample spanning 590 towns throughout India, reveals important facts about the impact of television in urban India: television viewing increased by 68 percent between 1978 and 1983, and the number of women viewers rose by 33 percent. The number of women who watched Doordarshan on a regular basis rose as well: while in 1978 only 46 percent of the women who owned sets watched television daily, in 1991 the figure was up to 62 percent. The NRS IV data also reveal that, on average, women watched up to eleven hours of Doordarshan a week.[8] But informative as these quantitative data are on the pervasiveness of Doordarshan, its reach among diverse regions and communities of India, and the gendered patterns of its spectatorship, they tell us little about the extent to which Doordarshan suffused relations of sociality within families and communities, the intensity with which viewers engaged with its narratives, or the degree to which its discourses constituted their subjectivities.

The entertainment programs analyzed in this study were drawn from the National Programme and were shown during prime time (that is, from 8:00 P.M. to 10:00 P.M. during weekdays, and from 9:00 A.M. to noon on Sundays).[9] The narratives ranged in genre from the mythological (*Ramayan* and *Mahabharat*) and the epic (*The Sword of Tipu Sultan*) to episodic sitcom series (*Yeh Jo Hai Zindagi*).[10] Many serials (*Hum Log* and *Buniyaad*, for example) resembled the Hindi film genre known as "the social" in their use of melodrama and social realism (cf. Vasudevan 1989 and Chakravarty 1989, respectively), and in their focus on the destinies of families, neighborhoods, and communities as well as those of individuals.[11] Most narratives had explicit "social messages," with themes relating to family planning, national integration, and the status of women woven into the narratives. At any given moment, more than half of the eight to ten serials and episodic series shown per week during prime time dealt explicitly or implicitly with nationalist themes. Although the social message woven into the narratives varied according to political contingencies (such as particular national crises or the needs of a ruling party), a significant number dealt quite centrally with women's issues.

A cross between American soap operas and popular Hindi films, these narratives spoke the "metalanguage" of popular Hindi films (evident, for instance, in the types of sets, dialogue, costumes, and music used [Krishnan 1990: 104]) and resembled soap operas in terms of audience engagement and narrative structure. Multiple plots, the deferment of narrative closure, and the buildup of suspense were important aspects of their narrative tone and texture. Further, like audiences of American soaps, those of Indian serials deeply identified with characters on the screen; unlike their more distant (although still passionate) attachment to film heroes and heroines, viewers' regular and relatively extended interactions with television characters fostered familiar, even intimate, relationships.[12] Since most serials and episodic series were telecast in the evenings rather than afternoons, however, they were not "targeted" exclusively at women or people who stayed at home, but rather at families.[13]

By focusing on the passions, fears, resentments, and aspirations that Doordarshan's narratives constructed for viewers, my aim was to engage the subjective bases of nationalism. As I commenced fieldwork, and as I started to look back on the creation of my own subject position as an Indian woman, I could recognize the power of nationalism—not as an "abstract" ideology of the realm of the so-called public sphere, but as a discursive practice that had material effects on the everyday lives of women. As my fieldwork and my memories of my own interpellation by Indian mass media nourished each other, I started to unravel the trajectory of Doordarshan's discourses in viewers' negotiations of their positions within their family, community, and nation. I began to trace how Doordarshan played a crucial role in the discursive slippages between "national culture" and "Hindu culture," and in the exclusion of experiences, memories, and modes of living not authorized by upper-caste, upper-class Hindu elites.

Although television constituted only one of many mass media, it was evident that it was one of the most powerful influences on how people perceived themselves. I became increasingly interested in understanding the relationships between the narratives of Doordarshan programs and those that viewers wove of their own lives, between popular culture and viewers' perception of themselves as Indian men and women. At the same time that I focus on the material effects of televisual representations of gender and nationhood, my analysis in this book highlights the fact that meaning is unstable: it is frequently contested by viewers who are historical subjects living in particular discursive formations rather than positioned by a single text.[14] While previous research on Indian television has generally dwelt on the political and cultural effects of texts (e.g., Krishnan 1990, Singhal and Rogers 1989), I have focused on the ways in which viewers interpret specific themes and images.

GENDER, CLASS, AND NATION

Indian Womanhood, exemplified in the ideal of the *Bharatiya Naari*, is an indigenous symbolic construct that predates the contemporary conjuncture.[15] Representations of Indian Womanhood were a major site of contention in colonial and anticolonial discourses, in which women were often represented as icons and "carriers" of tradition (Mani 1989) and nation (Chakravarti 1989, Sangari and Vaid 1989). Modified in the postcolonial context, notions of Indian Womanhood have continued to have profound significance for late twentieth-century constructions of identity. Not surprisingly, the state's efforts to harness television to the twin goals of national integration and national development have had a further impact on notions of Indian Womanhood.

Crucial among the policy and ideological shifts that occurred in the early 1980s was the resurgence and legitimation of laissez-faire capitalism, couched in the rhetoric of "freeing" the market in response to the pressures of global capitalism. Changes in economic policy at the state level coincided with (or, as some scholars argue, were necessitated by) the demographic expansion of the middle classes, who by the 1980s constituted more than 10 percent of the population. Being upper middle class myself, I was acutely aware that "the middle classes" were anything but homogeneous.[16] Indeed, some of the people I got to know in the lower-middle-class neighborhoods where I did my research were quite poor; others were relatively comfortable. Many were just a generation away from poverty. It seemed to me that they were precariously positioned along a slippery slope: all it would take was a layoff, a bad debt, or a failed examination on the part of one of their children, and many of them would slide right back into poverty. Those who were barely middle class nonetheless aspired to middle-class status via the acquisition of consumer goods (chapter 2); by their efforts to attain middle class "respectability" such as through the ways in which they socialized and disciplined their daughters and daughters-in-law (see chapters 2, 3, and 5); and in how they positioned themselves as citizen-subjects of the Indian nation. *All* the men and women I worked with were painfully aware of their financial vulnerability: their energies seemed to be focused either on striving to achieve a middle-class life or on sustaining it.

My research focused on the relationship between discourses and aspirations to "middle-classness" among the men and women I worked with, the discursive practices that embodied their struggles to achieve middle-class status, and their interpellation by hegemonic ideologies of gender and nation. In India, discourses of class and nation have been inextricably related from the outset. Partha Chatterjee characterizes anticolonial nationalism as a fundamentally middle-class phenomenon (1989); post-colonial nationalism has also been embedded in discourses of the middle class. It is hence not surprising that dominant visions of the future of the Indian nation are fundamentally middle class in their orientation. Even less surprising is the fact that Doordarshan officials, policy makers, serial producers, and advertisers conceptualized the expanding middle classes as their "target audience." Indeed, in its portrayal of "modern" middle-class lifestyles and its encouragement of consumerist desires, television seems to have played a crucial role in the cultural *constitution* of these middle classes as a powerful historic bloc.[17]

If the middle classes seemed eager to adopt modern lifestyles through the acquisition of consumer goods, they also became the self-appointed protectors of "tradition." This was especially striking in the case of the

Hindu middle classes, many of whom attempted to formulate their aspirations in the form of a strident, often exclusionary, nationalism. The 1980s had witnessed the reemergence of religious identities into the political arena. The communalization of nationalism seeped into Doordarshan's construction of "the Indian past" and its representation of national culture in terms of monolithic (and normative) Hindu identity. This hegemonic consolidation of a coalition of upper-caste Hindu power blocs into an aggressive, nationalist elite was accompanied by the state's deployment of its various apparatuses toward constructing a homogeneous national imaginary. Discourses of secularism, citizenship, patriotism, and modernity began to be reconfigured in the service of the vision of India held by this specific conglomeration of social forces.[18]

What were the consequences of the communalization of nationalism for notions of Indian Womanhood? Doordarshan occupied a central place in constituting female viewers not just as women but as *Indian* women. Thus, to understand the reconstitution of Indian Womanhood it is essential to unravel not just gender ideologies but also the construction of discourses of "Indianness." As nationalist discourses began to be reformulated from the perspectives of this increasingly powerful historical bloc, notions of Indian Womanhood were reconstituted accordingly. What (or whose?) experiences were projected as normative in representations of Indian Womanhood?

The material effects of Doordarshan's representational practices are underscored when we situate them in their sociopolitical context. The historical moment in which this study is located was marked by increasing repression by the Indian state. As secessionist movements in the Northeast, Punjab, and Kashmir gathered momentum, the constitution of *a* national culture acquired greater urgency for the state. And as discourses of national integration themselves became increasingly exclusionary, threats to the territorial unity of the nation increased. The state tried to use its manifold powers to squash dissent: the army brutalized thousands of helpless citizens in the Northeast, Kashmir, and Punjab in its campaigns to "weed out terrorists"; in states deemed "troubled areas," hundreds of innocent people were murdered in staged "encounters" with police and paramilitary forces that aimed, ostensibly, to "eliminate antinational elements." And when the custodians of law and order marched into riot-torn towns and villages all over the nation, they engaged in unabashedly partisan criminal acts of violence against the minority communities they had ostensibly been sent to protect. As I will point out in chapter 2, these acts of violence were erased in televisual narratives of national integration, thus indexing Doordarshan's complicity with the state's repression of all dissent.

Doordarshan played a critical role in the recasting and redeployment of the very notion of culture.[19] Struggles over definitions of identity, membership of community, and nation were often articulated in terms of culture wars. Doordarshan's role in these culture wars became evident to me as I traced the ways histories were rewritten, personal and collective memories recast, and notions of personhood, family, and sexuality reconfigured through viewers' active negotiations of televisual reconstructions of tradition and culture.[20] Viewers' engagement with television narratives was central to their constitution as gendered and national subjects, to their construction of national and communal pasts, and to their understanding of violence committed in the name of the nation—thus revealing the *political* significance of texts dismissed by many social scientists as fictive and therefore inconsequential, as "mere" entertainment or, less charitably, as kitsch. The viewers I worked with intimately engaged themselves with the characters and predicaments depicted in Doordarshan's narratives, thereby blurring the lines between fantasy and experience, fiction and reality. In the chapters that follow, I pay particular attention to the ways different narratives deployed specific televisual modes of address to "recruit" subjects as viewers,[21] as well as the culturally specific ways viewers derived pleasure from these texts.

The deliberate shaping and deployment of popular culture through a televisual mass medium enables us to trace the production of culture in historically specific fields of power. At the same time that this study focuses on the cultural and political significance of television in postcolonial India, it raises questions about how we may analyze the relationship between mass media and subjectivity and, more broadly, reconceptualize the place of culture in struggles over identity in the contemporary era.

THE ETHNOGRAPHIC CONTEXT: "THE SETTING"

From 1990 to 1992 I conducted ethnographic research with viewers of state-controlled Indian television who lived in two New Delhi neighborhoods, Vikas Nagar and Basti.[22] Working with urban women living in multiethnic neighborhoods enabled me to see how subjects negotiate and construct their identities in such contexts. New Delhi seemed a particularly appropriate setting for the study of nationalism: the presence of the nation-state was more overwhelming there than in any other Indian city I had known. Streets and parks were named after national leaders of India and, occasionally, other Third World nations (Kemal Ataturk Marg, Josip Tito Marg, Jomo Kenyatta Marg), testifying to postcolonial, ostensibly shared, dreams of national liberation and renewal. During the time that I conducted my research, the state was a major employer in New Delhi. At the time of writing this book, the city's landscape continues to be dotted with government buildings, government housing colonies, ministerial bungalows, and other reminders of the nation-state.

During the years I spent growing up there, and also during the time I did my research, it seemed as if New Delhi's identity issued primarily from its role as the capital of the postcolonial nation-state. At the center of New Delhi is India Gate: once a memorial to soldiers who fought in the colonial army during the First World War, an eternal flame now burns in commemoration of Unknown Soldiers who martyred themselves for the postcolonial nation. On hot summer evenings and sunny winter afternoons, middle-class families gather at the India Gate to sit on its lawns, eating peanuts and roasted chickpeas. If you look west from India Gate, the horizon is filled with the silhouettes of other markers of colonial and postcolonial histories. What used to be the viceroy's palace is now Rashtrapati Bhavan, the official residence of the president of India. Linking Rashtrapati Bhavan with India Gate is a huge avenue, Rajpath. If you move outward from Rajpath, you encounter other testimonials to the power of the nation-state: North Block and South Block, housing the Defense and External Affairs Ministries, respectively; the Central Secretariat; the cake-shaped Parliament building.

If you look at a map, it is hard to distinguish New Delhi from Old Delhi. But old-time residents can tell you exactly when they pass from one to the other: they say that the culture changes. People from New Delhi remark on the narrow streets and the press of pedestrians, cyclists, rickshaws, and cars in Old Delhi. (Of course, like cities throughout the world, New Delhi and Old Delhi perpetually reinvent themselves. Like many contemporary cities, they both seem to get busier, more crowded every year. And like cities all over the Third World, New Delhi and Old Delhi are gasping their way to the close of the millennium.) People from

Old Delhi characterize themselves as laid-back, courteous, and cultured, in comparison with the allegedly aggressive, rude, and brash residents of New Delhi. Old Delhi, they say, has "tradition"; New Delhi is a place where everything is in disarray. Folks from Old Delhi are quick to point out that New Delhi has no "regional culture" of its own. Unlike Old Delhi, which boasts communities claiming to be its "original" inhabitants, New Delhi's population is largely composed of migrants. Indeed, the regional and ethnic identities of New Delhi's migrant-residents exist in uneasy tension with the "national culture" encouraged by the state. For instance, even though Hindi was not the first language of most of the men and women I worked with, it was the language in which they communicated at their places of work, with their neighbors, with me, and to some extent even with their children. For all these reasons, New Delhi has the ambience of a quintessentially "national" city; in so many ways, it positions itself as the "center" of the imagined nation-space.

My mother, who lived in New Delhi, expected me to stay with her while I did my fieldwork in India. I had missed her terribly while I was in the United States, so I was only too glad to do so. Besides, my father had died recently and she was lonely; it felt right to live with her. I was introduced to the neighborhood of Vikas Nagar by Vani Krishnamurthi. While in India the summer before, I had mentioned my project to her and asked if she could suggest lower-middle-class neighborhoods consisting of people from different regional and religious communities. She enthusiastically proposed Vikas Nagar, the neighborhood in which she lived, and promised to introduce me to the people she knew there. I have used pseudonyms for the people I discuss in the following pages to protect their privacy.

When I started visiting the neighborhood, I realized that its class composition was not as homogeneous as I had first thought. Fine gradations and hierarchies were, quite literally, mapped onto it. On its northeast edge, Vikas Nagar was flanked by a very busy road on which was a cinema hall and some office buildings. If you entered the neighborhood from that side, you would find yourself walking through a cluster of two-story flats arranged around a small lawn. Most of the residents of this part of the neighborhood were employed as senior, or "upper-division," clerks in government offices, and were relatively securely ensconced in the lower middle class; they lived in one-bedroom flats with their own bathrooms, they often owned scooters (and, very occasionally, cars), and their children were likely to go to college. For the sake of simplicity, I will call this part of the neighborhood Division I. If you wound your way from this cluster of flats toward the center of the neighborhood, you would pass a huge dumpster, its contents overflowing onto the street. Chances are that you would find cows and stray dogs with their noses in the dumpster, rifling through its contents for food. Across from the dumpster was a narrow lane lined with more flats. These flats also had private bathrooms and one bedroom, but they were much smaller than the flats lining the main road. This part of the neighborhood I will call Division II. The residents of these flats usually worked as junior (or lower-division) clerks and secretaries in government departments. Beyond this lane was another cluster of flats, Division III. Vani and her family resided here, and this is where about three-fourths of my "informants" in Vikas Nagar lived. These flats were very small, about eight by ten feet, and each consisted of a tiny room, a kitchen, and a small verandah. Residents had to share bathrooms and latrines. Most of the residents were peons in government offices.

Obviously, the actual residential composition of each of the "divisions" within Vikas Nagar was far from monolithic and was a lot messier than I have described. Nevertheless, the areas did function as social divisions. One of the first questions people would ask when they made each other's acquaintance was: Which part of the neighborhood do you live in? Their behavior with each other would be shaped by the answer they received. Thus, even though both families were Bengali, the members of the Sengupta household, who lived in Division II, considered themselves a notch above the Dasguptas, who lived in Division III, and treated them with distant formality and reserve. Similarly, even though both Jayanthi Chandran and Sarojini Sukumaran took the same bus to work, they were not likely to socialize together: the Chandrans lived in Division I, Sarojini and her family lived in Division III. Jayanthi and Sarojini spoke of each other with regard, but they were both aware of their different statuses. Thus, I learned very quickly that even this interstitial group of people, all aspiring to become middle class, were divided by subtle class hierarchies.

When I started fieldwork, Vani took me on a tour of Vikas Nagar. She introduced me to the people she knew (as a longtime resident and an exceptionally gregarious person she had a large circle of acquaintances), who in turn introduced me to their acquaintances. Since she was popular and respected by her neighbors, I had little trouble establishing contacts and was able to make rapid progress in my research. Although most of the families I met in Vikas Nagar were struggling to achieve middle-class status, I was interested in talking to people who were still more precariously placed in terms of their class position. About three months later, I identified another neighborhood that suited my need.

Basti was a village until the city of New Delhi engulfed it. On one side was one of the busiest shopping areas of New Delhi. The other side of the neighborhood was lined by a wide drain containing the sewage of the entire area: the poorest inhabitants resided in tenements scattered along the drain. Unlike Vikas Nagar, however, in Basti the class positions of residents could not be predicted on the basis of where they lived. Like many other "urban villages" forced to coexist with middle-class neighborhoods, Basti had "developed" in an extremely uneven fashion. Scarce land and housing resulted in the sale of about a fourth of the plots to middle-class people who went on to build new, relatively fancy homes with modern plumbing and other indicators of upward mobility. All the people I worked with lived in the older, ramshackle houses. Much poorer than some of their middle-class neighbors, they all sublet tiny rooms within larger units. Yet most of them were relatively upwardly mobile: while many of the older generation were employed as household help in adjacent upper-middle-class neighborhoods, the younger men and women worked as assembly-line workers in factories or as clerks in private corporations.

A similar combination of personal contacts and luck enabled me to meet some of the residents of Basti. I began by contacting an acquaintance who ran a school for children there. Most of the teachers employed by the school were from Basti as well. My acquaintance introduced me to one of her teachers, Parmindar Kaur. Like Vani, Parmindar introduced me to her friends and neighbors, and, as in Vikas Nagar, I was able to meet a fairly large number of men and women with whom I could conduct my research.

In all, I worked with about twenty-five families, about half of whom were Hindu; the remainder were about equally distributed among Muslims and Sikhs. None of my "informants" was chosen "randomly": the people I worked with, the amount of time I was able to spend with them, and the intensity of our interactions were shaped by the circumstances in which we met, their willingness to work with me, the relationships we were able to forge, and a host of other contingencies. The families I worked with do not represent a microcosm of Indian television audiences: given the immense diversity of ethnicities and cultures in New Delhi, I deemed it neither feasible nor desirable to seek a "representative sample." Although I tried to meet a mix of people from different regions and communities, my "sample" reflects the volatile atmosphere in the city: the political context in which I did my research prevented me from working with as many Muslim television viewers as I would have liked. There were comparatively few Muslim families in Basti and Vikas Nagar, so I twice tried to conduct fieldwork in neighborhoods inhabited primarily by Muslim communities. Both attempts were frustrated because the escalating tensions between Hindus and Muslims resulted in curfew restrictions that prevented me from visiting these areas on a regular basis. I learned that political events can overtake even the most conscientious of research designs.

SELFHOOD AND SUBJECTIVITY

What subject positions were created for women at the center, so to speak, of nationalist discourses? As women living in the capital, and as urban, middle- and upwardly mobile lower-class women, most of the viewers I worked with constituted the core of the "target audience" of Doordarshan's nationalist discourses. The experiences portrayed as normative and "typically" Indian or Doordarshan *supposedly* represented those of the viewers I got to know. But how did these viewers respond to such depictions of "their" experiences? Further, televisual narratives seemed predicated on very specific, nationalist notions of Self and Other. What implications did these representations of identity have for women at the peripheries of these discourses; for instance, those belonging to minority or poor communities?

E. Valentine Daniel's theorization of Tamil personhood has been particularly helpful to me in analyzing the "fluid" boundaries of the selves that I encountered in my research.[23] According to Tamil notions of personhood, "a person is not . . . an 'individual.' A person includes his wife, his children, his kinsmen, his jati fellows, and even extends to include his ancestors and ancestral deities" (1984:103). I have expanded Daniel's notion of the fluidity of selves by focusing on how power, pleasure, and knowledge impinge on the construction of subjectivity at intersections of gender, sexuality, nation, class, and community. My conceptualization of subject constitution also draws in part, on the Althusserian notion of interpellation. Building on Lacan (1977), Althusser describes the process of interpellation in terms of the relationship between ideology and subjectivity: "Ideology 'acts' or 'functions' in such a way that it 'recruits' subjects among the individuals . . . or 'transforms' the individuals into subjects (it transforms them all) by that very precise operation which I have called interpellation or hailing. . . . The existence of ideology and the hailing or interpellation of individuals as subjects are one and the same thing" (1971:163). Stuart Hall explains interpellation as the point of recognition between subjects and ideological or signifying chains (1985:102). The concept of interpellation has enabled me to resist the notion of a unitary consciousness.

My understanding of the relationship between television and the formation of gendered subjectivities has been profoundly shaped by the critiques provided by radical feminists of color of the sovereign subject of Enlightenment epistemology and the monolithic Woman of Eurocentric feminist discourse (e.g., Alarcón 1990; Lorde 1984; Mohanty 1987, Sandoval 1990; and Trinh 1989).[24] In demonstrating television's place in the discursive construction of subjectivities, I draw on Trinh Minh-ha's notion of plural, nonunitary subjects (1989:22). I conceive of subjects in medias res, constantly being formed, never coming wholly to fruition. I reject the notion of a unitary consciousness, arguing that each person can be a contradictory subject "traversed" by a variety of discursive practices (Alarcón 1990:357, 365); thus redefined, consciousness is the space where forces of class, gender, race, ethnicity, age group, household position, and nation intersect.

My ethnographic research enabled me to understand the complex, sometimes unpredictable, links between televisual texts, viewers' interpretations of them, and the viewers' life experiences; in the chapters that follow, I demonstrate that viewers' semiotic skills were shaped by their positions along multiple axes of power. I posit that not only are texts polysemic, but subjectivities are multifarious as well. Since the position of the subject is an unstable, temporary one rather than a static sociological ascription, she is located in an interdiscursive space. Such a notion of subjectivity problematizes the relation between the text and the viewer: the notion of "one text/one subject" is changed to that of a "multiplicity of text/subject relations" (Morley 1980:166). In chapter 6 I analyze the role of televisual narrative in the construction of nationalist affect through the formation of ideas of romance, intimacy, marriage, conjugality, and duty to family. In chapter 7 I trace the role of a popular Doordarshan serial in reordering personal and collective memory through acts of remembering and forgetting. Throughout, my intention is to show how realms of our identities that we might mistakenly relegate to the "innermost recesses" of subjectivity might, in fact, be constituted through mass media such as television.

THE POLITICS OF THE POPULAR IN INDIA

At the same time that television played a crucial role in the state's project of constructing a pan-Indian culture, it was also condemned by cultural elites for "destroying" or "contaminating" Indian (high) culture. As Tejaswini Niranjana et al. point out, "culture has inevitably meant in our context the monuments of antiquity, the temple scriptures, all 'the wonder that was.' So when we turn to look at present-day cultural practices, weighed down as we are by the golden past and therefore by a certain notion of culture, we react with incomprehension, dismissal, embarrassment, or shame. Is it, perhaps, the very modernity of our culture that prompts this reaction?" (1993:1). What conceptions of class, modernity, and culture shaped these anxieties?

Discourses of class, gender, and nation seem to have been vital structuring principles in popular culture in India, and they have been *reconfigured* at specific historical moments. Feminist historiography reveals the centrality of discourses of womanhood to the politics of popular culture in colonial and postcolonial India. In nineteenth-century Calcutta, notions of "middle-classness" and gender converged in the "recasting" of the middle-class Bengali woman in popular culture (Bannerjee 1989). Discourses of middle-class womanhood based on the cultivation of genteel norms and domestic virtues were reformulated in terms of a new model of female education: "She must be refined, reorganized, recast, re-generated" (from "On the Education of Hindoo Females," in Bannerjee 1989:162). Feminist cultural critics point to two other moments when gender and nationhood were mutually imbricated in popular culture in India. As pointed out by Veer Bharat Talwar, discourses of gender and nationhood converged in Hindi women's magazines around the time of World War I, making a significant contribution toward the construction of regional women's movements and the nationalist struggle. Popular culture thus became a site for the nationalist "recasting" of womanhood. And in their edited volumes on women's writing in the nationalist and postindependence periods, Susie Tharu and K. Lalita highlight the articulation of discourses of gender and nationhood in terms of its implications for women's subjectivities (1993b:115), and posit that popular narratives provided a crucial site for the construction of notions of womanhood in postcolonial India (1991c, 1993b).

As I will argue in chapter 3, discourses of gender and nation in the anticolonial and postcolonial conjunctures have not been static or unchanging, but have been marked by sharp breaks, disjunctures, and reconfigurations. During the period of my study, representations of ideal Indian Womanhood in television narratives were essentially middle class, and were shaped by historically specific discourses on duty, family, and femininity. However, even as television's narratives seemed to reinforce dominant ideologies of gender, community, and nation, they sometimes opened spaces for subversive readings and, by creating opportunities for women to engage in social critique, enabled moments of rupture that forestalled ideological closure.

My conception of popular culture, subjectivity, and identity is indebted to Gramsci's emphasis on the force, as well as the contingency, of hegemonic ideologies. Hegemony refers not merely to conscious beliefs and practices but to a "whole lived social process as practically organized by specific and dominant meanings and values" (Williams 1977:109). More important, hegemony never exists passively: it is continually renewed, modified, and re-created in response to challenges from counterhegemonic forces. Indeed, alternative or oppositional elements are not merely important in themselves, they are central as "indicative features of what the hegemonic process has in practice had to work to control" (Williams 1977:113). For all these reasons, hegemonic forms are never static—they constantly work to transform or incorporate oppositional forces. In focusing on viewers' negotiation of televisual narratives, I have tried to emphasize the inherently unstable character of hegemonic discourses.

In the context of the culture wars ravaging India in the 1980s and early 1990s, the task of interpretation, and in particular the critical interpretation of popular culture, is itself a mode of intervention. Given Doordarshan's role in these battles over meaning and identity, to ignore the capacities of viewers to negotiate (and, occasionally, subvert) dominant discourses of nationhood and identity would be to discursively reinscribe the power of the state. Instead, by carefully examining the (limited) agency of national and gendered subjects, it is possible to forge theoretical and political strategies to resist hegemonic discourses. In this book, I explore the uses of ethnography as a strategy for constructing a political critique of the unspeakable violence carried out in the name of the nation.

Text and Context: The Pretext of Ethnography

Although I also interviewed producers, actors, policy makers, journalists, and activists, the analytical core of this study draws on my ethnographic research with lower-middle-class and upwardly mobile lower-class viewers. I engaged in "participant observation" with viewers as they watched their favorite television programs,[25] and followed up with repeated, in-depth interviews with them in which they offered interpretations of their favorite *"seeriyals"* and of their lives. I also "observed" their everyday practices and their interactions with the people around them. Rather than conceptualizing popular media in terms of a binary relationship in which meaning is "batted back and forth" between viewers/readers and texts (Hartley 1984:120), I have emphasized that the analysis of television cannot be reduced to the text on the screen, but instead must extend to the spaces occupied by television in the daily lives and practices of viewers. As we will see in subsequent chapters, these practices include viewers' personal and collective constructions of the past, their verbal and non-verbal interactions with each other, bodily enactments of experience, and the manner in which viewers organized space and time through their everyday routines and habits.

I deploy ethnography not to provide an empirical "record" of places or persons, but to explore how the production and reception of television texts are embedded in particular conjunctures. Indeed, the pretext of my ethnography is to evoke the contexts in which texts are interpreted and to demonstrate the inextricability of text from context. My strategy in this book is to *expand* conventional uses of ethnography by tacking between texts, contexts, and the interpretations of historically situated subjects, thus integrating textual analysis into my analyses of viewers' interpretative practices, the texture of their relationships, their daily lives, and their aspirations and fears. My intention is to demonstrate that by carefully reconstructing the relationship between mass media and the everyday practices, social relationships, and emotions of subjects, ethnography can enable the exploration of the material and discursive production of experience and, most important, the articulation of experience with structures of power and inequality.

My ethnographic research provided me with many instances of how television can create spaces for viewers to address what is happening in their own families.[26] Let me illustrate with an example. Surjeet Kaur and her husband Hardyal Singh were lower-caste Sikhs who lived in Vikas Nagar. A mutual acquaintance took me to visit them. Their home was the same size as others in that cluster of flats, yet it felt much smaller. The tiny kitchen was crammed with utensils and dishes; they hung from hooks nailed into the walls, and sat on the stone counter and on an old wooden shelf. The inner room was full of furniture. There was a narrow string bed on one side of the room. This was the only home in which I saw a dresser with a long mirror. Women's cosmetics lay on one side of the dresser; a set of teacups sat incongruously on its other side. In the center of the room was an ancient sofa and a plywood coffee table. Along another wall was a medium-sized refrigerator and a steel cupboard. Facing the bed, occupying pride of place, was a large plywood cabinet. A television set sat on one shelf; a second shelf contained a blender. It was an uneasy, claustrophobic space. Crammed with the bric-a-brac of upward mobility, the flat seemed to mirror the anxieties and aspirations of its inhabitants.

When I walked in, I saw Hardyal, very thin and with a flowing white beard, sitting by himself on the bed. He was wearing cotton pyjamas and a loose, striped T-shirt. My friend explained that I was there to talk to Surjeet and him about television. Hardyal said they had been expecting me and introduced himself. He said that he worked as a clerk in the Education Ministry but that he was on long leave because he had been sick. He was just beginning to tell us about his illness when Surjeet walked in. He immediately stopped talking. I instantly sensed the conflict between them; the room seemed to shrink further. As if to fill the heavy silence that hung in the room, I hurriedly and awkwardly introduced myself to Surjeet. I learned that Surjeet worked as an assembly-line worker in a garment factory.

Surjeet's relationship with her husband mediated her responses to television. Every time we met, she referred to her failing marriage in our discussions on television: indeed, she seemed to use our conversations about television to express her anger and, sometimes, to say things indirectly *to* her husband. One day, she began to describe a serial that dealt with a married couple (she couldn't recall its name but vividly recounted the story). She emphasized that the most important thing in any marriage is "understanding" and that without "understanding" marriage "is of no use." Her tone (anger? bitterness?) made it very plain to me that she was referring to her own marriage. She proceeded to say that she went to her neighbors' flat to watch television when she was upset and when she felt she "couldn't stand it anymore."

Her husband's reaction confirmed that she was talking about their marriage. He had walked out of the inner room in which we were sitting as she started speaking. But it was obvious to both Surjeet and me that he was listening to our every word. Suddenly, he started shouting at her to get back to work and accused her of wasting her time by talking to me. She shouted back to him to keep quiet and, ignoring my obvious discomfort, continued to speak to me. A couple of minutes later, just as she was talking about not being able to "stand it anymore," he started yelling for tea. At that point, I think, she felt that she could not ignore him any longer. She turned to me and said that he resented my being there, and that the best thing for us to do was to meet at another time at some other place. Surjeet had used our discussion of the serial as an opportunity to vent her feelings of frustration and rage at her husband; Hardyal's angry reaction made it clear that her shot had hit home. Their tiny room seethed with the tension between them.

Surjeet's experience of her own marriage deeply influenced her response to her favorite narratives; at the same time, what she watched seemed to enable her to reflect on the direction her life was taking. Almost all the women I spoke with had weathered many storms; before long, I began to see how they compared the tragedies and conflicts they watched on television with events in their own lives. In addition to provoking commentaries about the narratives, television seemed to create opportunities for surreptitious conversations among family members. In the chapters that follow, I analyze these commentaries and conversations in terms of their implications for relationships between the pleasures of television and cultural power, and between hegemonic discourses of family, community, and nation and the interpretive agency of subjects.

Although I conducted interviews with men as well as women, I have focused primarily on the constitution of women viewers as national and gendered subjects. Rather than look for hidden meanings or hermeneutic "truths,"[27] my aim is to represent women's narratives and practices as *enactments* of their interpellation by television's discourses. Their narratives and practices—as much as my own in recasting and retelling what I learned from them—were mediated by our particular gendered locations along axes of class, ethnicity, generation, and life experience, and by specific interpellations, positionalities, and agendas. At the same time, I want my ethnography to highlight the materiality of interpretive practices: women's responses to Doordarshan's discourses had concrete implications for how they made sense of their lives.

TOWARD A FEMINIST ETHNOGRAPHY OF MASS MEDIA

I have tried to theorize hegemonic constructions of subjectivity *through* my ethnography, and thus to problematize binaries between "description" and "analysis," empirical research and theory. Yet, at the same time that I have drawn on the theoretical and political insights of ethnography, I have struggled with several troubling questions relating to ethnographic authority and the representation of the people I worked with and grew to care for. My thinking about these issues has been guided by the rich traditions of feminist anthropology and ethnography, and feminist interventions in the cultural studies of mass media. Interventions in feminist ethnography have focused on the relationship between feminist politics and the politics of representation, and have engaged in an interrogation of the potentials, problems, and "failures" of cross-cultural feminist analysis (Visweswaran 1994), particularly the cross-cultural study of gender (e.g., Abu-Lughod 1990a, 1991; Behar and Gordon 1995; Mascia Lees et al. 1989; Stacey 1988; Strathern 1987a, 1987b; Visweswaran 1994). Two issues are most salient to the representational politics of this text: the interventions of this study in the larger context of the production and dissemination of discourses on Third World women, and my own positionality vis-à-vis the women I worked with.

Viewers as Critics

My emphasis on women viewers' capacity to actively engage and negotiate the hegemonic discourses of state-run television stems from my desire to strategically intervene against the production, in the First World academy, of colonial and neocolonial discourses on Third World women.[28] Even as I analyze the construction of exclusionary narratives of nation-hood that marked certain subjects and communities as irrefutably "for-eign" and Other, and at the same time that I trace the trajectories of these discourses as they suffused everyday practices and constituted realms of fantasy, desire, imagination, and pleasure, I have tried to craft a feminist ethnography of the creative ways in which viewers negotiated televisual narratives.

The women I worked with were able to critique televisual discourses at the same time that they intimately engaged them. Aparna Dasgupta was a middle-aged Bengali woman who lived in a tiny one-room flat in Vikas Nagar with her husband, two sons, three daughters, and two grand-children. She had never been to school but said that she had learned a lot from observing people. She thought that I, for all my "foreign" educa-tion, was extremely naive about "what really goes on in families." She was a gentle and wise teacher and often undertook to tutor me in the poli-tics of family relationships, the treachery of those "we" love, and, as she termed it, the "ways of the world." It was in this vein that she articulated her theory of television and its reception.

Aparna felt that television was powerful because one could learn from it (*shiksha milti hai*). When she was growing up, she said, women were not allowed to go to the cinema. Even though she had been living in Delhi for the past twenty-five years, she had never watched films until she started to see them on TV. In many ways, television was her window on the rest of the world. Not everyone, she told me, could learn from watching tele-vision: one had to have a particular *"bhaav"* (loosely, "feeling" or "emo-tion," although neither word quite captures the meaning) in one's heart.[29] One morning a couple of days after the last episode of her favorite serial, the *Mahabharat*, had aired, I asked her what she thought of it. She replied: "When you read the Gita, you should read it with a certain *bhaav* in your heart. It's the same thing when you watch something on television."[30]

But what was this *bhaav*? I pressed her for an explanation. Did it reside in the heart only to surface when we were touched by what we watched on television? Or was this a state induced by *what* one watched, that is, by experiencing something emotional unfold on the screen? If that were the case, wouldn't everyone learn something, the same thing, perhaps, from a particular serial? *Bhaav*, Aparna replied, was not quite so simple. She explained it with reference to her experience of Hindi films: "The first time I watched a Hindi film nothing much happened. But then I saw a second, then a third, then a fourth. Then one day as I watched, *bhaav* came to me [*bhaav aa gaya*]. . . . By then I too had a family. I was watching this film called *Bhabhi*. It was all about how this young woman suffers after she gets married. It was all about how you suffer in the world. How much the *bhabhi* [brother's wife] suffers! I just couldn't stop crying. I thought, suppose I have to face what she is going through, what will happen?"

This episode taught Aparna how to watch film and television narratives. One had to surrender to the mood of what was being watched; to learn from it, one had to be immersed in that state of being. And one had to be at a point in one's life where what was watched made sense *intimately*, at a level beyond mere empathy. This mode of watching, indeed of interacting, became clearer when Aparna recounted what had happened to her daughter Sushmita when she saw a scene from the *Mahabharat* in which the main female protagonist, Draupadi, is publicly disrobed in her in-laws' court. According to Aparna, when Sushmita saw what happened to Draupadi she wept for hours: the *bhaav* that "came to her" stemmed from her profound identification with Draupadi's plight and her fears about her own vulnerability as a young daughter-in-law.[31]

According to Aparna, we learn about life from the emotions (*bhaav*) that television's discourses arouse in us. However, interpretation operates within a larger set of discursive practices.[32] As Aparna patiently explained to me, one has to acquire the ability to learn from what is watched, and this ability comes from, among other things, frequent engagement. In addition, one must be at a particular point in one's trajectory, in one's development as a person; hence, the film *Bhabhi* would not have aroused *bhaav* in her had she watched it before she was married. She also insisted that not just anyone could learn: only those who, in her words, had an ability to "enter the soul" of what they watched could do so.

It is important to emphasize that *bhaav* does not emerge in a vacuum, a result of a text's "impact" on an isolated individual viewer; instead, we have to underscore the sociocultural bases of these experiences. Aparna was socially "habituated" to read the Gita and to watch the *Mahabharat* with a particular *bhaav* in her heart. Similarly, her unmarried daughter's tears at Draupadi's disrobing arose from her insecurity about her own future, a fear reinforced when she saw how other daughters-in-law (including her sister-in-law) were treated. These *bhaav*, these feelings and emotions, were products of the *social* relations in which they were embedded. In other words, emotions do not emerge from an "inner essence" distinct from the social world; emotions are "social practices organized by stories that we both enact and tell," and "persons are constructed in a particular cultural milieu" of experiences, meanings, relationships, and images, all of which are socially mediated (M. Rosaldo 1984:143, 138). Some of these experiences, "stories," and representations involve interactions between viewers located in particular sociocultural contexts and the texts of mass media such as television: far from being innate, many emotions are themselves produced by social practices mediated, and sometimes created, by television's narratives.

But are we to conclude that all women who watch television programs automatically assume the subject positions created by the discourses of television? I found that even as they deeply identified with characters on television, even as they experienced profound *bhaav*, many viewers were *simultaneously* able to stand back and critique what they watched. Neither they nor I saw any contradiction between these two apparently divergent modes of viewing. The women I spoke with loved to critique the acting ability of the cast or the competence of the director. Similarly, they would often comment among themselves that, for example, a particular set was "stagey," or that the "photographer" had done a "boring job" (in this case I think the person was saying something about camera angles).[33]

Many women had definite opinions about what TV "ought to" depict— that is, about appropriate or inappropriate subject matter. Surjeet Kaur was an accomplished storyteller who could narrate the sagas of *seeriyals* (and of her life) in intricate detail and with great flourish. But she complained that some *seeriyals* encouraged people's "superstitions." She felt that there was no place for "this sort of thing" (*aisi batein*) on TV *seeriyals* because "superstition" (*andh vishwas*) was "wrong" (*galt*).

Further, Surjeet Kaur, like many other women I spoke to, had definite ideas about the style in which stories should be told, how narratives should unfold, and, most of all, how tensions and conflicts in the narrative ought to be resolved. She thought TV producers were sometimes very careless about how they constructed stories: "You know how they make *seeriyals*—they pull from here, cut from there, try to patch a story together somehow." What she disliked most were the conclusions of many *seeriyals*. They concluded too abruptly; nothing seemed to be resolved (*koi faisla hi nahi hota*), and one never got a sense of "what really happened" in the end. She added that they all seemed to be cut off suddenly and speculated that perhaps most of the time they ended before "the original story" (that is, the script) had concluded.[34]

More important, most of the men and women I talked with were acutely conscious that the programs they watched had been selected, censored, and shaped by the state.[35] They often commented that when secessionist movements threatened the territorial unity of the nation-state, a spate of narratives dealing with Punjab and Kashmir appeared. One young woman complained that although she enjoyed the stories, she was getting tired of "the same old themes." Some of them saw even more direct connections between the plots of *seeriyals* and the political motivations of the ruling party. When I asked one viewer if he enjoyed watching these programs, he replied that he had enjoyed them until a few months ago but that ever since V. P. Singh, then prime minister of India, had come to power, the programs had deteriorated. "All they show now," he complained, "is villagers and their problems." Indeed, the prime minister was then making statements about a need to "bridge the gap" between cities and "the real India," that is, "village India." This person, along with countless others who pointed out the same thing, was quite astute in grasping why audiences were suddenly being subjected to a number of hastily produced programs set in villages.

Television watching, I sensed, had gradually become a site for people to complain about the power (and, very often, the stupidity: "They must be very stupid [*bewaqoof*] to think we're this gullible!") of the government. However, we need to be extremely cautious about concluding that this critical awareness signifies that people are somehow "outside" the reach of the state, or that they simply "resist" dominant discourses received through television. Viewers' responses to what they watch cannot be encompassed by categories such as "resistance" and "compliance." Oppositional readings, as I hope to demonstrate, are a lot more complex and a great deal more slippery.

For instance, the women I interviewed often "complied" with one of the multiple discourses constituting a serial but then appropriated another to criticize the government. One of my conversations with Surjeet Kaur began with her recapitulation of a particularly emotional episode of *The Sword of Tipu Sultan*, a controversial depiction of an eighteenth-century king. The main theme of that episode, according not just to Surjeet Kaur but also to the others present, was the loyalty of Haider Ali, an important character, to his friends. Surjeet Kaur used this story to contrast Haider Ali with present-day politicians who betrayed their supporters. She launched into a detailed description of the joy experienced by Haider and his friend Ramchander when they reunited after several years, and she pointed out that when he became king, Haider remembered his promise to help Ramchader. She exclaimed: "Haider never betrayed his childhood friendship [*bachpan ki dosti*], he bridged the huge divide between himself and Ramchander." Surjeet Kaur summarized the story thus: "This story is about a king and his friend, about a poor friend and a king" (*yeh kahani hai ek dost aur ek raja, ek garib dost aur ek raja ke bare mein*). She continued:

> Isn't that the way it should be? Not as it is in our country now. That's now how it is now. Whether it's a *raja* [king] or a P.M. [Eng.], they're only interested in keeping their seat [Eng.], their treasury. The people can starve to death, but they don't care. Who cares about the people? When it's time for their election, they [politicians] come with their hands folded and say, "We'll do this for you, we'll do that for you." What will you [politicians] do [*Kya karoge tum*]? You only come to us when you need us. Otherwise who asks about us? Now look, we have to pay five rupees a kilo for onions. Imagine [*bataiye*]! How are people like us to manage? It's true that the government has increased pay scales. But it doesn't make any difference. I would rather they kept prices down.

Thus, intense emotional involvement occurred *simultaneously* with a critical awareness that enabled some women to "see through" the narrative to the agenda of the state. At the same time, while many of the viewers I met seemed extremely aware of the power of the state, television, through *bhaav*, also informed them, in a frighteningly fundamental way, about their place in the world. They learned about their position as gendered subjects, and as Indians, from *bhaav* as it mediated their interpretations of television's discourses.

My insistence on foregrounding women's agency (defined here in terms of their ability to actively engage with, appropriate, challenge, or subvert the hegemonic discourses of Doordarshan) is not just an intervention against dominant conceptions of audiences of mass media as passive consumers; it is also an intervention against the representation of Third World women as helpless victims of a totalizing patriarchal "system" (cf. Mohanty 1984).[36] These stereotypes continue to haunt representations of Indian women in academic and popular literature, in which images of sati, purdah, and bride burning have become iconic of the subordination and passivity of "the Indian Woman." As we saw above, however, resistance and compliance are not mutually exclusive categories, and the role of television in the constitution of women's subjectivities cannot be conceptualized in terms of one or the other: with many women viewers, one level of engagement frequently slid into the other. The complexity of resistance has been well demonstrated by Lila Abu-Lughod, who talks of how Bedouin women both resist and support existing systems of power (1990a:47), and, in the context of popular culture, by Janice Radway (1984), who describes how women's resistance is embodied in the act of reading romance novels even as it is sometimes undercut by the content of the fiction. This reconceptualization of resistance and compliance has implications not just for how we interpret the constitution of women's subjectivities but also, more generally, for how we may conceptualize popular culture. Thus understood, popular culture is a *site of struggle* between dominant discourses and forces of resistance: popular culture contains "points of resistance" as well as "moments of supersession"; it forms a "battlefield where no once-for-all victories are obtained but where there are always strategic positions to be won and lost" (Hall 1981:233).

By charting the construction of identity in terms of hegemonic discourses of Self and Other, I analyze how Doordarshan texts produced or effaced differences *among* women: I underscore differences and inequalities among the women I describe by focusing on the positions they occupied along various axes of power. Further, by focusing on women's varying abilities to naturalize, appropriate, or subvert dominant discourses as they negotiate their positions in the family, community, and nation, I have tried to *problematize* (rather than efface or romanticize) women's agency as they responded to, and participated in, the construction of hegemonic discourses. I am interested in tracing what Richard Johnson calls "the subjective aspects of struggle," the "moments in subjective flux when social subjects . . . produce accounts of who they are, as conscious political agents, that is, constitute themselves, politically" (1986:69). Put another way, the narratives I want to construct are about women who construct their own (hi)stories, but not as they please and not in conditions of their own choosing.

Fieldwork and Positionality

Ethnographies conventionally begin with an arrival scene that invokes realist tropes of "the setting" and serves to introduce "the natives" to readers.[37] I begin and end this book with my *return* to New Delhi in order to problematize my project of doing fieldwork "at home."[38] Fieldwork, especially for those with long-standing emotional and political ties to our field sites, does not unfold in a linear trajectory, beginning with arrival in the field and ending with the publication of the book or the monograph, but instead consists of continuing engagements with our "informants." Our fieldwork is shaped by multiple temporalities. By using the trope of return, I highlight my positionality as an ethnographer trained and based "elsewhere."

My return to India was shaped not by a nostalgic search for roots or origins but by the complexities of doing ethnographic research in the cultural context that shaped my own subjectivity. My positionality as an Indian woman seeking to analyze discourses of "Indian Womanhood" is complicated, in part, by my own troubled nationalism. As subsequent chapters in this book will demonstrate, my examination of the structures of feeling that formed a large part of my own subjectivity has been fraught with ambivalence. In part, my hesitation stems from my discomfort about the uncritical use of personal experience that rests on unexamined assumptions about the individual as the locus of all knowledge:[39] ironically, texts that might otherwise build on poststructuralist understandings of subjectivity often display a curious narcissism and unproblematized assumptions about authorial intentions.[40] Personal experience, as Dorinne Kondo cautions us, is "itself a discursive production underlain by certain theoretical assumptions, and what is conventionally conceived as "theory" is always already a position in which a positioned subject has 'personal' stakes" (1990:303–304).[41] While I have built on feminist deployments of personal experience as a means to construct social analyses, this is not a study about my subjectivity or identity. Yet, as noted above, as a postcolonial Indian woman socialized into the very discourses of Indian Womanhood that I critique, my own subjectivity is inextricably entangled with this study.

In his discussion of the challenges of studying his own community, José Limón writes that his research has been shaped by his position in two sites: on the one hand, he is "born and bred of the place" that he studies; on the other hand, he has "also become simultaneously of another place as well, a child of the Enlightenment, of high literary modernism, of classical anthropology" (1991:116). Like Limón, my perspective on the men and women I worked with has been shaped not only by my upbringing as a middle-class Indian woman, but also by my training in anthropology and feminist theory, and by my participation in intellectual and political struggles within and outside the U.S. academy. In the chapters that follow, I present my experiences not as authentic referents for my theorizing, but as themselves implicated in the discursive formations that I analyze. Raymond Williams's conception of structures of feeling can be especially relevant to feminist critics who study our "own" culture: through the investigation of our structures of feeling, feminist critics may not just locate our positionalities, but may do so in order to stake claims, mark positions, and identify political and moral vantage points from which to launch our critiques.[42]

My attempts to denaturalize discourses of gender and nationalism in India have been mediated by an examination of the politics of my location as an ethnographer doing research at home.[43] In the 1980s, feminists such as Biddy Martin (1986), Chandra Mohanty (1987), Minnie Bruce Pratt (1984), and Adrienne Rich (1986) were instrumental in problematizing unexamined notions of community and home. More recently, Mohanty has urged feminists to redefine home "not as a comfortable, stable, inherited and familiar space, but instead as an imaginative, politically-charged space where the familiarity and sense of affection and commitment lay in shared collective analysis of social injustice, as well as a vision of radical transformation" (1994:353).[44] Drawing on these insights, my aim here is not to assume a unity of purpose vis-à-vis feminist scholars and activists working on similar issues in India and elsewhere, but to work toward the creation of alliances arising out of common intellectual and political struggles, and in so doing to redefine my home(s).

Martin and Mohanty have argued that just as a unitary notion of Feminism as an "all-encompassing home" is no longer tenable because of its repression of different temporalities of struggle, histories, and agendas, neither is the assumption of essentially different identities within feminism (1986:192). Immigrants and diasporic intellectuals such as myself, who maintain strong emotional and political ties to our "homelands" even as we strive to create new homes in the diaspora through our everyday practices and politics, must frequently reconfigure our positionalities as we negotiate multiple political terrains in both our homes. Elsewhere, I have spoken of the importance of a political bifocality that can enable us to forge transnational political alliances and relationships of solidarity with movements for social justice in the homeland as well as in the diaspora (Mankekar 1994; see Grewal and Kaplan 1994 for an excellent formulation of transnational feminist coalitions).[45]

Cornel West suggests that the decolonization of the Third World is a "world-historical process" that is "associated with the historical agency of those oppressed and exploited, devalued and degraded by European civilization," and is centrally implicated in the "dedisciplining" questioning of canonical texts and paradigms (1987:194, 200). This project, then, is shaped by at least two sets of (frequently overlapping) agendas: to intervene in the culture wars taking place in contemporary India by denaturalizing dominant discourses of gender and nation as constructed through television, and to deparochialize hegemonic anthropological and cultural studies assumptions about mass media, subjectivity, and culture within the First World academy.

While I endorse Kamala Visweswaran's call for turning "to our own neighborhoods and growing-up places" (1994:104), I see the project of doing fieldwork at home as extending not just to the "native" ethnographer, but to all scholars with enduring emotional and political ties to the communities in which they do their research. Further, even though I have personal stakes in this project arising from the fact that this research was done, in a sense, at home, following Kirin Narayan (1993), I do not claim the "insider" status of a "native anthropologist."[46] Narayan critiques the insider/outsider binary underlying the category of the native anthropologist by pointing out that "amid the contemporary global flows of trade, politics, migrations, ecology, and the mass media, the accepted nexus of authentic culture/demarcated field/exotic locale has unraveled" (1993:672–673). She argues that we must instead acknowledge the positionality of all researchers, including those who study their "own" cultures, in terms of "multiplex identities" (Narayan 1993:673). In addition to the factors of class, education, emigration, and life experience pointed out by Narayan, I would add that our positionalities "in the field" are also shaped by the emotional and political alliances we forge through our fieldwork practices.

This formulation of positionality critiques not just a simplistic insider/outsider distinction, but also the subject/object binary shaping much social science research. The following accounts are intended to explore my particular location vis-à-vis some of the women viewers with whom I worked, not as a "celebration of communitas" (Narayan 1993: 679) but as a reflection on the relationship between my positionality and the production of my analysis (cf. Gray 1995), and as a theorization of the potentialities and limitations of my "partial" perspectives (Haraway 1988).

My "Informants" and Me

In some ways I was an enigma to the women I met in the course of my fieldwork: I was married and lived in America, yet I had come to India to spend a whole year, "leaving" my husband and my comfortable life to live with my mother, ostensibly to speak to them about television! They constructed narratives of my life that bewildered, moved, amused, and eventually, frustrated me. For some, the mystery was solved when they learned that I had been married for six years and "still" hadn't produced any children; they thought I had been asked by my husband to leave because I was "sterile."[47] In the virilocal communities that many of them belonged to, married women returned to live in their natal homes only when they were destitute, that is, if they were widowed or turned out of their "husband's homes." My return to live with my mother was interpreted as proof that I had been turned out of my "husband's home." One woman in particular was extremely protective of me: she recommended several home remedies that would enable me to conceive a child when (and if) my husband "took me back." Aparna Dasgupta was convinced that I had been "thrown out" because my mother-in-law had "filled [my husband's] ears with poison" against me. All my protests served only to make Aparna more protective of me. She responded: "See how innocent she is! She has been thrown out. She has come to live with her mother. And she still won't see what he [my husband] has done!"

At first I was touched by the concern demonstrated by Aparna and some of the other women. But as time went on and they ignored my protestations about my "choices" to not have children and to return to India and live with my mother, I grew increasingly frustrated. I learned what it was like to be cast as a victim. I was able to persuade Aparna that I was indeed happily married only when, the following year, I brought my husband to meet her. After treating him with the nervous deference accorded to sons-in-law, she relaxed and reconsidered her constructions of me. Thus, I learned very early in my fieldwork of the potentialities and limits of the imagination in forging bonds between women of different structural locations, and of the power of "partial perspectives" in the construction of narratives.

There were indeed times when I felt like an "insider" vis-à-vis the cultural contexts that I wanted to analyze (cf. Kishwar 1990). This was especially true when my informants and I discussed the politics of gender, family, and kinship that young daughters and daughters-in-law had to negotiate in their daily lives. When one young woman told me that she enjoyed cooking her father's favorite dish because she knew that, before long, she would have to leave for her husband's home, I ached with the knowledge that my marriage had changed my relationship with my father forever: even though I often returned for short visits, my "departure" from my natal home at the time of my marriage had been marked with an irreversible finality. When young women sought me out and insisted on walking me to the bus stop so they could confide to me their fears about their impending marriages, I remembered vividly the sleepless nights I had spent worrying about whether or not my in-laws would "accept" me: I had known that even for "foreign-educated," upper-middle-class privileged women like myself, the success or failure of a marriage depended not just on the conjugal relationship, but on the complicated politics of gender, household position, and kinship surrounding young daughters-in-law as well. To the extent that there were similarities and unspoken understandings between us, my position with regard to some of these women was shaped not by an "ineffability of difference" (Visweswaran 1994:27) but by the shifting, often overlapping, and sometimes contradictory registers of our identities.

Thus, it should not have surprised me that some of these women assumed that I had been "hurt" by my "inability" to bear children.[48] In spite—or perhaps because—of being a silent witness to her husband's and son's brutalization of her young daughter-in-law, Aparna would insist on advising me about how to "shield" myself from the alleged "cleverness" of my mother-in-law. Although I tried my best to persuade her that I had no problems with my in-laws, I often pondered what differentiated me from Aparna's daughter-in-law. Was it "just" my class? Was it my "ability" to make decisions about marriage and motherhood? To what extent did my class protect me from the complex politics of gender and family?

And why did my claims about my *choice* to delay getting pregnant until after I finished my dissertation ring false to my own ears? As my protestations became increasingly shrill, my own agency suddenly seemed very fragile. Clearly, privileges of class and cultural capital enabled me to travel from the United States "back" to India. But what discourses of gender and kinship constrained my mobility between my "husband's home" and my "mother's home"? At the same time, the overwhelming support I had always received from my parents and my husband, and, more important, the security I derived from my class position, privileged me in ways that would always distance me from Aparna and her daughter-in-law. As I began to recognize how my subjectivity had been overdetermined by my class and my family position, I was forced to question not just my assumptions about my own agency but also to reconceptualize the subjectivities of the women I was getting to know.

Instead of analyzing the foregoing accounts as "halfie" ethnography (Abu-Lughod 1991, Narayan 1993), I prefer to focus on the conjunctural and shifting registers of subjectivity. Visweswaran argues that "identifying ethnography asks that we exhibit and examine our alliances in the same moment" (1994:132). At the same time that my tale of my interactions with women like Aparna Dasgupta and her daughter-in-law serves as a "fable of imperfect rapport" (Visweswaran 1994:29), it militates against the conventional anthropological project of the discovery of Otherness through the ethnographic encounter: my positionality vis-à-vis the women I worked with confounded binaries of Anthropological Selves and Native Others.[49] I offer this account as a preface to my study of representations of Indian Womanhood. By stressing at the outset the multiple and contradictory bases of subjectivity through the interpellation of women (including myself) by discourses of class, nation, community, and family, and by emphasizing the differences and inequalities among women, I hope to subvert claims about homogeneity underlying official, popular, and academic discourses of Indian Womanhood.

Indeed, there were times when differences between my life experience and structural position and those of my informants were so marked that they *precluded* the building of "rapport." My relationship with Bibi Satwant Kaur, for example, a Sikh woman whom I got to know in Basti, was marked by tension and suspicion. I first met her when her daughter Parmindar Kaur took me to her home in a narrow lane in the interior of Basti. When we entered Parmindar's home, only Bibi Satwant Kaur was there—a tall, stout woman, she was squatting on the kitchen floor knead-ing dough for that afternoon's chapatis. When I greeted her, she looked up at me, stared at me for a few moments, then returned to her task with a grunt. On subsequent visits, she acknowledged each of my salutations with a grunt or a sniff. Whenever I addressed her or tried to draw her into my conversations with Parmindar, she responded in monosyllables. No-body else I met in the course of my fieldwork was as cold to me as Bibi Satwant Kaur.

Bibi Satwant Kaur, or Bibiji, as she was known, was a forceful woman who intimidated most of the people who knew her. But the strain be-tween us was not just a result of her formidable personality. She lived in a neighborhood that had been terrorized by Hindu mobs in the 1984 anti-Sikh violence; I sensed that her coolness toward me arose from the fact that she saw me as representative of a community that had betrayed the Sikhs. Through her silence she constantly reminded me of the complicity of Hindu residents of New Delhi like myself who had watched our Sikh neighbors being murdered six short years ago.

Her daughter Parmindar, who had become my close friend and a favorite "informant," sensed the tension between us. Her solution was to throw us together as often as she could. To some extent, Parmindar succeeded in easing our relationship: Bibiji gradually started to treat me with the disdainful courtesy she extended to other young women she knew. When she found out one day that, like her, my mother had also been a refugee from West Punjab, she thawed somewhat and launched into a long interrogation of my mother's life. Interestingly, while earlier she had always spoken to me in Hindustani, after that day she insisted on talking to me in Punjabi. Again, I present this story not as "a fable of rapport," but to underscore the shared and divergent histories between women variably, and unequally, positioned along axes of class, ethnicity, and generation: for all the (somewhat tenuous) overlaps in our histories, the fact that I, a Hindu woman, represented the community that had ter-rorized Sikhs like herself always stood between Bibiji and me. As we will see later, her memory of Hindu violence against Sikhs was to mediate all our conversations.[50]

My ambiguous positionality was also brought home to me on those occasions when some of the people I worked with forced me to con-front my position as an upper-caste, upper-middle-class woman, and as an Indian woman now based in the United States. During the Mandal

Commission riots described at the beginning of this chapter, lower-caste viewers would point out, perhaps correctly, that I would never be able to understand their predicament. After they got to know me, viewers like Padmini and her husband, Selapan, who were lower caste and working class, described the anti-Mandal riots as the latest in a long trajectory of violence that upper-caste elites had perpetrated on marginalized groups. I know that they never really believed me when I said that I supported the Mandal Commission proposals. Similarly, my residence in the United States was often mentioned. When my questions about their responses to nationalist discourses got too probing or too direct, or when my comments revealed my struggles with my own nationalism, women like Padmini were quick to notice it. What were my stakes in talking to them about nationalism? they asked. What did I care, they seemed to demand; after all, I had *chosen* to leave India.

Despite my delineation of the differences in class, cultural capital, and life experience that sometimes distanced me from the women I worked with, the stories I presented above are also about our attempts to build relationships of community and solidarity. Martin and Mohanty redefine the notion of community as "the product of work, of struggle; it is inherently unstable, contextual; it has to be constantly reevaluated in relation to critical political priorities; and it is the product of interpretation, interpretation based on an attention to history, to the concrete, to what Foucault has called subjugated knowledges" (1986:210).

I offer these reflections as a prelude to the chapters that follow. These interrogations of my positionality are intended as a prolegomenon toward the forging of community through an acknowledgment of the differences between my structural location and privilege and those of my informants, and through a politics of solidarity that is accountable and cognizant of its limits.[51]

Feminist interrogations of the insider/outsider binary are especially relevant to the positions staked by critics of popular culture. Several scholars (e.g., Modleski 1986, Morley 1992, Morris 1990, and Williamson 1986) have critiqued the "populist" tendency of researchers who so identify with consumers of popular culture that they neglect their responsibilities as cultural critics.[52] In light of the tendency among some cultural studies practitioners to celebrate the "resistance" of consumers/viewers, it is essential that we disentangle our attempts to understand the pleasures a television text may provide to its viewers (and, sometimes, its critics) from our evaluation of the political construction and consequences of these pleasures. Yet, the panoptic position of a cultural critic voyeuristically "watching people watch television" is equally problematic. In the following chapters I underscore my complex positionality as a feminist critic of popular culture by holding the pleasures viewers obtained from the narratives of television in tension with my critique of these texts.[53]

I started this chapter by outlining some of the developments that marked the sociohistorical context in which I conducted my research. It is to those conjunctural conditions that I return as I underscore the urgency of this project. The 1980s and early 1990s witnessed the increasing violence of the Indian nation-state; the hegemonic construction of an exclusionary national past; the demonization of cultural "outsiders"; the creation of increasingly rigid subject positions for men and women in the family, community, and nation; and the persistence of the state's efforts to incorporate, and thus contain, oppositional ideologies such as feminism. Yet, the hegemonic practices of the nation-state are never uncontested: "Whatever its official discourses might proclaim, the nation (and its traditions) is constantly being recreated: contested, fractured, elaborated, redistributed, and rewritten, as new resolutions are negotiated or, as is more often the case, effected. Its closures, therefore . . . are never complete, never total. . . . The closures of government are strategic and always haunted by that which they write out of their schemes or delegitimate" (Tharu and Lalita, 1993a:52–53). It is my intention in this book to explore the closures as well as the interruptions of these hegemonic discourses.

The organization of this book enacts my perspective on subject constitution. While the analytical core of my study draws on viewers' interpretations of television narratives, I will present specific television narratives as illustrative of the discontinuous *nodes of discourses* within which men and women were constituted as national and gendered subjects: televisual narratives thus form a point of entry into my ethnographic study of the spaces they occupied in viewers' experiences, practices, and everyday lives. A major thrust of my critique of nationalist discourses is that, as hegemonic narratives, they seek to create unitary subject positions by denying men and women a complex subjectivity. My objective, therefore, is not to "recuperate" or "restore" a unified subjectivity to viewers of Indian television, but to ethnographically represent the manner in which women (and men) were constituted as multiply positioned subjects through their interpretations of televisual representations of Indian Womanhood. The trope of return weaves through my text as I trace how viewing subjects are *continually* constituted by discursive practices of nation, gender, community, and class.

The rest of the book is divided into four parts, each of which corresponds to a cluster or node of discourses articulated through Doordarshan's narratives. Part 1 describes television's reconstitution of family; part 2 examines how television engendered communities; part 3 consists of analyses of televisual narratives of violence. The Epilogue briefly examines how, through satellite television, Indian nationhood has been further reconstituted along transnational axes of capital and desire.

Kondo claims that "theory lies in enactment and in writing strategies, not simply in the citation and analysis of canonical texts" (1990:304). In their appropriation of particular epistemological and representational strategies, the following chapters deploy ethnography as *a mode of theorizing* and exhibit different narrative voices. Chapter 2, "National Television and the 'Viewing Family,'" focuses on the historical and institutional contexts in which television programs were produced. In it, I bring together policy analysis, perspectives of political economy, textual analyses of television commercials, and ethnographic examinations of consumer practices. Extending critiques of family and kinship in feminist anthropology, I argue that far from being a static "context" in which television was received, "the family" was crucially reshaped through viewing practices. In tracing the intersection of "local" and transnational fields of power, this chapter demonstrates the potential of conjunctural ethnographies of mass media. Chapter 3, "'Women-Oriented' Narratives and the New Indian Woman," begins by noting that the late 1980s and early 1990s were marked by a proliferation of televisual discourses on Indian Womanhood. Why was the Indian state so preoccupied with representations of women? What were the political and ideological imperatives that underlay what Foucault has termed this "incitement to discourse"? I analyze the crucial role of television in the production of postcolonial ideologies of ideal Indian Womanhood through an examination of a new genre, "women-oriented" narratives.

Part 2, "Engendering Community," enacts the strategic deployment of

ethnography in order to examine the role of gender and sexuality in televisual constructions of community, in particular, the "imagined" Hindu
community. Chapter 4, "Mediating Modernities: The *Ramayan* and the
Creation of Community and Nation," examines the intersection of discourses of communalism, secularism, and "the popular." I situate the *Ramayan*, the televisation of a Hindu epic, within a context marked by the
escalation of communal tensions between Hindus and Muslims and the
ascendance of Hindu nationalism. My primary objective in this chapter
is to examine the centrality of gender and sexuality to the construction of
a Hindu community that, for all its claims to antiquity, is fundamentally
modern. How did television enable the mediation of modernity through
its depictions of community? Since this analysis is empirically based in a
historical context characterized as "the crisis of secularism" in India, my
second objective is to interrogate modernist assumptions about the secular within prevailing anthropological and cultural studies perspectives on
"the popular" and "the political."

In "Television Tales, National Narratives, and a Woman's Rage: The
Multiple Interpretations of Draupadi's 'Disrobing,'"[54] I examine the televisation and reception of a second Hindu epic, the *Mahabharat*. Ethnographic analyses of the discourses of the producers of the serial (the
director and the script writer) are juxtaposed with a close examination
of the interpretations of Hindu women who deeply identified with Draupadi, a central character of the epic. I demonstrate that these processes
of identification reveal the profound impact of the serial on viewers' self-
perceptions, their experiences of violence in the public spaces of the city,
and their positions within the politics of their families. Several women
appropriated the example of the public disrobing of Draupadi to reflect on
their own subordinated positions, and in the process formulated powerful critiques of gender inequalities in their families and communities. I
argue that in a political context marked by the Hindu nationalist glorification of the "ancient Indian (read: Hindu) past," the critiques forged by
these women can provide feminist activists with opportunities to forge a
counterhegemonic praxis.

In part 3, "Technologies of Violence," I discuss Doordarshan's representations of violence perpetrated on behalf of the nation so as to examine their implications for the constitution of discourses of gender and,
in particular, Indian Womanhood. *Param Veer Chakra* was an episodic

series that dramatized the lives of military heroes, most of whom died in combat. In "'Air Force Women Don't Cry': Militaristic Nationalism and Representations of Gender" I turn to the production and interpretation of discourses of gender and nationalism in tales about violence enacted in defense of the nation. I inquire into the construction of nationalist affect through narratives of duty and martyrdom. What enables, indeed compels, men and women to sacrifice themselves for the nation? What affective processes endorse acts of dying and killing in the name of the nation? And how do these glorified representations of militaristic nationalism implicate women, especially the women "left behind"? I bring a feminist perspective to bear on these questions by examining the centrality of masculinity and femininity to the development of nationalist passion.

In "Popular Narrative, the Politics of Location, and Memory," I demonstrate that mass media such as television played a crucial role in the formation of personal and collective memories of the violence surrounding the "birth" of the postcolonial Indian nation. I examine the interpretations of the script writer and viewers of *Tamas*, a serial about the Partition riots that erupted when India and Pakistan achieved independence from British colonial rule in 1947. In focusing on the role of popular narrative in the casting of memories of violence, I emphasize that processes of remembering and forgetting are deeply shaped by one's position along axes of gender, community, class, and nation. Extending recent interventions within feminist ethnography, I interweave ethnographic analysis with autobiography to study how "the past" is constructed through practices of storytelling, forgetting, and silence.

In the Epilogue, I examine the implications of transnational satellite television for the reconstitution of nationhood in contemporary India. Transnational satellite television was first introduced in India in 1991, at the end of the first year of my fieldwork. At first, only the very affluent could afford satellite hookups; by the time I completed my fieldwork in mid-1992, entrepreneurs had set up cable operations that allowed some upper-middle-class neighborhoods to "catch" transnational satellite television networks such as Star TV, CNN, BBC, Zee TV, and Sony. For a while it seemed as if imported programs like *The Bold and the Beautiful, The Young and the Restless,* and *The Donohue Show* would defeat Doordarshan in the battle over middle-class and upper-class viewers' loyalties. Interestingly, however, once the excitement generated by the novelty of seeing imported television waned, viewers seemed to hunger for "Indianized" television narratives. By 1995, viewers were witnessing a proliferation of "Indianized" television serials, series, talk shows, game shows, and made-for-TV films. In the Epilogue, I ask how understandings of national sovereignty, gender, and modernity were once again reconstituted in response to transnational satellite television.

Part I *Fields of Power: The National Television Family*

Chapter 2 *National Television and the "Viewing Family"*

■ *November 1984: A hectic and rewarding year is drawing to a close for S. S. Gill, India's secretary for the Ministry of Information and Broadcasting. On a special mission authorized by Prime Minister Indira Gandhi, he has spent the year setting up hundreds of television transmitters that will draw the remotest corners of the nation into the ambit of Indian television's newly launched National Programme. Suddenly Mrs. Gandhi is assassinated. Ironically, the first TV images viewers nationwide see are of her body lying in state, and close-ups of her grieving son, Rajiv Gandhi. Within a few months, Rajiv Gandhi is elected prime minister. The queen is dead; long live the king. The magic of television has made itself felt.*

■ *December 1990: It is a cold, windy day. I sit with Selapan, a clerk in a government office, huddled over the charcoal stove that barely warms his eight-by-ten-foot flat. His wife, Padmini, sits near us, preparing the evening meal. Selapan tells me that as a lower-caste high school drop-out he has done well for himself. He has a government job and a government flat, his son is in school, he has a television set, he has applied for a loan for a refrigerator. His voice deepening with pride, he adds that his wife will never have to look for a job outside the home again. I look at Padmini, but she turns her attention to the onions she is chopping. It is evident that their meal that night will be meager. She senses my gaze on her. She looks away.*

■ *April 1992: Rasoolan Bi tells me in ghoulish detail about an occurrence unprecedented in her working-class Muslim community: a young bride has been killed for dowry. Eying my* mangalsutra, *the necklace Hindu women of my community wear as a marker of our married status, she says: "We Muslims never had dowry deaths." She adds: "Now our culture is changing. People see all sorts of things on TV; people are getting greedy; people are losing respect for women." Later that morning, after discussing the daring exploits of her favorite TV heroine, a woman police officer, she wants to know if there are classes where her twelve-year-old granddaughter can learn karate.*

In 1982, when heir apparent Rajiv Gandhi set up the team of scientists, bureaucrats, and communication experts that was to lead India into the "twenty-first century," Doordarshan was expected to play a key role in the building of modern India. The agenda was clear: on the economic front, a shift from capital goods investment to a consumer economy; on the cultural front, a concerted effort to focus on the aspirations and anxieties of the dramatically expanding middle classes. In the years that followed, the introduction of color television and commercially sponsored entertainment serials did indeed appear to serve that agenda, with noticeable effects. My fieldwork confirmed the magnitude of the cultural transformations that, I sensed, had occurred as a result of the spaces newly occupied by television in the everyday lives of people in Indian cities: I learned that television serials had set into motion a series of changes in the manner in which class consciousness and conflict were articulated, gender discourses reconfigured, religious and ethnic identities contested, and the politics of nation, family, and sexuality negotiated. I examine some of these changes in this chapter, focusing in particular on the construction of the "viewing family."

Building on feminist scholarship that has critiqued the "naturalization" of the family (e.g., Yanagisako and Delaney 1995; see also Collier et al. 1982, Collier and Yanagisako 1987, Rapp 1992, and Yanagisako 1984), I wish to draw attention to the ways in which the family, as a unit for reception of TV programs and as a unit of consumption of the goods exhibited in advertisements, was repositioned, perhaps even reconstituted, by *intersecting* local, national, and transnational fields of power.[1] As Jane Collier et al. argue, "The real importance of The Family in contemporary social life has blinded us to its dynamics." Thus, they add, the family needs to be analyzed as "an ideological construct constructed with the modern state" (1982:25). In this chapter I outline the ways in which television both participated in reconstituting viewing subjects as "family" and, simultaneously—by offering viewing subjects opportunities to connect imaginatively with larger collectivities—further blurred the boundaries of the family.

Recent ethnographic studies of mass media have enlarged our understanding of the cultural and political significance of popular narrative by attending to how readers/consumers/viewers actively interpret texts in specific "local" contexts. In light of the dominant trend in media studies, which has until fairly recently consisted of an almost exclusive preoccupation with the semiotics of texts, this attention to consumption and its contexts is long overdue (for an anthropological perspective on consumption, see Miller 1987, 1995b). However, the focus on viewer response needs to be pushed further to interrogate how "local" receptions of mass media,[2] whether conceptualized in terms of individual interpretations of texts or of those of collectivities such as family or community, are themselves produced at intersections of local and translocal fields of power. I will demonstrate how the entity of "the family" is repositioned and reconstituted by local, translocal, and transnational flows of capital, desire,[3] and knowledge, and thereby problematize the binary between the local and translocal.

My argument is part of a series of recent interventions that have critiqued the ubiquity of the local in anthropological studies of culture (Appadurai 1986b; Gupta and Ferguson 1997a, 1997b; Malkki 1992).[4] Studies of the constitution of audiences challenge the dichotomy between the local and translocal: the notion of audience carries within it tropes of locality as well as diffuseness (as in the Nielsen national audience ratings). Television "transgresses" (Morley 1992) the boundaries between the local, translocal, and transnational by drawing viewing subjects into larger economies of consumption and desire (cf. Miller 1995a).

The theoretical and political advantages of keeping the local and the translocal in tension have been outlined by Akhil Gupta and James Ferguson, who insist that the local is neither autonomous nor discrete, but is always already situated within hierarchical, interconnected spaces (1997b:35). They argue that bearing this in mind is especially important when one is tracing the contours of a "topography of power" that is simultaneously local and translocal (1997b:35). David Morley has described how television links the "domestic" and "the political" by constructing "an image of the unified nation, built around the experiences that we are all assumed to share, as members of families" (1992:255). In India during the late 1980s and early 1990s, the "viewing family" was constituted as the primary target audience for television, which was then put to the task of constructing a "national family."[5]

One important element of this construction was the creation of desires for different forms of modernity.[6] The meaning(s) imputed to modernity were neither imitative of the West nor assumed as self-evident, but were, in fact, constituted and contested through television's own discourses on gender, class, and nation. The postcolonial state's commitment to modernize the nation rested on the axiom that modernity would have to be "Indianized," thus bringing about a convergence between discourses of modernity and nationalism. In the early years after independence, modernity was to be achieved through development (Gupta 1998).

As Akhil Gupta argues, the discursive practices of development in postindependence India are specifically postcolonial for several reasons (1998). At the most superficial level, the project(s) of development is postcolonial because it is a creature of a historical conjuncture marked by the formal decolonization of the nation-state. More importantly, however, discourses of development in India are postcolonial because they are shaped by colonial constructions of linear time, teleological history, and the idea that Third World nations must follow First World ones in their march toward "progress." At the same time, these conceptions of development are postcolonial in that they ensue from the modernizing projects of formally decolonized nation-states as they struggle to shake off the yoke of "backwardness" imposed by and caused by colonial and neocolonial regimes (Gupta 1998). Discourses of development, then, are postcolonial because they mark a zone of continuous engagement with the colonial, simultaneously drawing upon and contesting colonial discourses and practices. In the postcolonial conjuncture in India, television was harnessed to the task of fostering national development and entrusted with the task of creating modern citizen-subjects.

After the mid-1980s, as liberalization opened the door wider to transnational flows of capital, information, and desire, postcolonial modernity became increasingly articulated in terms of consumerism. In television's discourses, modernity was frequently equated with, and expressed through, consumerist aspirations and desires: consumerism itself became an index of modernity. The family, henceforth conceived as a unit of consumption, would acquire a modern lifestyle, and the nation, through the boost consumers would give to the economy, would also "develop" and thus become modern. As the theme song of a popular advertisement for Bajaj scooters put it, the commodity was now a symbol of the "strength" of the nation: *"buland Bharat ki buland tasveer, hamaara Bajaj"* (the portrait of a strong India, our Bajaj). Television played a crucial role in the cultural constitution of "middle-classness" through consumerism. What were the implications of the slippage between modernity and aspirations for middle-classness for the viewing family? How were women positioned in these reconstituted "viewing families?" And how were television's discourses of modernity experienced by men and women in their everyday lives? The following analysis will examine how these negotiations of modernity implicated not just the "consumer habits" of viewing subjects, but also their longings, anxieties, and desires.

If we are to grasp the interdiscursive context in which viewers engage with television texts, it is essential that we situate viewing families within interlocking contexts of national and transnational cultural flows and political economies. In what follows, we will see the role of transnational forces—ranging from technological collaborations with international agencies to transnational flows of discourses of modernity, capital, and desire—in the production of television texts. Therefore, my intention in this chapter is to delineate a conjunctural ethnography of "the viewing family" by situating it within a broader sociohistorical conjuncture.[7] I will draw on diverse methodologies and sources ranging from policy analysis to interviews with key policy makers and Doordarshan officials, content analysis of media texts, and participant observation and repeated, in-depth interviews with viewers. I explore the potential of ethnography as an *evocative* genre of cultural analysis that aims to represent specific structures of feeling. For most of the men and women I worked with, the home became a landscape of their desires for modernity and of their anxieties about upward mobility. I pay particular attention to the relationship between viewers' ownership of commodities, their aspirations and desires to become middle class, and their constitution as modern subjects. For instance, the ownership of a television set (especially a color set) was for many itself an index of middle-classness and, as middle-class lifestyles became equated with modernity, of the modernity of their families (cf. Spiegel 1992). Similarly, their ownership of commodities—the amount of furniture and the number of kitchen appliances they possessed, whether they had gas or kerosene stoves, and the number of pots and pans they owned—became markers of their position along a slippery slope of upward mobility. Thus I describe the homes of these men and women not to provide an empiricist "record" of the commodities they owned, but to evoke the structures of feeling surrounding their aspirations to modernity and upward mobility.[8]

I begin my analysis by examining some of the assumptions underlying the postcolonial state's efforts to expand Doordarshan's reach by examining television policy and analyzing the deployment of Doordarshan as a hegemonic state apparatus. Next, I reconstruct the history of entertainment serials in terms of the role of private industry, the growth of the middle classes, and the spread of consumerism in order to demonstrate the ways in which "the viewing family" was reconfigured through local, national, and transnational fields of power and knowledge. I then delineate the different subject positions created for women as viewers and consumers, and conclude by pointing to the ways in which a conjunctural ethnography of the viewing family enables us to interrogate local/global binaries and problematize simplistic assumptions about how viewers/consumers are interpellated by the discourses of mass media.

VIEWING POLITICS: A VIGNETTE

The average sitting room . . . is, among other things, one of the principal sites of the politics of gender and age . . . the sitting room is exactly where we need to start from if we finally want to understand the constitutive dynamics of abstractions such as "the community" or "the nation." (Morley 1991:12)

My own introduction to the politics of viewing within the family came rather early in my fieldwork. Within a few days of starting my research, I saw that the family was a politically, and hence emotionally, charged context in which people watched television. The Dasguptas lived in a tiny flat in the southern end of Vikas Nagar (the poorer part of the neighborhood I have designated as Division III). Their home always seemed to be bursting at the seams with people: besides Shurojit and his wife, Aparna, the household consisted of their elder son, his wife and young daughter; their youngest son; and their three unmarried daughters (their two married daughters lived in Calcutta and Gauhati, respectively). In addition, Shurojit frequently had friends from his office over in the evenings and during the weekends. He would often ask them to stay for a meal, and I would see Aparna, their daughter-in-law, Beena, and their elder daughter, Sushmita, scramble to stretch a meal to feed their guests.

Shurojit, a short man with close-cropped white hair, was a clerk in a government department. He was about to retire, and this was a cause of serious concern for the rest of the family because his eldest son seemed unable to hold on to a job. The family hence depended on the earnings of Sushmita, a short, plump woman in her early thirties. Considered an "elder sister" by many young women in the neighborhood, Sushmita was the one they turned to in a crisis. She spoke with a quiet strength that always made me pause.

I had been working with the Dasgupta household for less than a month when I dropped in on them one morning just before the Sunday morning television serial was to begin. The neighborhood was buzzing with activity; people seemed anxious to finish their morning chores in time to watch TV. As I made my way toward the Dasguptas' flat, I passed Sushmita chopping vegetables as she sat in the handkerchief-sized concrete verandah that served as a backyard for a cluster of four flats. Aparna had finished washing the clothes. She had already taken her bath, said her morning prayers, and was now helping Beena cook the midday meal in the kitchen. When the opening notes of the song that heralded the beginning of the serial flowed through the neighborhood, Shurojit, who had been shaving in the backyard, wordlessly handed his mug of hot water to Aparna, and walked into the flat, ready to watch the show. On seeing me hovering about the door that separated the living area from the kitchen, he waved me in.

The serial telecast that morning was *Chunni*, a "family drama" about a feud between two Sikh men who had once been such close friends as to be "like family." One of many serials in which the family served as metonym for the nation,[9] *Chunni*'s enigma consisted of the disruption of the "fictive" family and its eventual resolution when the two male protagonists clear up their misunderstanding and reunite "as brothers."

As other members of the Dasgupta family started to trickle in, Shurojit drew the curtains. The flat seemed suddenly smaller as it became blanketed in a gray darkness made fluid by the moving images on the television set. I squinted to adjust my eyes to the patchy darkness of the room and looked around. On earlier visits, I had noticed that the Dasguptas seemed to have relatively little furniture. The room seemed even more bare in the shadowy light of the TV set. There were two wooden chairs against one wall; in a corner of the room was a bed and a metal desk, on which sat a small black-and-white TV set. Shurojit sat on one of the two chairs. Soon after the serial began, he was joined by Aparna, who sat with their grandson in her lap. Their younger son, who was lying on the bed, turned his head to the TV set. About ten minutes into the serial, the eldest son walked in and sat by his younger brother on the bed. The two younger daughters and their little niece sat on a jute mat on the floor.

I did not quite know where to sit, so I perched myself on a stool by the door. (I describe the politics of my location as I "watched people watching television" in the previous chapter; for now, it is sufficient to say that my changing status in this family was reflected by the fact that by the end of my fieldwork, I was sitting on the floor with the two younger daughters.)

While Shurojit's daughters were mostly silent, the sons kept up a running commentary throughout the show. When they talked too loudly or too long, Shurojit would grunt his disapproval to them. They would pause for a while, and then resume their conversation. Occasionally, one of the daughters would join in. Aparna was usually silent. As we watched that morning's episode, Sushmita and Beena flitted in and out of the room, bringing tea and snacks for all of us. At first I thought that they were unable to follow what was happening on the program, but when I returned the next evening to talk to them, I realized that despite the fact that their household tasks kept them too busy to sit down in front of the TV set, they were able not only to keep up with the show but to engage intimately with its narrative.

Hence, gender, household position, and age were the crucial factors influencing viewers' modes of interaction with what they watched. Who sat where, who spoke when, who kept silent, and who stayed on the peripheries of the physical and discursive spaces revealed the role of television in mediating relationships among the Dasguptas. Television created a site where relations of inequality were crystallized and reinscribed. And just as viewers' modes of interacting with television offered a lens to focus on the power dynamics within the family, so also could the cultural and political significance of viewing be traced through its role in the reinscription and, sometimes, the restructuring of social relations within the family.

But television's role in rearranging relations of sociality within the family went beyond the "topography of power" (Gupta and Ferguson 1997b) manifest in the ways in which people arranged themselves around the TV set. Even more powerful in reconstituting relations within the family were the discourses constructed, mediated, and reinforced by television. Many viewers believed that acquiring the goods advertised on Doordarshan was essential to their ascendance to middle-class status. The struggle to become middle class through the possession of consumer goods was played out with particular poignancy in the Dasgupta family.

In the course of my fieldwork, I saw the Dasguptas struggle with the dowries demanded by people who brought marriage proposals for their daughters. As I noted above, the Dasguptas themselves owned relatively little furniture and had fewer appliances than many of their neighbors. All of their meager savings, and a large part of Sushmita's earnings, had gone into creating dowries for the two daughters who were already married. Sushmita, as the eldest daughter still living at home, was very bitter about the fact that she was still unmarried. Even though she wished to get married, her father found every excuse to turn down proposals that came for her. She believed that this happened because he wanted to use her income to provide dowries for her two younger sisters.

About five months after I first met them, the family received a new marriage proposal for Sushmita. But Shurojit insisted on persuading the groom's family to consider one of her younger sisters instead. Sushmita confided to me that this had happened before. This time, the prospective groom's party asked for a refrigerator for the young couple, a scooter for the groom, and jewelry for the bride. Sushmita had saved a little money that she had managed to keep out of her parents' grasp, but Shurojit now wanted her to give it to him so that he could provide her younger sister "a nice husband and a nice home." In the ensuing weeks the family was shaken by many bitter fights between father and daughter; ultimately, Sushmita relented and handed her precious savings over to her father.[10]

About halfway through my fieldwork, while I was away in the United States, one of Sushmita's younger sisters got married. On returning to New Delhi, I visited the Dasguptas and was welcomed by Aparna, who immediately sat me down and showed me photographs of the wedding. She excitedly told me that they had agreed to all the dowry requests: the groom was presented with a scooter, there were gifts of saris and jewelry for the bride, and the couple started their new life with not just a refrigerator but also that ultimate symbol of middle-classness, a color TV.

All the time that Aparna was talking, I looked around for Sushmita, but she was nowhere to be seen. Later, as I made my way to the bus stop, I saw her walking in my direction. When she looked up and saw me, she stopped dead in her tracks and her eyes filled with tears. Memories of our previous conversations in which she had confided her feelings of loneliness and her frustration with her father raced through my mind. Perhaps they raced through her mind as well and proved too painful for her to bear, for, the next thing I knew, she put up a hand, as if to ward off any words of sympathy I might offer, and shook her head vigorously.

She turned her face away and crossed over to the other side of the road to avoid me. The next day I learned that she had had a bitter fight with her father that night in which she accused him of using her money to buy dowries for her sisters.

My objective here is not to draw a simple, causal relation between television and the rampant consumerism that resulted in widespread demands for increasingly ostentatious dowries. Rather, my vignette about the Dasguptas is intended to serve as a preface for the following questions: How did the dreams of upward mobility and modernity constructed through Doordarshan's discourses influence relations within the family? More broadly, how did local, national, and transnational fields of power and knowledge constitute viewing families? In particular, how did the images, discourses, and desires for commodities advertised on television position women within the viewing family?

THE NATIONAL PROGRAMME: FAMILY AS AUDIENCE, AUDIENCE AS FAMILY

The Expansion of Television

Audiences of mass media do not exist a priori. They are actively constructed through careful programming decisions and marketing strategies, as well as transnational flows of information, capital, and commodities, and in some cases, the agendas of the nation-state.[11] A brief narrative of the history of Doordarshan reveals some of the ways in which the "viewing family" was constituted as "national audience" through state policy, international communication organizations, and transnational discourses of modernity.

Indian television was first launched on September 15, 1959, as an experiment in social and national(ist) education. Initially, only two programs of one hour each were telecast every week. Twenty-one television sets were installed in community viewing centers in rural areas around Delhi, and teleclubs were set up at these centers. The following years saw a gradual increase in the number of TV sets in the nation and in the hours of transmission. The emphasis, however, continued to be on producing and airing educational programs: TV sets were placed in schools, and programs were designed to teach subjects such as physics, chemistry, Hindi, English, current affairs, and geography.

One of the first visionaries to conceive of the role of television in building a modern India was an eminent scientist, Vikram Sarabhai, who claimed that "if India wants to reduce the overwhelming attraction of immigration to cities, enrich cultural life, integrate the country by exposing one part to the cultures of the other parts, involve people in the programme of rural, economic and social development, then the best thing is to have TV via a satellite" (quoted in Chatterji 1991:126). The Satellite Instructional Television Experiment (SITE) was a major landmark in the history of Indian television. Based on an agreement between NASA and the government of India, the Application Technology Satellite (ATS-6) was deployed to beam TV signals to 2,400 direct-reception TV receivers installed in six Indian states. Here again, the objective was to broadcast informational and educational programs to rural audiences. The Indian Space Research Organization (ISRO) was responsible for the maintenance of these receivers and for the production of programs aired by the SITE service. In this manner, science and technology were hitched to national development—indeed to cultural production—from the outset.

Television was widely conceived as the panacea for most of the ills that beset "underdeveloped" India. Development information would enable modernization, and "exposing" citizens to each other's cultures through satellite television would foster national integration. Four hours of programs were telecast every day: one and a half hours of educational programming in the mornings, and two and a half hours of entertainment programs in the evenings. Although television receivers were initially clustered around New Delhi, low-power transmitters were later set up, on ISRO's insistence, to beam programs to audiences in surrounding villages. The 1970s witnessed a gradual expansion of the reach of television: TV centers, or *kendras,* were inaugurated in Bombay in October 1972 and in Calcutta, Madras, and Lucknow in 1975. For almost two decades, television was part of All India Radio; in 1977 it was instituted as a separate department, Doordarshan, with its own director-general.

The shadow of transnational information flows loomed large in the minds of policy makers. Immediately after the second TV center was set up in Bombay, stations were inaugurated in Srinagar (Kashmir) and Amritsar (Punjab) to counter the alleged propaganda of Pakistani television programs (produced in Lahore and Islamabad), which were rapidly gaining popularity among viewers in Kashmir and Punjab.

The groundwork was now laid for the introduction of national programming. SITE had forced Prime Minister Indira Gandhi to recognize the public relations possibilities of nationwide television, and in 1982 a second Indian satellite, commissioned by the Indian government and built by Ford Aerospace, was launched by the U.S. space shuttle *Challenger*. This satellite made it possible for television signals to be rebroadcast from ground stations in different parts of the country to surrounding areas. On August 15, 1982—India's Independence Day, a date chosen for its obvious symbolic significance—the National Programme was telecast for the first time. That day also saw the inauguration of color transmission. As if to foreshadow the partisan uses to which Doordarshan would be put in the years to come, the National Programme's first telecast consisted of Prime Minister Indira Gandhi's traditional Independence Day address from the ramparts of the Red Fort in Delhi. The National Programme depended almost entirely on programs produced in New Delhi and Bombay, and with its launching, Doordarshan became irreparably centralized.

The reach and shape of Doordarshan were also transformed by the Asian Games of 1982. The Asian Games, or the Asiad as they were popularly known, were perceived by the Indian state as a major public relations event, "a national showcase of India's technological and organizational abilities" (Pendakur 1989:182). The Asiad provided the state with an opportunity to convey its image as a modern nation capable of hosting and organizing an international sports event, not just to the rest of the world but also to its own citizens. According to television critic Iqbal Masud, who closely followed some of the policy decisions surrounding the event, the Asiad was deemed a perfect occasion to "prove that India was no longer a nation beset with poverty and unemployment"; with color television and satellite transmissions relaying programs via forty-one transmitters to different parts of the country, India could take its place among the most modern nations of the world.[12] Television thus became an icon of the modernity of the nation.

The deployment of another satellite, INSAT-1B, and the launching of the National Programme enabled a dramatic expansion in television viewership. The number of people reached by television had risen from 156 million in 1979 to 500 million by 1988 (Singhal and Rogers 1989:66). This dramatic expansion was fueled by low-power transmitters that relayed broadcast signals to remote parts of India. The number of television sets also increased dramatically, from 2.8 million in 1983 to 11 million in 1988. Sales of TV sets were brisk; in 1988, five sets were sold every minute.[13]

Television, Modernity, Development

Why did the state place so much importance on television? What was at stake? Communication policies in the first two decades of television were congruent with the modernist vision of India's future articulated by the first prime minister of India, Jawaharlal Nehru. Nehru's vision of modernity was predicated on a dependence on science, technology, and state-planned investment in heavy industry. Modernity became a synonym for progress, with the state assuming a central, coordinating role. The role of the state was legitimized "by a specifically nationalist marriage between the ideas of progress and social justice" (Chatterjee 1986:132). In addition to giving primacy to the economic sphere, Nehru's vision of modernity was based on a post-Enlightenment emphasis on "rationality" (defined in opposition to "superstition" and "tradition"). Nehru's cherished dream was to build a modern India on a foundation of scientific principles: this vision of modern India was reflected in the Science Policy Resolution adopted by Parliament in 1956, the success of which was predicated on the "propagation of scientific attitudes" among citizens.[14]

At first, Nehru was ambivalent about television, which he often described as an expensive toy that India could not afford. He was eventually persuaded to soften his attitude somewhat by scientists and media planners who argued that India could use television as a "powerful weapon for social change" (Chatterji 1991:52). What appears to have finally convinced Nehru was the argument that television could foster a major attitudinal change in the people of India: since social and economic modernization required a "scientific temper," mass media such as television could potentially be deployed to propagate "scientific values" and eradicate their polar opposites, "superstition" and "dogma."[15]

Scientific national consciousness was deemed the "principal architect" in the construction of a modern nation (Chatterjee 1986:158), and television programs were formulated to fulfill this objective. Educational programs on health, agriculture, and "other practices based on modern knowledge" were consciously formulated as an "antidote to superstition and dogma" (Chatterji 1991:135). These programs were primarily created for two different audiences: as school programs for children, and as "nonformal" educational programs for adults. In addition, Doordarshan production centers produced programs that aimed at providing elementary scientific information to general viewers. Thus, the state's communication policy rested on the axiom that information, rather than structural change, was the most essential ingredient required for India to modernize: disseminating development information would lead to a change in the attitudes of Indians, and this attitudinal change would, in turn, lead to a change in their practices. The linearity of this model was a manifestation of the teleology of the sequence of development that was to be followed for India to progress.[16] A UNESCO-sponsored campaign in social education launched in December 1961 reveals the extent to which ideas about development rested on premises derived from modernization theory. The campaign hoped to "add to the information of viewers on various topics, to influence, if possible, their attitudes towards aspects of issues and to encourage follow-up group action" (Reports and Papers on Mass Communication, UNESCO 1963:38, in Chatterji 1991:51). Thus, from the very outset, an emphasis on development was built into the conceptualization of television's social and political roles.

As with many development programs, the underlying goal was to provide entitlements to beneficiaries rather than to empower marginalized communities (Ferguson 1990). More generally, this model led to a determination to provide information to the "socially deprived," in this case, poor people living in rural areas, lower-class and working-class people, and women. Some development programs were aimed specifically at women, and hence created particularly gendered subject positions for them. For instance, Prabha Krishnan and Anita Dighe, describing a health education program about the importance of clean drinking water, claim that not only were the "structural constraints governing the use of clean water" ignored, but "women were assumed to be ignorant of basic hygiene" (1990:37). In general, women were conceived as "targets" and objects of development rather than as subjects and agents of social change.

Social justice was conflated with development and modernization — the telos of the Indian nation. Ideologies of development converged with discourses of citizenship. Citizens were entitled to development benefits from the state, but at the same time, it was also their *duty* to contribute to national development. One of the objectives of the First Five-Year Plan of

1951 was to publicize the state's agenda for development: "A widespread understanding of the Plan is an essential stage in its fulfillment. An understanding of the priorities of the Plan will enable each person to relate his or her role to the larger purposes of the nation as a whole. All available methods of communication have to be developed and the people approached though the written and spoken word no less than through radio, film, song and drama" (in Chatterji 1991:117). At stake for the state was the creation of a national subject whose understanding of his/her role was congruent with national goals, with "the larger purposes of the nation as a whole." Another UNESCO-sponsored experimental program in social education had as its general theme the "Responsibilities of Citizenship." The topics covered included traffic and road sense, community health, and encroachment on public property. "Each person" was to be reconstituted as a national citizen with certain expectations from and responsibilities to the nation-state: to this end, it was essential that citizens be made aware of the ways their roles, aspirations, and duties could articulate with the developmentalist goals of the nation-state. As a powerful participant in this national project, television's goal was not just to foster development but, ultimately, to construct viewing subjects as modern citizens.[17]

For a long time, the state's plans to persuade viewing subjects to adopt modernizing (and modernist) practices by providing development information were stymied by the fact that television reached only a very small audience. As S. S. Gill pointed out to me, until 1973 television was "merely a part of the drawing room furniture" of some upper-middle-class homes: "People switched on their TV sets only to watch the weekly Hindi films, other film-based programs like *Chitrahaar*" (which showed songs and dances from films), and the news.[18] In 1983, Prime Minister Indira Gandhi, her son, Rajiv Gandhi, and her closest advisers (including S. S. Gill) worked out a comprehensive plan—ranging from the installation of hardware to the training of personnel and the production of software—to expand television throughout India. According to Iqbal Masud, part of the impetus behind this expansion was political: Indira Gandhi's power base was becoming increasingly shaky, and, with national elections approaching, she was looking for ways to use broadcast media for propaganda purposes.[19] Masud claimed that the impact of television during the Asiad had further convinced Gandhi of the potential of broadcast media to reach a massive audience.

The Sixth Five-Year Plan of 1983 set aside Rs 869.5 million to increase the number of transmitters from 45 to 180 (Pendakur 1989:182). Gill informed me that on July 17, 1983, he started his campaign to build one transmitter a day. Gill also claimed that he encouraged the electronics industry to manufacture TV sets. This impetus, along with the liberalization of regulations making it easier to import color television technology, ensured that a large number of sets would be available for reception.

The state gave enormous importance to the introduction of color television. According to Gill, part of the reason color television had to be introduced was practical: it was difficult to replace black-and-white production equipment because manufacturers throughout the world were changing to color television. More important, however, color television was iconic of the modernity of the Indian nation. As Gill put it to me: "The old era of mechanical watches, steam engines, and black-and-white television had ended. India was now a modern nation." The introduction of color television meant that India had "kept up with the rest of the world."

In 1982, before the Asian Games, there were only 16 transmitters reaching less than 8 percent of the nation's population. By 1991, Doordarshan had 523 transmitters with the potential to reach close to 80 percent of the population. With an estimated 35 million TV sets in India by the early 1990s, "few countries in the world [had] seen such expensive bouts of television expansion" (Mitra 1985:103).

Television as Hegemonic State Apparatus

Information is power, and power is politics.
(S. S. Gill, interviewed on January 23, 1992)

The potentials of a nationwide audience of more than 500 million were staggering: for multinational corporations, such an audience represented an enormous market; for the Indian state, it represented a captive audience to whom it could legitimate its rule. The electoral politics of a mass democracy made television's potential as a hegemonic state apparatus particularly crucial. In addition to its modernist goals, the Indian state had more explicit political objectives in launching the National Programme in 1982. Relations between the central government and the states became very contentious after the rule of the Congress was destabilized and opposition governments were established at the state level in 1967.[20] As noted above, with the National Programme, Doordarshan was irreparably centralized. This became a source of frustration for state governments (particularly those run by opposition parties).[21]

The distribution of national economic resources has always been a major bone of contention between central and state governments. After 1982, however, the central government's communication policies, especially with regard to national programming, also became a source of tension. Speaking for other non-Congress governments, the minister of information and broadcasting from West Bengal said at a 1983 conference of Information Ministers:

> The two most important tools of opinion formation are AIR (All India Radio) and Doordarshan. Both are controlled by the Central Government. . . . The way these two media are being used now leaves much to be desired. The allegation of their partisan use cannot be dismissed lightly. We, in West Bengal, have felt on occasions that there was a serious misconception regarding the priorities of items in the all-India news telecast. There have been occasions when the State Government's news, including policy announcements by the Chief Minister, did not receive the attention due to them on issues where the opposition standpoint got elaborate coverage. (from Chatterji 1991:110)

Allegations of central-government media control found particular resonance in states where Hindi was not the first language, for, on average, 39 percent of the programs shown on the National Programme were in Hindi (except in Tamil Nadu, where Tamil programs made up 40 percent of the programs shown). In 1985, the breakdown by language of the programs shown during prime time was as follows: Hindi programs constituted 46 percent of the total programming, English programs 44 percent, Urdu programs 2 percent, Punjabi programs 1 percent, and programs in all other languages combined (including the languages of south India) 7 percent. Twenty-three percent of the programs shown on the National Programme were sponsored programs, 54 percent were produced by the Delhi Kendra, about 3 percent by the Bombay Kendra, and 10 percent consisted of imported programs. The contribution of other *kendras* was negligible.[22] In many parts of India, the National Programme, shown for two hours of prime time every evening, constituted the entire telecast.

Equally frustrating for opposition governments and for viewers in different parts of India was the National Programme's "Delhi-centric" perspective. The importance given by Doordarshan to events in different parts of the country seemed directly proportionate to their distance from the capital.[23] This perspective was also reflected in entertainment serials. For instance, most serials were set in north Indian cultural contexts. This was true even of such popular serials as *Hum Log,* which was criticized by none other than a former director-general of Doordarshan, Harish Khanna, for being restricted to a north Indian (or at least Hindi-speaking) audience (from Sethi and Mitra 1985:83). Doordarshan's response to such criticisms only added insult to injury: it tried to compensate for its north Indian bias by awkward insertions of "Bengali" and "Tamilian" characters in its serials. Although these insertions aimed at "approaching a national outlook," the amateur and clumsy ways in which these characters were portrayed only perpetuated regional and ethnic stereotypes.

Indeed, many men and women I spoke with complained that Doordarshan "distorted" their images. Sukumaran, a Tamil brahman, was in his mid-fifties when I first met him. He was a portly, gray-haired man who lived in Division III of Vikas Nagar with his wife, Sarojini, and daughter Lata. Sukumaran was very mild-mannered and was known in the neighborhood as a peacemaker: he never gossiped about his neighbors, and most people I knew respected him for this. He was a stenographer in a government ministry; Sarojini was a secretary in a private company. Like some other south Indians who had lived in the north for much of their adult lives, Sarojini and Sukumaran were accustomed to speaking in Hindi: it was the language in which they spoke to their neighbors and coworkers. But they were particularly anxious that Lata not forget Tamil: they sent her to a Tamil-medium school and insisted on speaking Tamil at home. They followed all the Tamil festivals and rituals, and cooked Tamil food.

One day, I asked Sukumaran what he thought about the fact that most of the programs were in Hindi. He replied, "We are all Indians, what does it matter?" I felt that he was giving me a "scripted" response; it might have come straight out of one of Doordarshan's national integration advertisements, I thought to myself in irritation. I suspected that because all our conversations took place in Hindi, he had identified me as a north Indian and did not want to hurt my feelings by making anti-Hindi statements. So I changed my approach and asked what he thought of the ways south Indians were depicted in TV serials. He replied that even though "many south Indians wear pants and work in modern offices," on the programs they were always presented as "wearing dhotis" (the loose waistcloth wrapped around the lower body) and speaking "in a strange way" (here, Sukumaran was referring to television programs' caricatures of south Indian speech patterns). He became increasingly angry as he spoke.

Sukumaran's response is dense with discourses about modernity, cultural difference, and Otherness. In his view, Doordarshan's representation of south Indians in dhotis (a "traditional" outfit, as opposed to trousers, which symbolized Westernized modernity) elided their claims to modernity (signified by the fact that they worked in "modern offices"). And in a cultural context in which national "mainstream" culture was frequently signified by (upper-caste) north Indian speech patterns, their exaggerated south Indian accents indexed their cultural difference from north Indians. As he warmed to this theme, the usually mild-mannered Sukumaran became quite agitated. I had obviously struck a nerve.

Selapan, who lived a couple of streets south of Sukumaran and Sarojini with his wife, Padmini, and young son Rajan, was also from Tamil Nadu. He was lower caste and worked as a junior clerk in a government department. He spoke Hindi more fluently than Sukumaran and Sarojini, but like them, he spoke Tamil with his family. Selapan was also very upset about Doordarshan's portrayal of south Indians. One Sunday morning, we were watching the last episode of *Param Veer Chakra*, a series about military heroes. This was his favorite television program, and we all watched it in silence and with appropriate solemnity. Padmini was folding clothes on the floor; Rajan was sitting in front of the nine-inch black-and-white television perched on a rickety wooden table; Selapan was on a wooden stool, I was sitting on a metal chair next to Rajan. As the episode drew to a close, Selapan let out a deep sigh: I could tell that he was sad the series was ending.

The closing shots of the series consisted of a list of all the soldiers who had died in action and had been awarded the Param Veer Chakra, the highest military honor. Some of these soldiers had not been portrayed in the series. When the voice-over read out the names of the martyred soldiers, it became evident that at least two were south Indian. Selapan's son repeated the names of the two soldiers in excitement. At that point, Selapan turned to me and said, "How come they did not show the two south Indian soldiers? See, they always do that!" When I responded, somewhat lamely, that perhaps they had run out of time, Selapan snorted scornfully. "No, I don't think so. They always do this. They only show Punjabis and UP-wallahs [people from the north Indian state of Uttar Pradesh]. They never show south Indians." Selapan seemed to think that the makers of *Param Veer Chakra* had deliberately omitted the south Indian soldiers. He thus revealed his resentment against the Delhi-centric—and, more generally, north Indian—bias of Doordarshan. And, although I did not know whether the series producers had intended to do so, I could not help agreeing with Selapan that most television programs depicted a preponderance of north Indian characters and cultural contexts. I knew that the narratives shown on the National Programme were seldom set in the south of India, and were invariably in Hindi.

Doordarshan could indeed be crudely partisan in its coverage of political events: the anti-Sikh riots that swept through north India in November 1984 and left thousands dead were ignored, as was the violence surrounding the Mandal Commission protests in 1990. Programs even indirectly critical of the current regime were never shown. Disproportionate attention was showered on politicians in power, and television was often flagrantly deployed to build personality cults, most glaringly in the case of Indira Gandhi and Rajiv Gandhi.

Between the mid-1960s and 1991, the Indian state established four different committees to address the cultural and political biases of Doordarshan. The first committee, the Chanda Inquiry Committee, produced its report in 1966. The report suggested that All India Radio be converted into a corporation run on the lines of the BBC; that a separate radio channel, Vividh Bharati, be set aside for commercialization; and that television be established as a separate unit from All India Radio and a twenty-year development plan be chalked out for it. The last two recommendations were adopted, but All India Radio, like television, continued to be government owned and managed. Next came the Verghese Working Group in 1978, set up by the Janata Party government that came into power immediately after Indira Gandhi's emergency was lifted. This group aimed at formulating safeguards against the repression experienced by the media during the emergency. Once again, the BBC was the model: the group recommended that All India Radio and Doordarshan be merged into a single trust called the Akash Bharati Trust and insisted that the trust's autonomy be incorporated into the Indian Constitution itself. It also recommended that All India Radio and Doordarshan be decentralized. But the Janata government collapsed before it had a chance to push a bill through Parliament to this effect.

When Indira Gandhi's government returned to power, it decided to expand the reach of television and, in December 1982, set up the Joshi Working Group on Software. The objectives of this group were to advise the government on how television programming could assist the process of "social and economic development of the country" (Government of India 1985:7). Significantly titled "An Indian Personality for Doordarshan," the report discussed three main concerns: the overcentralization of television, the dangers of consumerism, and transnational flows of information that threatened the "cultural purity" of the nation. The government, however, ignored the recommendations, and copies of the Joshi Report were not made easily available to the public. The next opposition government, the National Front coalition led by the Janata Dal, proposed yet another plan for the autonomy of broadcast media, the Prasar Bharati Bill, which was introduced in Parliament and modified. As with all the other plans, the BBC was the model on which the Prasar Bharati Bill's suggestions were based. The bill proposed that government control be replaced by an independent corporation whose chair was to be appointed by no less a personage than the president of India. At the time of writing this book, the fate of the Prasar Bharati Bill continues to be undecided.

The number of committees established to regulate Indian television indicates not just the highly experimental nature of television in the early days but, more important, the political stakes involved for the nation-state and for the ruling party. The formation of these committees was also a response to growing public criticism of the state's flagrant use of Doordarshan for propaganda purposes. Every opposition party promised in its election manifesto to "revamp" the broadcast media. And every party elected to power was obliged to set up yet another committee to review past performance and chart an agenda for future communication policies. No government in power, however, wanted to relinquish its control of the broadcast media.

"National Integration" as Repressive Discourse

In addition to using television to construct and broadcast discourses of development, the state deployed themes of national integration to consolidate its hegemony and repress dissent. Sarabhai had spoken of television's role in providing "continued stability and national integration" (1969:2, in Singhal and Rogers 1989:73). National integration was to be achieved by "exposing" inhabitants of one part of India to the culture of other parts. Several decades later, this objective continued to guide the formulation of national programming. This led to series such as *Ek Kahani* (One story), in which viewers were shown televised versions of short stories written in different languages which were then translated into Hindi. Discourses of national integration primarily reflected the state's efforts to create a pan-Indian national culture that could withstand the efforts of both the "enemy within" (separatist forces) and "external enemies" (the propaganda efforts of Pakistan and China and, equally dangerous, the "subversions" of U.S. cultural, economic, and political imperialism).

According to Gill, the National Programme aimed at "bringing Indian viewers onto a common national platform for at least a small segment of the total transmission time." Essential components of Doordarshan's project of national integration included travel programs that transported viewing subjects to different parts of India, dramatizations of anticolonial struggles, biographies of "freedom fighters" and national leaders, and the serials based on short stories drawn from different regional traditions. The national telecast of news programs was particularly significant because, as Krishnan and Dighe point out, "viewers are encouraged to think that what is presented in the news has happened to the nation and us" (1990:107) or, to put it slightly differently, to "us, the nation." In addition, long-running serials became part of the collective memory of entire groups of the population. This was particularly true of serials such as *Buniyaad, Mahabharat,* and *Tamas.*

Instances of blatant censorship of entertainment serials, using the charge that these serials would promote "communal tension" or posed a "threat to national interests" as the reason, abounded. For instance, *Tamas,* which focused on the violence of Partition, was temporarily pulled off the air because of the fear that it would reignite communal hatred between Hindus and Muslims. Similarly, *The Sword of Tipu Sultan* was surrounded by controversy regarding whether the protagonist, Tipu Sultan, an eighteenth-century Muslim king, had been "truly secular" or, as Hindu right-wing organizations claimed, a "demolisher of temples." Every episode of *Param Veer Chakra* had to be cleared by representatives of the military before it could be telecast. The state did not hesitate to repress even the most indirect criticism of power blocs: a film called *New Delhi Times* was kept off the air because it blamed a nexus of politicians and business interests for communal riots.

The (perhaps inevitable) irony of the National Programme was that, while national programming linked various parts of India with a central network, these programs, in fact, reflected the will of the state to homogenize local narratives into a central, hegemonic, pan-Indian national narrative. Thus it was not surprising that TV stations became emblematic of the stranglehold of the state and became a favorite target for bomb attacks by separatist militants in Punjab and Kashmir.

The National Programme's attempts to foster national integration also included the simultaneous telecast of "national events" such as the Republic Day parade, as well as coverage of the Independence Day speeches of the prime minister and major national festivals. Live telecasts had the potential to incorporate these events into the "calendar" of national life.[24] Significantly, all the viewers I worked with made it a point to watch the Republic Day celebrations, which were telecast live each January 26 to viewers across India. The Republic Day parade traveled through the heart of New Delhi. Beginning with different wings of the army, navy, air force, police, and paramilitary organizations—all marching to music played by their respective bands—the parade was a singularly impressive display of modern India's military might. The military and paramilitary troops were followed by groups of students from local schools (consisting chiefly of the National Cadet Corps). The high points of the celebration were the fly-overs organized by the air force, in which fighter planes engaged in acrobatic exercises, and the tableaux put on by the different states and union territories of India. At the same time that they showcased regional and ethnic diversity, the tableaux were intended to reinforce the theme of "unity in diversity" and thus enact the states' and union territories' allegiance to the nation.

I once watched the Republic Day parade with the Sukumarans, who watched the telecast religiously every year. The parade started very early in the morning, and as I set out, I grumbled to myself about having to leave the warmth of my home. In the past I had always watched the parade at home with my parents: my father would sit in his favorite armchair, and my mother and I would sit on a sofa opposite the television, our feet as close to the electric heater as we dared. This was my first Republic Day in India since my father's death, and I resented having to miss the family ritual at home with my mother. Besides, it had started to drizzle, and the scooter-rickshaw I was traveling in was old and poorly insulated; I was sure I would be frozen stiff by the time I reached Vikas Nagar. The streets, usually bustling with early-morning activity, were relatively empty. All I could see were a few vegetable vendors and some stray vehicles. The city was suffused with a smell I always associate with winter mornings in New Delhi: the smoke of charcoal stoves from the previous night hung stale and heavy over the streets. The neighborhood wore a forlorn air. By the time I arrived at the Sukumarans' house, my teeth were chattering.

Sukumaran and Lata greeted me with warmth; Sarojini, who was making tea for the family, smiled her welcome to me. I was happy to come in from the cold and the rain. The parade had just started: military music filled the Sukumarans' home. Sukumaran sat on the sole chair the family possessed, and the rest of us arranged ourselves on the bed facing the television set. Sarojini silently placed a mug of steaming tea in my hands; when I thanked her, she raised her eyebrows somewhat archly. As the Republic Day celebrations continued, I was flooded with childhood memories of watching the parade. The expression of wonder on Lata's face brought back the awe I used to feel when I watched as a child. I also remembered that once, years ago, I had commented to my mother that we were watching weapons of destruction. My mother had replied that yes, they are weapons of destruction, but they destroy our enemies; they keep us safe.

That morning, as I sat with Sukumaran, Sarojini, and Lata, my earlier ambivalence about my country's military prowess returned, laced with a sense of awe that I could not shake off. We said little as we watched; our silence was punctuated by occasional remarks about the might of the tanks and how smartly the soldiers marched. I found myself mesmerized by the music and, in a sudden moment of extreme discomfort with my own interpellation by militaristic nationalism, I joked that the president of India, who had to stand to acknowledge the salute of every battalion that marched by, was probably getting very tired. Sukumaran and Lata whirled around and glared their disapproval at my disrespect for the president and the parade. They said nothing, but they clicked their tongues in annoyance and I was appropriately silenced. From the corner of my eye, I could see Sarojini grinning slyly. When the groups of school students marched by, Lata turned to her father and said to him in a quiet voice: "I wish my school had participated. I would have been so proud to be part of the parade. India is so powerful. I wish I had marched." Sukumaran said nothing in response, but nodded his head as if he understood what she meant.

All morning Sarojini's behavior had been difficult for me to read: she had said very little; her ambivalence toward the parade was an invisible wall around her.[25] Later that morning, she frustrated all my efforts to find out what she felt about the parade by indifferently shrugging her shoulders and changing the subject. Sukumaran, on the other hand, had watched the parade with an awe, if not reverence, appropriate for religious rituals, an attitude I had disrupted with my uneasy disrespect. But it was Lata who seemed most moved by the parade and, as suggested by her longing to have marched in it, most enthusiastically engaged with the nationalistic pride it evoked. In this manner, the live telecast of events like the Republic Day celebrations contributed to the creation of a new genre of secular, national(ist) rituals that enabled the interpellation of viewers, particularly children and youth, as national subjects.

THE INTRODUCTION OF NARRATIVE SERIALS: CONSUMING NATION AND FAMILY

The "viewing families" who watched the narrative serials on Doordarshan were positioned not just vis-à-vis nationalist discourses but, simultaneously, at the intersection of national and transnational fields of information, capital, and desire.[26] In 1983, a commercial sponsorship scheme was introduced according to which, in exchange for ninety seconds of airtime, companies or advertising agencies could pay a set fee plus the production costs of a serial. Sponsors could also pay for the acquisition of the weekly Hindi film and film-based programs. Statutory guidelines limited the available airtime to 10 percent of the total transmission time. Advertisements were clustered at the beginning of programs and did not interrupt the flow of narratives as they do in U.S. television programs. Predictably, the sponsorship scheme firmly established the presence of commercials on television. But, more significant, by providing the means to acquire and maintain production facilities, sponsorship *enabled* the production of narrative serials.

The state approached with great urgency the production of "indigenous" programming explicitly oriented to constructing a national culture "untarnished" by foreign influences. Members of the Joshi Committee had been particularly afraid that Indian audiences would be "captured" by imported programs (primarily U.S. television programs). They were especially concerned that, as in other developing countries, Indian elites would "emulate" the lifestyles of richer countries after watching foreign television programs; this, they feared, would only widen the gap between the rich and poor within India. Further, there was great concern that television would create a comprador elite. The solution proposed by the state and by the nationalist elite represented in the Joshi Committee was to ensure that Doordarshan would acquire "a truly Indian personality."

The state's attempts to ward off the temptations of foreign-produced entertainment serials were most evident in its urgent attempts to produce "the Indian teleserial." But, as we will see shortly, these efforts were riddled with paradoxes and ironies. The following analysis demonstrates the way in which transnational cultural flows, private industry, and the demands of an increasingly vocal middle class converged to launch entertainment serials on Doordarshan.

Hum Log *and Transnational Discourses of Development*

The first dramatic serial ever to be shown on Doordarshan was *Hum Log* (We people), the story of a lower-middle-class family struggling to achieve upward mobility and become middle class. In keeping with the Indian nation-state's anxieties about the cultural imperialism of "the West," its allegiance to the Non-Aligned Movement, and its emphasis on cultural exchanges among Third World nations, policy makers turned to Latin American telenovelas for their "models."[27]

Doordarshan adopted a Peruvian telenovela, *Simplemente Maria,* as its model. Produced in 1969, the serial narrated the rags-to-riches story of a young woman who made her fortune by sewing (not surprisingly, the serial was sponsored by Singer Sewing Machines). The fortunes of Singer Sewing Machines rose along with those of Maria: by the end of the year there was an unprecedented rise in its sales. *Simplemente Maria* achieved very high ratings not only in Peru but also in other Latin American countries where it was shown, and it sparked a new trend in Latin American television entertainment. Mexico's Televisa was most successful in harnessing this unique genre to its goals of entertainment, high ratings (and hence high revenues), and development-oriented messages. Televisa producer Miguel Sabido produced several telenovelas, all of which received very high ratings. Supported by commercial advertising, these telenovelas incorporated into their narratives educational themes ranging from family planning and adult literacy to women's rights.[28]

Although the telenovelas took different forms in the countries where they were adopted, all shared the premise that information is the most important ingredient of development. Telenovelas also drew from social learning theory and aimed at influencing viewing subjects to "adopt" certain "pro-development" attitudes and behaviors with regard to birth control, literacy, and so on.[29] Like many other telenovelas that it inspired, *Simplemente Maria* was silent about the structural conditions responsible for "underdevelopment"; instead, it suggested that if individuals adopted certain "pro-social" behaviors, development would follow. The trajectory followed by *Simplemente Maria*'s protagonist was typical. Maria was conceived as a "positive role model" because, with hard work and idealism, she was able to rise from rags to riches: in a single year, armed with a sewing machine and plenty of grit, she sewed her way up the socioeconomic ladder to become the owner of a clothing boutique.[30] The assumption that viewers identifying with characters possessing "pro-development" attributes would emulate those characters was based on a particular conception of individual agency, according to which viewers could change their personal and social circumstances by adopting certain attitudes and behaviors.

Significantly, it was an international agency that first raised the possibility of introducing telenovela-style serials on Indian television. According to Gill, David Poindexter, the president of the Center for Population Communications-International, was convinced that telenovela-style serials could be deployed to encourage Indian viewers to practice family planning. Poindexter arranged workshops in Mexico City at which television producers from India (and other Third World nations such as Kenya and Nigeria) discussed various strategies with Miguel Sabido. The Indian contingent was led by Gill, who was then secretary to the Ministry of Information and Broadcasting. Gill was so convinced of the usefulness of the telenovela format that, as soon as he returned to India, he began planning an entertainment serial that would disseminate family planning information. He organized a workshop to which he invited Sabido, and introduced the concept of development-oriented soap operas to Doordarshan officials. The plan to produce *Hum Log*, an Indian-style telenovela, was launched.[31]

First, Gill went to Bombay to persuade professionals in the Hindi film industry to produce his serial. When he found no takers, he hired Shobha Doctor, an advertising professional, to produce the serial and commissioned anthropologist S. C. Dube to write a paper on the "negative and positive family values in the Indian family." The serial's production costs were to be met by corporations such as Food Specialties, Limited. A popular journalist, Manohar Shyam Joshi, was hired to write the script for the serial. Joshi came up with a formula that kept hundreds of thousands of families riveted to their television screens week after week.[32]

In addition to weaving development-oriented "social messages" into its narrative, *Hum Log* borrowed from many other narrative traditions: it used the melodramatic techniques of Hindi film; its narrative address and structure drew from U.S. soap operas. In this sense, *Hum Log* was a hybridized cultural text typical of the intersection of "indigenous" narrative techniques, the objectives of the Indian nation-state, and transnational cultural flows. Broadcast for seventeen months from 1984 to 1985, *Hum Log* spanned 156 episodes. Every episode ended with a popular film actor, Ashok Kumar, drawing out the moral of that day's story and responding to viewers' letters.[33] *Hum Log* achieved audience ratings unprecedented in the history of Indian television.[34] The *Indian* teleserial, born of a confluence of transnational cultural flows and the developmentalist objectives of the Indian nation-state, had finally arrived.

The success of *Hum Log* led to a proliferation of serials on Doordarshan. Gill claimed that it forced media planners and Doordarshan officials to realize that development information could be "packaged" in a "judicious combination" of entertainment and education. At the same time, *Hum Log*'s success also proved that teleserials could provide advertisers with a huge captive audience of middle-class families with the discretionary income to buy new products. Independent producers, media planners, and private corporations began to see Doordarshan as commercially viable. *Hum Log* was followed by another milestone, *Buniyaad* (Foundation), a serial that attracted a larger and even more loyal following. Set in the post-Partition years, *Buniyaad* followed the fortunes of a Punjabi Hindu family whose members came to north India as refugees; the "foundation" laid by the reconstituted post-Partition family was symbolic of the foundation of postcolonial Indian society and polity. *Buniyaad*'s popularity (it achieved 95 percent ratings) was surpassed only by that of the *Mahabharat* (99 percent ratings).

By 1987, forty indigenously produced serials had been produced and telecast on Doordarshan. *Buniyaad* was followed by *Tamas,* a serial that dwelled on the brutality of the Partition riots, and the two televised Hindu epics, the *Ramayan* and the *Mahabharat.* Journalists Sethi and Mitra commented at the time: "Suddenly this year, after more than twenty-five years of dishing out stodgy, listless, uninspired fare, Indian television has become the new addiction. And not only for the viewers. It is revolutionizing the advertising industry, threatening the traditional entertainment industry and titillating the giants of the consumer industry" (1985:78).

Hum Log's success also attracted the attentions of the Bombay-based Hindi film industry, which then proceeded to play a crucial role in producing serials for Doordarshan.[35] Many of the major serials mentioned above, along with many others that followed, were made by men and women who had proved themselves as directors, script writers, and actors in Bombay films. *Hum Log*'s success enabled the "film moguls" of Bombay to cast aside their initial skepticism of Doordarshan as a possible outlet for their work.

In fact, the introduction of entertainment serials on Doordarshan accelerated the financial recession the Bombay film industry was experiencing in the mid-1980s. The success of serials such as *Hum Log* affected the cinema habits of viewing subjects. According to a 1986 survey conducted by Operations Research Group, a major marketing research company, cinema going by its respondents decreased from 1.8 films before serials were introduced on Doordarshan to 0.9 films per month afterward. Gross box-office collections at Delhi's cinema theaters declined by 25 to 30 percent during 1984–1985.[36] In 1985, Ramesh Sippy, a filmmaker whose films had started to do poorly at the box office, said: "I am keeping a keen eye on developments in TV. If more money is being generated by TV, well, then I'd like to make TV serials with more money behind them."[37] By 1986 Sippy had started producing television serials, the most celebrated of which was *Buniyaad.*

Other filmmakers hastened to use their studios and their contacts in the government to make serials for Doordarshan as well. Relatively little financial risk was involved because there were countless advertisers eager for projects to sponsor. Further, producers did not have to deal with the problems that beset film production and distribution (such as box-office swings, video piracy, and so on). And by producing its serials in Bombay, Doordarshan did not have to invest in the expensive studio equipment re-

quired for well-produced programs. As Harish Khanna, former director-
general of Doordarshan, pointed out, it was "a marriage of convenience
between Bombay and Delhi."[38]

The new serials were targeted at families, which also became the
unit of reception for producers, advertisers, and the state. Several factors
served to position "the family" as the "primary viewing unit." Programming decisions dictated that serials would be aired only when the entire
family was most likely to be together: not surprisingly, many viewers told
me that they made plans to be home when TV serials were scheduled
to be aired. The narratives of many serials also revealed programmers'
assumptions about the family as the primary viewing unit. The most
popular genre among serials was the family drama, which depicted the
fortunes of one or more families. Family dramas sometimes represented
the family as a trope for the nation (e.g., in the immensely popular *Buniyaad* described above, the trials of a post-Partition family trying to stay intact symbolizes the struggles of the post-Partition Indian nation to "keep
united"). Several television industry officials emphasized that most programs were meant for "family viewing." A journalist who served on the
screening committee that evaluated proposals for television serials informed me that the most consistent criterion he and his colleagues used
for approving a serial was its appropriateness "for the whole family to
watch together."[39]

MIDDLE-CLASS DESIRES AND THE POLITICAL ECONOMY OF CONSUMERISM

> *Ten years ago, the political rhetoric centered on abolishing poverty; today it looks
> forward to the 21st century. Then it was a question of reining in monopoly capital;
> now the Government talks of industrial modernization and opening up the economy.
> Then the goals were more food, water, steel, aluminum, hospitals. Now, it is all that
> plus telephones, TV sets, scooters, cars, refrigerators. Then it was a question of tax-
> ing "luxury" goods to find money for the basics; now the Government has reduced
> the taxes on these so that more people can buy the things that make for a better life.*
> *(T. Ninan 1985:71)*

While the assumption that luxury goods provide consumers with a "better
life" is debatable, television contributed to the spread of consumerism
among the Indian middle classes.[40] The state's attempts to legitimate itself

in the eyes of the burgeoning middle classes articulated with the needs of private industry to create a market for its goods. The change in state policy from investments in capital goods to consumer goods production rested, in part, on the premise that India could become a modern nation when its citizens acquired middle-class lifestyles through the acquisition of consumer goods. How was the family, an ostensibly local site of consumption, permeated by translocal and transnational political economies and desires?

The Rise of the Indian Middle Classes

The 1980s saw the Indian middle classes expand to constitute more than 10 percent of the total population. Estimates of the actual size of the new middle classes vary.[41] In January 1993, the *Far Eastern Economic Review* put the figure at more than 100 million, or 12 percent of the population.[42] The new middle classes consisted of professionals, salaried employees of state bureaucracies, small-scale entrepreneurs, traders, and prosperous farmers, and represented households earning annual incomes between $400 and $1,867.[43] The middle classes were soon "captured" by television simultaneously as target audience for its serials and as market for the goods advertised in its commercials. The new economic policies enabled the middle classes to consume goods that had recently been luxury items but were now perceived as crucial indices of upward mobility: household appliances, toiletries, packaged foods, and other consumer goods.

From the 1950s to the early 1980s, the Indian state's economic policies had aimed at eradicating mass poverty (Indira Gandhi had won an election on the basis of the slogan "Abolish poverty" [*Garibi hatao*]) and had actively discouraged consumerism, which was described as wasteful and harmful to a growing national economy. By the mid-1980s, however, it became clear that the focus of economic policy had shifted from heavy industry to consumer goods. Indira Gandhi's regime took its first tentative steps toward "decontrolling" the economy by removing bureaucratic controls on private industry and opening the door to foreign collaboration. Economic growth picked up by 5 percent.[44] Rajiv Gandhi, first in his unofficial capacity as the prime minister's heir apparent, and later when he was voted prime minister, accelerated the reforms started by his mother. The rapidly expanding middle classes, whose earnings had increased during the late 1970s and early 1980s, were eager to spend their discretionary income on consumer goods and thus represented a huge market to advertisers. The expansion of the reach of television and the launching of commercials titillated the consumerist desires of viewing subjects by introducing them to a range of goods that promised to make their lives more modern, more exciting, more middle class. Analyst V. G. Kulkarni described the confluence of government policies on consumer expenditure and the demographic expansion of the middle classes: "Whether by design or default, a series of government economic policies has helped to give birth to [a] generation of Indians who have money to spend" (1992:45).

Some analysts insist that the middle classes, who by no means represented a homogeneous group with uniform interests, formed a lobby pushing for economic "reforms" and demanding more entertainment programs on television.[45] Their growing numbers and relative affluence endowed them with a "political voice" that politicians found difficult to ignore (Kulkarni 1992:45). Nobody understood the political importance of the middle classes better than Rajiv Gandhi, who recognized them as a significant constituency. "For the first time in India," one journalist pointed out, "a prime minister now feels that the middle class is a political force in even arithmetical terms because it has grown so rapidly in numbers, and that it makes political sense to satisfy its aspirations even at the risk of being portrayed as anti-poor" (T. Ninan 1985:71).

The demographic expansion of the middle classes was reinforced by its cultural constitution. Exposure to television radically transformed the media habits of the middle classes. In 1991, the results of NRS-IV, a mammoth survey undertaken jointly by the Indian Market Research Bureau and Media Search,[46] revealed that many respondents had reduced going to the cinema by 29 percent. This contrasted with television exposure, which for respondents drawn from urban and rural areas grew dramatically from 9 percent in 1978 to 68 percent in 1983. The exposure of women to television increased by 33 percent, compared with 26 percent for men. A leading advertising and marketing journal described the implications of the dramatic expansion of the reach of television: "A decade ago, less than half of all adult Indians were exposed to at least one mass medium while TV, yet in its infancy, was an upper class, metro, top-of-the-pyramid phenomenon. The 80s were the decade of a TV explosion in the country leading to the emergence of whole new sections of our society now being exposed to a commercial mass medium."[47]

The urban middle classes constituted the core of Doordarshan's target audience: in 1990, TV reached an estimated 75 percent of the urban adult population.[48] Because audience ratings translated into revenue for Doordarshan, serial producers, and the corporations sponsoring and advertising programs on Doordarshan, the urban middle classes became increasingly assertive and vocal with regard to television policy. The tone of the serials became less didactic, and their content slowly changed so that they became less concerned with development.

The middle-class (and, occasionally, upper-class) orientation of the most popular serials (with the notable exception of *Nukkad* [Street corner], which was unique in that it consciously attempted to appeal to a working-class audience) reveals a great deal about the class character of its target audience.[49] Close on the heels of *Hum Log*, which, with its focus on the trials and tribulations of an urban lower-middle-class family was explicitly targeted at middle-class viewers, were *Rajani* and *Khandaan* (Clan). *Rajani* narrated the reformist efforts of its upper-middle-class heroine, and *Khandaan* was a shorter, Indianized version of the U.S. soap opera *Dynasty*. The middle-class orientation of serials was commented on by no less than the minister of information and broadcasting, V. N. Gadgil, who noted that "their locale, the characters and their problems [are] too oriented towards an urban middle class audience."[50]

Several critics of Doordarshan voiced similar concerns. The Joshi Committee Report of 1985, for instance, condemned Doordarshan for neglecting stories about working-class women. Similarly, a series of reports brought out by the Research Center for Women's Studies at SNDT (Shreemati Nathibai Damodar Thakersey) University in Bombay criticized the "invisibility" of working-class women on Doordarshan (cf. Agrawal and Joshi n.d., Bakshi n.d., and Krishnan n.d.). According to Krishnan, when working-class or poor women were shown at all, they were generally portrayed as beneficiaries of welfare schemes (n.d.:16).

What pleasures did Doordarshan offer to its viewers? Put another way, how was it able to recruit viewing subjects? What sorts of spaces did it occupy in their everyday lives? The upwardly mobile working-class and lower-middle-class women I worked with often said that television offered an easy source of entertainment that had earlier been denied to them. This was especially true for women, many of whom spent a great deal of their time doing housework and working outside the home as well. They had neither the time nor the opportunity to socialize. Many viewers in Vikas Nagar and Basti were recent migrants to the city, transplanted into neighborhoods where they were forced to live with strangers from different parts of India: they frequently confided that they felt exceedingly isolated and lonely.

For women like Aparna Dasgupta, who was illiterate and thus could not read newspapers, television was a primary source of information about "the outside world." Aparna had moved from Calcutta to New Delhi thirty years ago. She frequently spoke of Calcutta with nostalgia: she missed hearing Bengali spoken in the streets; she craved the types of fish and vegetables that one could get only in Calcutta; most of all, she missed her extended family, all of whom still lived in and around Calcutta. She had not been able to find a community in New Delhi. She was rarely able to visit friends and relatives in New Delhi because she was afraid to travel alone by bus: she had heard too much about the harassment women, even middle-aged women like herself, had to face in buses. To add to her loneliness, her husband, sons, and daughters were away at their jobs most of the day, and her daughter-in-law was too busy with housework to spend much time with her. Despite the fact that she had lived in Vikas Nagar for the past seven years and was almost universally liked and respected by her neighbors, she had made few friends. When I asked her why that was so, she replied that it was because they were "too different" from her.

The diversity of languages and cultures in neighborhoods such as Vikas Nagar reinforced the isolation and loneliness of women like Aparna: there was only one other Bengali family in the neighborhood, and they were, according to Aparna, too "superior" to socialize with her. It was with considerable relief, then, that Aparna turned to television as a source of companionship. Her favorite time of the day was between 2:00 and 4:00 P.M., when she would watch the afternoon programs on Doordarshan. Indeed, she said that her day "really began" in the afternoon: she made sure that she finished her lunch by about 1:00 P.M. and helped her daughter-in-law with the dishes so that she could be ready for her favorite afternoon programs. By the time the afternoon programs finished, it would be time for the rest of the family to come home. Her words made it clear to me that the afternoon programs helped her get through the tedium and loneliness of the day.

Television was thus an important source of social connectedness for some women. As they arranged their schedules around their favorite programs, television became an integral part of their everyday lives. This, together with the fact that many of them could not go to the cinema or attend other public forms of entertainment, meant that television was also a major source of information. Through engaging with television's discourses, viewing subjects could imaginatively connect with larger collectivities.

The men and women I worked with felt a profound identification with the characters and predicaments in narratives that portrayed the lives of lower-middle-class and upwardly mobile working-class families like themselves. For instance, Shakuntala Sharma lived in Vikas Nagar with her husband, a clerk in the Finance Ministry, and her son and daughter. As brahmins who were precariously lower middle class, the Sharmas were very conscious of their caste and class positions. They considered themselves superior to some of their neighbors, and this sense of superiority was articulated most frequently in terms of how they had brought up their children. The children were the Sharmas' greatest hope for upward mobility, and they had accordingly invested all their meager resources in giving them an education: Poonam was going to college, and her brother had a master's degree in commerce. Shakuntala and her husband frequently commented that even though their daughter was outspoken at home, she was "well mannered," "modest," and soft-spoken in public. Their son had always done very well academically and was now working as an apprentice in a private company. Shakuntala related that, one day, her son's friends had come over on a scooter. The next morning, her neighbor, who had noticed the scooter parked outside the Sharmas' flat, asked, "Who was that who had come to your house?" Shakuntala recounted to me with pride: "I told my neighbor, 'That was my son's friend. Only people of class come to our house.'"

The Sharmas' self-constitution as middle class deeply influenced their preferences in television serials. Poonam and Shakuntala claimed that they had preferred *Hum Log* and *Buniyaad* (about a lower-middle-class family and a middle-class family, respectively) to *Khandaan*, which was about a rich, upper-class family. When I asked why that was so, Shakuntala replied that *Hum Log* was more "family oriented" (*paarivarik*) than *Khandaan* and was about a middle-class family. Poonam agreed; she explained that *Khandaan* was about "the business class," adding, "we don't understand the psychology of rich people. *Hum Log* was about people like us."

Moreover, like other viewers, Shakuntala and Poonam were acutely conscious of the fact that, given their limited financial resources, television was a crucial source of entertainment. For instance, Poonam once, in response to an upper-class person's criticism of television serials, retorted: "Television serials are to people like me what clubs and restaurants are for rich people." Hence, for Aparna Dasgupta, Poonam, Shakuntala Sharma, and many other women, television was a source not just of information and entertainment, but also of sociality.[51]

Commercial Sponsorship and the Spread of Consumerism

Thanks to the new sponsorship scheme mentioned above, major industrial companies, including prominent multinational corporations such as Nestlé, Brooke Bond, and Unilever, became important agents in the production of entertainment serials.[52] Since companies sponsored only those serials with the potential to draw large audiences, serial producers strove to get high ratings in order to attract and keep their sponsors. And sponsors, for their part, raced to get airtime on the most popular serials to ensure that they would reach the maximum number of viewers/potential consumers. Development-oriented educational programs on health, agriculture, and family planning began to fall by the wayside because they received extremely low ratings compared with entertainment programs.

Let me turn once again to the *Hum Log* story, this time to point to the relationship between the commercial sponsorship of entertainment serials and the spread of consumerism among the Indian middle classes. It was no accident that the production and telecast of the first development-oriented soap opera was made possible by a subsidiary of the multinational company Nestlé, Food Specialities Limited (FSL). This, in fact, was symptomatic of the shift from Indira Gandhi's quasi-socialist, protectionist policies to Rajiv Gandhi's promotion of the "opening up" of Indian markets to multinational capital. The famous Maggi Noodles story reveals the nexus between multinational capital, the Indian state, the advertising industry, and a largely middle-class audience primed to plunge into consumerism.

In 1984, the huge success of the marketing of a new, somewhat foreign food product through television commercials demonstrated the potential of commercial television for selling new products to a nationwide audience. Maggi Noodles were manufactured by FSL. When FSL first began advertising on *Hum Log* in 1984, the Maggi Noodles commercial was lost in the clutter of advertisements shown before the serial. By sponsoring the production of *Hum Log*, however, FSL was able to buy the crucial few seconds just before the show began, plus several more minutes of airtime. Two birds were killed with one stone: FSL met the production costs of *Hum Log*, and *Hum Log* became the vehicle that marketed Maggi Noodles. Maggi Noodles was thus introduced to a captive audience of more than 50 million people between 1984 and 1985, and sales rose from none in 1982 to 1,600 tons in 1983, to about 5,000 tons in 1984.[53] More significant, the success of Maggi Noodles made packaged foods not just acceptable but, because of their convenience and modern image, *desirable* to the middle-class audience.

This marketing success story launched a new era. In 1983, advertising agencies had scoffed at the prospect of making commercials for Doordarshan. By 1985, after the success of *Hum Log* and Maggi Noodles, there were about fifteen contenders for every prime-time slot.[54] R. Srinivasan, the marketing correspondent of the *Times of India*, informed me that the fastest growth in the Indian economy in the 1980s was in consumer production and spending.[55] Commodities such as cosmetics and packaged foods, deemed luxuries in the late 1970s, were "in demand as necessities" by the end of the 1980s. Although by the early 1990s the expansion of the rural middle classes had led to the establishment of rural markets, urban viewers still constituted as much as 60 percent of the market. According to Srinivasan, the consumer market first "took off" with the success of *Hum Log*, *Rajani*, and *Buniyaad*. Consumer spending accelerated most dramatically, however, when the *Ramayan* was telecast and urban viewership peaked. Hence, the spread of consumerism was inextricably related to the success of television serials.

Doordarshan charged advertisers Rs 36,000 ($1,440 at prevailing exchange rates) for ten seconds of advertising time; or, as noted above, advertisers could sponsor serials by paying for production costs in exchange for two minutes of free advertising time. The remaining advertising time netted $8,000 per minute of prime time.[56] Between 1985 and 1988, Doordarshan raised the cost of airtime three times.[57] In 1990, the total revenue Doordarshan received for advertisements amounted to $104 million.[58] The role of advertising agencies also expanded. In addition to producing and placing spots on television, some advertising agencies also located sponsors who would finance the production of serials. In other words, advertising agencies began to function as brokers, earning 15 percent commission from both Doordarshan and clients. Leading advertising agencies often retained the services of "full-time fixers," usually former bureaucrats, to use their contacts in Doordarshan to push scripts.[59] Thus, the partnership between industry and the bureaucracy and between the state and national and transnational capital in the production and shaping of national popular culture became firmly established.

The rapid expansion of the consumer market is also evident from the following statistics: sales of TV sets jumped from 2 million to 23.4 million between 1981 and 1990; the annual sales of new cars increased five times during the 1980s; and between 1984 and 1990, the annual sales of packaged consumer goods shot up by 220 percent.[60]

In spite of spiraling inflation, consumer spending continued to rise in the late 1980s and early 1990s. Increased consumer spending was also reflected in the fact that corporations increased their TV advertising budgets: the amount of money spent by corporations on TV commercials for toiletries increased from Rs 19.8 crore ($7.9 million) to Rs 27.1 crore ($10.8 million), for consumer durables from Rs 18.7 crore ($7.5 million) to Rs 20.4 crore ($8.2 million), and for textiles from Rs 5 crore ($2 million) to Rs 6.9 crore ($2.8 million).[61] Described by advertising industry leaders as the "most persuasive, the most cost-effective and the quickest medium,"[62] these advertisements catered to the urban and, later, rural middle classes.

The early 1990s saw the increasing presence of multinational and monopoly capital on Doordarshan. Most of the advertisers on Doordarshan consisted either of multinational companies and their subsidiaries, such as Colgate-Palmolive, Brooke Bond, Ponds, and FSL, or major Indian corporations such as Tatas, Birlas, Mody, Godrej, and TVS. In general, smaller companies were left out of the race for prime time. Close to 70 percent of Doordarshan's advertisement revenues came from the top twenty spenders.[63]

Several media critics commented on the spread of consumerism engendered by the commercial sponsorship of television serials. Arvind Singhal and Everett Rogers, for example, expressed their concern that consumerism "upsets the previous balance between the socio-cultural development goals of the mass media versus the mass consumer goals in India" (1989:81). Indian feminists entered the debate on the impact of consumerism on women and national development. For instance, Prabha

Krishnan and Anita Dighe argued that consumerism detracted from national development by focusing on the desires of upper-class individuals. Thus, they claimed, "educated articulate persons view their own and the country's progress and development in terms of the goods and services available to the elite. Consumerism arouses desires which distort economic priorities and lure people into artificial consumption patterns" (1990:113).

As I noted above, advertisements were clustered at the beginning of the serials. Depending on the popularity of the program, these ads could last for ten to fifteen minutes. The following inventory of advertisements framing a single episode of *Param Veer Chakra* lists the products advertised and the languages in which they were telecast. The target audience for the advertisements may be surmised from the kinds of products advertised:

Mikado Suitings: fabric for suits; featured upper-class men and women; in Hindi

Natura Mango Bar: fruit candy; featured middle-class children; in Hindi

BTex Ointment: analgesic ointment; featured middle-aged and senior adults who seemed middle class; in Hindi

Amul Badambar: chocolate-covered almond bar; featured upper-middle-class children; in English

Cibaca Toothbrush: featured middle-class man and a little girl; in Hindi

Parle-G Biscuits: featured middle-class extended family; focus on seniors and children; in Hindi

Vespa Scooter: featured a middle-class little girl and her father; in Hindi

Kisme Toffee Bar: candy; featured middle-class children; in Hindi

Nutramul: chocolate-flavored beverage; featured upper-class children; in English

Safi: unani skin tonic; featured Hindi film actress; in Hindi

Hajmola: ayurvedic digestive tablets; featured middle- to upper-class adults; in Hindi

Tractor Distemper: house paint; featured upper-middle-class extended family; focus on happy housewife; in Hindi

Lehar Pepsi: Pepsi Cola; featured celebrated Hindi film actress Juhi Chawla and Goan rap singer Remo Fernandes; in Hindi

Hawkins Pressure Cooker: featured middle-class housewife; in Hindi

Pan Pasand: betel nut product; featured middle-class housewife and her husband; in Hindi

Drainex: drain cleaning powder; middle-class family; in Hindi

Nixoderm: ointment for skin rash; featured middle-class adults; in Hindi

Hero Honda: moped; focus on middle-class young man; in English

Hot Wheels: toy cars produced by the multinational Leo-Mattel; focus on upper- to middle-class little boys; in English

Rajkamal Aggarbattis: incense sticks; class of target audience unclear; in Hindi

The foregoing were the advertisements lumped together in a cluster. After the advertisement for Rajkamal Aggarbattis came advertisements of the companies that sponsored this particular episode of *Param Veer Chakra:* Allwyn; Paras Pharmaceuticals; Marico, Ltd.; and Eureka Forbes, Ltd. Because these advertisements were shown in the last five minutes before the episode began, they were likely to be seen by the maximum number of viewers:

Aquaguard: water-purifying appliance for home use; featured an upper-class woman and her family; focus on salesman played by actor Nitish Bharadwaj, who played Lord Krishna in the serial *Mahabharat;* in Hindi

Eureka Vacuum Guard: vacuum cleaner; focus on upper-class home; in English

Parachute Coconut Oil: personal grooming product; featured Hindi film actress and middle-class teenage women; in Hindi

Sweekar Refined Sunflower Oil: cooking oil; featured middle-class housewife; in Hindi

Moove Pain Ointment: featured middle-class family; focus on seniors; in Hindi

Stopache: analgesic tablets; set in a busy office; focus on young, upper/middle-class young man; in Hindi

Allwyn No-Frost Refrigerator: featured middle/upper-class family; in Hindi

Allwyn Quartz Watch: wristwatches; voice-over in English.

Of the twenty-eight advertisements listed above, seven were for candy, snacks, other packaged foods, and beverages; six featured high-end consumer durables such as refrigerators, scooters, and so on; and four pertained to other kitchen appliances. Although it did not strike me at the time, six of the advertisements featured children, thus indicating the identification of children as an important segment of the market. In general, the focus in *all* these advertisements was on upper- and middle-class families and, more generally, on modern lifestyles and homes; indeed, the advertisements seemed to equate middle-class lifestyles with modernity. While the English advertisements were explicitly aimed at upper-middle-class viewers, the fact that many advertisements for expensive products (e.g., Allwyn No-Frost Refrigerator, Aquaguard, and Eureka Vacuum Guard) were in Hindi indicates the expansion of the middle class to include viewers relatively less fluent in English. There were two advertisements for "traditional" medicines (the unani Safi and the ayurvedic Hajmola) that were now being manufactured and sold with modern packaging.[64] Typically, the advertisements for home appliances featured middle-class housewives. These advertisements naturalized the gendered division of labor within the middle-class family and the relationship of the desire for modern and middle-class homes and lifestyles with the acquisition of these products. Finally, while some advertisements portrayed the personal comfort, glamour, or convenience that individuals could acquire through commodities (as in the advertisement for Parachute Hair Oil or Mikado Suitings), for the most part they focused on the lifestyles of families rather than of individuals, hence illustrating how viewing families were constituted as units of consumption.

Many advertisements explicitly linked modernity with "Western" technology. The voice-over in the advertisement for Allwyn Quartz Watches claimed: "The technology that gave the world the very first quartz watch. Allwyn Quartz Watch. Yours." Similarly, the voice-over in the advertisement for Eureka Vacuum Guard claimed: "India's most wanted home-cleaning system, the Euroclean Multi-Vac. The protective power your family needs against dirt, dust, and health hazards," and promised that the "protective power" of European technology was now available in India.

Significantly, the voice-overs in both of these advertisements were male, in contrast to female voice-overs in some of the advertisements for kitchen gadgets and appliances. The voice-over for Hawkins Pressure

Cooker was that of a woman, and the advertisement featured a young, middle-class woman who emblematized a selective blending of "tradition" and "modernity": despite the fact that the housewife used a modern pressure cooker, she was "traditional" in that she was shown in a sari and had long hair modestly arranged in a bun. Illustrating a significant and typical slippage between tradition and Hinduism, the *tikka* on her forehead and a *mangalsutra* around her neck signified her Hindu (and married) identity.

Packaged foods such as Maggi Noodles, Fryums (fried snacks), and MDH Masalas (preground, premixed spices) became increasingly popular with some of the lower-middle-class women I worked with, because of their convenience. Advertisements for textiles, for polyester saris, and for cosmetics were especially popular among younger women, for whom these commodities signified an entry into modern lifestyles.

Almost all the women I worked with were from families precariously poised on the threshold of middle-classness. How did advertisements such as those described above reinforce their anxieties about financial security and affect their dreams for upward mobility? How did the advertisements mediate their aspirations to acquire middle-class lives? I now turn to the example of two lower-middle-class women, Rehana Ahmad and her daughter, Razia. Rehana's husband worked in a garment factory on the other side of town; her elder son, Bashir, had a high school degree and had been unemployed for three years. For most of the time that I knew the family, Bashir was away visiting his grandfather in Moradabad. Rehana and her husband also had a younger son still in school; Razia had finished high school the previous year. The family lived in a small one-room tenement in the northeast corner of Basti. The single room functioned as a living room by day and a bedroom by night; it was linked by a narrow corridor to a tiny kitchen. Every time I visited, Rehana was either working in the kitchen or sewing clothes in a corner of the main room. She always seemed to be working, and I used to feel very guilty about taking up her time.

My anxiety about being intrusive was somewhat alleviated by Rehana's warmth and by the enthusiasm with which Razia would greet me. Rehana and Razia seemed more like friends than mother and daughter; yet, I often got the feeling that Razia was lonely. When I first met her, Razia had just become engaged to a cousin who lived in Moradabad. While her mother was working in the kitchen, Razia would talk to me about her fiancé. She would speak about him in whispers: it was hard to miss the excitement, tinged with anxiety, in her voice. Razia was worried because her fiancé had been in and out of jobs several times in the past two years; she seemed especially concerned about her financial future.

Rehana was also anxious about Razia's upcoming marriage. We talked about it one sleepy afternoon when Rehana was embroidering a *dupatta* for Razia's trousseau.[65] Razia was very beautiful: according to her mother, she was so beautiful that the prospective groom's parents had said they expected no dowry. "Is it the custom in your community to give dowries?" I asked. Rehana replied: "No, it never used to be. But now people are imitating others. Now they know what to ask for." She said that while the practice had not existed in her generation, it was becoming more common nowadays. "Why do you think it is becoming common?" I persisted. Rehana repeated what she had said earlier: that members of her community were now imitating "others." She kept her gaze averted from mine when she said this, and I realized that the "others" her community members were imitating were the majority Hindu community, but she was hesitating to say so to spare my feelings.

Then, perhaps because she sensed my discomfort, she said that there was more money coming into her community from people who had migrated to the Middle East. She added: "Also, don't forget that these days people lead more ostentatious lives. Earlier, people lived more simply. Even if they were rich, they didn't know where to spend money. Now, with TV, they know." Rehana reverted to Razia's upcoming marriage. "We were so relieved when they didn't ask for anything. We would have been ruined if they had" (*hum to bik jaate*). She bent her head to her embroidery and repeated the last phrase several times, the needle and thread flying through her fingers, "We would have been ruined. I thanked God they didn't ask for anything. We would have been ruined."

I watched television with Rehana and Razia one Sunday morning. Rehana's husband was away for the entire day, so she seemed less harried than usual. As we waited for that morning's serial to start, an advertisement for Tractor Distemper (house paint) came on. The advertisement showed a (Hindu) family consisting of a woman, her husband, her two children, and their grandmother gathered in a spacious living room with freshly painted, white walls. At the time, I did not pay any attention to the advertisement. Weeks later, Razia was telling me about a childhood friend who had married and gone to live with her husband in Bombay.

Her friend's husband worked for a private company; Razia did not know exactly what he did, but she knew that he made a "good income." Razia said that her friend was very happy; she had a beautiful flat, "just like the one we saw in the paint ad." At first I could not remember what paint advertisement she was talking about. It was only later, when I was looking over my fieldnotes, that I realized that she had been referring to the advertisement for Tractor Distemper.

I knew that Razia had never been to Bombay, and therefore had not visited her friend's house. But it was evident that the house in the advertisement represented to Razia the benefits of a "good income": unlike her parent's house, the house in the advertisement (which became transposed onto her friend's house in Bombay) was spacious; unlike the peeling, yellow walls that surrounded her, it had sparkling white walls. Unlike the room in which we were sitting on a sheet spread on the floor, the living room in the advertisement had modern furniture consisting of a sofa and upholstered armchairs. In Razia's discourse, the qualities of the house in the advertisement were transposed onto her fantasy about her friend's house in Bombay, that city of opportunity and glamour, and signified a distant dream of comfort, affluence, and modernity.[66]

This exchange with Razia was one of many (sometimes poignant) conversations I had with women in which I gleaned how television commercials had shaped their desires for the financial security promised by upward mobility into the middle class, their anxieties about the future, and their dreams of modernity. The extent to which television might have interpellated viewers as consuming subjects may be gauged from the rapid proliferation of commercials and the kinds of products they advertised. Operations Research Group, one of India's largest marketing research companies, claimed that Doordarshan averaged about three thousand spots a month during 1986–1987. Thirty percent of these ads were for food products, 22 percent were for toiletries, 10 percent were for pharmaceutical products, and the remaining 29 percent were for consumer durables and services.[67]

The first direct impact of this proliferation of advertisements was on the lifestyles of families: the home became the site for the fulfillment of their dreams about middle-class security and, more than that, their desires for modern lifestyles. A news report claimed that "the rise of the middle class in India is amply reflected in the country's shopping centers and malls. On offer today are whole new ranges of processed foods, and a previously undreamt of choice in domestic appliances, including washing machines, vacuum cleaners, slow and fast cookers, mixer-grinders that come in 75 brands, room coolers, hot water geysers, and that ultimate sign of middle class decadence, the 24 chime doorbell" (T. Ninan 1985:73).

Programming decisions, the content of serials and the advertisements that framed them, and, most significant, the imperatives of the transnational consumer market thus converged to position (and perhaps reconfigure) the viewing family as viewers of national programming; viewing families were simultaneously recruited as units of consumption for the ever-widening range of consumer goods marketed through the advertisements. What subject positions were created for women by the representations of middle-classness and modernity enacted in television advertisements?

THE MODERN INDIAN WOMAN AS VIEWER/CONSUMER

Desire, as soon as there is exchange, "perverts" need. (Irigaray 1985:177)

As I noted above, advertisements on Doordarshan frequently targeted women viewers. According to the 1991 NRS-IV survey undertaken by two major marketing research organizations, Indian women's exposure to television increased fourfold between 1983 and 1991. While only 46 percent of the women who owned television sets watched every day in 1978, in 1991 62 percent watched television for at least one hour a day. On average, women watched up to 11.4 hours of TV a week in 1991. The discourses of advertisements (and, where available, of advertising agency personnel) reveal the ways in which Indian Womanhood was categorized and reconstituted. What do these categories tell us about underlying ideas of class, modernity, and tradition? In this section I will focus on the structural and discursive factors that positioned women viewers as consumers, drawing on my ethnographic research with women viewers/consumers, content analyses of advertisements, and analyses constructed by feminists and media critics within and outside India.

Categories of Womanhood

In her essay on advertisements in the United States, Mary Ann Doane points out that advertising keeps alive the desire to consume because it goes "beyond the aim of selling a particular commodity" and serves to "generate and maintain an aptitude for consumption in the subject" (1989:28). That middle-class Indian women were firmly ensconced in circuits of consumerism was evident in the sharp rise in women's consumer spending that occurred after the introduction of commercials on Doordarshan. Reflected in the growth of markets such as those for kitchen gadgets and packaged food and beverages, it was particularly evident in the case of the market for women's cosmetics, which grew sixfold, with the index of growth rising from 258 points in 1985 to 590 in 1990.[68]

Indian advertisements created spectatorial subject positions that were crucially mediated by culturally specific discourses of gender, modernity, and tradition. Yet, given the transnational character of the industry, it is not surprising to also find some broad similarities between Indian and U.S. advertisements. Doane suggests that three types of relationships exist between the commodity form and the female spectator/consumer. In the first relationship, the woman is herself a commodity in a patriarchal system of "exchanges." This involves "the encouragement of the woman's narcissistic apprehension of the image of the woman on the screen. The female spectator is invited to witness her own commodification and, furthermore, to buy an image of herself insofar as the female star is proposed as the ideal of female beauty" (Doane 1989:24–25). The second type of relationship ensues from the contractual arrangement between advertisers and studios. In the case of Doordarshan, the commodity is "tied" to the production of the serial. The third relationship exists in the film/serial itself and "its status as a commodity in a circuit of exchange." The film, or in our case the television serial, is itself a commodity that is produced, bought, and sold for a profit (compare the case of *Hum Log* and Maggi Noodles described above). In its commodity form, the film/serial promotes a certain mode of perception that, for the female spectator, initiates a particularly complex dialectic of being, having, and appearing (Doane 1989:25). There are, therefore, profound interconnections between the different economies at work in the relationship between the serial/film text and the consumer: the economy of the text articulates with the economy of the commodities that are advertised and bought, as well as with the purchase of the text-commodity itself. The relationship between the "economy of the text, its regulation of spectatorial investments and drives, is linked to the economy of tie-ins, the logic of the female subject's relation to the commodity—her status as consumer of goods and consumer of discourses" (Doane 1989:25).

In the context of Doordarshan, sponsor tie-ins and the advertisements framing serials resulted in a range of categories, and subject positions, of modern Indian Womanhood. In some cases, as in serials like *Rajani* (discussed above), there was a continuity, or "flow," between the subject positions offered to women in the narratives of serials and those of the commercials.[69] In these serials and in the advertisements that framed them, women were depicted as simultaneously modern and traditional: even as they ran their homes with modern appliances, they were portrayed as traditional because of their fidelity to their roles as dutiful housewives and nurturing mothers. In the process, the advertisements *constructed* the meanings of "modernity" and "tradition" in explicitly gendered terms.

In one serial discussed by Krishnan and Dighe, the marginalization of the woman protagonist and her containment within the home "with men controlling all the action" was comparable with the passivity of the women in the commercials that preceded the serial (1990:48–49). At other times, there was a contradiction between the "messages" contained in serials and commercials, respectively. This was particularly acute in the case of "women-oriented" serials shown on Doordarshan, many of which, ironically, tried to make a case against dowry. Similarly, *Swayam-siddha*, a serial that aimed to depict the empowerment of a divorced woman, was sponsored by a company that manufactured saris: every episode was framed by advertisements that fetishized the female model's body by lingering voyeuristically on it.[70]

Discourses of advertising frequently hinged on the objectification of the female body. As in the United States, many Indian advertisements segmented the female body into hair, face, legs, breasts, and so on.[71] Several feminist critics of Doordarshan have commented on this sexual objectification of women. For instance, Krishnan and Dighe describe how in many advertisements, "the caressing movements of the camera sweeping over women's bodies engage the male viewer as voyeur, evaluator and subject, and the female viewer as object" (1990:90).

Marketing strategies targeting women viewers/consumers created subject positions that were marked as much by class as by gender, most frequently through the category of "housewife," which was further divided into "traditional housewives" and "modern housewives" (cf. Miller 1995a). The market segmentation strategy followed for Procter and Gamble's Ariel detergent was typical of the ways women viewers were categorized as consumers in terms of their class positions. The target audience was divided into two segments: all housewives, and housewives with a monthly household income of Rs 750 ($27) and at least a high school education.[72] Another marketing strategy for packaged foods segmented its target audience in terms of a "typology of housewives" depending on how they used modern convenience foods: "traditional" housewives, "nutrition-conscious" housewives, and "convenience-seekers" (MARG, from the *Economic Times*, July 8, 1992).

The segmentation of women viewers by class is also illustrated by the contrast between advertisements for two laundry detergents, Surf and Nirma. The advertisement for Surf featured Lalitaji (played by Kavita Choudhry, the lead actress in the "women-oriented" serial *Udaan*),[73] a shrewd housewife who ran her household according to the norms of modern efficiency but was at the same time traditional in that she wore a sari, wore her hair in a bun, and had a *tikka* on her forehead. Lalitaji was the quintessentially *upper*-middle-class urban woman who had successfully blended modern housekeeping with "traditional" traits. This advertisement contrasted with the advertisement for Nirma, which marketed itself not as "laundry detergent" but as "washing powder." In marked contrast to Lalitaji, the women in the Nirma advertisement were *lower* middle class. Further, and more significant, unlike the Surf advertisement, which showed Lalitaji haggling with vegetable vendors (thereby establishing that she was a frugal housewife), the Nirma advertisement frequently showed women actually washing clothes. Evidently, the two advertisements were aimed at different segments of the audience: while the more expensive Surf was for the upper middle classes, Nirma was aimed at lower-middle-class women.

In a paper presented at an international seminar on advertising and marketing, marketing experts Bijapurkar and Ahluwalia advised their audience on how *different* consumer goods could be marketed in terms of specific semiotic codes. The experts suggested that cooking oils could be promoted in terms of purity, taste, economy, and "good housewifelyness [*sic*]"; cosmetics, on the other hand, would have to be "positioned" so as to "target the new, modern Indian woman promoted in advertising as westernized and independent." They claimed that "the core values of ABC as a company [and a brand] that got established as a result of its lead products, were: 'modern, westernized . . . women's or working women's products.'"[74]

In these recommendations, modernity was explicitly associated with Westernization. As we have seen above, however, in most of the advertisements shown on Doordarshan, modernity was visually represented so as to encapsulate "Indian" virtues such as modesty (signified by the sari and the hair bun), tradition (signified by the ubiquitous *tikka* and *mangalsutra*), and duty (signified by the female characters' fidelity to the role of the conscientious wife/mother/daughter-in-law) in the very person of the female model, who hence represented the "new, modern Indian woman."

The transference of symbolic values associated with "the new, modern Indian woman" to, for instance, cooking oil or cosmetics reveals what Luce Irigaray describes as the superimposition of "symbolic and imaginary productions upon, and even substituted for, the value of relations of material, natural, and corporal (re)production" (1985:171). Invested with meaning, commodities "speak" to consumers. The symbolic meanings of commodities and consumption have been analyzed by scholars such as Arjun Appadurai (1986a) and Dick Hebdige (1979), who focus on the "social life of things" and of the communicative aspects of consumption, respectively. Since it is embedded in larger significatory chains, consumption necessarily involves the production of meanings. For example, an advertisement for the ayurvedic cleansing cream Vicco Turmeric Creme was extremely popular among the young women with whom I worked. In this advertisement, a young bride-to-be beautified herself in preparation for her marriage by using Vicco Turmeric Creme. The next scene showed a large, spacious home bustling with the festivities of what seemed to be a lavish marriage. The camera then cut to the face of the bride, her eyes turned demurely to the floor: artfully made up and resplendent in heavy jewelry, she was a beautiful bride.[75]

The combination of turmeric, oil, gram flour, and milk contained in Vicco Turmeric Creme is a "home remedy" that many middle-class women (including myself) put together for cleansing our skin. Packaged in this manner, however, Vicco Turmeric Creme televisually combined discourses of femininity, beauty, and, last but not least, a desire for ostentatious weddings in a seamless semiotic chain. In a quintessentially modernist move, the Vicco commercial encapsulated both the traditional and the modern by creating and inserting the product into discourses of gender (iconicized by the modest and, therefore, "traditional" bride), class (indexed by the spacious, ostentatiously modern home), and modern forms of conspicuous consumption (symbolized by the lavish festivities and, most vividly, the ostentatious jewelry and makeup).

Women viewers were themselves positioned as commodities because they were "sold" to sponsors and advertisers as prospective consumers. In her ironic use of Lévi-Strauss's model of the "exchange" of women, Irigaray claims that the "economy of exchange—of desire—is man's business" (1985:177). But, as Doane suggests, perhaps Irigaray goes too far: she neglects to leave room for the construction of women's desires. Theories that focus exclusively on the objectification of women ignore the construction of women's subjectivities through the constitution of *their* desires. Through their location in the circuit of exchange and their fetishization in terms of specific commodified values, women viewers were positioned as both objects and subjects of consumption. Encapsulating discourses of tradition and modernity, advertisements for Surf, Vicco Turmeric Creme, and Hawkins Pressure Cooker commodified Modern Indian Womanhood for the consumption of viewing subjects. These discourses positioned women viewers as subjects who "consumed" not just the commodities being advertised, but also notions of Modern Indian Womanhood constructed through semiotic chains of images and desires.

From the perspective of the advertising industry, middle-class women had to be "seduced" to consumerism. This seemed especially critical in the case of women like Aparna Dasgupta who, because of time constraints, economic limitations, or social custom, could not go to the cinema for entertainment. However, I do not want to imply that only women were targeted by television commercials and interpellated by desires for the middle-class and modern lifestyles they promised. For men as much as for women, television advertisements conferred on goods values that resonated with their aspirations and anxieties at a time when they were struggling to consolidate their middle-class status.

Yet, many men claimed that women were the ones who "craved" the commodities offered in the advertisements. In fact, some of the men I spoke with claimed that middle-class women who worked outside the home did so for the express purpose of acquiring consumer goods. Selapan told me that only men who were "greedy" for consumer goods "permitted" their wives to work outside the home. His statement struck me as very interesting for several reasons: first, he completely divested women of all agency—they would or could take up jobs only if their husbands were "greedy" enough to "permit" them to do so. More important, I had observed on several occasions that Selapan spoke of the commodities he owned with great pride: he clearly attributed a great deal of value to them.

While Selapan was not the only man who yearned for consumer goods (see Miller 1995a:34 for the gendering of consumer subjects), his position along axes of caste and class seemed to have been refracted through his interpellation by consumerist discourses. Like some other lower-caste men and women I worked with (for example, Surjeet Kaur), Selapan's attempts to acquire consumer goods signified (potential) access to the middle class, entry into which was hampered not only by his low income but also by his low-caste status. I could see that his family was very hard up, but he had just purchased an iron and had applied for a loan to buy a refrigerator.[76] I never heard his wife, Padmini, express a desire to buy anything she saw on TV—as we will see shortly, her primary goal was to ensure that the family had enough to eat.

Women as Subjects

The desire of the men and women I met in Vikas Nagar and Basti to buy consumer goods seemed deeply embedded in a desire to attain middle-class status. As suggested in my vignette about the Dasgupta family, these aspirations had profound consequences for the dynamics within many of these families. A few months before I concluded my fieldwork, I arrived at the Selapans' home unexpectedly one weekday morning to find a lock on their door. When I met them the next evening and asked Padmini where she had been the previous morning, she replied that she had gone grocery shopping. A couple of days later, I returned to their house in the afternoon hoping to spend some time alone with her. I found that she was out this time as well. When I inquired about Padmini's whereabouts from the woman who lived next door, I was told that Padmini had started working part time as a maid in the upper-class neighborhood adjacent to Vikas Nagar. She had lied to me about going shopping; she did not want her husband to know about her job. My sense was that their plans to acquire consumer goods had pushed their resources to the limit: Padmini had found it impossible to manage on Selapan's meager income and, as a last resort, had found a job on the sly. I remembered that one Sunday afternoon I had dropped in while Padmini and her family were eating their lunch and had been struck by how meager it was: they were eating coarse boiled rice with a very watery vegetable curry. I had also noticed that the tea they served me had very little milk. I remembered that Padmini's saris always looked very faded and threadbare, and that her son Rajan wore shirts that looked like hand-me-downs. So when I heard that Padmini had risked her husband's wrath to get a job, I interpreted it as her effort to take control of the family's finances so as to ensure that her husband's aspirations to buy appliances did not drive them into bankruptcy.

Some of the other families I met in Vikas Nagar and Basti were better off than the Selapans. In keeping with the expansion of the middle classes in the early 1980s, many women earned incomes over which they had varying degrees of control. Some women had entered the labor force in order to gain upward mobility and become middle class—indeed, most of the families I worked with *needed* two incomes to stay middle class. Jayanthi Chandran worked as a stenographer in a government department. Her husband had retired as a government clerk. She, her husband, and their daughter, Uma, lived in a one-bedroom flat in Vikas Nagar. As a senior stenographer in her department, Jayanthi was entitled to a relatively large flat, an achievement that somewhat established her middle-class status. One of a cluster of about fifteen flats nestled in the northeast corner of Vikas Nagar, the Chandrans' flat had a verandah, a separate kitchen, and that unmistakably middle-class luxury, its own bathroom. One entered the home through a door that opened into a living room. Against one wall were a settee, two cane chairs, and a coffee table. The furniture was arranged to face a color television. The Chandrans were the only family I knew in Vikas Nagar with a VCR. Immediately beyond the living room was a narrow passageway: the first door on the left led to a small kitchen, in which I could see a gas stove and a mixer-grinder; a few feet down the corridor from the kitchen was a bedroom with a large bed and a wooden closet. One of the bedroom walls had a line of hooks on which were hung some clothes. Outside, against the wall between the kitchen and a bedroom, was a refrigerator that hummed and rattled with the fluctuations in power supply.

Jayanthi was very proud of keeping a "neat and clean" house, and, indeed, I never saw a thing out of place. There was always a clean bedsheet spread over the settee and a fresh table cover over the coffee table.

The Chandrans' personal appearance also marked their middle-class aspirations. Jayanthi and Uma were always well dressed, Jayanthi in polyester saris and Uma in crisp, well-starched (if sometimes faded) salwar-kameezes (the loose tunics and trousers worn by women in many parts of north India). A neighbor once jokingly remarked that Jayanthi and Uma looked "smart" even when they went to the nearby market to buy vegetables. The fact that they had acquired middle-class status clearly filled them with pride, and this pride was reflected in how they kept their home and presented themselves to the world.

Uma had just graduated from college: as the first of her generation to get a college degree, she was a source of great pride and joy to her entire extended family. She had been successful in school and college all along, had always received good grades, and was popular with her friends and cousins. But being "the best" was clearly a source of great stress for her, and she frequently spoke to me about feeling pressured always to do well and not disappoint her friends and family. After getting her college degree, Uma managed to find a job in a multinational company. Far from bolstering her somewhat fragile self-confidence, however, Uma's job actually made her even more unsure of herself. Even though she was regarded as "smartly dressed" by her lower-middle-class neighbors, she frequently confided in me that she was the most poorly dressed of all her colleagues, many of whom wore expensive clothes. She was ashamed of the fact that she lived in a lower-middle-class government colony (most of her colleagues lived in upper-class south Delhi neighborhoods), and was particularly embarrassed that she had to travel by bus (unlike her colleagues, who either owned cars or could afford to take scooter-rickshaws). When she first started working, Uma used very little makeup; within a few months, I noticed that she had begun to wear lipstick to work and had shed her cotton salwar-kameezes for polyester saris. She was clearly trying very hard to fit in with her upper-class colleagues.

Jayanthi had worked outside the home all her life. The daughter of a poor rural family, she had somehow passed middle school, been trained as a stenographer, and, through family connections in Delhi, had obtained a government job. She had married soon after. Jayanthi often told me that having an independent income had been a source of tremendous "strength" for her: not only did her husband respect her more, her in-laws were also "careful" around her. She insisted that it was her income that enabled their family to achieve middle-class status. With great pride, she once told me that their family was the only one in the neighborhood to own a VCR and that they had been the first to buy a refrigerator. "Could we have afforded all this without my salary? On his income we would barely have scraped by. But because of me we have a decent life. They [her in-laws] know that. They behave with me because they know I can help buy things for my sister-in-law's marriage." Even though she was under constant pressure to buy consumer goods for her in-laws, she used her ability to do so as a way of commanding their respect. In this manner she was able to jockey for a better position within her larger extended family.

In contrast, Sarojini was less lucky with her in-laws. Sarojini and her husband, Sukumaran, earned considerably less than Jayanthi and her husband. They lived with their teenage daughter, Lata, in a tiny one-room flat in the center of Vikas Nagar: like all the other residents in their cluster of flats, they had to share a bathroom with the others in their quadrangle. One of the first things they bought when they set up their household twenty years ago was a mixer-grinder. But they had gone without a gas stove for several years, and had bought their refrigerator only recently. They had had to obtain a loan to buy their color television set and when I met them were still paying installments on it.

All the household appliances they possessed had been bought with Sarojini's salary: Sukumaran's was barely enough to cover their basic needs. Sarojini's income had enabled them to achieve a precarious middle-class status. Like Jayanthi's family, their middle-class identity was explicitly measured by the consumer durables they owned. But Sarojini claimed that her in-laws, who lived in distant Hyderabad, had never appreciated her contribution to their family. Every now and then they would demand that she give them an appliance she had bought for her own home. Most of the time she complied. But it angered her a great deal. "They are greedy," she once complained to me. "Don't they know how difficult it is for us? If I say anything they tell me, 'Why should you care for us. You are rich now. Why should you bother about us!' But don't they know we have no extra money? That we have to save for Lata's education?"

Certainly, owning kitchen gadgets such as mixers and pressure cookers made life more convenient for lower-middle-class women, many of whom put in a double day working both in the home and outside it. But these commodities were also proud markers of the upward mobility of their families. While women such as Sarojini and Jayanthi valued the convenience of household appliances, for younger women like Uma, makeup and polyester saris were equally important indices of middle-class status: how a woman dressed reflected not just on herself but on the position of her family.

Consumerism was not the only set of discursive practices perceived by these viewing families as middle class: for example, in the following chapter, I describe how notions of respectability and sexual modesty, duty to the family, and service to the nation participate in the creation of middle-class and gendered national subjects. Nevertheless, many men and women, upper-caste as well as lower-caste, believed that consumerism would provide their children with middle-class lifestyles. As noted in the list of advertisements presented above, some advertisements explicitly targeted children. It was not surprising, then, that a number of children and young people I met had been interpellated by middle-class desires. For instance, Shakuntala Sharma said that even though their income had been lower earlier, they were less comfortable now (*barkat kam hoti hai*) because of the pressure to buy the things that helped them maintain a "standard of living." The Sharmas' children frequently pressured them to buy things. They had insisted that their parents buy a refrigerator and an air cooler on credit: they complained that they were ashamed to invite their friends home because there was no cold water to offer them, or because the house was too hot. These things, they said, would reflect poorly on their family. Shakuntala also felt that even though her husband was just a junior clerk, it was important for them to maintain their "standards" because their children were growing up, and "when the time comes for their marriages to be arranged, these are the things that people will look at to evaluate our family."

Sometimes, the spread of consumerism had brutal consequences for the position of women in middle-class families. Although the practice of demanding large dowries existed before liberalization and the advent of commercials on television, women's groups, social scientists, and journalists all believe that television commercials whetted people's appetites for such consumer durables as washing machines, expensive kitchen appliances, and, most important, color television sets. Thus, while earlier dowry demands took the form of cash, jewelry, and, in some cases, scooters, recent dowry demands consisted of consumer durables that had become available only after liberalization. In 1985, the popular proindustry newsmagazine *India Today* claimed that "increasing acquisitiveness in society has led to the spate of bride burnings" (T. Ninan 1985:74).[77] Other critics explicitly related violence toward women (especially young brides) in the family to consumerism. For instance, the Joshi Report quoted a viewer complaining about Doordarshan and consumerism: "Why should Doordarshan promote consumerism? Is it not aggravating the dowry problem? There are atrocities on young girls who are not able to satisfy the growing appetite for these well-advertised goods and gadgets" (quoted in Chatterji 1991:176–177).

As indicated in my conversations with Rehana, some women perceived the connection between television commercials and the rise in dowry demands. Shakuntala Sharma was emphatic that the practice of dowry (*dahej*) had increased since commercials started on television. Late in the afternoon one October day, I accompanied her to the neighborhood market. She was looking for some fabric for a blouse, and I tagged along, grateful for an opportunity to talk to her. We looked in several textile shops before Shakuntala found something that she considered reasonably priced. Walking around the market gave me an opportunity to see what was sold in working-class and lower-middle-class neighborhoods like Vikas Nagar. I was struck by the fact that even though the market was relatively small (it could not have contained more than thirty shops), there were three large shops selling kitchen appliances and utensils, and two shops selling television sets, vcrs, and other electronic goods. Obviously, shopkeepers deemed it profitable to open businesses in that neighborhood. Even more striking was the fact that, at three o'clock in the afternoon on a weekday, these shops were full of people.

I shared my observations with Shakuntala. Where do people get the money to buy so much? I asked. Shakuntala attributed the desire to buy commodities to television. Commercials, she explained, increased people's "greed" (*laalach*), and this greed led to their making "unreasonable demands" for dowries. She described the last family wedding she had attended where she had been amazed to see how much dowry had been given to the bride. She reprimanded her relatives for "spoiling things" for other people (*bigarh rahe ho aap log*): she was afraid that when her daughter got married, people would compare her dowry to theirs. According to Shakuntala, consumerism led not only to greed but also to competitiveness among families: middle-class parents and their daughters were hence becoming victims of their own competitiveness.

TOWARD A CONJUNCTURAL ETHNOGRAPHY OF THE "VIEWING FAMILY"

Indian television acquired multiple semiotics in the mid-1980s. It symbolized the state's goal of constructing a hegemonic, pan-Indian culture; it was iconic of the modernity of the Indian nation; at the same time, like the commodities it advertised, television was also an index of the upward mobility of the middle classes. My first objective in this chapter was to outline how television viewers were interpellated as "family subjects" by discourses of the state, political economies of consumption, and transnational communication flows.[78]

How did television participate in the constitution of the viewing family? Families do not consist simply of biological relationships between kin, they are also symbolically and politically constructed in historically specific contexts. As a unit for the reception of TV programs and as a unit for the consumption of the goods exhibited in advertisements, the family was repositioned by multiple fields of power. "The family" was not just seized on as a target audience for television. Through marketing strategies, state policy, programming decisions, and transnational flows of information, capital, and desire, relationships within the family were reconfigured, and the entity of the family was re-created as metonym for nation, as unit of reception, and as unit of consumption.

Moreover, as Collier et al. (1982) point out, families have never existed as bounded or discrete social units. Television further blurred the boundaries of the family by offering viewers opportunities to imaginatively connect with larger collectivities such as community and nation. My project of delineating "the viewing family," therefore, is intended not to reify The Family as a fixed sociological entity but to trace how viewing families and viewing subjects were reconfigured at the intersection of local, national, and transnational fields of power.

Gupta and Ferguson point out that the contemporary transnational public sphere has "rendered any strictly bounded sense of community or locality obsolete" (1992:9). They insist that anthropologists should focus on the *production* of the local through global forces engendered by late capitalism and new communication technologies. My delineation of how the family, as a site of local relationships and practices and as a local field of analysis, was itself constituted within transnational fields of power and knowledge thus serves a second objective: to problematize the binary between the local and the translocal. Further, my intention in this chapter has been to show how the so-called micropolitics of women's everyday lives are permeated by the macropolitics of political economy and global cultural flows. Foregrounding the *articulation* of women's experiences, dreams, and anxieties with the agendas of the nation-state and the discourses of transnational advertising agencies interrogates distinctions between micro and macro, and local and translocal.

Third, my delineation of the discursive and material contexts into which viewers were inserted contextualizes my subsequent analyses of their negotiation of televisual discourses. Some recent studies of mass media have tended to exaggerate (and thus reify) viewers' oppositional interpretations of texts.[79] This has tended to slide into a somewhat romantic insistence on reading resistance into every instance of viewing subjects' active interpretations of hegemonic texts. Such conceptions of resistance are problematic because they ignore the multiple contexts in which these processes occur, and hence implicitly reinscribe viewers as sovereign subjects. Because this book aims at foregrounding viewing subjects' active engagement with television, it is especially imperative that we locate viewing subjects in larger, often overlapping, fields of meaning and power. Tracing the constitution of the "viewing family" and hence locating viewing subjects in broader sociohistorical conjunctures compels us to see that viewers' interpretations are "set within and, in part, determined by wider pressures and contexts" (Carragee 1990:92). Highlighting the overdetermined political context in which these negotiations take place is particularly crucial given the Indian nation-state's deployment of increasingly violent strategies of repression in the late 1980s and early 1990s. It is this interdiscursive context that we need to hold in view when we focus on how viewing subjects actively negotiate television's texts.

Finally, in order to explore the articulation of several agencies—the state, industry, advertisers, and power blocs within audiences—I have attempted to construct a *conjunctural* ethnography of Doordarshan and its viewers.[80] My construction of a conjunctural ethnography has important methodological and conceptual implications for the anthropological analysis of mass media. As I noted in chapter 1, studying mass media presents particular challenges for those committed to doing ethnographic research. Ethnographies of mass media require us to expand our repertoire of methodologies and combine participant observation and repeated in-depth interviews with policy analysis, archival research, and textual analysis. An unorthodox methodological strategy is necessary because such projects entail a broadening of conventional anthropological conceptions of "ethnographic context" based on fieldwork in "face-to-face" communities.[81] Focusing exclusively on the local makes it too easy to ignore the larger contexts of power, such as state policy and transnational flows of capital, in which subjects are located. But holding the local (the family/audience) and the translocal (national policy, transnational fields of power) in tension enables us to trace how audiences and, more specifically, viewing subjects are constituted.[82]

Chapter 3 *"Women-Oriented" Narratives*

and the New Indian Woman

I had just returned to New Delhi for fieldwork and was explaining my project to a colleague. When I told her that I was going to study the role of Doordarshan in the reconstitution of Indian Womanhood, she responded wryly: "You should have no problem finding programs to analyze. We've been asking ourselves, 'Is this Doordarshan or *stri-darshan* [woman-watching]?'"[1] She explained that viewers were currently being subjected to a "virtual blitzkrieg" of "women-oriented" programs. As during the encounter between colonial administrators and the indigenous male elite in the nineteenth century, there now seemed to be an "incitement to discourse" (Foucault 1978:18) on women in official and popular nationalist discourses. Yet, it was clear that the representations of Indian Womanhood that proliferated in the late 1980s and early 1990s were not simply an extension of colonial and early nationalist ideas of gender.

As Hall points out, the postcolonial is not an epochal stage "when everything is reversed at the same moment, all the old relations disappear forever and entirely new ones come to replace them" (1996:247). Indeed, as constructed and articulated on Doordarshan, postcolonial representations of gender and nation illustrated the discontinuous and multiple temporalities of decolonization. Relationships between nationalism and gender were distinctly *post*colonial in that they exhibited neither a clean break from colonial discourses nor a simple continuity with them (Hall 1996, Frankenberg and Mani 1993). Postcolonial discourses of gender and nation differed as much as they drew from colonial and preindependence discourses in the subject positions they created for women within the family and the nation.

Partha Chatterjee emphasizes the primacy of constructions of family to notions of culture and nation by suggesting that "the home . . . was not a complementary but rather the original site on which the hegemonic project of nationalism was launched" (1993:147). In chapter 2 I described the ways in which notions of modernity, articulated in terms of consumerism, created particular subject positions for women within the family. This chapter continues my examination of the reconfiguration of family by focusing on representations of women's "uplift" and emancipation in Doordarshan's women-oriented narratives. I explore what these narratives reveal about the postcolonial state's attempts to reshape gender politics within the Indian family and examine how these discourses intersected with women's experiences in their families and communities. Notions of "Indian culture," as formulated in women-oriented narratives, created specific ambivalences and anxieties regarding women's place in the home and the world. My analysis of women-oriented narratives in postcolonial India thus focuses on the centrality of family, in particular "the Indian family," in discourses of Indian culture and, therefore, of nationhood.

This chapter is divided into four sections. In the first, I situate postcolonial constructions of Indian Womanhood within their broader historical contexts; next, I examine the articulation of discourses of gender, nation, and family in women-oriented narratives and ethnographically demonstrate their intersection with the sentiments, relationships, and everyday practices of viewers.[2] In the following section I analyze viewers' responses to Doordarshan's representations of the formal education of women and examine how some viewers of women-oriented narratives negotiated the anxieties provoked by women's formal education and employment outside the home. Next I study Doordarshan's construction of the emancipated New Indian Woman (the *Nai Bharatiya Naari*) by presenting two ethnographic examples: first, I analyze the interpretations of a director of a popular women-oriented serial; this is followed by an examination of how one woman appropriated representations of the New Indian Woman to her own life. In the final section, I analyze how postcolonial nationalism constitutes women as gendered citizen-subjects who are expected to participate in the state's projects of nation building and serve as custodians of national integration.

MODERNITY, NATIONHOOD, AND INDIAN WOMANHOOD

We need to situate the proliferation of women-oriented narratives on Doordarshan within a political context marked by the state's monopolistic control over television production and its conscious deployment of television to construct a pan-Indian culture based on hegemonic ideologies of community and identity. When I asked producers and Doordarshan officials why they had been so intent on telecasting women-oriented programs, many replied that (middle-class) women constituted a large part of their target audience and they felt that Doordarshan's programs would have to resonate with those women's experiences.[3] Further, bureaucrats and policy makers in Doordarshan were aware that women's issues were an *intrinsic* part of the state's project of nation building. A former director-general of Doordarshan revealed that the "uplift" of women had formed an important part of the agenda of Prime Minister Rajiv Gandhi, who claimed that he wished to take India into the "twenty-first century." During the mid-1980s, the state launched comprehensive strategies to modernize not just economically, but also technologically, through the import of computers and communications infrastructure, and culturally, through the formulation of careful and detailed cultural policies. The "uplift" of women became a crucial component of the state's agenda to construct a modern national culture. The "Woman Question" of Indian nationalism was thus recast in terms of the construction of the modern Indian woman who would participate in the nation's entry into the "twenty-first century." But what kind of gendered subject was being created? On what elisions and renegotiations of class, caste, and religious identity was the modern Indian woman of postcolonial nationalism predicated?

This was also a historical moment when the relationship of feminists and women activists to the Indian state was fraught with ambivalence. During the late 1980s and early 1990s, several committees were set up and reports written that focused exclusively on women's issues (e.g., the National Perspective Plan for Women 1988). As pointed out by feminist scholar and activist Sujata Patel, the post-1985 period was marked by the growing significance of women as a political constituency, and by the state's attempts to appropriate the political spaces created by feminists and other activists for women's empowerment.[4] These years witnessed the inclusion of women activists in state bodies that formulated economic and technological policies (e.g., the appointment of grassroots activist Ela Bhatt of SEWA, the Self-Employed Women's Association, to the influential Planning Commission that draws up the national five-year plans).[5] These years thus saw the incorporation, and in many cases the co-optation, of women activists into the state's projects of policy planning and implementation. Instead of confronting the state, some dissenting groups, leaders, and movements attempted to work within the mechanisms provided by it.[6] Through a combination of populist rhetoric and the co-optation of grassroots leadership, then, women's issues were accommodated within the nation-state's agendas of development and nation building.

Further, secessionist movements gathering momentum in Punjab, Kashmir, and the Northeast made it all the more urgent for the state to develop strategies that would enable it to extend (or, in some cases, maintain) its hegemony. Discourses of national integration were crucial to this process, and the position of women in the national community had to be reconstituted accordingly. Women-oriented programs reflected the state's need to mobilize women not just toward the twin goals of development and modernization, but also as custodians of the unity of the nation; women thus had to be constituted as loyal and patriotic citizens who would protect the integrity of the nation.

Finally, some of Doordarshan's ostensible preoccupation with women's issues was also rooted in the long-standing relationship between ideologies of gender and Indian nationalism. It is hence crucial that we relate Doordarshan's reconstitution of the New Indian Woman to historically specific discourses of gender and nation.

Gender in Colonial and Postcolonial Discourses

Conceptions of nation and gender in India in the late 1980s and early 1990s were in some respects consistent with earlier discourses. For example, Lata Mani has suggested that in nineteenth-century colonial discourses on sati, women were neither the subject nor the object but were the "ground" for discourses of tradition and modernity. In some of the televisual narratives examined later in this chapter, women are indeed represented as "emblematic of tradition" (1989:117,90). Mani also points out that in colonial discourse, satis were portrayed as "pathetic or heroic victims" (1989:97). As analyzed below, similar discourses of victimology emerge in the countless Doordarshan programs on the uplift of women's status.

These continuities notwithstanding, significant shifts occurred in the subject positions created for women with the deployment of nationalism to mobilize different sections of the population into joining anticolonial struggles. Early encounters between colonial authorities and indigenous elites generated a proliferation of discourses on women. This was followed by a period of relative silence, indexing what Partha Chatterjee (1989, 1993) terms the nationalist "resolution" of the Woman Question. In the aftermath of the colonial encounter, the indigenous male elite made a sustained effort to insulate the home, perceived as the repository of authentic Indianness, from the world. As an inner sanctum, the "home" epitomized "Indian" spirituality; the "world," on the other hand, represented the material struggles waged by the nationalist elite in an environment dominated by colonial rule. Predictably, while the "world" represented the domain of the male, women were reinscribed in the "home."

By the time Gandhi entered nationalist politics, a crucial break had occurred in this perception of women. From being construed as victims in need of rescue by social reformers, women emerged as active participants in nationalist struggles. Gandhian nationalism played an important role in creating spaces for women's agency and continued to have currency in postcolonial discourses on gender.

Woman in Gandhian Nationalism

Feminist analyses of Gandhian nationalism point to the tensions inherent in its discourses on women. Gandhi has been credited with validating women's participation in nationalist politics. Tanika Sarkar points out that although women might have had to struggle with their inhibitions in order to actively enter nationalist politics, they did so with the "sure knowledge" that their conservative, upper-caste families endorsed their participation in the Gandhian independence movement (Sarkar 1989, from Tharu and Lalita 1991a:180). Further, Gandhi respected women's "personal dignity as individuals" and, "without belittling their roles as mothers and wives, he proclaimed . . . that they had an equal role to play . . . in the achievement of freedom and social justice" (Mazumdar 1976:58). He insisted that women should not be objectified as sexual playthings and claimed that their "superior" spiritual strength would provide the basis for the construction of Indian society. Gandhi's invocation of traditional symbols of female power enabled women from orthodox families to enter the freedom movement (D. Jain 1986). Gandhi employed these symbols to address women "not as objects of reform and humanitarianism, but as self-conscious subjects who could, if they chose, become arbiters of their own destiny" (Kishwar 1985:1691).

Although Gandhi made it possible for women to participate in nationalist politics, he also subscribed to essentialist notions of women and glorified the place of the mother in the national community. Analyzing the ideologies of caste, class, and religion that mediated Gandhi's attitudes toward women, Sujata Patel claims that his conception of women's agency, both within the home and in the public world of politics, was "drawn from a space inhabited by an urbanized middle-class upper-caste Hindu male's perception of what a woman should be" (1988:378). His religious and class affiliations were evident in his invocation of icons of feminine power in Hindu mythology and his insistence on the honor and purity of women. Gandhi's deployment of the spinning wheel as an "instrument for the woman-in-the-home to participate in political life from within the home" led to an "unresolvable tension" in his discourse. He glorified the position of women in the home, but when, in the 1930s, hundreds of women came out of their homes to participate in nationalist struggles, the "sanctity of the home was brought into question" (Patel 1988:379). Gandhi tried to resolve the tension this created by reconstituting the patriotic Indian woman as one who channeled her energies to the service of the nation. He claimed that the patriotic Indian woman's *dharma* (duty) was to dedicate herself to the nation even at the cost of disobeying her husband: "Today . . . the *dharma* of the country reposes in your hands. And for this *dharma*, the higher moral good, the women have the right to even question her husband's authority, if he does not let her take the Swadeshi vow" (Patel 1988:380). Thus, after the 1930s, the nation began to take precedence over the family in Gandhi's discourse on women (Patel 1988:380). He created new roles for women by *invalidating* their confinement to the home if, and only if, such seclusion had detrimental consequences for the nation. At the same time, as pointed out by Madhu Kishwar (1985) and Patel (1988), he conceived of women's oppression exclusively in moral terms and ignored the social and material conditions in which it occurred. Further, and more pertinent to my argument in this chapter, Gandhi conceived of "women's problems as an extension of the national question" (Patel 1988:381). What were the legacies of Gandhian nationalism for Doordarshan's representations of Indian Womanhood?

WOMEN-ORIENTED NARRATIVES: SOME COMMON THEMES

Significantly, almost all women-oriented narratives shown on Doordarshan in the late 1980s and early 1990s were set in the family. Some serials drew on the Hindi film genre of the "family drama."[7] The first of these to be serialized was *Hum Log*. Spanning 156 episodes, *Hum Log* ran for seventeen months during 1984–1985. Set in a neighborhood very much like Vikas Nagar, *Hum Log* narrated the dreams and anxieties of a lower-middle-class family struggling to find a foothold in urban India. *Hum Log*'s family consisted of Basesar, a self-employed carpenter who spends most of his money on alcohol, his parents, his long-suffering wife, and their five children. They all live together in a tiny two-room flat. Every episode ended with a commentary by popular octogenarian Hindi film actor Ashok Kumar, who drew out the moral of the story and responded to the letters of viewers who commented on story lines or advised characters on how to solve the latest crisis in their lives.

In its powerful depiction of the neuroses and claustrophobia experienced by this lower-middle-class family and its struggles to acquire upward mobility, *Hum Log* was didactic: it aimed at informing and persuading viewers about the importance of family planning (Basesar is miserable because he has more children than he can support); the evils of alcohol (the entire family suffers because of Basesar's fondness for drink); the scourge of dowry (the eldest daughter, the plain Badhki, who, at first, is rejected by prospective in-laws because her parents cannot afford a "decent" dowry for her); the ills that befall young women who venture outside the protective control of their families (the second daughter, Majhli, defies her parents by going to Bombay, where she is sexually exploited); the importance of women's education (Badhki rails against her parents for not allowing her to study further, while the perky youngest daughter, Chutki, is determined to become a doctor and thus avoid the fate of her two older sisters).

Ironically, although one of *Hum Log*'s purported objectives was to bring about a change in the status of women, its most important women characters are all depicted unsympathetically. The grandmother, Dadi, contrasts with Dadaji (the grandfather): where he is wise and selfless, she is vain, greedy, and lacks "common sense." More important, while Dadaji often takes up the cause of his granddaughters and daughter-in-law, Dadi is insensitive to their suffering. Basesar's wife is a docile doormat who never asserts herself and is unable to protect her daughters from their father's tyranny: at the end of one episode, the commentator, Ashok Kumar, criticizes her for not protesting Basesar's injustices to her and her daughters. Majhli's ambitions blind her to the predatory intentions of the men who promise her a break in films. Kamya, Nanhe's friend, is a rich, spoiled young woman who is ruthless in her pursuit of power. Badhki and Chutki, the eldest and youngest daughters, are somewhat redeemed by their strength of character and their ability to stand by their respective principles; yet they are completely marginalized by the politics of their family. Chutki comes into her own only when she leaves her biological family and is adopted by a childless doctor and her husband. Badhki's battle for self-respect is a lonely one: she is committed to feminist activism, but after she gets married her political commitments lead to conflicts with her husband.

The figure of Dadaji is a foil to the character of Basesar. Dadaji represents the benevolence of tradition; Basesar symbolizes the rootlessness and chaos of modernity. Dadaji is the moral center of the narrative: retired from the army, he tries (usually in vain) to bring order into the lives of his family. He articulates, indeed personifies, the "wisdom" of the ideal extended family. As he says in an episode early in the serial, it is essential for members of a family to live together and share their resources in order to survive. *Hum Log* thus reinforces a nostalgia for the benevolent patriarchy, order, and harmony supposedly represented by the extended family of the past. The "traditional values" Dadaji symbolizes have been eroded by the chaos of contemporary urban life.

Close on the heels of *Hum Log* was *Rajani,* a sitcom series telecast in 1985. Shown every Sunday morning, it was about the reformist efforts of its upper-caste and middle-class heroine, Rajani. The series, set in Bombay, portrayed Rajani fighting against corrupt bureaucrats, dishonest cabdrivers, brutal wife batterers, and so on. As the strong-willed, socially conscious New Indian Woman, Rajani epitomized the confluence of liberal discourses of women's agency with ideologies of reformist nationalism.

Buniyaad (The foundation), telecast in 1987, was another milestone in Doordarshan's discourses on women and the family. Haveliram (remembered by viewers as Masterji), the younger son of a wealthy family in pre-Partition Punjab, is a freedom fighter who is frequently imprisoned for his participation in anticolonial struggles. He is thrown out by his extended family when he marries a young widow, Lajoji. The core narrative of the serial relates Masterji and Lajoji's attempts to hold their family together despite the turbulence of the times in which they live. *Buniyaad* left a long-lasting impression on the viewers I interviewed: even though they could not always recollect details of its plot, characters such as Masterji, Lajoji, and, to a lesser extent, Masterji's sister, Veeranwali, remained in their memories.

Buniyaad evoked in many viewers' minds a nostalgia for the idealism of the independence struggle in pre-Partition India, a nostalgia embodied in the patriotism and integrity of Masterji and Lajoji. The series contrasted life in pre-Partition Punjab with the decline of values in contemporary times, allegorized, in turn, by the tragedy and corruption of the lives of Masterji and Lajoji's children. Television critic Iqbal Masud commented that *Buniyaad* "showed the rotten foundations of our polity" and was "more ambitious than *Hum Log*."[8] The serial was, indeed, ambitious in its attempts to construct a social history of the postPartition conjuncture. Significantly, *Buniyaad* did not dwell on the brutality of the violence surrounding Partition: Partition is merely the backdrop for the saga of the survival of Lajoji's family. The consolidation of the extended patriarchal family serves as a trope for the construction of the fragile, postcolonial nation. Despite the marked tension and mutual suspicion among the next generation, Lajoji's family, like the nation, struggles to survive the trauma of Partition.

Even as *Buniyaad* was praised for its gripping script and excellent production values, some feminist critics pointed to its conservative depiction of women. Feminist journalist Mrinal Pande, for example, wrote that "the breakup of the patrilineal family structure and the rise of the nuclear family has constantly been presented (through films and popular literature) as the symbolic beginning of some horrifying future, which will destroy morality . . . which will masculinize the females by allowing them the choice of an identity and, horror of horrors, extend to them the freedom to exercise that choice" (1991:64). Lajoji contrasts with at least two other women who are foils to her devotion to the nation-family. Despite being ostracized by her husband's family, Lajoji is a docile and respectful daughter-in-law. In the first half of the narrative, we see her elder sister-in-law, Shano, fueling the hostility between Masterji and his elder brother. If the docile Lajoji is the pivot that keeps the family united, Shano represents the greedy, shrewish woman who is (at least partly) responsible for its disintegration. She is petulant and spoiled. Worse, her greed and jealousy result in the breaking up of the extended family: she provokes her husband into throwing Masterji and his new bride out of the family home, and attempts to disrupt Lajoji's relationship with their mother-in-law. Her antagonism to Lajoji is exacerbated when Lajoji gives birth to two sons. Lajoji, the loyal daughter-in-law, is also an ideal mother in that she is able to produce sons who will carry on the family lineage; in contrast, Shano can produce only daughters. In the second half of the serial, another woman is set up as a contrast to Lajoji: her daughter-in-law Sulochana. The rebellious Sulochana prefers her theater career to her family and is directly responsible for the breakup of Lajoji's family because she forces her husband to separate from his parents.

Hum Log, Rajani, and *Buniyaad* set the stage for the other woman-oriented programs that followed, the most notable of which were *Stri, Adhikaar, Swayamsiddha, Udaan I, Pukaar, Udaan II,* and *Humraahi* (which was supposedly modeled on *Hum Log*). *Stri* (Woman) was actually a docudrama depicting the life narratives of women, famous and unknown, who had triumphed over adversities, and *Adhikaar* (Rights) aimed explicitly at informing women about their legal rights. What subject positions did the programs described above create for women viewers? Below, I examine viewers' interpretations of women-oriented narratives by focusing on the convergence of class and discourses of gender, the position of women (especially young daughters and daughters-in-law) in the family, and the problematic value of higher education for women. I am particularly interested in the overlaps and disjunctures between Doordarshan's discourses and viewers' relationships and everyday practices.

Gender and "Middle-classness"

In Amitav Ghosh's novel *The Shadow Lines,* the protagonist accompanies his family to visit long-lost relatives who live in a poor part of Calcutta. As he is dragged away from staring at the landscape of poverty and hopelessness surrounding his relatives' home, he reflects on his own anxieties about his middle-class status: "I was already well schooled in looking away, the jungle-craft of gentility. But still, I could not help thinking it was a waste of effort to lead me away. It was true, of course, that I could not see that landscape or anything like it from my own window, but its presence was palpable everywhere in our house; I had grown up with it. It was that landscape that lent the note of hysteria to my mother's voice when she drilled me for my examinations. . . . I knew perfectly well that all it would take was a couple of failed examinations to put me where our relative was" (1990:131–132).

This passage from *The Shadow Lines* has always held a particular resonance for me — it has helped me understand my own nervousness when I visit relatives who are considerably poorer than my family; it reminds me of my anxieties about exams, "doing well," being successful. This passage repeatedly surfaced in my mind when I visited families in Vikas Nagar and Basti who occupied a much more interstitial class position than I ever had. Barely lower middle class or upwardly mobile working class, their desperate attempts to acquire middle-class security were driven by their fear of sliding back into poverty — from which most of them were barely a generation away.

Being middle class was not just about acquiring financial security; it was also about attaining and maintaining respectability, sexual modesty, family honor. Put another way, middle-classness was a *moral* virtue, a structure of feeling, the habitation of a safe space that distinguished one from less fortunate (less worthy) Others, and therefore a vantage point on the world. And since respectability, sexual modesty, and family honor were predicated on the conduct of women, women's behavior was monitored especially intently. Hence, the aspirations of families to acquire middle-class status resulted in a particularly close watch on women's bodies, movements, behavior, clothes, and speech patterns.

An overwhelming majority of Doordarshan's women-oriented programs focused on middle-class families and their struggles to acquire or maintain upward mobility and middle-class respectability.[9] With a few exceptions, Doordarshan's images of Indian Womanhood were almost entirely middle class.[10] The narratives of these serials held tremendous significance for the men and women I worked with, all of whom were struggling to acquire and retain middle-class status.

How were these struggles for upward mobility and middle-classness enacted in the self-conceptions and daily practices of families? As described in chapter 2, Jagdish and Shakuntala Sharma were brahmans and were first-generation migrants from a Himalayan region of Uttar Pradesh. I vividly remember the evening that Sarojini first took me to their home in Division III of Vikas Nagar. Sarojini was keen that I meet them: she was impressed with their children and wanted to get to know them better so she could introduce them to her daughter, Lata. I gathered that the Sharma children had a reputation for being very studious, and it was plain that Sarojini thought they would be a good influence on Lata who, she alleged, "didn't study hard enough."

A middle-aged woman answered our knock. Her wispy gray hair was held back in a braid, and her face was lined with wrinkles. She was wearing a well-ironed but faded and threadbare sari. She opened the door just a crack and peered out at us, then broke into a smile when she recognized Sarojini. As she opened the door wider to let us in, the sunlight fell on her face and I saw with a start that she was younger than she first appeared. She welcomed us in soft-spoken, Sanskritized Hindi and ushered us in through a curtain.

The Sharmas' home embodied their aspirations toward upward mobility and their desire to create a middle-class world of their own. We walked past a kitchen filled with stainless-steel cooking utensils so shiny that they sparkled. A second curtain separated the kitchen from the inside room where a man and a young woman sat sipping tea and reading. The windows were shut and lined with curtains. It was a pleasant October evening, a foretaste of the cooler weather that would soon relieve a long month of heat and humidity, and I could not understand why, unlike their neighbors sitting in the courtyards outside, this family chose to be indoors.

As in most other homes in Vikas Nagar, the space in the inner room was arranged around the television set. The tiny inner room was crammed with rickety old furniture: against one wall was a bed that doubled as a divan during the day; an old wooden closet stood against another wall; a coffee table that swayed dangerously every time someone set something down on it sat in the center of the room opposite two creaky cane chairs. But this flat looked very different from all the others I had seen in that neighborhood. What struck me most was the interiority of this space: unlike other homes, where doors and windows let in the sun, wind, and dust, and neighbors constantly flowed in and out, in this home the layers of curtains and the firmly shut doors and windows seemed to keep out the rest of the neighborhood. Further, despite the fact that everything, from the faded curtains that had clearly been tailored from old cotton saris to the rickety furniture, looked well worn, the flat was extraordinarily neat and orderly. Nothing seemed out of place: the old magazines and books stacked on the shelves against one of the walls were held from spilling into the room by a faded muslin curtain; the kitchen was one of the neatest I had ever seen; the floor shone as if it were scrubbed every day. When I entered the inner room, Jagdish was leaning back on the divan reading a newspaper as he drank his tea. Their daughter, Poonam, about twenty years old, was curled up in a chair reading a Hindi novel by the famous nationalist writer Saratchandra. That night I wrote in my notes that if there was ever an image that embodied dreams of middle-classness, this was it. The neatness of the home; the inner room, separated from the rest of the neighborhood by layers of curtains; the books and magazines lining the walls; the stainless steel utensils gleaming in the kitchen; a man and his daughter reading.

When he saw us, Jagdish stood and asked us to be seated. Poonam sprang to her feet: she seemed excited to see us. Sarojini introduced me to the family and, as she loved to do, explained my project to them with great enthusiasm and pride. Before I could edge a word in, she had enlisted their help and had set up a time for me to begin my interviews. Sarojini then turned to me to say how impressed she was with the Sharmas' children. "They are so quiet and well behaved," she said. "You never see them hanging around. Otherwise one often sees young men hanging around the streets. But that is not the case with their children." Visibly pleased, the Sharmas concurred with her. Both said that they kept the doors of their flat shut: the children stayed indoors and either studied or talked among themselves.

Jagdish claimed that the children were kept indoors because of the "atmosphere" (*mahoul*) in the neighborhood. He spoke about one of the neighbors, a drunkard who constantly fought with his wife and children. Shakuntala added that this family made the atmosphere in the neighborhood very unpleasant; because of "the sort of people around" she did not encourage her children, especially her daughter, to go out much. In fact, she said, Poonam was now so used to staying indoors that, during the winter, she had to coax her to go out to dry her hair in the sun.

It was clear that the Sharmas felt that they were more respectable, more middle class, than their neighbors, and considered themselves superior to them. They expressed contempt for most of their neighbors, who, Shakuntala alleged, "did not know how to live." Shakuntala and Jagdish were particularly critical of how their neighbors allowed their children to loiter about the streets. They expressed a very strong sense of being "different" from their neighbors. Nowhere was this difference more marked than in the way they brought up their daughter.[11]

Unmarried Women as Daughters

The sexuality of daughters was an important concern in many Doordarshan narratives that focused on the position of women.[12] For instance, as noted above, in *Hum Log* the middle daughter, Majhli, "ruins" her life because of her ambition to work in Hindi films. A disobedient daughter, she defies her parents by seeking fame and fortune in Bombay, where she becomes fair game for men who sexually exploit her. She returns to Delhi a "fallen woman," chastened and deeply depressed. In the rest of the serial she remains a symbol of what happens when daughters defy their parents' authority and parents are unable to control their daughters' sexuality. She is redeemed only when she gets married and becomes a passive, dutiful wife. Similarly, in a subplot of *Buniyaad*, Veeranwali, Masterji's sister and the daughter of the house, is seduced by her fiancé, who is later lost in the turbulence of Partition. Veeranwali discovers she is pregnant and attempts to commit suicide. Her mother finds out and, in an attempt to prevent her daughter's pregnancy from bringing dishonor to their clan, leaves her at an ashram; she informs the rest of the family that Veeranwali is dead. Veeranwali changes her name, becomes an ascetic, and dedicates her life to community service. The daughter with an uncontrolled sexuality, the fallen woman, is rehabilitated only after she renounces all worldly pleasures and attachments.

The discourses of sexuality articulated in *Buniyaad*, as well as in other women-oriented narratives, resonated with themes that pervaded conversations I had with viewers in Vikas Nagar and Basti, where the place of daughters in the family was inextricably tied to aspirations to middle-class respectability. It was most marked in the case of the Sharmas. The intimate relationship between notions of middle-class and upper-caste respectability and discourses of gender, honor, and sexuality was evident in the manner in which they had raised their daughter. More significant, Poonam's own everyday practices enacted middle-class notions of femininity and modesty. Even though her mother complained that she was sometimes "too sharp-tongued," she was soft-spoken, polite, and reserved in public; she did not mingle with "outsiders," she dressed modestly, she stayed indoors. Shakuntala frequently claimed that daughters had to be "extra careful" because their sexuality made them susceptible to dishonor: as unmarried women, daughters had to live under the protective control of their families.

One afternoon while Poonam was still away at college, Shakuntala and I spoke of the vulnerability of young women. Shakuntala was preparing the evening meal. As always, she turned down my offer to help; I sat by her, nursing a cup of tea in my hands. I remarked that the previous evening I had returned home later than usual to find my mother standing by the entrance to our house, waiting anxiously for me. Shakuntala nodded knowingly. "Daughters are always a source of anxiety for mothers. Even after they are married. But when they are unmarried they are really vulnerable." She added: "If someone says something bad, the girl's honor is the first to go. . . . I see girls and boys around me and feel very proud about my children. They never wear flashy clothes. When Poonam sees her friends wear expensive clothes, she says, 'Doesn't matter. I'd rather be simple.' She always wears loose *kurtas* [the loose tunics worn by many women in north India]. She *never, never* wears fitting clothes that are tight over here [Shakuntala indicated her breasts with her hands]" (emphasis in original). I instinctively looked down at my own clothes, and remembered that when I was in college I had been chastised by my mother every time I wore tight kurtas. I realized that when I visited this neighborhood, I always wore a sari, a considerably more modest (and, not incidentally, more "grown up") outfit than a salwar kameez: I was careful to dress with modesty not just out of deference to the expectations of the people I worked with, but also because of my own middle-class and upper-caste concerns about appearing modest, and therefore respectable.

For the most part, discourses of sexuality articulated in the narratives and practices of lower-middle-class viewers converged with those found in serials such as *Hum Log*. These discourses drew from, and reinforced, prevailing representations of the sexuality of daughters in many north Indian cultures.[13] In many Doordarshan serials, unmarried women were usually represented as daughters. "Good daughters" always deferred to the authority of the patriarchal family; in contrast, those who transgressed their assigned "place" in the patriarchal family were severely punished by exile, profound emotional anguish, or suicide. The moral of these stories—that unmarried women had to be "protected" by their families—reinforced the patriarchal family's authority to control their sexuality.[14]

At the same time, programs such as *Udaan* (Flight) and *Rajani* portrayed women who ostensibly stepped outside the confines of the home to intervene in public life. Indeed, the heroines of these narratives embodied ideal Indian Womanhood because they channeled their energies

Figure 1 Kalyani,
the disciplined
police officer

into reforming Indian society. Yet, these narratives expressed an ambivalence that converged with the dilemmas of many lower-middle-class families who were struggling between the economic compulsions to permit their daughters to seek employment and their anxieties about the surveillance and "protection" of the young women's sexuality. This tension was somewhat resolved in one of the Sharmas' favorite serials, *Udaan*, which was unique in its portrayal of a man who defies his extended family when he insists on educating his daughter, Kalyani, and allows her to join the police force (fig. 1).

How did lower-middle-class families experiencing similar dilemmas respond to portrayals of ambitious, single women like Kalyani who apparently transgressed their culturally sanctioned place as obedient daughters? Although Poonam and her mother criticized Majhli of *Hum Log* for being "too ambitious" and not keeping to her "place" as a daughter, they praised Kalyani for her "courage" in fulfilling her ambitions and joining the police. The moral framework in which the two serials portray ambitious women gives us a clue to these viewers' contrasting responses to Kalyani and Majhli. For one thing, Majhli's ambitions are depicted as self-centered: after all, it is her desire for personal success that drives her to show business. Further, and perhaps more important, her parents are

unable to control her sexuality. Once in Bombay she is outside their surveillance and is, predictably, sexually exploited by sleazy film producers.
In contrast, *Udaan*'s Kalyani is portrayed as an ideal daughter and citizen. Early in *Udaan I*, after Kalyani's father is beaten up by his enemies,
she realizes "what it like for people from the lower and middle classes"
who have to struggle to seek redress for the injustices committed against
them. She resolves to make her father's battle her own; her father's
struggles are synecdochic of the struggles of the disempowered "lower
and middle classes" of India.

Kalyani channels her energies toward national and community service
by joining the police. Every episode of *Udaan II* begins with scenes that
show her slow transformation from a little girl to a police officer. In the
first shot we see the door to a birdcage being lifted by a young girl: a
bird flies out of the cage and into the sky. The camera then cuts to the
face of the young girl, Kalyani, who turns her gaze upward to the birds
soaring above her. In quick succession, we see flashbacks from her childhood: we see her and her family being thrown off their ancestral lands;
the next shot consists of an older Kalyani standing next to a bicycle giving
her father a cheerful thumbs-up. The camera then cuts to a close-up of
her father: he looks exhausted, yet determined. Next the camera cuts to
a flashback of her as a young girl: as the camera zooms in on her face,
she looks serious, resolute. Immediately afterward is a close-up of her
as an adult: we see her looking out a window, her expression once again
serious and resolute. Next, we see her donning her police uniform: she
ties the laces of her boots, puts on her belt and her cap with its police
crest, and places her baton under her arm. The next three shots consist of
close-ups of her face in quick succession. With her hair carefully pinned
beneath her police cap, she is transformed from a woman to a police officer: her sexuality is subsumed by her police uniform. In the rest of the
serial, we see her disciplining and surrendering her body to the service
of the nation: she learns karate so she can engage in hand-to-hand combat with a bandit (fig. 2); even though she is romantically attracted to a
colleague, she concentrates all her energies on fulfilling her duties as a
patriotic police officer. We rarely see her as a sexual woman. She is, above
all, a disciplined police officer.

Further, while Majhli's parents and brothers vehemently oppose her
desire to join films, in contrast, Kalyani's ambitions are unequivocally endorsed by her parents. Even after she is transferred to a distant district,

Figure 2 Kalyani learns karate

she seeks her father's advice on professional matters. Every time she is confronted with an ethical dilemma, she asks herself what her father would do. As I will describe shortly, Kalyani's father provides the moral resolution of the narrative: he, rather than Kalyani, is the hero of the serial. He retains his moral authority over her, and by extension over the narrative; for all her ability to assume the "masculine" role of a police officer, Kalyani remains an obedient and loyal daughter. *Udaan* thus resolves the middle-class tension between women's agency and the surveillance and control of their sexuality by effacing Kalyani's sexuality; as an unmarried daughter, she remains (morally) subordinated to the protective control of her father.[15]

The specific positions of daughters within the family frequently surfaced in the discourses of serials and in the interpretations and everyday practices of viewers.[16] I turn, once again, to the example of Shakuntala Sharma and her daughter, Poonam. Shakuntala would often claim that "you have to take a lot more care of girls." Daughters had to be protected because their sexuality could potentially bring dishonor to their families. Moreover, they also had to be "trained" to stay in their appointed "place" in the family and the community.

In most lower-middle-class and working-class families, daughters had to share in the housework and to be "trained" in it.[17] Like many other lower-middle-class daughters, Poonam, who was working toward a master's degree in history, juggled her studies with housework. Her mother described a typical day to me: Poonam woke every weekday at 5:00 A.M. and studied for an hour. While her father and brother went for a walk or read the newspaper, she ironed the clothes of the rest of the family (with characteristic middle-class concern for looking neat, Poonam once said to me, "It looks nice if the clothes you wear are well ironed; you feel good all day"). Then she helped her mother prepare breakfast for the family. After breakfast, she left for the university. She returned home around 4:00 P.M. and, after resting for half an hour, started the evening meal. Shakuntala explained to me that she was usually too tired to do much work in the evenings, so Poonam always cooked dinner. The family watched the evening television serial while eating dinner; after studying for a couple of hours, Poonam retired for the night. When I asked Poonam what she did for relaxation, she replied that she liked to read novels during the weekends. She had some friends at the university and, very occasionally, went to the university cafeteria with them. But there was little time to socialize: she found the master's program in history very demanding and, because she had to help with housework, had to do most of her studying in the university library.

One day, I accompanied Poonam to the neighborhood market, where we ran into some of her neighbors. While I met them with enthusiasm, she greeted them with a gentle, yet formal courtesy that was full of reserve. As we walked back to her home, I noticed how she held herself: her *dupatta* draped carefully around her shoulders, her eyes downcast, her body tense and stiff.[18] She was unfailingly courteous to people when they did speak to her (indeed, several of her neighbors had described her gentle dignity with admiration), but her aloof and formal manner seemed to discourage them from initiating a conversation. When we returned home, I asked her if she had any friends in the neighborhood. As I expected, she replied that she did not; in fact, she did not even know the names of many of the young women I had met while doing my research.

When I inquired why that was the case, she replied that her parents dis-approved of her talking to neighbors. She explained: "Who has the time to socialize? . . . Besides, they're different from us."

Poonam wanted to be a schoolteacher when she finished her studies. It seemed to me that these ambitions were circumscribed by her percep-tions of her role as a daughter and, after her (inevitable) marriage, her duties as a daughter-in-law. Of all her career options she felt that teach-ing was most appropriate because it would not be "too strenuous," and after she was married, she would be able to "adjust" the demands of her job to her obligations to her family. Like many other young women I met in Vikas Nagar and Basti, Poonam worked hard to help her family main-tain their middle-class status: she studied diligently so she could get a teaching job; she dressed and behaved with modesty to ensure that her reputation and that of her family were never tarnished.

How was the tension between the expectations of "good daughters" and middle-class compulsions to enter into the labor force negotiated in women-oriented serials such as *Udaan*? Kalyani's parents actively en-courage their daughter to join the police force. In fact, Kalyani's father had been ostracized by his extended family for insisting on making avail-able to his daughter all the opportunities given to sons. How was this narrative interpreted by viewers? One Sunday afternoon, on the heels of a long discussion about *Udaan* in which Shakuntala and Poonam praised Kalyani for having the "courage" to join the police force, I asked if they thought women should take up any career they wished. Shakuntala re-plied that she thought it was important for women to have a job because it gave them an independent source of income. "This is a harsh [*sakht*] world," she said. "A woman never knows what she might have to face." But a job should never consume too much of a woman's energies: her first priority should be her family. She continued: "I have struggled all my life. I was suppressed [*main to dab gayi*]. But I made sure my family was always in peace."

For all their aspirations to middle-class status, the Sharmas were clearly struggling to make ends meet. They did not indulge in conspicuous con-sumption in quite the same way as Surjeet Kaur, who dressed in flashy polyester salwar kameezes and whose home was filled with furniture; they had fewer appliances than Sarojini or Jayanthi Chandran. The Shar-mas' clothes were shabby; their furniture was old and worn. The stainless steel utensils in their kitchen seemed to be their one indulgence. And the books and magazines filling their tiny home reflected their investment in their children's education (Shakuntala once recounted that she had told her children, "These books are our investment" [*jama-punji*]). Everything about Shakuntala spoke volumes for how hard she had worked to save money for her children's education: her faded saris, the lines of fatigue permanently etched in her face, the austere expression in her eyes that softened only when she spoke about the people she loved. I sensed that the children were their parents' only hope for upward mobility.

At the same time, it was clear to me that Jagdish and Shakuntala had invested a lot more, emotionally and financially, in their son, Ramesh, than in Poonam.[19] Ramesh was about two years older than Poonam; after finishing his bachelor's degree he had been unemployed for a year. When I first met him, he had just got a temporary job in a financial corporation. Jagdish and Shakuntala were willing to educate their daughter, and in fact had indulged her desire to obtain a master's degree.[20] But there seemed no doubt in Shakuntala's mind that it was her son who would ensure his parents' comfortable old age; after all, Poonam would soon be married, and her attachments and duties would then be transferred to her husband and in-laws. Shakuntala differentiated, in word and in deed, between Poonam and Ramesh.

Shakuntala's bias in favor of Ramesh frequently surfaced in the way she would effusively praise his achievements and slight Poonam's. She would describe her son with great tenderness and pride, and often spoke of how intelligent he was. He had always topped his class, he had been a favorite with all his teachers and classmates, and he never did anything without his parents' permission. One winter evening, the three of us were sitting in the kitchen. Ramesh and his father had gone for a walk. I was sitting on my heels hugging myself to keep out the chill that was rapidly closing in on us; Shakuntala was kneading dough for that evening's chapatis; Poonam was chopping vegetables. Shakuntala recounted that she had accidentally met a former teacher of Ramesh's, who inquired about him. "Everyone who has ever taught him still remembers him. I still keep all his report cards," Shakuntala said. I cringed in embarrassment and mortification as she proceeded to compare Ramesh and Poonam: "He is very intelligent. But Poonam is okay. He would get very good marks with very little effort. But she has to study late into the night to do well. And even then her marks are not as good." All this was said in the presence of Poonam, who sat with a blank expression on her face and continued to chop vegetables for the evening meal.

Married Women as Daughters-in-Law

If daughters were discriminated against and expected to juggle house-work with studies or career, daughters-in-law were further marginalized by the politics of the extended family.[21] The tyranny of the double day—of working both within and outside the home—was accentuated in the case of daughters-in-law, most of whom lived with their husbands' parents and returned to their parental homes only for brief visits. Doordarshan programs often provided a discursive space in which women would talk to each other and to me about their positions within their families. After observing the daily practices and family relationships of the viewers I worked with, I discerned at least three ways in which daughters-in-law were marginalized by the politics of the extended family: through in-laws' demands for dowry; the exploitation of their labor; and the fundamental, usually unspoken, assumption that a woman's sexuality was the property of her husband's clan.

Dowry was a very common theme in government-produced public in-formation spots, in nonfiction magazine programs, and, most frequently, in women-oriented narratives.[22] For instance, *Hum Log*'s Badhki is repeat-edly humiliated by prospective in-laws because of her parents' inability to provide her with a sufficiently large dowry. As noted in the previous chapter, programs criticizing the practice of dowry were often framed by advertisements that tempted viewers to procure consumer products. By titillating viewers' desires to acquire consumer products, these advertise-ments indirectly encouraged them to ask for increasingly lavish dowries. Indeed, many feminist critics have commented on how dowry demands for kitchen appliances and scooters increased after the introduction of commercials on television.[23]

The dowry demands of prospective in-laws evoked a very tangible fear in many of the men and women I worked with, and in fact dominated our discussions about serials such as *Hum Log*. For instance, Jagdish and Shakuntala Sharma were extremely worried about their ability to provide Poonam with a dowry that would satisfy her future in-laws. One of the reasons why they were so anxious for Ramesh's job to become permanent was because they wanted to start saving for Poonam's dowry. Similarly, as described later in my analysis of responses to *Mahabharat*'s Draupadi (chapter 5), viewers such as Sushmita Dasgupta were very nervous about the "dishonor" they might be subjected to once they went to their in-laws' home: they were terrified that their lower-middle-class families would be unable to provide them with dowries that would satisfy their future in-laws.

Discussions about Doordarshan programs enabled parents to vent their fears that their daughters would be harassed by their in-laws for dowries, and provided young women with opportunities to express their apprehensions about what they might face once they got married. At the same time, as Sushmita pointed out, programs about dowry always depicted harassed daughters-in-law as helpless victims. Sushmita wished to know why these programs did not portray greedy people being "caught" and "punished" for harassing their daughters-in-law. Her response underscored the manner in which Doordarshan, perhaps unwittingly, perpetuated a discourse of victimology about women who were harassed for dowry, reinscribing these women as "dowry victims" who had to be rescued by the state. The efforts of the scores of grassroots organizations that have fought to empower women who are harassed for dowry were either completely ignored by these narratives or presented as ineffective.[24]

Interestingly, Doordarshan programs did not dwell on the patriarchal extended family's exploitation of women's labor to the same extent that they narrated the sufferings of "dowry victims." In fact, serials such as *Buniyaad* normalized the exploitation of daughters-in-law. For instance, after running a restaurant during the day, Lajoji's younger daughter-in-law comes home and does the housework. Her capacity to work a double day uncomplainingly, in fact, indexes her status as an ideal daughter-in-law. She helps manage her husband's business and is able to bring in additional income. She is a "good" daughter-in-law because she takes on a major part of the housework, is constantly at hand to fetch and carry for her in-laws, and is always polite and respectful even when she and her husband are insulted by her brother-in-law.

The relative silence surrounding the exploitation of women's labor in these narratives contrasts with its prominence in the life narratives constructed by women viewers. For example, *Yugantar* focused on the place of daughters-in-law in an upper-class extended family in nineteenth-century Bengal. I was talking about it with Shakuntala and Poonam when, as invariably happened in our conversations, we switched from talking about the serial to discussing our own lives. Shakuntala began to compare her life in the city with her experiences as a young daughter-in-law in her husband's village. She had been raised in a small town in central India but was married at the age of sixteen to a man of her own caste who lived in a distant village in the Himalayan foothills. She described how terrified she was when she left her parental home to live with her husband in a remote place. She added that there was very little she missed of her life in her in-laws' village. As a young bride she had been unfamiliar with most of her in-laws' customs and had frequently annoyed them by unwittingly doing or saying the wrong thing. For instance, she was never able to keep the edge of her sari on her head while she worked in the fields (as a daughter-in-law she was expected to cover her head in front of her in-laws). Even though she was often bitter about the loneliness and isolation she felt in the city, she spoke of her life in the village with little nostalgia.

Shakuntala went on to describe how hard the women in her husband's village worked. In addition to doing all the housework, they had to work outside the home as well. Although women did not plow the land, they did all the other agricultural work, collected fodder and fuel, and looked after the animals. Even though they had to veil themselves in front of their male affines, like many peasant women in India, they were also expected to work in the fields.[25] But the women of her community also had access to the "outside world" because they were usually responsible for marketing the agricultural produce. Most of the men were away in cities; the few who remained did very little work and "only sat and smoked and drank." Shakuntala told me that "intelligent" women were able to control the financial resources, such as they were, of their families. But, she added, in the city, women like her were confined to the home. When I asked why that happened, she explained: "First of all, we don't have any land to work on. All our work is at home. What do we do all day. Second, our husbands are always around us." When she first moved to the city to join her husband, Shakuntala hoped to find a job outside the home. This met with disapproval from him and his family, and she soon realized that her "place was in the home." The sense of claustrophobia lurking behind her words, "our husbands are always around us," revealed her sense of marginalization and confinement in the city. Even though I could see how hard she always worked, her self-deprecating remarks about house-work, "what do we do all day," did not surprise me; her terse words simply underscored how she devalued her labor within the home.

Finally, even fewer serials raised the question of the sexuality of daughters-in-law in the context of the politics of the extended family. *Buniyaad* showed how the sexuality of women is put to the service of the patriliny when daughters-in-law are pressured to produce sons to con-tinue the lineage. The *Mahabharat* was unusual in its explicit portrayal of the sexuality of women as the property of the Hindu extended family. Early in the serial, we see Queen Satyawati insist that her widowed daughters-in-law have intercourse with her son from a previous marriage so they can conceive heirs to the dynasty. The "disrobing" of Draupadi (described in chapter 5) brings the place of the sexuality of daughters-in-law in the patriarchal family more explicitly to the forefront when Drau-padi confronts her in-laws with the question: "Is a woman her husband's property that she can be used as a stake in a game of dice?"

My observations of the relationships and everyday practices of the men and women with whom I did my research made it obvious that the sur-veillance and control of women's sexuality did not cease when they got married. It simply acquired another form. Sometimes it was manifested as sexual exploitation; in one case, it assumed the more brutal form of rape. The predominantly lower-middle-class women I worked with rarely discussed their sexual experiences explicitly: I had to learn to read their gestures and body language, the furtive movements of their eyes, and the innuendoes they employed to talk about sex. What struck me most was that they often represented sexuality in the idiom of power, as the "hold" men had on women, as the reason for their vulnerability, or in terms of the ways the men in their families abused them.[26] Married women some-times alluded to how their sexuality was perceived as the property of their husbands' families, either because they were expected to produce chil-dren to continue the lineage or because aspersions cast on their sexual "purity" would bring dishonor to their husbands' clans.[27]

Occasionally, the bodies of daughters-in-law became sites for elder male affines to exert their patriarchal authority. One day, when Surjeet Kaur was talking to Sarojini and me about Draupadi's disrobing, she compared Draupadi with herself. My initial interpretation of her com-ments was that, like other women who had been moved by Draupadi's plight, she was talking in a general way about the disempowerment of

daughters-in-law or the sexual vulnerability of women. But then she proceeded to tell me about how she had experienced Draupadi's plight (*main
khud us dour se guzri hun*). At first I was puzzled; then I realized that she
was telling me that she had been sexually assaulted by her father-in-law.

About a year before her wedding, her father-in-law had married for
the third time. Shortly afterward, his new wife ran away. Surjeet and
her husband moved into her father-in-law's home immediately after their
marriage. Surjeet recounted that her father-in-law had a vicious temper.
He would get drunk every night and rail against the rest of the family.
"One day, he [her husband] did not come home until very late at night.
The old man [her father-in-law] got very drunk. When he [her husband]
came home I was lying in another room, bruised and in pain. He saw
what had happened but did not say anything. After that, he would frequently return home very late at night."

Sarojini clicked her tongue sympathetically (I got the impression she
had known about this), and I was dumbstruck with horror and pain. Surjeet Kaur proceeded to tell us that it was she who had insisted that they
leave her father-in-law's home; her husband had refused to do so. After
several months of quarreling with her husband, her will to escape the
clutches of her father-in-law prevailed and they moved out. But, she said,
she had learned that she had to be "self-sufficient." Nobody was going to
protect her, "nobody, not even my husband": "He knew what had happened. But *I* had to insist that we move out. I know what Draupadi had
to go through. I have emerged from that reality [*main khud us haqiqat se
nikal kar aayi hun*]. I was not in the shadow [*parchayeen*] of anyone's protection. What I have gone through nobody can survive, especially not in
this society." Sarojini turned to me and commented, "What she has had
to live through is worse than any serial." Surjeet Kaur added that she had
become a very strong woman and could "take care of" any man who tried
to "come near" her: "I am a very brave woman, I never lose courage. I
always feel I have enough strength in my hands, in my body. And I can
earn my living."

She thus narrated, in an elliptical manner, what had happened to her
decades ago, when she was a young bride. I already knew from previous fieldwork in a north Indian village that fathers-in-law and other
elder affines sometimes sexually assaulted young daughters-in-law who
were not in a position to resist them. I was deeply distressed by Surjeet Kaur's story, which reiterated the vulnerability of women who suffer

sexual abuse within the family. Surjeet Kaur had appropriated the story of Draupadi to speak of her sexual abuse at the hands of her father-in-law. Like Draupadi, she had been dishonored by an in-law: instead of protecting her, her father-in-law had assaulted her. And like Draupadi's husbands, who watched passively while she was being disrobed, Surjeet's husband had pretended not to notice what had happened. He was complicit in his father's rape of his wife because he had failed to protect her and had, in fact, resisted her wish to move out. Even more noteworthy was the manner in which Surjeet Kaur told this story. She did not narrate what happened to elicit my sympathy: her matter-of-fact, unsentimental narrative defied me to pity her. Indeed, she used the story to describe herself as a survivor: despite being abused by her father-in-law, she had "emerged from that reality" a brave, strong woman who did not need the "shadow" of anybody's protection.

Education and the "Uplift" of Women

All the programs that propagated the "uplift" of women's status devoted a fair amount of time to the issue of women's formal education. *Yugantar*, a serial based on the novel *Sei Samay*, written by well-known Bengali writer Sunil Gangopadhyay, dealt explicitly with women's formal education and the position of widows in the nineteenth century. Telecast in fall 1990, it depicted the crusades of social reformers such as Iswarchandra Vidyasagar and other members of the (male) nationalist elite for widow remarriage and the formal education of women. The serial was unequivocally nationalist: anticolonial struggles formed the mise-en-scène for the portrayal of "women's issues," and commentaries about important events of the anticolonial struggles were inserted throughout. For instance, a song about the defeat of the mutineers of 1857 situated the serial in a particular nationalist narrative of the past; similarly, one important subplot concerned the Indigo Rebellion. What were the politics of telecasting a narrative of nineteenth-century campaigns for women's education on Doordarshan? Most viewers I worked with enjoyed watching *Yugantar* and, although it was set in the previous century, appropriated its discourses to comment on the position of contemporary women.

While *Hum Log* and *Udaan* portrayed education as crucial to the upward mobility of the family, *Yugantar* made an explicit plea about the centrality of women's education to the "progress" of both the family and the nation: when women are formally educated, their families acquire middle-class status and the nation edges closer toward modernity. Through its depiction of "women's issues" in the nineteenth century as an integral part of a larger nationalist project, *Yugantar* represented women's education both in terms of its benefits for the family and in terms of social reform, an important part of the modernist project of the *post*colonial nation. The implication was that the future of postcolonial India rested on the formal education of its women and, eventually, the constitution of modern gendered subjects who could participate in the building of a modern nation; thus, even as conceptions of Indianness reconfigured notions of womanhood, discourses of the emancipation of women shaped the envisioning of the future of India.

Most of these narratives, however, also reflected an ambivalence toward the agency of educated women that overlapped with the tension between middle-class viewers' acknowledgment of the necessity for formal education and their fears that educated women represented a threat to the "traditional" family. For instance, even though Shakuntala devalued her labor as a homemaker, she was unequivocal in her view that housework should have top priority in a woman's life. This surfaced several times in my conversations with her and Poonam. I present extracts from one such exchange below.

Shakuntala, Poonam, and I had been talking about *Yugantar's* emphasis on women's education. I referred to an earlier conversation in which Shakuntala had expressed her ambivalence about Poonam's desire to pursue a master's degree. Didn't she think that girls should be well educated before they were married, so as to not be financially dependent on others? Shakuntala agreed that it was important for a woman to be educated in order to be "able to earn and eat. At least she won't have to be dependent on someone else." But it was clear that Shakuntala felt that women should be educated only to the extent that they could support themselves. I responded that, perhaps because of inflation and other socioeconomic pressures, young women sometimes faced a dilemma. On the one hand, they had to contribute to their family's income by working outside the home; on the other hand, they also had to perform their duties as wives, mothers, and daughters. No sooner were the words out of my mouth than Poonam became very excited and seized on what I said: "You're absolutely right! This is just what I keep saying. We are in the middle, we are neither very modernized, nor have we been able to leave behind our old culture. That old culture which, in many matters, is not all that good. So we are caught in the middle. We're neither here nor there."

Shakuntala did not seem to grasp what Poonam and I were talking about. The following exchange occurred between mother and daughter:

> *Shakuntala:* Yes, for instance if a girl has to study all the time, when will she get time to learn stitching and embroidery? They have to know all these things. After all when the prospective mother-in-law asks, "What does she know?" she has to be able to say something! . . . At the very most, they will only learn to cook, and that too when they have time. *All girls learn to cook.* But the thing is there are other things like stitching, embroidery. When will she learn those things? And then work [outside the home] too? (My emphasis.)
>
> *Poonam:* Mothers-in-law should also realize . . .
>
> *Shakuntala interrupted her:* Yes, mothers-in-law should be understanding and accommodating. Like, if there are children she can look after them. Then, when she [the daughter-in-law] returns [after working outside the home] in the evening, she will realize that the mother-in-law has worked all day, she will take over . . .

Thus, like other women of her class and generation, Poonam expressed her sense of being "caught in the middle." Lower-middle-class women were now expected to earn for their families as well as fulfill their "traditional" responsibilities within the home. These expectations not only exhausted women, both physically and emotionally, they also led to conflicts within the family. Poonam felt that women like her were "neither here nor there," neither "modern" nor "traditional." Shakuntala, on the other hand, was oblivious to Poonam's feelings of entrapment.[28] There was little doubt in her mind that women who worked outside the home also had an obligation to fulfill their traditional roles as housewives and mothers. Shakuntala naturalized these roles by assuming that "all girls" had to learn cooking; knowing how to cook was the minimum skill required to qualify as a daughter-in-law. When prospective mothers-in-law asked about the qualifications of their future daughters-in-law, they wished to know what *other* homemaking skills they had: Could they sew? Could they knit? These were the skills that were valued in the marriage market. When Poonam tried to articulate her own opinion on what mothers-in-law ought to look for in a potential daughter-in-law, Shakuntala interrupted her to continue her own train of thought. She maintained that mothers-in-law ought to be magnanimous and help with raising the grandchildren if their daughters-in-law worked outside the home. But there was no question that once they returned home from their jobs, daughters-in-law ought to "take over" the housework. The double day faced by most women who worked outside the home, and the fact that many middle-class and lower-middle-class men did little to help with housework, was thus completely taken for granted by Shakuntala.

While Poonam, for all her apparent acquiescence, occasionally questioned some of her family's self-consciously middle-class values, Renuka Sengupta, who was about the same age, seemed a lot more conservative. An upper-caste Bengali Hindu woman, she had grown up in New Delhi and, when I first met her, was working on a master's degree in philosophy. Renuka and her family lived in Division II of Vikas Nagar. Division II flats were a little larger than Division III flats, and they contained a much-envied luxury: individual bathrooms and latrines. Renuka and I would usually sit and chat in her living room; there also seemed to be one bedroom, a small front verandah, and a handkerchief-size lawn in the front.

Renuka's mother suffered from a number of chronic ailments. She had suffered a heart attack the previous year, and was plagued by chronic high blood pressure and diabetes. Since she was no longer able to do all the housework by herself, Renuka helped. Like Shakuntala, Renuka's mother described Renuka's help as a necessary apprenticeship for what she would do "all her life": "After her marriage, this is what she'll have to do" (lag jayegi). When I first met them, Renuka's parents were looking for a "suitable match" for her. In the meantime, they permitted her to study (in her mother's words: "We think until we find someone suitable she might as well study"). Renuka's mother was worried that it might be difficult to find a bridegroom for her because people in their community did not favor highly educated girls; instead, they preferred high school– or college-educated women with jobs.

Renuka shared her mother's ambivalence toward women who were "too highly educated" and frequently talked about how such women represented a threat to the "unity" of the family.[29] It was difficult for me to assess what Renuka meant by "highly educated." She agreed with Yugantar's discourses about the importance of women's formal education. I gathered that she felt it was essential for women to have a college education; however, she seemed to think that women pursuing doctoral degrees or other demanding programs of study were clearly indifferent to the welfare of their families. I used to wonder if she wasn't using our discussions about *Yugantar* to express her disapproval of me and my commitment to my studies: there was always some tension between us, and I sometimes came away from her house feeling defensive about having "left" my husband to do fieldwork in India. Renuka often claimed that it was important for women to be educated so they could be worthy companions to their (inevitably) better-educated husbands. Here again, her views seemed to mirror *Yugantar*'s perspective on the relationships between women's education, companionate marriages, and the modernity of the nation: when women acquired formal education, they became worthy companions to their husbands; companionate marriage was deemed a necessary feature of the modern Indian family.

One day, we had just finished watching an episode of *Yugantar* and were talking about the two male protagonists, Ganga and his younger brother, Navin. I commented that even though Navin was portrayed as an intellectual, he never encouraged his child bride to learn to read and write. Ganga, in contrast, pushed his widowed cousin to study and encouraged his wife to read literature. Renuka agreed with me. She explained that Ganga asked his wife to read literature so she could become "worthy" of him (*mere layak bano*). Since I did not recollect Ganga saying this, I tried to clarify if he had indeed used those very words. Renuka replied impatiently, "I mean . . . yes . . . obviously!" She continued: "When he is so educated . . . he thought his wife should walk side by side with him [*usse kadam milaake chale*]. With education, she can sit and talk with people, the two can discuss things together. So like that, he wanted to educate his wife." Navin, on the other hand, had been married while still a child but, unlike his child bride, was able to attend school. Renuka pointed out that even though Navin's wife was intelligent, she was no companion to him.

Yugantar was unusual in its portrayal of Navin's attraction toward his elder brother's wife. This had caused quite a ripple among viewers. But Renuka was quite matter-of-fact about it. She explained that Navin was attracted to his sister-in-law because his own wife could not be a companion to him: he could not talk to her about literature and the other things he felt passionate about.

While Renuka felt that women should be educated in order to be "worthy" companions to their husbands, she maintained, as did her mother, that "problems" arose if a woman was "too" highly educated.

After all, she claimed, a man will not start helping his wife with housework just because she is well educated. In fact, that will only cause conflict in a marriage, because an educated woman will get frustrated with housework. And, she added, a highly educated woman who is frustrated with her life is more likely to "shatter" her husband's family by antagonizing his parents. When I disagreed with her, she continued: "If, by chance, someone has studied a lot and is also working, it's not as if the husband will share the work. Because he's also working. . . . It's not as if they're partners who should divide the work. *That can't be possible*. . . . There's the mother-in-law, the father-in-law. You have to look after them. So she has double work. It becomes frustrating. The woman has to do everything at the same time" (my emphasis).

According to Renuka, although husband and wife can be companions to the extent that the wife is "worthy" of the man, they cannot be partners because the wife has the added responsibility of doing all the housework and serving her in-laws. Renuka believed it was essential to take care not to antagonize one's in-laws because without their support a woman was very vulnerable. Describing how, in *Yugantar*, the educated daughter-in-law was loved and supported by her in-laws, she added, "They give her a helping hand. *That's* why she is able to flourish. When you don't get that support from the family, you can't do anything" (emphasis in original). It was therefore important, she felt, to "merge" with the husband's family. That was the way *Yugantar* depicted "good" daughters-in-law: as women who were educated and were companions to their husbands but who also "adjusted" to the ways of their in-laws and never antagonized them.

. I wanted to know if Renuka approved of the freedom some contemporary women enjoyed. She replied, "The way it is now, it's okay. It should not be more than this." She added that educated women demanded "lots" of freedom. This was "not right" because "lots" of freedom would incite them to "spoil" families. She then told me that she did not plan to work full time when she got married: she would look for a teaching job in a school that would allow her to be home by the afternoon. That way she would be able to fulfill her responsibilities toward her in-laws, husband, and children. Regardless of her education, she intended to give her family priority. Thus, I saw striking parallels between Renuka's views and the liberal-nationalist discourses of serials such as *Yugantar*. Both conceived a woman's education in terms of its role in consolidating her marriage: a woman should be educated, but just enough to be a "worthy companion" to her husband. "Too much" education would make her "too independent" and would threaten the purported unity of her family.

What was the role of formal education in the historical construction of the New Indian Woman, a woman who was both modern and retained the "true essence" of Indian Womanhood? According to Partha Chatterjee, anticolonial nationalists believed that the "essence" of Indian Womanhood had to be "recovered from the morass of bigotry and superstition into which tradition had fallen, and [that] reform and education would accomplish this" (1993:144). But Renuka's discourses set clear limits both to the ends to which women should put their education and, more important, how much education they should obtain. If women studied "in continuation," Renuka said, they would get so used to the freedom they enjoyed as students that they would be frustrated by the restrictions imposed on them in their husbands' homes. I disagreed with her. Did women get frustrated because they were highly educated, I asked, or because of the restrictions imposed on them? She responded: "If you go into another family, there are bound to be new restrictions. Educated women will rebel. In your family, the rules were different, in the new family they will be different. It happens everywhere. Now look at you, you've studied so much. If someone was to impose restrictions on you, would you like it? . . . [Women with higher education] start thinking too much about themselves, their own self, their own child. It [the family] gets shattered. Higher education is one cause." Renuka conceded that there were other reasons why families broke up ("such as temperamental incompatibility between a man and a woman"); however, she felt that higher education was "the cause, to a large extent, of the disintegration of families."

I thus saw an ambivalence toward women's education, and in particular the agency of educated women, expressed in women-oriented narratives as well as in the opinions and practices of viewers such as Renuka. On the one hand, in keeping with the state's official commitment to "uplift" women, serials such as *Yugantar* overtly encouraged women to obtain formal education. On the other hand, these narratives displayed an anxiety that educated women, by stepping outside the confines of the family, would transgress their appointed places as daughters/daughters-in-law and threaten the patriarchal family's authority to monitor their energies, their bodies, and their subjectivities. In their analysis of gender discourses in nationalist ideologies of social reform, Tharu and Lalita point out that "the whole question of women's education was . . .

riddled with contradictions. On one level education promised freedom and equality and was projected as a program that would shape the child for responsible citizenship. Yet underlying much of the discussion in the nineteenth century was the need felt as urgently by missionaries . . . as by the new Indian men to break into the *zenana,* or the private spheres of household and family, and make women into more fitting homemakers, mothers, and companions for the emerging urban middle-class men" (1991a:163–164). An "enlightened" middle-class woman was expected to be formally educated; at the same time, however, her education was oriented toward making her a companionable wife and a mother who could raise her children to be modern, middle-class Indians.

As in the social reform discourses of the colonial era, women's struggles for access to education appear in postcolonial discourses to be accommodated and subsumed within master narratives of family and nation. Further, at the same time that "the family" is configured as essentially Indian, discourses of modernity (the modern nation, the modern Indian woman, the modern Indian family) provide new norms for social governance. A form of subjectivity is created for the New Indian Woman who participates in the nation's march to modernity and, at the same time, preserves all that is unique and authentic about "Indian culture."

THE CONTAINMENT OF WOMEN'S ENERGIES: A LOOK AT *UDAAN*

Unlike the late nineteenth century, when the Woman Question was "resolved" by demarcating the private sphere (of women) from the public sphere (of men), late twentieth-century constructions of the New Indian Woman *complicated* notions of women's agency by valorizing "emancipated" women who dexterously straddled the "home" and the "world." In this section, I trace the figuration of the New Indian Woman of postcolonial nationalism by analyzing the discourses of the script writer and director of two of the most popular serials shown in the late 1980s and early 1990s, *Udaan I* and its sequel, *Udaan II.* The core narrative of the two serials portrayed the efforts of Kalyani, a young, lower-middle-class woman, to qualify for the police force and, later, to function as an honest, conscientious officer in a corrupt environment. In presenting my discussion with Kavita Choudhry, the script writer and heroine of *Udaan,* it is not my aim to reify authorial intention (Foucault 1988:113–138) but, on the contrary, to situate her interpretations within larger discourses of nationalism and gender.

Udaan I began with a depiction of a feudal family in which one of the sons is determined, at the risk of incurring the wrath of his father, to give his daughter the same educational opportunities as his son. As a result of his defiance, he and his wife and children are thrown out of their ancestral home and cheated of their rights to the family property. They move to the city, where they struggle to make ends meet and educate their children. Their daughter, Kalyani, is sensitive and intelligent. She sees that her father is unable to seek legal redress for the injustices perpetrated on him by his brothers. In a crucial episode, her father is beaten up by hired hoodlums, and she goes to a local police chief to seek justice. He refuses to see her. At that moment she resolves to join the police so she can sit "on the other side of the table" and have the power to help people who have been cheated of their rights. *Udaan II* showed her as a police officer struggling to retain her idealism and her commitment to her job in the face of pressures put on her by corrupt senior officers, politicians, and landlords.

Udaan had a tremendous impact on the viewers I worked with.[30] Men and women alike were impressed with Kalyani's idealism and self-confidence, and many described with admiration her courage in fighting corruption. Kalyani became a household name during the time that the serial was aired; the actress was so deeply identified with her television persona that when I asked for directions to her flat in Bombay, the little boy who ran up to help me pointed to it, saying, "That is where Kalyani lives."[31]

I met Choudhry in the flat she shared with her brother and his family in an upper-middle-class neighborhood in Bombay. We had our interview in a somewhat austere living room, where we sat on an old, faded sofa. The other furniture consisted of a couple of old armchairs, a coffee table and two small end tables, a television set, and an old dining table. Choudhry herself was very casually dressed. Without makeup she looked much younger than she did on screen, and in a plain, long black skirt she looked anything but glamorous. I found her more straightforward (and certainly a lot more introspective) than the other film industry professionals I had met during the course of my fieldwork. We talked all afternoon and I came away struck by her candor and perspicacity.

My discussions with Choudhry helped me to appreciate the constraints faced by activists who *choose* to intervene through mass media. Moreover,

Udaan was exceptional in its construction of a complex and introspective protagonist, Kalyani, whose observations on corruption in the police force coexist with the pleasure she derives from her own ascent to power. However, even though I do not subscribe to the dichotomous view of texts as either subversive or dominant, I continue to feel disturbed by *Udaan*'s participation in the hegemonic construction of Indian Womanhood through its valorization of Kalyani's father, its discourses of middle-class citizenship, and, in particular, its role in the containment of oppositional subject positions that it might have created through its story about a courageous and idealistic woman police officer. Looking back now, four years after my meeting with Choudhry, I see how my ambivalence toward *Udaan* mediated our conversation and continues to frame my analysis.[32]

As I noted in chapter 2, at the time that I was doing this research, the popular film industry was facing a serious recession caused in part by the success of entertainment serials on Doordarshan. Since the state exercised monopolistic control over television production, Doordarshan was the only means available of reaching a "mass" audience. State-appointed review committees carefully scrutinized proposals for all entertainment programs (and, in the case of programs depicting "sensitive issues," screened every episode before it was telecast). *Udaan* was produced at the crest of the wave of women-oriented narratives. I was curious to know how Kavita Choudhry, as director and script writer, had negotiated with the state, with the politics of feminism, and with dominant discourses of family and nation.

Gender and Family in Udaan

Kavita Choudhry was candid about the fact that, because she was working with Doordarshan, she had made a conscious decision to "soften" her critique of gender politics in the family. She added that she aimed to situate gender inequality in the context of other social and political inequalities, acknowledging that confronting "gender issues" head-on was difficult because "in India we're very proud of our heritage. To touch that is very sensitive [because] chauvinism is there everywhere. [It is] especially difficult with regard to gender. Therefore, I did not frontally tackle gender."

Choudhry thus expressed a dilemma confronting other activists and feminists attempting to work with Doordarshan.[33] On the one hand, working with television was critical to their political project because it gave them access to a huge, captive audience. On the other hand, engaging with mass media compelled them to craft a message that would appeal to a cross section of viewers. Often, making their programs accessible and acceptable to an audience consisting of a broad spectrum of viewers meant having to "blunt" the critical edge of their work. Clearly, there were advantages as well as disadvantages to working with such a medium. What made Choudhry's task still more delicate was the fact that the discourses of gender that she wanted to "tackle" were, as she suggested, deeply embedded in notions of Indian culture. Hence, Choudhry felt that she had to be cautious: critiquing gender relations, especially within the context of family, was a "very sensitive" matter because it was perceived as an attack on "our heritage."

Yet, she aimed to focus explicitly on the role of the family in the normalization of gender inequalities at an everyday level. She was particularly concerned with the "upbringing" of "the girl child" and the ways that women were raised to assume certain roles in the family. In comparing the socialization of girls with that of boys, her objective was "to show that the discrimination is there everywhere." She wanted viewers to "feel" the discrimination girls faced "through the narration" of her story: instead of engaging in overt feminist polemic, she aimed to make the discrimination against girls so "transparent" that viewers would "feel that rather than hear" her critique. She pointed out that when Kalyani's father resolves to educate her, her grandfather responds that it is not her fate to receive an education because she is a girl (*sab kismat ki baat hai*). This, according to Choudhry, was "the dialogue heard in every Indian home; putting it that way makes one see the fallacy of the sentence." Her objective was to "make the viewer feel it [gender inequality within the family] through emotion." Alluding to what she termed the "emotional reservoir" of narratives, she felt that certain emotions "could be used to communicate" one's political ideologies and, in fact, had to be constructed or evoked in order to bring about social change.

Udaan's representation of the family is complex. Kalyani's father breaks away from a "feudal" extended family to establish a nuclear family, which he tries to run according to the ostensibly "modern" principles of equality and democracy. His moral authority over his family is not only left intact, however, but, as we will see shortly, valorized. Choudhry decided to "soften" her critique of the family because: "the family being so dear to us, we see him [the father] also as a devoted son. So [we were]

Figure 3 Kalyani confers with her father; her mother is in the background

toeing the line, yet making room for progressive ideas without being too radical."

Choudhry also pointed out that Kalyani's father is committed to giving her the same educational and career opportunities available to his son. She reiterated her position on the importance of expressing one's political ideas indirectly rather than explicitly: "The viewer must see it before you put it into words." The most explicit expression of the way *Udaan* softened its feminist critique was its depiction of Kalyani's relationship with her mother. Like Kalyani's father, her mother is also a very idealistic, strong person. But while her father is presented as her inspiration and role model, her mother is represented as a supportive companion. When I asked her if she had deliberately sidelined the mother's role in Kalyani's life, Choudhry initially responded that she was "not making a statement" by showing the mother as "less passionate" than the father. Later in our conversation, however, she mentioned that she had wanted to foreground the father's role and not make *Udaan* "an out and out women's film" because she did not want to "make it too radical" (fig. 3).

At one point in the narrative, Kalyani meets the uncles who cheated her father of his rights to the family land. She is now a powerful police officer and is tempted to use her authority to take revenge on them. But she is prevented from doing so by her father, who gives her a long lecture on the evils of abusing her power. His sermon moves her to tears, and she whispers to him that his integrity and generosity to his brothers reveal that he is morally "above" her. As noted above, the narrative's hero is not Kalyani but her father.

Kalyani, the Emancipated Indian Woman

Choudhry tried to be "careful" in her portrayal of Kalyani. She claimed that part of her caution stemmed from the fact that she was working within a serial format: while film allowed one to show the transformation and development of character, the serial format imposed specific constraints. Because there was a one-week gap between telecasts, the note on which an episode ended had to leave a "lasting impression" on viewers. Therefore, it was essential that Kalyani not appear "too pompous or negative." But I was curious to know if some of Choudhry's insistence on depicting the "slow unfolding" of Kalyani's persona into a tough policewoman stemmed from her hesitation to construct an explicitly feminist message about the empowerment of women. I therefore asked about the images of ideal womanhood constructed in *Udaan.*

Interestingly, Choudhry responded by asking me whether I wanted her to speak "individually" or "in terms of *Udaan.*" Clearly, she wanted to differentiate between her position as the director of a television serial and her personal opinion as a feminist. When I replied that I wanted to know what she felt in her capacity as both a director and a feminist, she responded that on a personal level, she felt that ideal womanhood must be conceived of in terms of both "personal evolution" and activist work with a community or collectivity. She added that personal growth went hand in hand with political activism, and that the two could "go on simultaneously." But if one was "not wise or strong enough to contribute at a broader level," it was possible to "take time off" to focus on "personal evolution." At a personal level, she emphasized, she believed that true emancipation came with "an inner liberation, that is, a liberation from [emotional] attachments in a spiritual sense. But," she added, "this is not something I would present to viewers. These attachments are what give energy and are the main link with the viewer." Thus, in providing narrative energy, emotions enabled viewers to identify with characters in the serial. Interpreted in light of her earlier statement on the "emotional reservoir" of narratives and their potential to bring about political change, the deployment of emotions—the "main link" with viewers—was essential for media activists such as herself.

She added that she wanted to emphasize that individuals who wished to transform their idealism into political action needed to get involved with organized, collective struggles. This is what she wanted to stress in *Udaan*: "In the end, the moral is that it should be a collective effort. A single individual cannot clean up the system." In this sense, *Udaan* contrasted with *Rajani*, which focused on a single individual's efforts to campaign against "social ills." It also contrasted with the explicit hostility to collective political action demonstrated in *Swayamsiddha*.

Choudhry insisted that in *Udaan II*, the woman "has to become a social entity, have status," before she can do anything to fight social injustice. At first I thought she was referring to Kalyani's resolution to "get to the other side of the table," that is, to acquire a policewoman's powers. But Choudhry clarified that she meant that one had to "work *within* the system" (my emphasis) and "clean up the system." But choosing to restrict her activism to reforming "the system" limited the kind of critique she could present. *Udaan I*, which showed Kalyani's transformation as she resolved to fight injustice by joining the police, constructed its heroine as a rebel. In comparison, *Udaan II*, in which Kalyani became a police-woman and tried to fight corruption "within the system," was unable to construct an effective critique of the structural relations underlying the marginalization of women and other disempowered social subjects. Television critic Iqbal Masud noted in his weekly review column that "the earlier serial *Udaan*, showing Kalyani rising above the despair and ruin of her family, had a tang of freshness, spontaneous revolt and genuine youthfulness. Kalyani the outsider was marvelous. Kalyani the insider, the cop, simply failed to take off in *Udaan II*."

Masud pointed out that *Udaan II* was unable to focus on "the dilemma of an honest person in an immoral administrative set-up" because television's "framework of discourse simply doesn't permit such dissent."[34] Indeed, as suggested above, rather than engaging in radical social critique aimed at changing specific relations of power, *Udaan*'s social critique was contained within the reformist, liberal nationalist framework of working "within the system." Further, it is important to note that *Udaan*, in particular, was as much an attempt to put a human face on the police as it was a story about a middle-class woman's empowerment. Given the prevailing political context, with the state becoming increasingly repressive, valorizing the police, even through the character of a maverick policewoman, precluded a critique of the state.

Discourses of Sexuality

In my interview with her, Choudhry described one of the episodes of *Udaan* that dealt with violence against women. In one of the few scenes in which we see Kalyani out of uniform, a drunk businessman, unaware that she is a policewoman, tries to molest her as she walks down a street. The businessman turns out to be a friend of her colleague Harish Menon, who claims that Kalyani's treatment of his friend is "too harsh." But she is adamant about punishing the man who tried to molest her. Choudhry explained that she was determined to devote an entire episode to this event because, having grown up in north India, she could never lose sight of the vulnerability of women in public spaces: "I've lived in the North. The girl student, her whole life is structured around the fear of the dark."

She recalled that her costars, many of whom had lived in Bombay all their lives, were puzzled about her determination to structure a whole episode around this incident. But she had been resolute in making it the focus of that episode because she felt it was essential to draw attention to the sexual harassment of women. The vulnerability of young women in public spaces, she suggested, reinscribed their confinement to the home and consolidated the ability of male relatives to "protect" them and, thereby, to control their activities. She explained, "In Bombay it's very different—the unit [her co-workers on the set] didn't understand. But for most girls in the North, it has [a] very serious fall-out in terms of her relationship with her family, her father and her brothers."

Apart from this episode, however, *Udaan* did not further explore the relationship between discourses of sexuality and the marginalization of women in either the family or the so-called public sphere. As I noted earlier in this chapter, Kalyani's sexuality, both as a teenager and as an adult, was left unexplored. Even when she is attracted to Harish Menon and agonizes about how she will juggle her personal life with her commitment to her career, the arbiters of her sexual destiny are her parents:

the serial ends with the information that Harish's parents are to visit her parents to arrange their marriage. Kalyani the policewoman is subsumed by Kalyani the daughter and potential daughter-in-law.

For Choudhry, Kalyani's romance with her colleague was a means of "balancing" Kalyani's private life and public persona. The relationship between them is implicit, their attraction to each other hinted at rather than explicitly depicted. This suggests that Choudhry wished neither to deploy generic conventions of popular romance nor to delve into the sexual needs and desires of Kalyani, who lives by herself in a remote part of the country. Interestingly, some viewers criticized the portrayal of Kalyani's relationship with Harish Menon. A metropolitan newspaper reported that Kiran Bedi, a New Delhi police officer who had acquired a legendary reputation for her integrity and professionalism and who was rumored to have inspired the character of Kalyani, criticized Udaan for "including romance." Although she watched the serial avidly, she had mixed feelings about it. On the one hand, she felt the serial provided an "authentic insight" into interactions among police officers. However, "she didn't care particularly for the romantic ending." Kalyani, she felt, was not portrayed as tough as she should have been and the romantic conclusion seemed to imply that Kalyani caved in eventually to the pulls and pressures of the system.[35] Similarly, television critic Maithili Rao alleged that Kalyani's romance with Menon revealed that she had to "ultimately give in to a system in which marriage is the final destination" for all women, including those who are committed to their careers.[36]

Gender and the Politics of Liberal Nationalism

Udaan demonstrated the importance of situating gender inequality in broader sociological contexts of corruption and injustice in contemporary India. As Choudhry explained, "Udaan I saw it from one side of the table. Udaan II is about what happens when a woman gets to the other side of the table." Choudhry wanted to focus on the dilemmas and struggles of an idealistic police officer trapped within a corrupt system. Indeed, Udaan was unique among Doordarshan serials in its attention to the introspection of an individual character. Viewers often heard Kalyani ponder aloud about her work, the pressures she had to cope with, the dilemmas she confronted as a woman and a police officer. Although

Kalyani never loses her integrity or idealism, she openly enjoys her fame and celebrity status. The pleasure she derives from her newfound status makes her dilemmas all the more poignant.

Choudhry wanted viewers to identify with Kalyani's "move from being a have-not to a have" and to derive vicarious pleasure from her success. Two scenes show this transformation. Early in the serial, when she is frustrated with her vain attempts to seek justice for her father, she throws herself in front of the car of a minister in an attempt to confront him about her father's plight. When the minister's assistant tells her to plead her case in his office, she shouts back, "I plead no longer! I ask for my and my father's right." The minister is impressed with her tenacity and agrees to meet with her. Later in the serial, after she has become a police officer, she and her father meet by chance in a court building. She is there as a police officer and her father is there to plead his case. They see each other across the corridor and smile. She smartly and confidently walks toward him, acknowledging the salutes of all the policemen she passes. Her father is proud to see how much respect and authority she commands; she is pleased that he has had an opportunity to see all that she has accomplished. (When I watched this scene with Jayanthi and Uma, I could tell they were profoundly moved by it: they watched in silence; Uma's eyes misted with unshed tears.[37])

Udaan's message, Choudhry claimed, was to show a woman "overcoming [the] odds" stacked against her. Certainly, all the women I worked with were very impressed with Kalyani's physical prowess. Several women could describe in vivid detail her training in the police academy; some women derived obvious satisfaction from recounting her battles with a dangerous bandit. Without exception, all the women derived pleasure from her rise to power as a police officer.

In an interview with the Hindi newspaper *Dainik Jagaran*, Choudhry claimed that *Udaan* was the story of a middle-class woman's ability to rise above adversity by dint of her persistence and hard work. But this, she insisted, was only half of the story. The other half was about Kalyani's struggles to be a conscientious police officer despite pressures from her senior colleagues to compromise her idealism. Choudhry's ultimate objective was to show that a single idealistic individual cannot achieve much: what is required is collective struggle. She wanted to emphasize that it is the responsibility of all citizens to fight corruption.[38]

Toward the end of the serial, we see Kalyani increasingly disillusioned with the corruption in the police force, the ability of politicians and businessmen to bribe their way through the judicial system, and her own inadequacy in bringing justice to the oppressed. She is particularly despondent after she is unable to arrest the in-laws of a childhood friend who is burned to death. She feels that being a policewoman does not give her the opportunity or the political space to participate in social activism. In the last episode, we see her at a political meeting. Her appearance is particularly significant: she wears not her uniform but a salwar kameez; her hair is in two braids, and she looks very slight and girlish. We see her not as a professional but as a child-woman. At the end of the meeting, she hears a man stand up and make an impassioned speech about the responsibility of citizens to organize to fight for their rights and to prevent "injustice" from occurring. As we follow her gaze to the man standing among the crowd, we see that it is her father. Even though he is a short man, he seems to tower above the heads of those around him: he is truly "above" her and other people. Her father's speech transforms Kalyani the policewoman into Kalyani the citizen-activist. The voice-over takes up from where he finishes: citizens must collectively organize to cleanse society of corruption. It their *responsibility* to do so.

In the end we see Kalyani as a young, admiring daughter and a citizen rather than as a police officer or feminist activist. When I asked Choudhry why she chose to end on this note, she replied: "The second half is more [about] collective existence rather than ambition in an individualistic sense. After all, becoming an officer is not an end in itself but [one] has to be a good officer. In the end, the blame is on the common man [sic] for not doing anything about it or on the enlightened for not being passionate enough—a lot of it was to touch that chord." She referred to a poem by W. B. Yeats, "The Second Coming," and said that she wanted to emphasize that idealistic people should not lose the "passion" to work against social injustice (here, she was alluding to the poem's line "The best have lost all conviction"). She added that it is "not enough to just say that everyone is corrupt" but that, as citizens, it is our responsibility to actively fight corruption. Significantly, although the serial makes much of fighting corruption and thus reforming "the system," it leaves no space for discourses about the oppression of marginalized subjects (such as dalit, lower-caste, tribal, and working-class communities) or about changing existing systems of domination and exploitation.

The note on which the serial ended drew a mixed response from viewers. Some were disappointed that it did not explicitly depict the resolution of Kalyani's romance with Menon. Others praised the "social conscience" of Kalyani, who realizes that she must fulfill her duty as a citizen by taking to political activism. And a few viewers, including myself, felt that *Udaan* did not go far enough in its advocacy of feminist activism. I was struck by the fact that women's struggles for empowerment had been subsumed under a general, somewhat vague, platform of "political activism" and was disappointed that, once again, Kalyani sought the guidance of her father in order to resolve her sense of inadequacy as a police officer. Television critic Maithili Rao criticized the resolution of the narrative as a "liberal, facile answer to societal problems." When Kalyani joins a citizens' group as an activist, Rao said, "we are left with the idea that [there are] no ideological wars left; the only ideologically-valid activities left are civil liberties or women's rights or environment. We are left in an ideological vacuum. Kalyani falls into the fashionable trap: to be part of [the] police plus do voluntary work. It is a trap, rather than a compromise on the director's part" (interviewed on April 15, 1992).

My objective in interpreting the discursive terrain in which *Udaan* was conceptualized was to present an example of how the Woman Question was accommodated and subsumed in a liberal, nationalistic framework. *Udaan* was made by a reflective media activist who strategically chose to "soften" her political message in order to reach a mass audience. Because she was apprehensive about constructing an explicitly feminist serial ("an out and out women's film"), Choudhry chose to "blunt" the critical edge of her narrative. At the same time, Maithili Rao's comments bear repeating: rather than representing a "compromise" on the part of the director, the resolution of the serial's narrative demonstrates the *traps* inherent in liberal feminism and nationalism. The oppositional energies of feminism are contained within the discursive frameworks of discourses of family and nation; as a result, the narrative is ineffective in *critically* engaging dominant discourses of family and national culture.

The serial ended by reinforcing liberal notions of political activism and nationalist discourses of citizenship. The moral of *Udaan*'s narrative is that, rather than struggle to change existing relations of power, "emancipated" women must join mainstream struggles to fight for their rights. They must "work within the system," not as women or as disempowered social subjects, but as citizens of the Indian nation. According to *Udaan*'s narrative, dissent can (and should) be domesticated within discourses of citizenship that enable "emancipated" Indian women to negotiate both "the home" and "the world."

Udaan exemplified Doordarshan's discourses on the New Indian Woman. In its search for heroines, Doordarshan created new stereotypes of women who managed to rise above adversity, achieve success in fulfilling their individual goals, and channel their energies toward selfless social activism. Feminist Vibhuti Patel describes this trend as the "valorization" of the patriotic New Indian Woman; instead of depicting strategies for mobilizing women as a collectivity, such programs advocated their "upliftment" in terms of discourses of liberal-nationalist politics and citizenship.[39]

RAJANI AND THE RE-FORMING OF SELF AND NATION

The representation of the New Indian Woman as a patriotic citizen whose primary duty lay in social reform was clearly illustrated by another popular serial, *Rajani*. By all accounts, this serial had a tremendous impact on its viewers; for instance, shortly after the episode featuring her fight against cheating cabbies was aired, taxi drivers in Bombay went on strike, alleging that the serial had libeled them.

At the same time that she is a feisty social reformer, Rajani remains a dutiful (and therefore "traditional") wife, daughter-in-law, and mother (fig. 4). In fact, she draws the moral authority to engage in her reformist crusades from her fidelity to "traditional" roles. At the time the series aired, marketing sociologist Meena Kaushik claimed that "Rajani represents the new woman, the new female stereotype who combines the traditional values of the housewife with the more aggressive, championing traits of a working woman" (from Sethi 1985:34). Rajani was, above all, an icon of the New Indian Woman as citizen: she idealistically directs her energies into correcting the "social ills" around her.

Rajani inspired other middle-class women to assert themselves. At the level of everyday practice, some women viewers appropriated the constructions of women's agency portrayed in the serial to assert themselves in, what were for them, unprecedented ways. Shakuntala Sharma, who felt that she had been "suppressed" all her life, claimed that *Rajani* instilled in many women the courage to "speak out."[40] When I asked if she approved of that, she replied: "Yes, they have to. Now I myself speak out"

Figure 4 Rajani, a loving mother, with her daughter

(*ab main to khud bolti hun*). She constructed the following narrative to illustrate how she had been inspired by Rajani's fearlessness and assertiveness and had, even if only temporarily, transformed herself into a socially responsible New Indian Woman.

There was a government-run Delhi Milk Supply (DMS) depot near the Sharmas' house where Shakuntala and her neighbors went to collect milk. One day, with no prior warning, the men running the depot started to distribute milk at 7:00 P.M. instead of 5:00 P.M. This was inconvenient for all the women because they had to be home at that time to cook dinner. Shakuntala learned somehow that the delivery truck carrying the milk left for the depot around 2:00 P.M. Why, then, she asked, should it reach there so late? She spoke to the other women gathered at the depot and insisted that they refuse to buy the milk in protest. At that time, they agreed to support her. When they got together at the milk depot the next day, the women seemed to have changed their minds, but Shakuntala, inspired by Rajani's success in mobilizing harried housewives to protest against the corrupt distributors of gas cylinders, again succeeded in preventing them from buying the milk. She confronted the man in charge of the depot and said that the women would refuse to buy milk until he gave them an explanation for why he sold it so late in the day, at a time so inconvenient to them. He replied that he had no choice since this was when the milk was delivered. But Shakuntala refused to accept his excuses and, following Rajani's example, asserted herself. She responded that he was trying to mislead the women because she had learned that all the trucks left for milk depots at 2:00 P.M. She scolded him and accused him of being incompetent. Shakuntala recalled that the man was so ashamed that he promptly promised to improve the service.

"From then on," she claimed, "till this day, there has been no delay. So you can see why we need to speak up." She recounted that a couple of days after this incident, her husband overheard one of her neighbors describe her as a "sharp" (tez) woman. When he got home, he asked her if she had quarreled with someone. When she explained what had happened he kept quiet. But he approved of what she had done. On several occasions, I had observed that Shakuntala's husband exerted his authority within the family through long silences and terse reprimands. She was usually quiet in his presence and always deferred to him. In fact, whenever I asked her questions in his presence, her husband usually responded on her behalf! Indeed, she was one of the gentlest, most self-effacing women I met in the course of my fieldwork. She claimed that her husband never asserted himself outside the home ("he never likes to say anything to anyone"). Hence, she felt that, like Rajani, she would have to start asserting herself to take care of her family. She continued: "When one person is not assertive [the word she used was sust, which translates to "slow" or "lazy"], then the other person has to be assertive. Otherwise how will the household [grihasthi] run?"

Shakuntala's account of how she was inspired by Rajani's rebelliousness problematizes analyses of agency. She was able to channel her frustration at the DMS official and take the initiative to assert herself on behalf of her family and her neighbors. Normally a soft-spoken, somewhat timid woman, she was able to confront him and scold him for ignoring his responsibilities. Significantly, her attempts to assert herself were consciously aimed at the welfare of her family; by her own admission, women needed to be assertive in order to take care of their families—they had to assume the power to "speak out" in order to "run" their households. But at no point did she indicate that women should assert themselves within the family: women's assertiveness must be contained within the parameters of service to the family.[41]

Most ethnographic contexts, within which life narratives are constructed, entail the performative unfolding of dialogic selves. Shakuntala constructed a particular narrative of herself to show how she had been inspired by Rajani's fearlessness; I have interpreted her story as an allegory of her (temporary) self-transformation from a shy, self-effacing woman to a New Indian Woman.[42] It is important to note that I do not think that Shakuntala Sharma and I share the same notions of women's empowerment; nor do I intend to construct a hierarchy of notions of empowerment by contrasting her views with mine.[43] Yet, it is clear to me that even as Shakuntala's narrative illustrates that the subject position of the New Indian Woman entails a renegotiation of the self, it evades a critique of power relations within the family.

As illustrated by Rajani's self-confident persona, the New Indian Woman's energies are channeled to the service of not just the family but also the nation. The kinds of problems Rajani attempted to reform and the strategies she used to solve them were conceived in essentially middle-class, liberal terms. For instance, in an episode featuring her crusade against a corrupt and inept administrative apparatus, we see her turn her anger against officials occupying the lowest rung of the bureaucracy: her mode of protesting their harassment is to complain to senior (upper-class) bureaucrats about the corruption of their minions. Similarly, the series raised the issue of domestic violence by portraying Rajani's patronizing efforts to protect her maid from her abusive husband. This underscored the middle-class bias of Rajani's social reform efforts by constructing poor and working-class women as victims who need to be rescued.[44] In addition, by representing domestic violence as a feature of working-class, and therefore supposedly less enlightened, families, the narrative ignores its prevalence across classes.[45] By focusing on the reformist efforts of a single individual, *Rajani* failed to critique the institution of the patriarchal family or, as in the case of the corrupt officials, broader contexts of state and political economy.

What I have highlighted here are the implications of Doordarshan's representations of women's agency and empowerment in the quintessentially modernist project of self-making on the part of the New Indian Woman. At stake was the constitution of not just a modern self, but a subject formed at the intersection of discourses of gender and nation. The New Indian Woman was middle class and modern but not Western.[46] Most important, her agency was harnessed to the service of her family, to social reform, and to the nation. As in the case of anticolonial nationalism (P. Chatterjee 1993:130), issues of social responsibility acquired salience in the constitution of the New Indian Woman. *Udaan* and *Rajani* were about women who overcame obstacles to fight not for their individual rights but against "social ills" (however vaguely defined). But both narratives were also reformist in that they located political agency squarely "within the system." Their discourses of middle-class citizenship implied a collective, national "we" that evaded any discussion of the place of Others (such as poor or minority women) in the construction of the national imaginary. And when women like Shakuntala appropriated these depictions of women's agency, their efforts were channeled toward service to the family rather than toward reflecting on, or addressing, inequalities within the family.

My representations of Kavita Choudhry and Shakuntala Sharma also illustrate how a progressive media activist and a woman from an upwardly mobile lower-income family were interpellated by *discontinuous* discourses of gender, nation, and family. Kavita and Shakuntala occupied different class positions and had unequal access to cultural capital. Kavita was an activist and a media professional who had chosen to intervene politically through mass media. Shakuntala, on the other hand, was able to (perhaps temporarily) reconstitute her subjectivity as she asserted herself in unprecedented ways so as to take better care of her family. Taken together, the foregoing accounts represent how women's agency is at once enabled and domesticated by larger master narratives of nation and family: these narratives show how nationalism created the "horizon" for women as it constituted them as citizen-subjects (Tharu and Lalita 1993b:53).

THE RECONSTITUTION OF INDIAN WOMANHOOD

This portrayal must take note of women in all facets of their lives: as workers, and significant contributors to family survival and the national economy. (Government of India 1985, from Punwani 1989:231)

The foregoing excerpt from the Report of the Doordarshan Software Committee, set up in 1982 to formulate programming policies, illustrates the conceptualization of women by the nationalist elite. Significantly, the representation of women in "all facets of their lives" extends to their roles as workers and as "contributors" to the national economy and their families. This directive illustrates the manner in which ideologies of nation and family circumscribe notions of women's agency. In this section, I will argue that in the context of the ongoing battles over identity, community, and nation prevailing in India in the late 1980s and early 1990s, the construction of Indian Womanhood was itself a political intervention: discourses of the New Indian Woman left very little room for radical critiques of women's positions within the family and nation. Equally significant, these representations foreclosed any discussion of inequalities among women along axes of religious identity, caste, or class.

Recasting Women's Political Agency

Tharu and Lalita trace the persistence of nineteenth-century concerns with women's "uplift" in the policies and initiatives of the postcolonial nation-state, which have ranged from propaganda against dowry, purdah, child marriage, and sati to policies encouraging the formal education of women (1993b:84). As noted above, most of the women-oriented narratives shown on Doordarshan articulated the notion of women's emancipation in terms of the New Indian Woman whose energies were harnessed to the service to nation (as in the case of Kalyani and Rajani), or in terms of the uplift of women by the state.

Hum Log, the first teleserial about the uplift of women, is an instructive example of how women's political struggles were depicted on Doordarshan. An ambivalence toward women's *struggles* (as opposed to an endorsement of the conferment of women's *rights* by the patriarchal state) lay at the heart of Hum Log's narrative. The question of women's position in the family, cast in the liberal discourse of women's rights and the "uplift" of their status, was explicitly raised and provided most of the narrative energy of the serial. However, when the serial did present women's efforts to improve their positions within the family and community, these struggles seemed to result only in suffering and loneliness for those who participated in them. For instance, although Badhki is represented as admirable in her commitment to women's rights, the serial focuses on the suffering that results from her engagement with activist politics. She is constructed not as a role model for women in similar predicaments, but instead as a victim of an unkind fate. In its discourses of the uplift of women, Hum Log was typical of Doordarshan narratives that ostensibly aimed at propagating the emancipation of women. As observed by feminist scholar and activist Vibhuti Patel, the representation of women's issues in such serials resulted either in the marginalization or trivialization of women's struggles or, when such struggles were depicted, in their accommodation within hegemonic discourses of family, community, and nation.[47]

The case of *Swayamsiddha* (Self-sufficient) is particularly illuminating for its depiction of women's struggles to improve their conditions. *Swayamsiddha* promised to be very radical because it was about the efforts of a single woman to overcome the trauma of divorce, become self-sufficient, and live a life of dignity. However, it focused so much on her woes that it ended up constructing her as a helpless victim. As pointed out by feminist critic Jyoti Punwani, "*Swayamsiddha* conveyed only pessimism. The heroine's constant long-suffering, martyred expression, the difficulties real and imagined she encounters all the time, made many viewers wonder whether it wasn't easier to suffer in a bad marriage rather than suffer after divorce" (1989:229).

Further, the serial was notable for its hostility to women's collective struggles for social justice in that it constructed a very negative and trivializing portrayal of feminist activists, who came off as hysterical, "anti-family" harridans—so much so that women's groups in Bombay felt compelled to launch a protest.[48] As Vibhuti Patel points out, the serial's title, *Swayamsiddha,* itself illustrated a disregard for women's *collective* action because it (ostensibly) emphasized the "self-sufficiency" of individual women.

Udaan was unusual in its efforts to situate gender inequality in contexts of other social inequalities. Most other women-oriented narratives restricted themselves to depicting the efforts of individual women to "rise above adversity" (e.g., *Stri*). These portrayals of the New Indian Woman left no space for the depiction of the mobilization of women as a collectivity or the forging of alliances between different women's groups battling for radical social change. The efforts of hundreds of grassroots organizations struggling for the empowerment of women in diverse sociopolitical contexts was either ignored or, as in *Swayamsiddha,* trivialized. Further, Doordarshan's advocacy of women's rights was constituted according to the political contingencies faced by the nation-state or by the regime in power.

Tharu and Lalita point to the dismantling of the "frames of mind and structures of feeling that underwrote disobedience, resistance, and revolt" in postcolonial India; they claim that "oppositional energies were consciously diffused" as the nation-state established its hegemony (1993b:44). Doordarshan's women-oriented narratives reveal how the "oppositional energies" of feminism were attenuated by nationalist discourses on the emancipation of women. Earlier in this chapter I described how, in Gandhian nationalism, the "spiritual strength" of the nation rested on women's capacity for strength, tolerance, and nonviolence (Patel 1988:385, 386). This conception of women's agency was to have profound implications for postcolonial discourses on gender. The construction of emancipated Indian Womanhood on Doordarshan was often based on "quiet strength" rather than militancy (e.g., Lajoji of *Buniyaad*). As noted above, social change was conceptualized in terms of middle-class conceptions of reform rather than a radical restructuring or even a critique of power relations within the family, community, or nation.

The New Indian Woman: Custodian of the Nation's Integrity

I have argued that with the establishment of the nation-state, women were to be constituted as citizen-subjects who would participate in the task of nation building. In order for this to occur, they had to be unyoked from those aspects of "tradition" that potentially impeded the nation's predestined march toward modernity. However, at the same time that women were to be "uplifted" and modernized, they also represented the spiritual core, the authenticity of Indian culture. Representations of the New Indian Woman in postcolonial nationalism drew on notions of Indian Womanhood in anticolonial nationalism. Partha Chatterjee describes how Westernized women were pilloried in anticolonial nationalism as dangerous because of the threats they posed to the Indian family, and therefore to Indian culture (1993:122–123). Many Doordarshan narratives also predicated discourses of ideal Indian Womanhood on the essentialized construction of the Westernized woman as Other.

The women I worked with had clearly been interpellated by ideologies of cultural nationalism. For example, Renuka Sengupta's conception of the attributes of the ideal woman was explicitly cast in terms of *Indian* womanhood: "An ideal woman, an ideal Indian woman, will . . . generally, the way she respects the husband, the elders, the way she blends into his family [*usi mein rang jaati hai*]. . . . But in joint families, if the daughter-in-law doesn't understand her husband, if she doesn't fit into his family and upsets his parents, then the family is shattered. That's how it happens. It shouldn't be like that." According to Chatterjee, in nineteenth-century discourses on Indian Womanhood, the authenticity and cultural superiority of the New Woman lay in her difference vis-à-vis both "Westernized women" and the "common women" of the lower castes and classes (see also Bannerjee 1989). Chatterjee adds that the "attainment by her own efforts of a superior national culture was the mark of woman's newly acquired freedom. This was the central ideological strength of the nationalist resolution of the women's question" (1993:54). Renuka's views on women's education seem to illustrate a similar perspective on modernity: the New Indian Woman had to be modern but non-Western.

Essentialist discourses of national culture surfaced again when we talked about why families "broke up." I asked her why she thought women were responsible for the disintegration of families. Renuka insisted that "outside influences" were responsible for families breaking up. At first, I could not follow what she meant so I pushed her to clarify. She replied, "Foreign influence and higher education." Indeed, some of what she said resonated with what I had been hearing all my life: that Westernization (what she glossed as "foreign influence") was responsible for women "going astray" and "breaking up" families. Her representation of families was fundamentally essentialist in its opposition of "the Indian family" with "foreign" or "Western" families:

> *Renuka:* They're very advanced in foreign countries. But they don't have the unity you have in India.
>
> *PM:* You mean family unity?
>
> *Renuka:* There you have everyone doing all the work together. But the wife will leave the husband and go off with someone else. . . . Here it's still there, that culture, that unity, that respect for elders, all this is still there.
>
> *PM:* So are you saying this is special about Indian culture, that there's a lot of unity, family unity, respect for elders? What's the role of women in this culture?
>
> *Renuka:* Yes. In Indian culture the family is always united. And she is the one who unites it all [*samarth hai*]. She is the one who ties it all up in one place [*ek jagah mein baandhe rakhti hai*].

Figure 5   Lajoji, a dutiful wife, with her husband

Renuka's notion of ideal womanhood was clearly embedded in her conception of the united Indian family as a symbol of the uniqueness and
strength of "Indian culture."

Similarly, in *Buniyaad,* the nationalist Lajoji (fig. 5) contrasts with her
Westernized daughter-in-law Sulochana, who neglects her duties to her
family and is disrespectful of Indian culture. Sulochana is full of contempt for the traditional joint family; she speaks Hindi with an English
(convent school) accent; she is full of admiration for all things foreign.
Sulochana's ostensible lack of loyalty to her family is coterminous with

her lack of loyalty to "Indian culture": she is a foil to the *khadi*-clad Lajoji, whose devotion to the nation is matched only by her loyalty to her family. In addition to embodying all that was authentic and pure in Indian culture, the New Indian Woman was made actively responsible for preserving the unity of the postcolonial nation. When the unraveling of the nation seemed imminent, the New Indian Woman was entrusted with actively protecting its integrity. The representation of the New Indian Woman as custodian of the nation's integrity was effected through the metonymy of family and nation.

The Metonymy of Nation and Family

The metonymy of nation and family was particularly evident in Doordarshan's representations of anticolonial struggles and crises faced by the postcolonial nation.[49] Some of these representations of family and nation overlapped with viewers' own discourses of women's agency. For instance, in her discussion of *Amar Desh,* a Bengali serial on the independence struggle that was telecast on Doordarshan's second channel, Renuka claimed that it was "okay" for women to participate in liberation struggles. I asked her what she imagined happened to the family when women joined "revolutions."

> *PM:* About these revolutionaries. Didn't they have to leave their families? Like when they went to jail. Did that break up their families? . . . What about the revolutionaries who were married? What happened when they had to leave home?
>
> *Renuka:* It is possible that they had their in-laws' support. That is how she would go. I don't think it's happened that without any support a woman has gone forward. Or there must have been some financial help—like the father-in-law or the husband would have supported.
>
> *PM:* You mean, because of their [the family's] support [*unhi ke bal par*] they would become revolutionaries, otherwise they would not have been able to become revolutionaries.
>
> *Renuka:* I don't think so.

In Renuka's opinion, when women left their families to join liberation struggles, they did *not* subordinate their responsibilities to their families in order to serve the nation; further, they almost always had the support (if not the permission) of their families, in particular, that of their

Figure 6 Citizen-
mothers like Lajoji
strive to keep the
nation-family united

husbands and in-laws. The family circumscribed the agency of these revo-
lutionary women: indeed, they were able to "step out" as revolutionaries
only because their actions did not threaten the purported unity of their
families.

Renuka equated women's duties to the family and nation. This became
clearer when she explained why women "came forward" to participate in
the nationalist movement: "At that time, what was good for your country
was good for your family. That was okay. And the British were here so it
was okay to fight for the country. There were women who came out. . . .
Like Sarojini Naidu. Like the women who participated in revolutions."

The imminent threat of the disintegration of the nation added a new
dimension to representations of the patriotic New Indian Woman. For
example, Lajoji of *Buniyaad* symbolized the nationalist citizen-mother
who subordinated her own desires to protect the precarious unity of the
nation-family (fig. 6). In the opening episode, set in 1947, Masterji is lost
in the riots that have erupted in Lahore. Lajoji is torn between her desire
to wait for Masterji to return and her duty to accompany her children to
India: it is their last chance to escape to safety. She decides to leave with
her children because dissension has already sprung up among them and
she is worried that, left to themselves, the family will disintegrate. In the

aftermath of Partition, she constantly reprimands her sons for quarreling amongst themselves and pleads with them to "stay together" (*katthe raho*).

Lajoji's struggle to keep her family together produced most of the narrative tension in the serial: as suggested above, the trials of the displaced family became metonymic of the struggles of the post-Partition Indian nation to rebuild itself and "stay together." Teleserials such as *Buniyaad* placed the onus of keeping the nation-family together on women, the citizen-mothers.

The Reconstitution of Hindu/Indian Womanhood

Given the rise of Hindu majoritarianism after the 1980s, it was no accident that the New Indian Woman represented in Doordarshan programs was invariably Hindu. Minority women were conspicuously absent from the women-oriented narratives I described above. In part, this silence regarding the emancipation or uplift of minority women was due to reasons of realpolitik: after burning its fingers in the Shahbano case in 1985, the state had deliberately avoided constructing (purportedly) emancipatory discourses on Sikh and Muslim women.[50] Another reason for the absence of minority women from these narratives was that, as with other representations of Indian Womanhood analyzed elsewhere in this book, the New Indian Woman was constructed on the basis of the normative experiences of Hindu, middle-class, upper-caste (and, often, north Indian) women (cf. Tharu and Niranjana 1996).

The idealized New Indian Woman's commitment to national integration was never in question. This was true not only of Hindu women, whose Hindu identity represented the center of nationalist articulations of identity, but also of the Sikh and Muslim women located at its margins. Thus, although Sikh and Muslim women did not feature prominently in women-oriented narratives, they were often central to the national integration programs produced after 1985. In these narratives, minority women's loyalty to the nation overrode any claims their community or ethnicity could make on them: it was for this reason that they represented ideal Indian Womanhood rather than ideal Sikh or Muslim Womanhood. The unitary subjectivity imposed on them by nationalism left no room for any other sources of identity. Thus, the Sikh and Muslim women in two particularly masculinist national integration narratives, *Chunni* and *The Sword of Tipu Sultan*, stand out as exemplars of loyalty to the nation.

Chunni was about the relationship between two Sikh friends, Karamjeet and Hardayal, who fall out with each other. While Hardayal is anti-Hindu (and, through a crucial discursive slippage, antination), his wife is steadfast in her loyalty to the nation. Similarly, Muslim women sacrifice their lives for the nation in *Tipu Sultan*. As examples of ideal Indian Womanhood, these women were constructed as heroines for other minority women to emulate.

In a context marked by the reemergence of the politics of religion and ethnicity into the national arena, the very project of constructing discourses of *Indian* Womanhood was inherently hegemonic. Two parallel discourses may be traced in this regard. On the one hand, in (ostensibly) secular women-oriented narratives such as *Udaan* and *Rajani,* the protagonists' Hindu identity was naturalized and presented as normative: the heroines' names and, as in the case of Rajani, their *tikka* and *mangal-sutra*[51] immediately fixed their identity as middle-class Hindu women. Their Hindu and Indian identities were equated: by implication, Sikh or Muslim women were the Other. On the other hand, serials such as the *Ramayan* and *Mahabharat* represented "the Hindu past" as "the Indian past" and effected the marginalization, if not demonization, of cultural (that is, non-Hindu) Others.

In this chapter, I explored the role of Doordarshan in the construction of postcolonial Indian Womanhood by focusing on "women-oriented" narratives that aimed, ostensibly, to propagate the uplift of women. My focus was on how these narratives intersected with womens' experiences in their families and communities, and, more broadly, on how the notions of women's agency and empowerment articulated in these narratives resonate with or contradict the ideologies of modernity, nationhood, and class circulating at the time. As we have seen, the nation-state's project of reconstituting Indian Womanhood was deeply imbricated with the culture wars over national identity in post-1980s India, a period marked by the escalation of ethnic conflicts and the consolidation of Hindu nationalism. In the next two chapters, I will analyze how the *Ramayan* and *Mahabharat* may have participated in the engendering of community.

Part II *Engendering Communities*

Chapter 4 *Mediating Modernities: The* Ramayan *and the Creation of Community and Nation*

On January 25, 1987, the first episode of the *Ramayan,* a serial based on an important Hindu epic, was telecast on Doordarshan's National Programme.[1] Spanning seventy-eight weekly episodes and produced and directed by Ramanand Sager, a successful Hindi film producer and director, the *Ramayan* received unprecedented ratings.[2] The *Ramayan* was condemned by many media critics and secularists as a "communal" text that had enabled the consolidation of Hindu nationalism. Three years after the telecast, tensions between Hindu and Muslim communities, which had been exacerbated by Hindu nationalist attempts to "reclaim" the site of the Babri Mosque as Lord Rama's birthplace, exploded in a series of riots all over the nation. In December 1992, in one of the most tragic outbreaks of violence since the Partition of India, Hindu nationalists stormed the Babri Mosque.[3]

In this chapter, I situate the televisation of the *Ramayan* within a socio-historical context marked by the escalation of tensions between Hindus and Muslims and the ascendance of Hindu nationalism.[4] In this historical moment, Hindu nationalists seized on civil society as "a terrain for civil war" (Simeon 1994:232) whose ultimate aim was to redefine the Indian nation as a Hindu nation (Hindu *rashtra*). The slippage between Hindu and Indian nationalisms, while not unprecedented, acquired tremendous potency in the late 1980s and early 1990s.[5] It was in this context that two Hindu epics, the *Ramayana* and the *Mahabharata,* were serialized on state-run television. In what follows, I examine how the *Ramayan* shaped "commonsense" conceptions of Indian culture, belonging, and identity in an unfolding war of position. I do not wish to propose a simple causal connection between the televisation of the *Ramayan* and the outbreaks of communal violence that have ravaged the Indian subcontinent in the last decade; instead, I am interested in examining *how* this television serial might have participated in a reconfiguration of discourses of nation, culture, and community that overlapped with and reinforced Hindu nationalism. At the time the *Ramayan* was telecast, culture in general and national culture in particular became ideologically weighted constructs. Culture was no longer just a "site" in which ferocious, often bloody, battles over identity were waged; it had become the object of struggle itself. Belonging, citizenship, and identity were recast as the content, the very substance, of national culture was redefined.

My primary objective here is to bring feminist analysis to bear on the exclusionary discourses of tradition, community, and nation constructed by the *Ramayan*. What were the politics of telecasting a Hindu epic on state-run television at a time when religious tensions were at an all-time high? How was the *Ramayan* deployed in the construction of discourses of Self and Other, nation and community? How did the serial participate in the relationship between notions of Indian Womanhood and the construction of hegemonic discourses of community and national culture? In focusing on the narratological and symbolic techniques of the *Ramayan* as a televisual text, I argue that the gendered iconography of the serial created moments of suture for Hindu viewers when it resonated with hegemonic discourses on gender and caste, and "sacralized" existing inequalities by ascribing to them an immortal and divine status. I further suggest that we need to examine not only the repercussions of Hindu nationalism for gender and sexuality, but also the manner in which gender and sexuality were *central* to the construction of militant Hindu identities.

Like many "popular" texts, the *Ramayan*'s interpretations were circumscribed by the political context in which it was produced and received. Unlike most other televisual texts, the *Ramayan*'s narratives were received by many Hindu viewers with profound faith and reverence.[6] Some secularist cultural critics either dismissed these Hindu viewers' reverential viewing or condemned it as evidence of their interpellation by Hindu nationalism. The televisation and reception of the *Ramayan* occurred during a historical moment marked by what many observers have termed "the crisis of secularism" in postcolonial India, during which it was perceived that secularism had failed to engage the *cultural* politics of Hindu nationalist rhetoric and practices. This "crisis" was accompanied (and in some cases precipitated) by an attack on secularism as a modernist discourse par excellence by some antimodernist scholars, who turned to the "traditional community" as repositories of tolerance and as antidotes to the violence of communalism (e.g., Madan 1995, Nandy

1990). Contemporary Hindu nationalist rhetoric also recharged the binary between tradition and modernity by resurrecting "the traditional community," emblematized as Ram Rajya (the rule of the divine King Ram) depicted in hegemonic versions of the *Ramayana*.[7] Therefore, my second objective in this chapter is to clear a strategic space for feminist cultural analysts to negotiate the highly charged, politically fraught terrain of discourses of modernity and antimodernity. Attacks on secularism by antimodernist scholars and Hindu nationalists were countered by cultural critics and activists who attempted to redefine and reclaim discourses of secularism so as to engage with questions of faith and cultural politics (e.g., Agrawal 1994, Bharucha 1998). I build on these efforts and conduct a feminist analysis of the "traditional" community depicted in the *Ramayan* with the intent to interrogate both Hindu nationalism and antimodernist critiques of secularism. I demonstrate that feminist analysis of the *Ramayan's* imagined Hindu community reveals not only that it is fundamentally modern, but also that it is predicated on violence, repressions, and exclusions.

My third objective is to explore what the televisation of a Hindu epic on state-run Indian television might tell us about the relationship between mass culture (as conceptualized in the work of Horkheimer and Adorno 1969), popular culture (cf. Peter Burke 1978), and culture. Modernist discourses on culture have tended to create binaries such as high/low culture, classical/popular culture, authentic/mass culture, and tradition/modernity. Indeed, according to Andreas Huyssen, modernism is an "adversary culture" because it is predicated on an anxiety of "contamination" by mass culture (1986:vii). But when the Indian state deployed television in the quintessentially modernist project of creating a national culture in the late 1980s and early 1990s, the lines between high culture, popular culture, and mass culture were at once transgressed and re-created. More than the other serials shown on Doordarshan, the *Ramayan* confounded distinctions between popular culture, mass culture, and an organic and "authentic" culture. At the same time that it was dismissed as mass culture or kitsch by some critics, many Hindus claimed the *Ramayan* as part of their heritage and culture. And for many Hindu nationalists, the *Ramayan* represented culture at its most organic, authentic, and pure.

Finally, this chapter addresses the question of the role of methodology in feminist evaluations of "popular" mass-mediated texts that engage in the production of exclusionary narratives of identity. In addition to describing the historical and discursive contexts of the telecast of the *Ramayan,* I engage in a close examination of its narratological features and its televisual strategies of representation. I have devoted more attention to the textual analysis of the *Ramayan* than the other serials that I analyze in this book, first, in order to understand why it was able to capture the attention of so many viewers in India and, second, and more important, to investigate the representational strategies through which it may have participated in the consolidation of Hindu nationalism. My study of the televisual techniques of this serial (e.g., as the use of sound, music, the framing of mise-en-scène, the combination of computer-simulated graphics with folk performance techniques, and the iconography of calendar and poster art) reveals that the "preferred" viewing of the serial, the structure of feeling it aimed to produce, was that of devotion, or *bhakti.* Moreover, my analysis of the narratological and symbolic aspects of the serial reveals how it participated in the production of discourses of community, tradition, and nation that were predicated on the marginalization of women and lower-caste people and violence toward cultural Others.

Ethnographies of mass media sometimes tend to provide a catalogue of particularistic readings, so much so that the presentation of "multiple readings" becomes an end in itself.[8] Such studies are not just theoretically "banal" (Morris 1990), but can have politically deleterious consequences as well, as when they slide into a naive celebration of the "subversive" readings of viewers and reify and romanticize their agency. My intention here, however, is to deploy ethnography *strategically.* I use ethnographic material to demonstrate both the power of the *Ramayan*'s representational techniques in producing hegemonic readings or viewings, and the fact that these representations were not totalizing in their effects.

Further, I use ethnographic material to *tactically* intervene in larger debates within cultural studies about the politics of "the popular." While it is important to underscore that many viewers' interpretations were shaped by the representational strategies of the televisual texts and circumscribed by the specific political contexts in which they were received,[9] I problematize assumptions of "the popular" as monolithic by representing the different ways in which viewers engaged the *Ramayan.* I am concerned with why the *Ramayan* was so popular among the men and women I met during my fieldwork in New Delhi. Why did this narrative "work" as a hegemonic text, to whom did it speak, and whom did it exclude? I intend to foreground the dangers of "popular" texts like the *Ramayan* that create exclusionary discourses of identity.

In addition, my deployment of ethnography serves a third strategic function: I present some Sikh and Muslim viewers' critiques of the *Ramayan* and its implied moral framework in order to problematize the totalizing claims of Hindu nationalism. For, although I focus on how Hindu viewers responded to the *Ramayan's* construction of a homogeneous and militant Hindu national identity, I also represent and examine the interpretations of Sikh and Muslim viewers. Did they feel excluded by the *Ramayan's* mode of address, and how did they respond to these modes of exclusion?[10]

This chapter is divided into three sections. I begin by examining the extent to which the *Ramayan* may have participated in the consolidation of Hindu nationalism. Next, rather than simply dismiss it as a communal or Hindu nationalist text, I attempt to understand how and why the serial was able to construct exclusionary discourses of culture and nation. Finally, I show how feminist analyses of representations of tradition and community constructed by the *Ramayan* enable us to negotiate modernist and antimodernist discourses of identity, community, and culture.

THE RAMAYAN

The extraordinary cultural import of the *Ramayana* (as well as the *Mahabharata*) may be gleaned from the fact that millions of Hindus in the South Asian subcontinent (and in several parts of Southeast Asia) turn to it as a moral and cultural resource in their everyday practices, decisions, and relationships.[11] To use Anthony Giddens's formulation, this epic is part of the practical and the discursive consciousness of Hindu communities across the South Asian subcontinent.

The core narrative of the television *Ramayan* is as follows: King Dashrath of Ayodhya has four sons—Ram, Bharat, Lakshman, and Shatrughan—from three wives.[12] Soon after Ram attains adulthood and is married, he is exiled to the forest for fourteen years because of a vow his father had made many years earlier to his favorite wife, Kaikeyi (the mother of Bharat). Ram's wife, Sita, and younger brother Lakshman insist on accompanying him into exile. In the forest Sita is abducted by Ravan, the powerful demon-king of Lanka. Ram and Lakshman defeat

Ravan and his family in a battle and rescue Sita. Years later, after they return to Ayodhya, Ram banishes the pregnant Sita because of rumors that she was unchaste while a captive of Ravan. Sita finds shelter with a sage in the forest and gives birth to twins. When the twins become teenagers, they vindicate her honor and the family is reunited. But Sita refuses to return to Ayodhya with Ram: the earth splits and she is swallowed by it.

Stories derive meaning not only from their narrative structures and semiological practices, but also from the sociohistorical contexts in which they are enacted and narrated, and thus they must be analyzed as *social* texts. Paula Richman argues that "*Ramayana* tellings provide a set of resources on which people have drawn—in their own way and for their own purposes—in order to accuse, justify, meditate, debate and more" (1991a:12). What sorts of reflections, debates, and social commentaries did the television *Ramayan* enable among its viewers?

The Ramayan *and the "Imagined" Hindu/National Community*

> *Narratives are not for all to hear, for all to participate. It has a self in which it origi-*
> *nates, a self which tells the story. But that self obviously is not soliloquizing or telling*
> *the story to itself. It implies an audience; a large self towards which it is directed,*
> *and we can extend the idea to say that the transaction of a narrative creates a kind*
> *of contractual space, a sort of narrative contract. For just anybody cannot be the re-*
> *cipient of narrative bounty/grace, it is only some people who belong to categories who*
> *are in some ways privileged by the narration. (Kaviraj n.d.:80)*

Who was the larger self at whom the *Ramayan* narrative was directed, and whom does it exclude? What is the relationship between the emphases, displacements, and elisions within the text and the voices they represent, marginalize, and exclude? While the television *Ramayan* appeared to successfully invoke an "imagined" Hindu/national community that was markedly militant and exclusionary, the macropolitical consequences of this narration have proved exceedingly difficult to fathom.

Sanskritist Sheldon Pollock has pointed out the "ready availability" of the *Ramayana*'s core narrative for political struggles occurring at different moments in the history of South Asia. According to Pollock, during the eleventh and twelfth centuries, after a long period of relative hypertropy, the *Ramayana* was redeployed as a "language in which the [Hindu] political imagination expresses itself" (1993:264). During this time of (what Pollock terms) the Turkic invasions of the subcontinent, some indige-

nous ruling elites responded by employing two kinds of tactics: militariz-
ing the polity, and attempting to draw a homology between rulers and the
divine kingship of Ram. This enabled them to legitimize and strengthen
their political and moral authority in the face of military, political, and
cultural invasions. The *Ramayana* attributed to Valmiki became the hegemonic narration in the northern part of the subcontinent. The Valmiki
version offered both a vocabulary for conceptualizing a divine political
order and a framework within which a "fully demonized Other" could be
"categorized, counterposed, and condemned" (Pollock 1993:264). In this
manner, the *Ramayana* provided ruling elites with a vocabulary to consolidate their hegemony over the peoples they ruled in their encounter
with "alien" invaders. Although we can hardly conflate what happened in
the eleventh and twelfth centuries with the political developments of the
late twentieth century, the core narrative of the televised *Ramayan* also
offered a semiological framework for the construction of exclusionary
discourses of community and nation, Self and Other. Thus, examinations
of the "popularity" of the serial must begin with the following question:
What version of the *Ramayan* was telecast on a popular and authoritative
state-controlled medium, and whom did it represent?

Unlike, for instance, the compositions of Homer in the Greek tradition, the *Ramayana* has never been frozen into a single literary text (Richman 1991a). The *Ramayana* was always recast to comment on ongoing
cultural developments. Various versions, refracted by local histories and
commentaries and expressing the aspirations and struggles of the communities that articulated them, were created at different times and places
(e.g., the Bhargava narrative, the Buddhist rendering in the Jatakas, and
the Jaina narrative). In an early Tamil version by Kampan, the demon-
king Ravan is as much a tragic hero as a villain; many versions represent
Ram as an incarnation of Vishnu.[13]

Several analysts contend that the Doordarshan version "homogenized"
the *Ramayana* tradition by imposing a hegemonic north Indian, upper-
caste narrative on its captive audience.[14] They allege that it excluded regional and "folk" traditions, and critical, heterodox interpretations (for
instance, some versions adopt the perspective of Sita, who is constructed
as an emblem of the harsh treatment of women [P. Agrawal 1994]). Yet,
every episode claimed that the serial's narrative was collated from several
versions: the *Ranganath Ramayana* in Telugu, Eknath's *Bhavarth Ramayana* in Marathi, the *Kritivas Ramayana* in Bengali, and Malayalam, Urdu,

and Kannada versions.[15] And indeed, every single viewer I spoke with believed that the director, Ramanand Sagar, had made an effort to draw on all these versions. I was particularly surprised to hear Tamil viewers affirm Sagar's claims because I expected that his version of the Ram story would be different from the Kampan *Ramayana* popular in Tamil Nadu.

The televised version was in the Sanskritized Hindi associated with upper-caste north Indians and, for the most part, portrayed upper-caste, north Indian practices. For example, the wedding rituals portrayed in the Doordarshan *Ramayan* were those of contemporary middle-class and upper-caste north Indians, and the verses (*chaupai*) framing every episode were from the Tulsi *Ramcharitmanas*. The *Ramayan* was full of devotional songs sung in the north Indian traditions. The serial may hence be said to represent the dominant culture of north Indian, upper-caste Hindus who, in the postcolonial era, have "define[d] themselves as the norm-setters and value-givers, the cultural mainstream" (Oomen 1984:17, in Krishnan 1990:103).

Ramayana tellings have been a crucial site for contestations of north Indian cultural hegemony. For instance, Dravidian nationalist E. V. Ramasami's exegesis of the *Ramayana* focused on the moral failings of its brahman characters in order to emphasize the moral inferiority of north Indian, brahmanical Hinduism. It appears that for Ramasami, "northern" Hinduism (and "northern" culture generally) represented "brahmanical, caste-ridden, and Sanskritic" culture, in contrast to southern "nonbrahmanical, egalitarian, and Tamil" culture (Richman 1991b:181).[16] Indeed, Ramasami's critique of Ram stories was crucial to the development of the Self-Respect movement in Dravidian nationalism and cultural separatism in Tamil Nadu in the 1950s.[17]

How did south Indian viewers respond to the Sagar *Ramayan?* Sukumaran was a Tamil brahman: although he had lived in New Delhi all his adult life, he had grown up speaking and identifying as Tamil. Interestingly, Sukumaran found few problems with the *Ramayan:* he felt that the serial was an "accurate" rendition of the Ram story and that it depicted "Indian history" and "Indian culture." When I interviewed him, I was aware of other south Indians' responses to north Indian versions of the *Ramayana*. Members of my family who lived in southern metropolitan centers such as Madras and Bangalore had informed me of considerable local resentment against what one of them described as "compulsory viewing" of a "Hindi version" of the *Ramayan:* the Hindi version of the

Ramayana was alleged to be a manifestation of the continuing cultural hegemony of north India through Doordarshan, particularly through the National Programme.[18] I was thus surprised at Sukumaran's response and persisted in my questions. I asked if this version of the *Ramayana* resonated with Tamil tellings of the story. Sukumaran replied that there were some differences, but the "basic story" was the same. "What is the basic story?" I inquired. Sukumaran responded that the "basic story" was about a "good king and a good man trying to do his duty to his kingdom and his wife and his family." In Sukumaran's view, therefore, the story was fundamentally a story about conflicts surrounding duty, or *dharma*.

Still puzzled over Sukumaran's apparent acceptance of the television *Ramayan* as the authoritative version, I decided to speak to other viewers who identified as Tamil. I told myself that Sukumaran, after all, was brahman and was less likely to be interpellated by Dravidian, antibrahmanical readings of the story. Besides, he had lived in Delhi for almost all his adult life: it was possible that he had been less influenced by Dravidian struggles against north Indian hegemonies.

I thus turned to Selapan and Padmini, who were also from Tamil Nadu but were lower caste. To my surprise, they too seemed to have few objections to the serial. Selapan seemed to be persuaded by Sagar's claims to have drawn from regional tellings of the story, including Kampan's narrative. Further, Selapan said that he found several similarities between the Sagar *Ramayan* and Kampan's narrative. Since Padmini rarely spoke in Selapan's presence, I sought her out one afternoon when her husband was at work.[19] It was November, and we sat in the courtyard outside her flat, drinking hot, sweet tea and trying to get as much warmth as we could from the setting sun. She had just finished a load of washing and was resting; I had just finished a long and frustrating visit with one of her neighbors and was exhausted. We made small talk for a while, and then, when the sugar and the caffeine in the tea kicked in, I asked if she was familiar with the Kampan *Ramayana*. When she replied that she had grown up hearing it, I asked the same question I had put to Selapan: Do the differences between the Sagar *Ramayan* and the Kampan *Ramayana* outweigh their similarities? Padmini replied that she remembered some differences; most important, she remembered that in Kampan's version Sita had been "stronger." What did she mean by "stronger"? "Well," Padmini replied slowly, as if measuring her words, "When [in Kampan's story] Rama asks her to go through fire, she is very angry with him. She does it, but she is very angry." For this reason, Sagar's Sita seemed different from Kampan's Sita.[20] While my own feminist critique of the Sagar *Ramayan* converged with Padmini's views, it is important to note that Padmini's interpretation of Sita was not "feminist." Besides, Padmini did not seem to attribute much significance to the different portraits of Sita constructed by Sagar and Kampan: like Selapan, she insisted that "apart from this difference" there was little to distinguish the Sagar *Ramayan* from Kampan's version.[21] "The main difference," she added, "is [that] this *Ramayan* is televised."

Since I have never read Kampan, and my own understanding is based entirely on my reading of scholarly analyses of his work, I am not sure how to interpret the reactions of the south Indian viewers of the Sagar *Ramayan* who insisted that there were few differences between the two. Were they less likely to be interpellated by Dravidian critiques of north Indian versions of the *Ramayana* (and therefore more receptive to the Sagar *Ramayan*) because they had lived in north India for so long? I cannot offer a simple explanation for their views. But I find it striking that the Doordarshan *Ramayan* represented itself as an authoritative representation of not just the Ram story but also, for many Hindu viewers, of Hindu/Indian culture. The serial's claim that it drew on regional versions of the *Ramayana*, in fact, seemed to impose a master narrative of a unified Hindu community. It focused on the commonalities between the different versions of the Ram story: by narrative sleight of hand, the serial emphasized the *unity* of all these versions rather than their differences.

This attempt by Doordarshan to invoke a unified Hindu community was politically significant. Unlike religions based on a unified theological framework, and in contrast to the monolithic community constructed by contemporary revivalists, Hinduism was relatively flexible until fairly recently. According to historian Romila Thapar (1989), most of the attempts to construct a monolithic and modernist Hinduism occurred during the colonial conjuncture. Christian missionaries confronted with the "looseness" of Hinduism strove to integrate Hinduism into a single monolithic framework, and Orientalist scholarship attempted to "fit" the plethora of sects and cults into a "comprehensible whole." Further, the colonial state's attempt to codify customary law resulted in the superordination of certain texts over others. At the same time, social and religious reform movements in the eighteenth and nineteenth centuries strove to "purify" Hinduism by eliminating its heterodox practices. The colonial state's establishment of separate electoral colleges on the basis of religious affiliation further accelerated the growth of the political concepts of majority and minority communities. Finally, drawing on Orientalist discourses, early nationalist ideologues employed a monolithic definition of Hinduism in their conceptualization of a national culture. The effort to consolidate a Hindu community that paralleled Muslim and Christian communities enabled a change from earlier, segmented identities to one that subsumed differences of caste and sect, and identified itself as Hindu.

In other words, contrary to the claims of Hindu revivalists, "the Hindu community" does not have a long ancestry.[22] Hindu communities of the past that existed as a "mosaic" of diverse local sects and cults emphasizing "social observance rather than theology" (Thapar 1989:215) enabled a relatively "loose" cosmological imaginary. In contrast, modern Hinduism started to elevate ecclesiastical authority, endorse conversion, favor the notion of a single sacred text, and seek historicity for its deities: these developments allowed the modern version to claim an identity that could (theoretically) transcend caste, sect, and region, and hence include more devotees (Thapar 1989:228–229).

How might we characterize the implications of televising a conservative version of the *Ramayana* in a sociohistorical context marked by rising Hindu nationalism? As noted above, past appropriations of the *Ramayana* reveal that it has long provided a language not only to articulate political struggles but also to demonize cultural Others, as during encounters with Islamic peoples from western Asia in the eleventh and twelfth centuries. Indigenous rulers were identified with Ram, and Islamic Others with the demons (*rakshasas*). In this manner, the political world came to be "read through—identified with, cognized by—the narrative provided by the epic tale": the demonization or "rakshasizations" of the Muslim "outsiders" became an enduring feature of various versions of the text (Pollock 1993:272). For example, in the late seventeenth-century version of Ram Das, the Moghul emperor Aurangzeb is cast as the villain Ravan, and in Kavi Bhusan's version, Aurangzeb is represented as an incarnation of Ravan's brother, the demon Kumbhakarna (Pollock 1993:287).

Consistent with this tradition, the television *Ramayan* also depicted *rakshasas* as racial and cultural Others. In it, *rakshasas* are portrayed as extraordinarily strong, larger than human beings, and with big, protruding teeth and bushy eyebrows; their physical appearance is an important index of their bestiality. This is particularly striking in the case of "their" women, the *rakshasis*, who are depicted as sexually aggressive, physically strong, dark complexioned, and attired in feathers and beads. With their loose, flowing hair, the *rakshasis* look wild, masculine, and "barbaric." For instance, Taaraka, who is killed by Ram and Lakshman, is portrayed as a very large woman who has the "strength of ten elephants."[23] Her wavy, waist-length hair is matted, and she wears a garland of human skulls around her neck. Ram's success in killing her emphasizes his divinity.

But more than their physical appearance, the Otherness of the *rakshasas* is indexed by their "culture," lifestyle, and, most important, their moral inferiority. They are usually depicted as antagonistic to brahmans and as sexual predators. Their Otherness is emphasized by the contrast drawn between their "culture" and the kshatriya and brahmanic codes of conduct followed by Ram's clan and its priests. The conflict between the two kinds of "morality" is laid out in one of the opening scenes when Vishnu descends to the earth to rid it of all the *rakshasas:* his reincarnation, Ram, is the embodiment of Good, and Ravan and other demons represent unmitigated Evil. As Shakuntala Sharma, one of the Hindu viewers I interviewed, remarked: "Men have two qualities [*gunas*]: Ramji and Ravan. This is what they've showed in the *Ramayan*."

Thus, cultural difference is cast in a moral discourse of Good versus Evil, such that the Other is implicitly evil. The political significance of discourses of cultural difference is particularly evident from the ways in which Hindu nationalist organizations have reified and manipulated the notion of culture. For instance, the RSS (Rashtriya Swayamsevak Sangh), one of the most powerful "grassroots" Hindu nationalist organizations, self-consciously and deliberately presents itself as a cultural organization. But as Purushottam Agrawal argues, "culture in RSS discourse is not a vibrant reality energized by common experiences, creative interventions and the conflicts of power, but a system for the concealing of conflicts and oppressions that works by deploying a rhetoric of hatred and destruction" (1994:260). I will trace some of the implications of these constructions of cultural difference in the next section.

The Ramayan and Hindu Nationalism

Although arguments about "historical revivification" do not always include a consideration of issues of agency, intentionality, and political action (Pollock 1993:280), the *Ramayana*'s history of the demonization of Muslims is certainly suggestive of the kinds of readings it may have enabled during the culture wars in late twentieth-century India. Pollock argues that the television *Ramayan* may have provided "a language of mythopolitics—not because it was inherently such a language but because there is now a history of its doing that specific symbolic work—available for encoding the paired forces of xenophobia and theocracy" (1993:293). Put another way, it is very likely that the *Ramayan* text, because of the spaces it has historically created for discourses on Self and Other, lent itself to easy appropriation by forces of Hindu communalism and nationalism. Indeed, some Hindu nationalist activists credited the serial with contributing to their cause. Balbir Singh, one of the secretaries to the RSS, said that "Sagar's *Ramayan* created an awakening. *People who were sleeping were forced to wake up.* There is not one Hindu in this country who hasn't seen the serial. We should have more of such serials so that people can appreciate their religious heritage" (from Philipose 1990:13; emphasis added).

What are the social and cultural bases of Hindu communalism and nationalism? Communalism draws from the "belief that because a group of people follow a particular religion, they have as a result, a common social, political and economic interest" (Chandra 1984, from Chhachhi 1989:568).[24] Communalism is based on a purportedly unified religious identity and "supports a programme of political action designed to further the interests of that religious community" (Thapar 1989:210–211). The postindependence years have been marked by the growth of communalisms of different hues—Hindu, Muslim, and Sikh versions—which have been accelerated by electoral politics.

Hindu nationalism, on the other hand, is marked by attempts to redefine the identity of the Indian *nation* in terms of a monolithic Hindu culture. As Peter van der Veer points out, religious nationalism "equates the religious community with the nation and thus builds on a previously constructed religious identity" (1994:80). Like Hindu communalism, Hindu nationalism draws its potency from constructions of an antique past in which Hindus existed as a clearly defined, "unified" community; derives its legitimacy from history;[25] and is predicated on discourses of a demonized Other. Hindu nationalism is based on the belief that India's Hinduness unites its diverse cultures: "Hindu culture," or Hindutva, is thus the substratum, the essential culture underlying the "influences" of

Islam, Buddhism, or Christianity. Some discourses of Hindu nationalism claim that all Indians, regardless of their present religion, are "basically" Hindu. Further, they assert that India's unity is contingent on the strength of its Hindutva: to be a nation at all, India has to be a Hindu nation (Hindu *rashtra*). The cultural essentialism of Hindu nationalism is evident in the assertion that the nation's strength is predicated on maintaining its "inherent" cultural characteristics. The essential characteristics of Hindutva, the Hindu way of life, are based on claims to a heritage of deep spirituality (dependent, in turn, on physical discipline) and on the premise that ties between individuals must be subordinated to loyalty to the collectivity (the family, community, and nation). Hindu nationalists allege that the Hindu/Indian nation has been weakened by Islamic influences, Westernization, the policies of secularist national leaders such as Nehru, and, above all, by a failure to recognize the Hindutva "uniting" the "diversity" of Indian culture (Fox 1990:65–69).

Early Hindu nationalism, formulated largely by upper-caste ideologues, began as a form of "cultural resistance" to Westernization and British colonialism (Fox 1990:65). The perception of the Muslim as the "enemy within" grew after the 1920s with the rise of the Hindu Mahasabha and the RSS. These organizations, with their primarily urban, lower-middle-class membership, became increasingly militant immediately before independence, but temporarily lost legitimacy after the assassination of Mahatma Gandhi by a Hindu nationalist. The popular appeal of Hindu nationalism accelerated after the 1970s. In the post-1970s years, support for Hindu nationalism has come from urban, lower-middle-class Hindus. Fox attributes the socioeconomic bases of the growth of Hindu nationalism to the "intermediate regime" characterizing the Indian economy.[26] Unlike capitalist or socialist economies, Fox says, intermediate regimes have neither a "well-developed" bourgeoisie nor a "well-developed" proletariat but are instead marked by the dominance of the lower middle class. The Indian lower and upper middle classes, who acquired national prominence during the anticolonial movements, dominated the post-independence intermediate regime (Fox 1990:72). By the late 1980s, the supporters of Hindu nationalism were largely lower middle class, middle and upper caste, and were primarily north Indian.[27]

Insecure about their upward mobility, members of the lower and upper middle classes proved to be the backbone of the growth of Hindu nationalism in the 1980s and 1990s. In October 1990, three years after the telecast of the *Ramayan,* a crucial politico-religious march (the *rath yatra*) undertaken by L. K. Advani, the leader of the Hindu nationalist Bharatiya Janata Party, was phenomenally successful in mobilizing Hindus in favor of "reclaiming" the birthplace of Ram in Ayodhya at the cost of the destruction of the Babri Mosque. The BJP and its allies, the Sangh Parivar, claimed that the mosque was built after a Ram temple was razed to the ground during the reign of the sixteenth-century Moghul emperor Babar; historical and archaeological evidence, however, proves otherwise.[28] At least part of the success of the *yatra* can be attributed to its strategic timing: it was conducted in the wake of riots against the government's attempts to extend affirmative action quotas to lower castes other than "untouchables" (the Mandal Commission proposals described in chapter 1) in the teeth of widespread opposition from upper and middle castes.

The political ascendancy of Hindu militancy was also facilitated by its seizure of the public sphere. The past two decades have been marked by the organization of several mass rituals (*yajnas*), politico-religious marches (*yatras*), and mass pilgrimages to sacred Hindu sites, all of which have greatly accelerated the growth of Hindu militancy. Militant organizations such as the Bajrang Dal, with its loyal following among the lumpen proletariat, further widened the class base of right-wing organizations such as the Bharatiya Janata Party, traditionally a stronghold of the urban petite bourgeoisie. In addition, after the mid-1980s, strategic alliances were forged among Hindu nationalist organizations across the country (e.g., the Bajrang Dal, Vishwa Hindu Parishad [or World Hindu Organization, a transnational, militant Hindu nationalist organization at the forefront of the movement to "reclaim" the Ram Temple at Ayodhya], and Bharatiya Janata Party) under the banner of making India a Hindu *rashtra* (Hindu nation). The Sangh Parivar was successful in evoking images of consanguinity to suggest that all Hindus are united by "primordial" bonds. Some of these organizations developed paramilitary wings, and all espoused an ideology of Hindu expansionism; for instance, the Vishwa Hindu Parishad openly declared that "Hindus are the only people who accept India as their motherland . . . national integration is synonymous with Hindu consolidation" (Chhachhi 1989:569).

Hindu nationalism gained ascendancy in part through the struggles its supporters waged over the content of national culture and nationalism. In the early years of the formulation and consolidation of anticolonial nationalism, leaders and ideologues drew from Hindu revivalist discourses (illustrated, for instance, by a notion of Mother India based on the Hindu concept of the mother goddess).[29] Further, Indian nationalism shared with Hindu nationalism the essentialist belief in an "innate" difference between the "materialist West" and the "spiritual East": to this extent, both nationalisms drew on Orientalist scholarship on "Indian culture." The differences between Hindu nationalism and mainstream Indian nationalism were further blurred in the early 1980s when, in a major strategic shift, the Bharatiya Janata Party appropriated some elements of Gandhian nationalism and consequently acquired public symbols of great authority: this "ideological hijacking" provided Hindu nationalism with a "new legitimacy" (Fox 1990:69).[30] From being one of several contending nationalisms before the 1970s, Hindu nationalism grew into one of the dominant forms.

In his assessment of the *Ramayan,* RSS ideologue Sitaram Goel equates Hindu nationalism with Indian nationalism: "Just like Attenborough's *Gandhi* gave our middle class an idea of what Gandhi was all about, even though in a far from satisfactory way, Sagar's *Ramayan* gave our westernized urbanites an idea of who Ram was. The other point I'd like to raise in this context is the tendency of our ruling elite to dismiss nationalism, of which such serials are a part, as communalism" (Philipose 1990:13).

In a similar vein, V. H. Mathur, a Bharatiya Janata Party activist, is reported to have explained the appeal of the serial thus: "I think it roused the consciousness of Hindus to their religion and definitely led to their pondering over various aspects of their heritage" (from Philipose 1990:13). Below, I will trace how the *Ramayan* serial evoked images of a pristine Hindu culture and enabled the popular imagination of the Hindu *rashtra* through its portrayal of the utopian ideal of Ram Rajya, and of Ram and Sita as icons of ideal Hindu manhood and womanhood. The *Ramayan* conflated "national culture" with "Hindu culture" and constructed a "prehistory" of the Hindu *rashtra* sought by Hindu nationalists. How did viewers with different religious affiliations interpret the *Ramayan?*

Viewers' Discourses of Self and Other

In their responses to the television *Ramayan,* most Hindu viewers conflated their Indian identity with their Hindu identity. Renuka Sengupta was an upper-caste, Bengali Hindu woman who had grown up in New

Delhi. As noted in the previous chapter, her family's upward mobility was indexed by the fact that they lived in one of the larger flats in Division II of Vikas Nagar and by her pursuit of a master's degree. She considered herself superior to most of her neighbors, many of whom described her to me as "cold" and "snobbish." It seemed to me that, even more than her class position, she was proud of being "cultured": her speech was often peppered with references to Sanskrit texts, and it was clear that she was particularly proud of her Hindu heritage.

One conversation stands out in my memory. It was late afternoon; we were sitting in her living room talking about her favorite serial, *Yugantar.* Our conversation was frequently interrupted by a tempo (a three-wheeled automobile) that was going back and forth on the streets advertising a Vishwa Hindu Parishad meeting, scheduled for later that week, on a loudspeaker. At one point in our conversation, when we had been interrupted for the umpteenth time by bombastic exhortations to Hindus to "rise" and "claim our rights," Renuka turned to me and said that she wanted to attend the rally because she thought that the VHP was right in asking Hindus to claim their "cultural rights." She felt that "the government" was making "too many concessions" to Muslims. The government allowed them to have four wives and made the Hindus feel like "guests in their own homes." She added: "The *Ramayan* has taught us a lot about Hinduism." She claimed that, until recently, many of her friends had felt ashamed of exhibiting their Hindu identity, but of late, most of them felt it was "alright to be traditional. . . . *Ramayan* has taught us to be proud of our heritage." Her discourse equated tradition and heritage with the notions of Hindu culture constructed by the *Ramayan.*

Like many of her Hindu neighbors, Renuka felt that the *Ramayan* serial was "authentic." Moreover, she insisted that the serial was "valuable" because it taught "Indian values." I pressed her to explain how a Hindu epic could teach "Indian values." She clicked her tongue impatiently and replied: "But Indian culture is based on Hindu culture!" While attributing Renuka's Hindu nationalist leanings exclusively to the television *Ramayan* would be an oversimplification, the serial seemed to have participated in her understanding of "Hindu culture" and reinforced her tendency to conflate Hindu culture with Indian culture.

Similarly, Sukumaran claimed that the *Ramayan* represented "the best of Indian culture." When I pointed out that the *Ramayan* was, after all, a Hindu epic, he replied, "Yes, it may originally be Hindu. But it is now part of our common heritage." What about Muslims? I asked. Was it part of their "common heritage" as well? He replied that the *Ramayan* was part of their "heritage" because Indian Muslims were "basically" Hindus who had converted to Islam.

The Hindu men and women I worked with tended to have two kinds of discourses about Muslims. Some insisted that Muslims were the same as Hindus: according to this perspective, although Muslims had converted to Islam, basically they had the same culture. Others claimed that Muslims were *essentially* different and that everything about them—their family life, their habits, and their political allegiances—was alien or foreign. According to Renuka, Muslims were "alien" because they had four wives, they could "divorce easily" ("all they have to do is say *talaaq, talaaq, talaaq* [here Renuka snapped her fingers], and they can get rid of one wife and acquire another"), and they "did not bathe every day," and hence were unclean. Further, she claimed, during the cricket matches between India and Pakistan, Muslims always cheered for the Pakistani team. At this point, Renuka got very agitated. "Tell me, how can we trust them?" she exclaimed. For Renuka, the alienness of Muslims was represented in terms of discourses of sexuality, hygiene, and their alleged loyalty to the Pakistani cricket team (and therefore to Pakistan).

Both kinds of responses—that Muslims were basically the same as Hindus or that they were essentially foreign—struck me as equally disturbing.[31] The former perspective homogenized the differences between Hindus and Muslims in terms of a monolithic notion of "Indian culture." Viewers espousing the second point of view excluded Muslims from their conception of the "national community." Again, while I hesitate to attribute these conceptions of Self and Other entirely to the discourses of the television *Ramayan*, the serial's creation of a discursive slippage between Hindu culture and Indian culture overlapped with Hindu nationalist discourses of "culture," belonging, and nationhood. For example, Shakuntala Sharma said that it gave her great satisfaction to watch the serial with her children because it provided "young people of today" an opportunity to acquaint themselves with "their culture" (*sanskriti*). Sukumaran went even further by telling me that the *Ramayan* represented the "history" of the nation. The discourses of these viewers exhibited yet another instance of the conflation of the Hindu community with the nation.

Such responses were fairly standard among the lower-middle-class Hindus with whom I worked. Even those who criticized the performative styles in the serial (for example, the "stilted dialogue" of Ram and Sita) or its construction of gender discourses at some time or other mentioned that it represented "our" culture, and, occasionally, "our" history. None of the Sikh or Muslim viewers I interviewed ever mentioned the term *history* or *culture* in their discussions of the *Ramayan*. They were even less likely to claim it as *their* culture or history. But the discourses of culture, Self, and Other constructed in the *Ramayan* seemed to have enabled most of the Hindu viewers I interviewed to consolidate their Hindu identity and, further, to naturalize the slippage between Hindu culture and Indian culture.

Yet, as many observers pointed out, the serial's viewership was not confined to Hindus. For instance, soon after the telecast it was reported that "a Madras-based Muslim entrepreneur is engaged in subtitling the *Ramayan* in English describing this as a labor of love and an act of faith" (Krishnan 1990:114). I cannot generalize about all Muslims who watched the *Ramayan,* of course, but those I worked with were a lot more critical of the serial than the Hindu viewers. While they appreciated the multiple narratives of the *Mahabharat* serial, their reactions to the *Ramayan* were more mixed and revealed a greater range of positions than those of Hindu viewers.[32] For instance, although Hindu women commented on Sita's misfortune, they tended to dwell on her devotion to her husband and his lineage (that is, her *pativrata* qualities); most Muslim women, however, focused almost exclusively on Sita's sorrows and the way in which she had to "suffer all her life." Some interpreted the *Ramayan* as an interesting (if quaint) story about an ancient Hindu king and his family.[33] One woman told me that she learned things about Hinduism that she had not had the opportunity to find out about before. Most important, these viewers never described the *Ramayan* as representative of "Indian culture": most of them claimed that the *Ramayan* was simply a story.

At least two women told me that they had refused to watch the *Ramayan*. Rasoolan Bi was a forty-nine-year-old widow who lived with her son, daughter-in-law, and five-year-old granddaughter. One March afternoon, about two years after the telecast of the *Ramayan* had ended, Rasoolan Bi, her daughter-in-law, Shahida, and I were sitting on a bedsheet spread out on the floor of the room that served as the dining area at meal times, the bedroom for the young couple and their daughter at night, and the living room during the day. I had been visiting the family for about a month, and after first being received with courteous but distant curiosity,

I now felt that I was being treated with a little less formality; nonetheless, my Hindu identity frequently shattered any complacency I might have felt about my "rapport" with them. When I asked Rasoolan Bi and Shahida if they had watched the *Ramayan* serial, they replied that they had "refused" to watch it. In my notes that night I recalled that they did not say that they had not watched it, but that they had refused to do so: the term they used was *inkar* (refusal), denoting their active choice in not watching it.

When I asked why they had refused to watch it, Shahida immediately retorted, "Why should we? What does it have to do with us?" Rasoolan stared coldly at her for a moment—perhaps she felt that Shahida had spoken too quickly, too frankly—then turned to me and said in a calm and matter-of-fact tone that they had simply not been "interested" (*hamein koi dilchaspi nahin thi*). But I knew that, except during Ramadan, their television set was always turned on and they often watched programs regardless of whether they found them entertaining or not. I sensed that they had refused to watch the serial not because they found it boring, but because this was their way of claiming indifference, and perhaps resistance, to the *Ramayan* and all it represented. Shahida's outburst in particular revealed her sense of exclusion from the *Ramayan* and its narratives of culture and belonging. When I tried to push them further, they evaded my questions by saying that it was too "boring" to watch and even more "boring" to talk about. It was obvious that they did not want to openly express their hostility because I was Hindu.[34] At the same time, however, they clearly wanted to register their antagonism to the serial. Indifference seemed to be one way in which these Muslim viewers, who perhaps perceived the telecast of the *Ramayan* on state-controlled television as an invasion of their homes, could negotiate its discourses on community and nation. The responses of Rasoolan Bi and Shahida contrasted with the views of the Hindu viewers who had conceived of the *Ramayan* as the "heritage" not just of Hindus but of the entire nation.

The Ramayan *and the State*

Given the care with which all serials were screened and monitored both before and during their telecast, the airing of the Sagar *Ramayan* on Doordarshan suggests that the state was not just complicit but actively endorsed the propagation of this hegemonic narrative of the "national past."[35] Further, the serial's invocation of Ram Rajya, or the rule of King Ram, reinforced Hindu nationalist exhortations to recuperate a Ram Rajya through the construction of a "pure" Hindu national culture: the recovery of the Ram Temple in Ayodhya was to serve as a first step and an emotive symbol of Hindu nationalist plans to reclaim the "glorious Hindu past."

The meanings of Ram Rajya have shifted according to the sociohistorical contexts in which the concept has been employed and received. Ram Rajya has been appropriated by varying political movements ranging from a peasant uprising in Avadh in the 1920s (Pandey 1990) and the Indian National Congress during its anticolonial struggles, to Hindu revivalist organizations like the Sanatan Dharma in the nineteenth century, communal organizations like the Jana Sangh founded in 1951, and Hindu nationalist coalitions like the Sangh Parivar in the late 1980s. In his anticolonial discourse, Gandhi invoked the concept of Ram Rajya as a utopian ideal to denote the rule of the people. In most interpretations, Ram Rajya represents a "harmonious but hierarchical order, in which the privileged confidently enjoy their status and the dispossessed know their limits, or conversely as a kingdom of universal righteousness, in which the possibilities of freedom are accessible to all" (Lutgendorf 1991:374). In the contemporary context of rising Hindu nationalism, however, Ram Rajya denotes a nation united by devotion to Ram, or *Ram bhakti*. Ram Rajya symbolizes a recuperation of all that was pristine and glorious about Hinduism before the onslaught of cultural Others, exemplified first by the Turkic and Moghul "invaders," and later by British colonialism.[36] The *Ramayan*'s Ram Rajya symbolized the ideal Hindu state.

Although issues pertaining to the legitimacy of the state and the ruler are central to the core narratives of both the *Mahabharat* and the *Ramayan*, they were depicted very differently in the two serials. The *Mahabharat*'s first few episodes contained a long discussion of the transfer of power in terms of the qualifications of an able ruler rather than his or her genealogy. Since this episode was telecast at a time when Prime Minister Rajiv Gandhi, who had succeeded his mother, was being criticized for his incompetence and corruption, viewers were able to recognize its relevance to contemporary politics. Similarly, the *Mahabharat* contained several discussions on the complicity of the ruler and the state in the spread of corruption: once again, viewers were quick to discern a subtext of political commentary on prevailing scandals involving Prime

Minister Rajiv Gandhi's alleged acceptance of kickbacks from a Swedish arms manufacturer. In comparison with the *Mahabharat,* the *Ramayan's* discourses about the state were extremely conservative. While other versions of the *Ramayana* express some ambivalence toward the authority of ruling elites and the state, the Doordarshan version validated an authoritarian political ethos. Unlike the *Mahabharat,* it offered no Draupadi-like figure to question the competence (indeed, the complicity) of a state that passively allows violence against women; similarly, there was no Eklavya to defy and implicitly critique the oppressive power of brahman teachers.[37] And while there was no idealized figure in the *Mahabharata* (even Yudhishtra, called Dharmaraja because of his integrity, is so addicted to gambling that he will stake his kingdom, his brothers, and his wife in a game of dice), the *Ramayan* presented Ram as an ideal (a loyal son and a noble king) and the paragon of *dharma* (appropriate conduct).[38]

The hegemonic version of the Ram story was conservative at several discursive levels. In the name of Ram Rajya, the television *Ramayan* validated a hierarchical polity by extolling the benevolent authority of rulers over the ruled, husbands over wives, fathers over their families, upper castes over lower castes, and teachers over pupils. In fact, it excluded the possibility of any critique of hierarchies within Ram Rajya (Thapar 1990:441). Viewers of the *Ramayan* often appropriated the representation of Ram Rajya in the serial to critique the current political regime. For instance, praising Ram's ability to relinquish his claim to the throne, Jayanthi Chandran said: "That was the way things were in that era [*zamana*]. These days everyone clings to their chair. Those days things were different." By its idealization of Ram Rajya, the *Ramayan* evoked a strong nostalgia for a "glorious Hindu past" in which the state was benevolent and its rulers just and honest.

The Ram Rajya depicted in the serial validated the existence of a pristine, antique Hindu community. By portraying Hindu culture as national culture and Ram Rajya as the Hindu *rashtra,* or Hindu nation, the serial's narrative converged with the attempts of the historical bloc represented by middle-class (and predominantly upper-caste) Hindus to construct a hegemonic national culture.

THE POPULAR AND THE SECULAR

As I noted above, the televisation of the *Ramayan* generated a great deal of controversy among Indian media critics, feminists, secularist activists, and intellectuals, who condemned the use of state-controlled television to show a Hindu religious epic at a time when Hindu-Muslim relations were so volatile. They feared, quite rightly as it turned out, that the televisation of the Hindu epic would encourage a religious revivalism among the increasingly aggressive majority community, which in turn would exacerbate tensions between Hindus and minority communities, particularly Muslims.

Although these critics were astute in alleging that the *Ramayan* prepared the ground for a resurgence of Hindu nationalism, their analyses were sometimes inadequate and reductionist. In part, these critiques were shaped by a modernist contempt for mass culture: for example, in an interview with the video magazine *Newstrack*, leftist activist Suhasini Ali condemned the serial as kitsch. Many critiques of the *Ramayan* were predicated on conceptualizations of viewers as homogeneous and passive consumers, and of "mass culture" as monolithic and essentially manipulative, in implicit contrast to a notion of culture that was conceived as organic and authentic. Such critiques made little attempt to comprehend why so many men and women of different classes, castes, ethnicities, and generations had become such avid viewers of the *Ramayan*. Thus, while I agree with critics who allege that the television *Ramayan* may have participated in the creation of a militant Hindu identity, I believe that a more effective intervention against Hindu nationalism can be forged not by dismissing serials such as the *Ramayan* as kitsch or "inauthentic" mass culture, but by attempting to understand why this particular narrative became popular and how it participated in battles over national culture and, indeed, culture.

It is not my intention to construct a binary between viewers and critics or to valorize the opinions of the viewers of the *Ramayan;* instead, I want to interrogate the disjuncture that existed between these different perspectives. My position as a cultural critic is complicated by my own location as a middle-class Hindu woman; my horror at the violence that haunts the landscapes of my childhood compels me to be vigilant of my own interpellation by Hindu nationalism. It is tempting to ally myself with the critics of the television *Ramayan*—especially since I, too, have

concluded that the serial participated in the resurgence of Hindu revival-ism. But while I am cognizant of the dangers of valorizing the responses of the *Ramayan*'s viewers or of taking their interpretations at face value (Brunsdon 1990, Gray 1987, Morris 1990, Williamson 1986), I have also learned the value of paying careful attention to the interpretations of the men and women I met during my fieldwork.[39]

The Construction of the Popular

The *Ramayan* achieved unprecedented ratings. Several people informed me that shops in New Delhi pulled down their shutters during the serial, and a stillness fell over streets and markets that usually bustled with ac-tivity. Stories abounded of important meetings being postponed in order to accommodate the schedule of the telecast on Sunday mornings. Several years later, observers are still unable to explain the serial's phenomenal success in drawing viewers to television sets week after week. For many viewers, the fascination of the *Ramayan* appears to have resided not so much in its plot—that is, in "what happened"—as in how the story was told. In some instances, viewers' familiarity with the epic created mo-ments of suture that interpellated subjects and rearticulated the "existing symbolic order in ideologically orthodox ways" (Krishnan 1990:105).

Figure 7 Representation of Ram in a north Indian religious poster
Figure 8 Representation of Ram and Sita's wedding in a north Indian religious poster
Figure 9 Representation of Ram, Sita, and Lakshman in a north Indian religious poster

The men and women I worked with were drawn to the *Ramayan* for a multitude of reasons. The serial's popularity rested at least in part on its combination of narrative strategies, including the cinematic techniques of popular Hindi film (Krishnan 1990), the performative traditions and choreography of folk performances (in particular, *ramlila* and *katha* conventions), and popular religious iconography (such as poster and calendar art; see figs. 7, 8, and 9).[40] The serial's televisual techniques ranged from the use of background music and songs to invoke specific moods and emotions to the use of special effects to depict the divinity of gods. The power of these televisual techniques stemmed from the fact that the semiotic skills of many of the *Ramayan*'s viewers had been honed by an enduring engagement with popular film.

Music played a very important role in the *Ramayan*'s ability to create specific structures of feeling and modes of viewing. Many episodes had prologues consisting of a *bhajan,* or devotional hymn, whose purpose was to produce a devotional *bhaav,* or structure of feeling, in viewers. In addition, as in some folk plays and Hindi films, background music was deployed to induce a particular mood or to emphasize a character's emotional state (for instance, Dashrath's grief at Ram's exile, Sita's fear when she is abducted by Ravan, or Ravan's rage when he hears of Shurpanakha's mutilation by Lakshman). The very first episode used a combination of

imagery and music to establish the purportedly pan-Indian character of
the *Ramayana*. Early in its prologue, we see saints and poets from all over
India writing and singing passages from regional "tellings" of the *Ramayana*. In all instances, images of the poets and saints are superimposed
on still photographs of temples. In the first frame, we see Tulsidas sitting
on the banks of the Ganges, writing the *Ramacharitmanas*. His image is
accompanied by a voice-over singing passages from that work: the song
aims both to establish the serial's authenticity and to invoke the religiosity of viewers. A couple of frames later, we see an image of Valmiki
while a passage from the Valmiki *Ramayana* is sung in the background.
The next few frames aim to establish the pan-Indian character of the epic.
First, we see a poet singing in Telugu (the implication is that this is the
poet Ranganath, who wrote the Ranganath *Ramayan*). The camera zooms
in on his hands as he writes, then pans back to show him against the
backdrop of a south Indian temple. The next few frames depict Krutivas,
Kamban, and Eknath, who wrote in Bengali, Tamil, and Marathi, respectively, and use identical techniques of image and song. In this manner,
the combination of audio and visual techniques (the songs, the camera movements, the temple in the background) posit the authenticity of
Sagar's claims that the television *Ramayan* drew on regional tellings and
tradition.

Computer-simulated graphics were used to establish Ram's divinity.
For instance, during Ram's battle with Taaraka, we learn of Taaraka's
supernatural powers from the manner in which she is depicted. She occu-
pies the entire screen; Ram and Vishwamitra look like ants in comparison. She first exhales smoke that completely envelops them. Next, we are
given a close-up of Ram's face: his expression is calm and self-confident.[41]
Then we get a medium shot that shows him taking aim at Taaraka, who
has lifted a huge boulder to throw at him. In the following frame we see
his arrow moving through the air; it stops the boulder in its tracks and
shatters it to pieces. Next, we see Taaraka uprooting a tree and hurling
it toward Ram and Vishwamitra. Again, Ram's arrow meets the tree in
midair and destroys it. Vishwamitra then commands Ram to kill Taaraka.
This frame is followed by a medium long shot of Ram as he takes aim,
closes his eyes in prayer, and shoots an arrow toward Taaraka. This arrow
has even greater supernatural powers than the previous ones: as it pierces
Taaraka's stomach, it proliferates into several small arrows and kills her.

Camera movements in some scenes were extremely slow; other sequences resembled choreographed dance versions of *ramlila* traditions. As in plays in which actors perform against a curtain, in some scenes images were superimposed on a still background. In the scenes described above, for example, the images of saints and poets from different parts of India are superimposed against still photographs. The acting in many scenes was very stylized and resembled the performative traditions of folk plays rather than the particular brand of realism characteristic of contemporary Hindi film. Several viewers commented on the serial's unique combination of computer-simulated graphics, cinematic techniques from Hindi films, and the performative traditions of indigenous theater. For instance, Uma Chandran described the "war scenes," which combined computer-simulated graphics with *ramlila*-type depictions of battle: "Those war scenes, they were horrendous. They showed those bows and arrows going—they used to take hours to show just those three arrows crossing each other. And it went so slow." Similarly, Surjeet Kaur found the serial "artificial" because it was too "stagey." Yet, the stylized acting and tableaux-like sequences were exactly what appealed to many other viewers. The serial evoked a nostalgia in some viewers for the tales they had heard and the folk performances they had watched as children. For instance, Bhisham Sahni, a leftist writer and intellectual who otherwise disapproved of the serial, informed me that he enjoyed the "gaudy" sets and melodramatic performances in the serial because they reminded him of the village *ramlilas* he had seen as a child. The *Ramayan* was also a huge success among the children I interviewed: the adventure and "action" of the war scenes, narrated with all the special effects of Hindi films, kept them enthralled.

The television *Ramayan*, with its opulent sets, brightly colored costumes, and the facial expressions and postures of its main characters, also drew from the iconography of religious calendar and poster art. Although some upper-class viewers complained that the *Ramayan*'s sets, inspired by the tinsel and glitter of *nautanki* performances and the bright colors of calendar art,[42] were kitschy and that its colors were gaudy, many lower-middle-class viewers I worked with described the sets as "glorious" or "magnificent." This was especially true of lower-middle-class north Indian viewers. Similarly, while upwardly mobile and English-educated Uma Chandran complained that she was "bored" with the "plastic expressions" of Ram and Sita, Poonam Sharma, who was precariously middle class, said: "What was amazing about the *Ramayan* serial was that Ram

Figure 10 Evoking Ram *bhakti.*
Courtesy of Ramanand Sagar.

and Sita looked exactly like I had imagined. Sita [had a] peaceful expression. Ram also [looked] peaceful. Lakshman [looked] angry. Ravan [looked] frightening. It was just as I had always imagined. How did the actors manage it?" Her mother, Shakuntala, agreed and said that the actor playing Ram had "Ramji's form" (*Ramji ki chhavi*).

Indeed, several scenes in the serial focused on the divinity and grace of Ramji's form. For instance, the prologue to episode 4 consists of a four-minute hymn. Ram has just completed his education, and this scene introduces us to him as an adult. But he is no mere adult: he is godhead in human form, an incarnation of Vishnu, an embodiment of virtue. A frame-by-frame examination of this prologue reveals that its explicit purpose is to induce Ram *bhakti,* or devotion (fig. 10). The first frame consists of a long shot of Ram as he appears among the clouds: the camera takes in his dazzling gold crown and his bow and arrows. Next, the camera zooms in to give us a close-up: his expression, which combines serenity, self-confidence, masculinity, and dignity, typifies his divinity and grace. As the camera pans back to portray him in his entirety, it seems to take

Figure 11 Ram as a warrior-ascetic. Courtesy of Ramanand Sagar.

its cue from the hymn in the background and reverentially caresses his form, his bow and arrows, his "mighty arms," and his "bejewelled limbs, splendid in proportion." The following frame portrays Lord Brahma in the sky floating toward Ram: Brahma is accompanied by other gods, all of whom praise Ram. Cut to Lord Shiva smiling benevolently down on this scene of adulation from the skies. The camera then zooms in to give us a close-up of Ram: his expression is unwavering. For the next six frames, the camera slowly moves between showing us the adulation of the other gods, Ram's form, and the expression on his face. Then, as the hymn reaches a crescendo, the camera movements pick up speed and zoom between Ram's face and his entire form.

With his eyes half-closed, his hand raised in benediction, a faint smile playing around his lips, Ram was often shown in the peaceful form (*shaant mudra*) in which gods are portrayed in popular iconography (fig. 11). I remembered that when I first saw the *Ramayan* during a brief family visit in May 1987, I too had been struck by how "familiar" the depictions of Ram, Sita, and Lakshman had seemed. In my own case, my

Figure 12 Ram and Sita: the ideal couple. Courtesy of Ramanand Sagar.

sense of familiarity had been shaped in my childhood by my voracious consumption of *Amar Chitra Katha* comic books, whose brightly colored illustrations had brought many Hindu gods to life for me,[43] and by the icons my mother kept in her bedroom. When Poonam and Shakuntala claimed that Ram, Sita, and Lakshman looked exactly as they had imagined them, I looked around at the religious calendars and icons on the walls of their tiny flat and understood in an instant what they meant.

For some viewers, the *Ramayan*'s appeal lay in its portrayal of the relationship between Ram and his wife, Sita (fig. 12). Ram and Sita's marriage is put to the test several times. Shortly after they are wed, Ram is banished to the forest for fourteen years. Sita insists on accompanying him into exile, and she is abducted there and kept in captivity by Ravan. After she is rescued and returns to Ayodhya with her husband and brother-in-law, aspersions are cast on her chastity and she is banished from the kingdom. Years later, when Ram finds her again, she refuses to return with him. Sita's story resonated with some viewers whose life experiences drew them to the serial. Harbhajan Kaur, a young Sikh widow with whom I became particularly close, saw herself as a woman wronged. Her husband had died two years earlier and left her, a young woman of thirty-two, with two small children and a huge debt. Harbhajan worked very hard to make ends meet: she sewed clothes for women of the middle-class neighborhood adjacent to Basti and, when the opportunity arose, did assembly-line work in garment factories. She was very bitter that her husband's family, who lived across the street from her, did nothing to help her. Instead, whenever she worked outside the home, her husband's uncle would come over to reprimand her. Her husband's family seemed to keep a close watch on the comings and goings in her little sublet; they went so far as to gossip about her "lack of modesty" to me, a relative stranger. I was not at all surprised that Harbhajan chafed under their surveillance.

Harbhajan told me that she watched the *Ramayan* regularly because it depicted the trials of "a good woman who was always misunderstood by her family." She added that the *Ramayan* provided important clues for the negotiation of family conflicts. Thus, it was not faith in Lord Rama, much less a predisposition toward Hindu nationalism, that made Harbhajan such a fan of the *Ramayan*. As far as she was concerned, the serial was the story of a woman who, like her, had been betrayed by her husband and mistreated by her in-laws and her community.

Harbhajan's response to Sita contrasted with that of Shikha Vaswani, one of the few upper-class Hindu viewers I interviewed. Shikha said that the *Ramayan* was "very artificial" and "too full of sermons." I asked her what she found artificial about the serial: was it the sets, or was it the style of acting? She replied that it was the characters. She continued: "Can there ever be anyone like Sita? She was not at all lifelike."[44] In contrast to Harbhajan Kaur, Shikha's class position had provided her with life choices: she had just finished a degree in business management and was learning French while she applied for jobs—she hoped to get a position in one of the many multinational corporations that were mushrooming all over New Delhi. An only daughter, she was her parents' pride and joy. Shikha's life experiences, which had been shaped by her privileges of class, cultural capital, and family position, enabled her to interpret Sita's life story very differently from Harbhajan.

The serial may have been popular with some Hindu viewers because it provided them with an easily comprehensible version of Hinduism. For instance, Sukumaran told me that the *Ramayan* provided a philosophy of "living in the world." But in some cases, this version of Hinduism converged dangerously with the discourses of Hindu/Indian culture formulated by Hindu nationalists. Shikha's mother, Bina Vaswani, while complaining about the "loud colors" and "vulgar sets" of the serial, also praised the television *Ramayan* for making "young people aware of our culture. . . . [It] has instilled a pride in them."[45] Bina's response illustrates the discursive overlap between the *Ramayan* and Hindu nationalism, and demonstrates the growing hegemony of Hindu nationalism among Westernized, upper-class Hindus in late twentieth-century India. The collective self implicit here, the "our" she referred to, obviously consisted of people like herself, upper-caste Hindus, who represented the normative "voice" in which the narrative was performed. Further, and more significant, her words were a chilling echo of the slogan used by Hindu nationalist organizations to mobilize potential supporters: "Proclaim with pride that we are Hindu" (*Garv se kaho ham Hindu hain*).

I am particularly concerned about the positions cultural critics can create and adopt while attempting to study "popular" narratives such as the television *Ramayan:* this "popular" text in fact created exclusionary discourses of identity and belonging. Therefore, my purpose in presenting the different responses of viewers is not intended as a collation of "multiple readings"; instead, my objective is to show that "popular" narratives do *not* yield an infinite range of interpretations. At the same time, the heterogeneous responses of viewers (including those of Hindu viewers) reveal that the "popular" is not a monolithic category: viewers' modes of engagement were shaped by their life experiences, gender, and class. To complicate things further, the *Ramayan* was obviously very powerful—both in its ability to create an imagined Hindu community and in its ability to keep many (though not all) non-Hindu viewers engaged. The *Ramayan*'s participation in the creation of exclusionary discourses of national culture and belonging underscores the importance of politicizing the notion of "the popular" even as we deconstruct it.

The "Crisis" of Secularism

Many critics of the *Ramayan* dismissed the role of faith in some Hindu viewers' engagements with the serial. But before I analyze the serial's construction and evocation of Ram *bhakti*, I must situate its reception in the debates about religiosity, faith, and secularism that were going on in India during its telecast. Until the 1980s, secularism had embodied the utopian dream of peaceful coexistence between different religious communities and, more generally, the heady promise of modernity.[46] *Dharm nirpekshata*, or a separation of church and state, modeled on the experi-

ences of European nations became the model for the postcolonial polity
and a cornerstone of the modern secular nation.[47]

By the time the *Ramayan* was telecast in 1987, heated debates were
taking place about the role of religiosity in the public sphere, the relationship between the state and religion, and the relevance of secularism
to the Indian polity. Academics, activists, and "laypeople" were all concerned with the potentials and limitations of secularism as an effective
strategy against communalism. Critiques of secularism were organized
along the following lines: secularism is "unsuited to Indian conditions";
it is "deeply insensitive to religious people"; and "a secular state pretends
to be neutral but is partial either to the unbeliever or to the minority
community" (Bhargava 1994:1784). Since critiques of secularism have
emerged from sources ranging from anticommunal scholars engaging
in comprehensive evaluations of modernity to religious fundamentalists,
communalists, and Hindu nationalists, it is essential that we disentangle
these critiques on the basis of their political objectives.

Here I will focus on the critique of modernist secularism presented
by antimodernist scholars who are motivated by concerns that orthodox
secularist ideologies and practices have been an inadequate intervention against the cultural politics and violence of communalism.[48] One of
the most trenchant critiques of secularism has been provided by Ashish
Nandy, who hopes to "recover" the notion of ethnic and religious tolerance from the "hegemonic language of secularism" (1990:70).[49] His
attack is directed against state secularism, which, he alleges, excludes
religion from "public life" and relegates it to "private life."[50] He adds:
"Implicit in this ideology is the belief that managing the public realm is a
science which is essentially universal and that religion . . . is an open or
potential threat to any modern polity" (Nandy 1990:74).

Nandy's criticism of the exclusion of religion from public life and the
purportedly antagonistic relationship between governance and religion
is thought provoking.[51] His larger argument, however, is analytically and
politically problematic: he equates "nonmodern" Indians with "believers,"
and claims that Indian "believers" are provoked into communal violence
because of their "feelings of impotence, and . . . their free-floating anger
and self-hatred while facing a world which is increasingly secular and desacralized" (Nandy 1990:79). Thus, he attributes religious zealotry not
to "primitivism" or a "pathology of traditions" but to modernity (Nandy
1990:83).[52] For secularists, he claims, "religion is an ideology in oppo-

sition to the ideology of modern statecraft and, therefore, needs to be contained" (Nandy 1990:72). Nandy proposes tolerance as an alternative to secularism and posits the "traditional community" as the repository of tolerance. Given the invocation of the traditional community by Hindu nationalists, this conceptualization of the traditional community is extremely troubling (see below). Nonetheless, his critique of the refusal of orthodox secularists to engage with questions of faith deserves serious consideration.

Indeed, critics' refusal (or inability) to engage with some Hindu viewers' devotional viewing of the *Ramayan* can be explained in part by the fact that orthodox secularists persist in dismissing the power of faith and everyday religiosity. In an insightful and provocative essay, activist Purushottam Agrawal describes the overlap that existed between "left-liberal" and communal reactions to a slogan that was coined by a New Delhi–based anticommunal organization, the Sampradayikta Virodhi Andolan (SVA). In 1989, in the thick of the Hindu nationalist agitations to "reclaim" the Ram Temple, Agrawal, a member of the SVA, created a slogan that he hoped would strategically acknowledge and appeal to the everyday religiosity of Hindus and would enable them to resist Hindu nationalist rhetoric: "*Kan kan mein vyape hein Ram, mat bhadkao danga lekar unka naam*" (Ram permeates every atom of this universe, don't instigate riots in his name). Interestingly, this slogan was criticized both by Hindu communalists and by their leftist and liberal opponents. Agrawal notes that while it was clear that Hindu communalists perceived the slogan as an appropriation of their attempts to construct Ram as a symbol for their campaigns, "the hostility of the left-liberals was rooted in their facile understanding of communalism as merely the reprehensible politics of religious identity" (1994:345). He adds that the inadequacy of "left-liberal secular discourses" is most marked in their inability to understand the cultural strategies of communalists: "The fundamental assumptions of the dominant secular discourses can be summed up thus: Communalism is the false consciousness of religious community with common socio-religious interests, and is channelized through irrational religiosity into violent intolerance of other religious communities. Communal consciousness is the politically motivated distortion of the economic and political competitiveness among sections of the social elite, who try to sidetrack any progressive political agenda by inventing imaginary problems and offering imaginary solutions" (1994:247–248).

My own interpretation of the *Ramayan* is shaped by the work of the secularist scholars and activists who responded to the "crisis of secularism" in more constructive ways than the theorists and activists criticized by Agrawal. Rajeev Bhargava has made a powerful argument about "giving secularism its due" because of the urgent need to find ways in which people of different faiths can live together (1994). Bhargava argues that the coercive character of the state makes it critical that religion be separated from politics (1994:1785–1786). He distinguishes between political secularism, according to which a "more liveable polity" may be attained by the separation of religion from politics, and ethical secularism, which enables us to "live together well" by working toward the "ultimate ideals" of equality and democracy (1994:1786, 1786–1790). Cultural activist Rustom Bharucha endorses the concept of ethical secularism, which can be "enhanced by a transfusion of the principles of tolerance to be found in all religious traditions, though one cannot automatically assume a transference of values between the religious and the political domains of life without the appropriate mediations and interventions at the levels of concept and practice" (1998:3). Bharucha redefines and reclaims secularism as a "respect for differences cutting across class, caste, community, and gender, in which religion is a component in the shaping of identity but not the determining criterion" (1998:6). I base the following analysis of the *Ramayan* on these efforts to reclaim and redefine a secularism that engages questions of faith at the same time that it remains vigilant about the ways in which coercive states and hegemonic discourses of nation and culture can mobilize everyday religiosity to create exclusionary notions of identity and belonging.

The Ramayan *and Everyday Religiosity and Faith*

Bhakti, the personal relationship of surrender and absolute devotion between a devotee and the subject of her worship, seemed to be an important form of engagement for many of the *Ramayan's* Hindu viewers; the fact that their *bhakti* was electronically mediated seemed to make little difference to them. Indeed, as suggested in my earlier analysis of the audiovisual representation of Ram, the televisual medium seemed to encourage a particular form of *bhakti* through the visual process of seeing, or *darshan.*[53]

Darshan is crucial to the *bhakti* between a devotee and the guru or deity she worships. Diana Eck points out that *darshan* "refers especially to religious seeing, or the visual perception of the sacred. When Hindus go to a temple, they do not commonly say, 'I am going to worship,' but rather, 'I am going for *darsan*'" (1985:3). *Darshan* is not simply a passive act of seeing; it encompasses an interaction, a relationship, a profound engagement with the sacred. It entails both seeing and being beheld by the deity (Eck 1985:3). The viewers I worked with engaged the *Ramayan* with the same reverence they would have accorded a religious ritual: seeing Lord Rama on television became a form of *darshan* for them.[54] From what I gathered from news reports, this response was far from unusual.[55]

Academic discourses on South Asian religion have a long-standing scholarly tradition of the study of *bhakti*.[56] As noted above, however, orthodox secularist critics of the *Ramayan* were unable to engage with the concept and dismissed viewers' *bhakti* as irrational fantasy, false consciousness, or, worse, as evidence of interpellation by militant Hindu nationalism.[57] I focus on *bhakti* not as a system of signification per se, but as part of the everyday religiosity of (some) modern subjects. How was *bhakti,* as a mode of engagement and as a structure of feeling, constructed by the Sagar *Ramayan?*

As sociohistorical narratives enacting cosmological and ethical conflicts and dilemmas, epics are not just religious per se (Thapar 1990:39). In the case of the Ramayana tradition, however, Valmiki's *Ramayana* and Tulsidas's *Ramcharitmanas* are primarily religious texts. This is particularly true of the *Ramcharitmanas,* which is steeped in *bhakti* toward Ram. Ram *bhakti* is the dominant mood in Sagar's rendition, which was based largely on this version. As noted above, it was invoked at the beginning of many episodes with a devotional discourse (*pravachan*) or hymn. Further, viewers were encouraged to have *darshan* of Ram: the grace and beauty of Ram's form (his *chhavi*) were emphasized throughout the serial. Early in the serial, when Ram and Lakshman walk through the streets of Mithila, a background song describes how the people of Mithila are mesmerized by Ram's beauty and grace. A *bhajan,* or devotional hymn, at the beginning of episode 7 describes how the "form of the Lord" is the embodiment of grace. Similarly, when Ahalya, a woman who is turned to stone, is "redeemed" by Ram, she expresses her gratitude, exclaiming: "My eyes have feasted on Ram." Indeed, the serial invites all Hindu viewers to have Ram's *darshan* by "feasting" their eyes on his form.

The serial is full of examples of how *bhakti* enables devotees to attain personal salvation. For instance, in their search for Sita, Ram and Lakshman meet Shabri, an old, lower-caste devotee of Ram's who has spent her whole life worshipping him and is filled with bliss at his *darshan*. Because he is hungry she brings him berries, but only after she has tasted them to ensure that they are worthy of him. While Lakshman is reluctant to eat the half-eaten berries, Ram doesn't hesitate for an instant because he recognizes Shabri's *bhakti*. Ram comments that *bhakti* transcends all boundaries of community and caste: as complete and absolute surrender of the self, it provides all devotees with a means of attaining salvation.

The predominance of *bhakti* in the television *Ramayan* was further reinforced by its emphasis on Lord Ram's divinity and the miracles he is able to perform. The serial opened with a scene of the Hindu god Vishnu in the heavens. Blue hued and reclining on a huge serpent, he is represented through computer-simulated graphics in terms of the iconography of religious poster and calendar art. A group of gods, sages, and devotees floats through the sky to beseech him to rid the earth of the demons that have been unleashing a reign of tyranny and chaos. Through a combination of representational techniques drawn from the iconography of calendar art and Hindi film, we see Ravan striding menacingly across the earth (represented by a globe). These shots are interspersed with images of his soldiers wreaking havoc, superimposed on a larger-than-life close-up of his face as he laughs the diabolical laughter of Hindi film villains. In response to his devotees' prayers, Vishnu agrees to descend to earth in an incarnation to rescue it from demons. He is born to Dashrath, the King of Ayodhya, as Ram, his eldest son. Ram reveals his divinity several times in the serial: to list but two of his miracles, he kills demons like Taaraka whom no human was ever able to defeat, and with the touch of his foot he is able to redeem and free Ahalya.

Bhakti toward Lord Krishna was one of the multiple thematics of the narrative of the *Mahabharat:* it existed alongside philosophical discourses on the significance of human action and commentaries on family politics, the corruption of rulers, and gender inequality.[58] In contrast, the television *Ramayan* aimed at establishing a mood of *bhakti* to Lord Ram that precluded counterhegemonic interpretations or commentaries (e.g., feminist revisionist interpretations, or lower-caste critiques such as those constructed by Dalits).[59] Great emphasis was placed on absolute loyalty toward brahman sages, and kshatriya *dharma* (code of conduct) was constantly valorized as chivalrous and honorable. Unlike the *Mahabharat,* in which lower-caste characters such as Karna protest upper-caste dominance, the lower-caste characters in the *Ramayan* exhibit nothing but unwavering loyalty and devotion toward their upper-caste rulers. One scene presents Nishaad, a lower-caste chieftain who was a childhood friend of Ram's, as reluctant to eat with Ram and the brahman sage Atri until he is persuaded to do so with a patronizing lecture on the equality of all people. Clad in beads and feathers and speaking a vernacular non-Sanskritized Hindi, Nishaad is depicted as self-effacing and servile. Even as the *Ramayan* glorified Ram's love for lower-caste people like Nishaad and Shabri, lower castes and tribal members (indeed, all "non-Aryans") were depicted as primitive, in sharp contrast to the "civilized" and learned kshatriyas and brahmans. As a personal relationship between the devotee and his or her object of devotion, *bhakti* sometimes provides lower-caste devotees access to religious communion and thus circumvents the authority of priestly castes and their rituals. In the television *Ramayan,* however, *bhakti* was embedded within the larger discourses of Ram Rajya; far from being counterhegemonic it in fact reinforced the authority of the upper castes.

I found that many viewers' *bhakti* was embedded in their everyday religiosity. For instance, Sunita Chandra, a middle-class woman of twenty, told me that her mother and grandmother would bathe and purify themselves before the serial came on, and would sit in front of the television set with their heads covered and hands folded, just as they would while participating in a Hindu ritual or while getting the *darshan* of a deity. For them, there was little difference between reading the *Ramayana* and watching it on TV.

In another case, Ram *bhakti* was a remedy for a sense of disempowerment and feelings of helplessness and desperation.[60] Poonam Sharma and I were sitting in her flat in Vikas Nagar one afternoon. She had just returned from college. Usually, she would gulp down her tea and start helping her mother get the evening meal ready. That day, perhaps as a concession to my presence, she permitted herself to relax over her tea. We talked about her day, and she told me about a professor who was hostile to her. She was afraid that this professor would give her a failing grade in the upcoming exams. Poonam was acutely aware that her parents had invested their hopes and meager financial resources in their children's education: failing her exams would spell shame and disaster for the entire family. Poonam had started to study later and later into the night as the year-end exams drew closer. As time went by, she also prayed more fervently. It was in this context that Poonam brought up the television *Ramayan*. She said that the *Ramayan* had reminded her of the power of faith and that she was now a fervent devotee of Lord Ram. She sometimes dreamed of him, and in her dreams he looked just like he did in the serial.[61] She said that Lord Ram spoke to her in her dreams and reassured her that she would pass her exams. As in the case of Sunita Chandra's mother and grandmother, Poonam's *bhakti* did not automatically translate to Hindu nationalism; it was much more complex.[62] For Hindu viewers like Poonam, *bhakti* was a structure of feeling, a mode of being in the world, a cosmological location that was deeply rooted in the relationships, practices, dilemmas, and anxieties that constituted their subjectivities.

Some viewers articulated highly complex analyses of their multiple engagements with the text even as they sought *darshan* from it.[63] Aparna Dasgupta, an elderly Bengali woman I became particularly close to, told me that watching the *Ramayan* was like "getting *darshan* of God." She said that religious meanings exist in many "great books," but "you have to be able to understand them." She explained to me that although the *Mahabharat* had a lot less *bhakti*, it was important to watch both epics with certain "emotions [*bhaav*] in one's heart," in particular the emotions of *bhakti* and reverence (*shraddha*), in order to understand the philosophical and religious "meanings" (*arth*) they contained.[64] Like Sukumaran, she claimed that these "meanings" gave one guidance as to how to "live in the world."

Aparna also felt that it was important to make a distinction between the religious meanings of the *Ramayan* and the fact that it was a television serial: "It is about god—this is one thing; it is a TV story—that is another thing." Hence, while she felt that it was important to watch the *Ramayan* with "particular emotions in one's heart," she was able to distinguish between the multiple thematics of its narrative. I would suggest that it was precisely this ability to separate the various levels of the *Ramayan* that enabled viewers such as Aparna to "feel" the *bhakti* of the text: on the one hand, they were able to engage with, for instance, the way Ram pined for Sita after she was abducted by Ravan; at the same time, they could focus on the *bhakti* expressed in devotional songs and illustrated by incidents such as Ram's encounter with Shabri.

If we are to begin to understand the power of texts like the Sagar

Ramayan, we can ill afford to dismiss the *bhakti* of viewers like Poonam and Aparna as "false consciousness" or irrational fantasy. Agrawal has pointed out that the secularist dismissal of religiosity is "a logical outcome of treating communalism as a politically motivated and yet *natural* extension of religiosity" (1994:248; emphasis in original). Agrawal's critique is perhaps even more pertinent to the modernist dismissal of faith.[65] At the same time, it is important to note that faith is not impermeable to mobilization by religious nationalism.[66] Therefore, my point is not that faith is "innocent" of politics, but that we need to expand our understanding of the reception of popular texts such as the *Ramayan* by acknowledging the power of faith, as a structure of feeling, in the interpellation of viewers as subjects of mass media.

A FEMINIST ANALYSIS OF TRADITION, CULTURE, AND COMMUNITY IN THE *RAMAYAN*

Feminist historian Uma Chakravarti has pointed out that the nineteenth century was a period when a new "script for the past" was prepared. The late 1980s and early 1990s represent another such juncture in which a specific version of "the past" was constructed to create a (Hindu) national identity: as in the nineteenth century, the place of women in the community and nation became central to the way the past was reconstituted and identities constructed. How did the *Ramayan* participate in the reconfiguration of gender and nation, and how did this reconfiguration implicate the resurgence of Hindu nationalism?

Hindu nationalists assert that the Ram Rajya, predicated on the fundamental inseparability of faith, religious identity, culture, and politics, is the exemplar of the utopian "traditional community." In their discourses, the pristine Hindu community becomes coterminous with the Hindu nation, or Hindu *rashtra*. On what sorts of elisions, marginalizations, and repressions are these invocations of the traditional community constructed? In this section I will use feminist analysis to demonstrate how, in the "imagined" community invoked by the *Ramayan*, violence was exerted not just toward cultural Others, but also against women and lower castes within the (Hindu) community through the production of discourses of patrimony and primogeniture, racist and casteist accounts of an Aryan past, essentialist notions of femininity and masculinity, and the representation of racial and cultural Others as sexual predators.

Patrimony, Primogeniture, and the Patriarchal State

The essence of Ram Rajya lies in the benevolent rule of the father/king over his children/subjects. The night before his scheduled coronation, Dashrath advises Ram on the rules of ideal kingship: "He who wears a crown has to surrender himself to his subjects. A king should be like a renunciate: he has nothing of his own. Everything he owns belongs to his kingdom." Dashrath explains a king's readiness to sacrifice everything to his kingdom by comparing the kingdom to the family: "The nation is . . . [a king's] family. Like a good father, a king should be fair and gener-ous." Thus, in the *Ramayan*, kingdom and family became metonyms for each other: the essence of Ram Rajya lay in the benevolent rule of the father/king over his children/subjects, and in the obedience of the chil-dren/subjects to their father/king.

Both the *Ramayan* and the *Mahabharat* were full of examples of wise (male) elder statesmen (the court guru Vashistha in the *Ramayan* and Bheeshma and Vidura in the *Mahabharat*) who constantly valorize the patriarchal rule of the state. As pointed out by Krishnan, the serial vali-dated the rule of the state at the cost of marginalizing (sometimes deci-mating) autochthonous peoples (1990:108). Interestingly, while conflicts around patrimony and primogeniture were central to both,[67] these con-flicts were resolved differently in the two epics: the tragedy of the *Ma-habharat* lay in the fratricidal war between cousins; in the *Ramayan*, tragedy was averted because Ram persuaded his younger brother Bharat to rule as regent, thus reinforcing the rule of primogeniture. The stability of the Ram Rajya depends, in large part, on following the laws of patri-mony and primogeniture.

Racist and Casteist Accounts of an Aryan Past

The *Ramayan*'s depiction of Ram Rajya as an exemplar of a "traditional community" depends on racist and casteist accounts of the "Aryan past" and overlaps with Hindu nationalist rhetoric. Hindu nationalism has sought historicist and mythological justification from the theory of an

Aryan past according to which Hindu civilization was established by Aryans who settled in the subcontinent. The theory of the Aryan race acquired scholarly and popular currency chiefly through the efforts of German Indologist Max Muller. In the nineteenth century, when anti-colonial struggles were just beginning to be formulated in terms of a specifically nationalist imaginary, indigenous elites appropriated Muller's work on the Aryan/Hindu past with great enthusiasm. This evocation of past glory enabled indigenous elites to claim that they were of the "same stock" as their rulers and boosted their morale by providing "a sense of self-esteem, and a means by which all Indians of the upper strata could, in opposition to their colonial rulers, gain a sense of 'national' identity" (Chakravarti 1989:46).

Racist theories of the Aryan past have frequently converged with discourses of masculinity. Early nationalist thinkers associated colonial subjugation with emasculation. It thus became imperative for them to forge a new masculine identity based on the evocation of the glorious Aryan/Hindu past. In nineteenth-century cultural nationalist ideologies, the men of the Aryan/Hindu golden age were portrayed as "free, brave, vigorous, fearless, themselves civilized and civilizing others, noble, and deeply spiritual," and the women as "learned, free, and highly cultured" (Chakravarti 1989:46). Muller's representation of "Aryan" civilization as the "golden age" of Hinduism has continued to be very influential in dominant Hindu representations of the past.

How did the *Ramayan* participate in racist, casteist, and masculinist constructions of the Hindu/Indian past? The serial explicitly and repeatedly characterized Ram's clan and their "culture" and lifestyles as Aryan. As one of the pillars of Aryan/Hindu civilization, Ram is said to have laid the foundation for a superior society and polity both through his establishment of Ram Rajya and through his personal example as the embodiment of perfect manhood. The continuities between Hindu nationalist assertions of a masculine Aryan/Hindu/Indian identity and the *Ramayan*'s depictions of masculinity were most striking in the serial's portrayal of the *kshatriya dharma,* or code of conduct of the kshatriyas, the second highest caste in the *varna* scheme. The serial's depiction of the glory of pristine Hinduism drew largely on its portrayal of Ram and his clan as embodying the masculinist kshatriya (and, therefore, upper-caste) *dharma.*

Like the *Mahabharat,* the *Ramayan* extolled the virtues of kshatriya

manhood in terms of physical strength, martial prowess, and a willingness to take up arms to fight for a "just cause." The political significance
of such representations is underscored by the fact that Hindu nationalists
have invoked the so-called kshatriya tradition to counter the alleged perception of Hindus as emasculated cowards (Anderson and Damle 1987).
In addition to being exclusionary vis-à-vis "non-Aryans," the television
Ramayan's construction of ideal masculinity was also intrinsically patriarchal in that it was based on militarism and the masculinist "protection"
of women (along with brahmans, lower castes, and all other social groups
that are vulnerable and therefore depend on kshatriyas for their protection). Again, it is possible to trace the legacy of earlier cultural nationalist discourses at work here. For instance, nineteenth-century nationalist
ideologue Bankim Chandra asserted that the British were able to colonize
India because Indian men had become effeminate; his construction of
ideal masculinity combined the militancy of the kshatriya and the spirituality of the renouncer (*sannyasi*).[68] The portrayal of Ram in the Doordarshan *Ramayan* bore a striking resemblance to this image: not only was he
depicted in terms of popular iconography with a bow and arrows slung
on his shoulder, he was frequently shown meditating, praying, and leading the ascetic life of a renunciate.

Essentialist Discourses of Masculinity and Femininity

The *Ramayan*'s essentialist polarization between masculinity and femininity is illustrated in its depiction of ideal fathers and mothers. Before
their sons are born, Dashrath's eldest wife, Kaushalya, pleads for a son
because "a woman can never feel complete if there is no [boy] child to call
her mother." Later, when Dashrath decides to send his four sons away for
their education, their mothers are very upset. His favorite wife, Kaikeyi,
taunts him for attempting to prove how courageous he is by trying to control his emotions; controlling one's emotions is thus associated with masculine courage. Dashrath's reply to her further essentializes the purported
difference between the nature of mothers and fathers: "This is the very
difference between a mother and a father. A mother equates her duty with
her attachment to her child [*mamata*]. But a father? A father has to think
of the child's future . . . he will control his emotions and not reveal the
weakness of his feelings. He derives his strength from his sense of duty."
Kaikeyi responds by saying that mothers cannot understand matters of

duty; they are ruled only by their maternal attachment. In this representation, mothers are essentialized as emotional and weak beings blinded by their attachment to their children. Exceptional women, however, derive their strength and honor from their sons. When Kaushalya consoles a lonely Dashrath, he praises her for being restrained in her sorrow. "After all, you are Ram's mother," he adds by way of explanation. Sita's sons grow up to vindicate her honor. The songs they sing about her reduce the people of Ayodhya to tears of shame and guilt: only then do the people of Ayodhya realize their error in suspecting her of infidelity.

The Sagar *Ramayan* glorified the code of conduct (*dharma*) as practiced and exemplified by Ram, who was repeatedly hailed as *maryada purushottam* (roughly, "ideal man of propriety" [Lutgendorf 1991:355]), and allowed no space for the criticism of any of his actions. But while ideal masculinity was depicted in terms of militancy and physical strength, ideal femininity was predicted on the containment of women's energies.

This containment is exemplified in the *lakshman-rekha*, the boundary Lakshman draws around Sita's hut to protect her. In his pursuit of Sita, Ravan compels a sage to disguise himself as a beautiful golden fawn. When Sita sees the golden fawn, she wants it as a pet and insists that Ram bring it to her. While Ram is in the forest chasing it, Sita hears a voice pleading for help and is tricked into believing that it is the voice of Ram. When she asks Lakshman to find him, he initially refuses because Ram had left him explicit instructions to remain with Sita; but when she taunts him as a selfish coward who is afraid to go to Ram's aid, he is provoked into going. Before he leaves, he draws a line, the *lakshman-rekha*, around her cottage with his arrow. This, he claims, is the boundary that will always protect her: nobody will be able to cross it, and as long as she stays within it she will be safe. Soon after Lakshman leaves, Ravan appears disguised as a brahman sage and asks Sita for food. When he tries to follow her into her hut, he is prevented from doing so by the magic of the *lakshman-rekha*. He sits outside the line, and when Sita appears with his food, refuses to walk up to her to get it. When she expresses her reluctance to cross the *lakshman-rekha* (significantly, she describes it as the line of *maryada* [appropriate conduct] that her brother-in-law has drawn around her), he threatens to curse Ram. She is thus compelled to cross the *lakshman-rekha*. But as soon as she does so, Ravan kidnaps her, saying, "Once a woman steps outside the line of *maryada* she can never go back."

In dominant Hindu discourses on gender, the *lakshman-rekha* is a commonly used trope for the control of women's conduct (whether self-imposed or as a result of overt external constraints). I frequently heard it used while I was growing up, sometimes sardonically but often in dead earnest, to denote the code of conduct Hindu women had to subscribe to in order to protect themselves from "dishonor." The primary characteristics of this unofficial, often self-imposed *lakshman-rekha* were containment, sexual modesty, and self-control: once a woman transgresses it, it was said, it is impossible for her to redeem her honor by "stepping back" into it. The concept of the *lakshman-rekha* provides the basis for the code of conduct (*naari dharma*) prescribed for the ideal Hindu woman which, through a critical slippage, comes to represent the ideal Indian woman.

Like the *Mahabharat,* gender discourses in the *Ramayan* suggest that female sexuality has to be controlled in the interests of the patriarchal family and state.[69] The *Ramayan* made several references to the relation between female sexuality and the integrity of the family, community, and nation. The story of Shurpanakha illustrates the narrative's emphasis on the control of female sexuality.[70] Shurpanakha, the sister of the demon king Ravan, is attracted first to Ram, and, when she is unable to seduce him, then to Lakshman. When she threatens to kill Sita in jealousy, Lakshman angrily slices off her nose. He justifies his transgression of kshatriya *dharma* by claiming that it is not a sin to kill such an evil woman (*dushta naari*). Ram responds: "No one is more terrifying than a shameless woman overcome by lust. Such a woman destroys not just herself but others as well."[71]

Kaikeyi also embodies malignant female sexuality. Sagar anticipated the intertextual manner in which the serial would be interpreted in his casting of Kaikeyi: the actress he selected to portray her, Padma Khanna, had had a successful career in Hindi films portraying vamps and prostitutes. Kaikeyi's powerful sexuality is highlighted by her swaying walk, voluptuous figure, pouting lips, and seductive demeanor. Her overt sexuality is a foil to the more demure charms of her co-wives and her daughters-in-law, especially Sita. The most beautiful and youthful of Dashrath's wives, Kaikeyi is able to manipulate him into banishing Ram, his heir and eldest son by another wife, so that her own son can ascend to the throne. For this she is berated by Dashrath, Bharat, and the people of Ayodhya. Dashrath describes himself as "an old man who was blinded by the love of a woman" and condemns her as a "destroyer of the clan" (*kulna-shini*). Kaikeyi demonstrates the dangers of female sexuality, which if left unchecked can destroy not just the patriarchal family but the state itself.

Indeed, malignant sexuality and the manipulations of women are identified as "woman's character" (*triya charitra*). Kaikeyi's maid, Manthara, incites her into asking Dashrath to exile Ram by persuading her to use her "feminine wiles," her *triya charitra*. Dashrath's subjects are devastated when they hear of his decision to exile Ram, which they attribute to his blind attachment to a woman (*stri moh*) and to her *triya charitra*.

Sita as the Ideal Hindu/Indian Woman

Psychoanalyst Sudhir Kakar describes the "intimate familiarity" of Sita to Hindus thus:

> This intimate familiarity is not meant to suggest historical knowledge, but rather a sense of the mythical figure as a benevolent presence, located in the individual's highly personal and always actual space-time. From earliest childhood, a Hindu has heard Sita's legend recounted on any number of sacral and secular occasions; seen the central episodes enacted in folk plays like the Ram Lila; heard her qualities extolled in devotional songs; and absorbed the ideal feminine identity she incorporates through the many everyday metaphors and similes associated with her name. Thus, "She is as pure as Sita" denotes chastity in a woman, and "She is a second Sita," the appreciation of a woman's uncomplaining self-sacrifice. (1988:53)

While I agree with Kakar's analysis of the "intimate familiarity" associated with Sita, I found that some women contested the depiction of Sita as emblematic of "ideal womanhood."[72] Nonetheless, the power of her image may be assessed from the fact that, long after the telecast of the *Ramayan*, many Hindu men and women were still debating the extent to which the "values" associated with Sita were pertinent to their own lives.

Drawing from Valmiki's and Tulsidas's texts, the television *Ramayan* depicted Sita as the epitome of ideal Indian Womanhood by focusing on her chastity, passivity, fidelity to her husband and his clan, and, most important, her forbearance. The serial hence characterized Sita as a devoted wife (a *sati*) rather than a powerful woman (*shakti*) (Das 1981, in Krishnan 1990:104). In his portrayal of Sita, Sagar combined the cinematic tech-

Figure 13 Sita, the bashful bride. Courtesy of Ramanand Sagar.

niques of Hindi film with calendar iconography and drew on hegemonic discourses of sexuality. We are first introduced to Sita in her father's palace in Mithila with a long shot that shows her at some distance from the camera: her slight figure seems almost overwhelmed by the grandeur of her father's palace. As she walks down the hallways of the palace, the camera moves in to give us a closer look: as befits a princess, she walks with dignity, her head held high. In the next frame we get a close-up of her face: she is fair skinned, her eyes are downcast, and a shy half smile plays about her lips; her hands clasped in front of her, she holds herself with a demure grace. Her modesty is indexed by her innocent expression and downcast eyes. When she and Ram first see each other, they fall in love instantly but she does not express her feelings for him. In an editorial appearance at the end of the episode, Sagar praises both Sita and Ram for their self-restraint.

Her modesty and self-restraint are emphasized throughout the serial both aurally and visually. When she walks toward Ram during their wedding ceremony, a background song describes her modesty and innocence in detail (fig. 13). She speaks very little, and when she does, it is in a very soft, childlike voice. The only time we see her angry is when Ravan threatens her chastity. The narrative contrasts her modesty and chastity with the overt sexuality of Kaikeyi and Shurpanakha. Sagar is reported to have mentioned that although "during that period women did not cover their torsos . . . it was impossible for him to allow that on the screen since the image of Sita as a pure, chaste and ideal wife was so strong and important that showing her without a blouse would violate the moral message of the serial" (Chhachhi 1989:570).

As pointed out by Krishnan, both the *Ramayan* and the *Mahabharat* portrayed woman's honor as located exclusively in the control of her sexuality, an honor that is "fragile and easily fractured" (1990:107). Even Sita, who embodies modesty and self-restraint, is vulnerable to the evil designs of Ravan and other *rakshasas* because of her youthful sexuality. The *Ramayan*'s depiction of female sexuality seemed to have resonated with several women viewers who frequently spoke of their own vulnerability as women. When Uma Chandran asked her mother why Sita had to "face the situation she did," Jayanthi had no hesitation in explaining that Sita was vulnerable because "she was so beautiful." Uma disagreed, exclaiming, "That means our being beautiful is itself a sin!"

Jayanthi replied, "Beauty is the cause of the destruction of everything [*sarvnaash*]. Sita was such a simple lady. She wasn't glamorous like Draupadi. Even then Ravan abducted her. After all she was beautiful, and he was a demon." Obviously, Jayanthi had no doubt that Sita's beauty was the cause of all the troubles that followed; because she was beautiful, it was inevitable that demons like Ravan would be tempted by her. Thus, even though Sita was simple and chaste, her beauty tempted demons like Ravan to abduct her.

Before Sita leaves for Ram's kingdom as his bride, her mother, Sunaina, advises her. Sunaina claims that *naari dharma* will stand her in good stead because it will always guide her in her duties as a woman, which she defines exclusively in terms of her role as a loyal and loving wife: "A woman's foremost duty is toward her husband: you should always remember that for a woman, there is no god greater than her husband. A woman doesn't have to pray to any god if she fulfills her duty toward her husband. Thus, you should sacrifice all selfish desires and dedicate yourself to worshipping and pleasing your husband. Only a *pativrata*, a woman who devotes herself to her husband in thought, word, and deed, can be a true companion to her husband. A woman should also dedicate herself to her in-laws' happiness." For many viewers, Sita was the embodiment of

Figure 14 The long-suffering Sita contrasts with the willful Draupadi of the *Mahabharat*.

naari dharma, as indexed by her modest deportment and her loyalty to her husband's clan. When I asked her what she liked most about Sita, Sushmita Dasgupta, who was unmarried and in her early thirties, replied: "Her nature [*svahhav*] had humility, she spoke in a loving manner [*baton mein pyaar tha*], she respected her elders. The best thing was that she was very loyal to her husband. After all, who goes with her husband these days to roam in the forest? Only a woman like Sita could have gone [to the forest]."

Sita insists on accompanying Ram to the forest in order to fulfill her duties as a wife (her *pativrata dharma*). Sagar was so determined to emphasize Sita's *pativrata dharma* (and at the same time to absolve Ram of all blame) that, instead of having Ram banish her (as in other versions of the *Ramayana*), he portrayed Sita as insisting on going into exile. He focused on Sita's "choice" in leaving Ram: she leaves Ram in order to defer to the will of "the people" and not because Ram has banished her. The serial also portrays Sita asking for Ram's permission to leave, and hence leaves intact the control of husbands over the activities of their wives. Sita's father praises her for "choosing" to leave. He claims that she has now become the paragon of Indian Womanhood for all the ages to come (*naari dharm ka kirti-sthamb sthapit kiya*): because of Sita's "decision" to leave Ram, the forest where she lives in exile will henceforth become a pilgrimage site.

Viewers were divided on the contemporary relevance of Sita's *pati-vrata dharma*. The following discussion between Uma Chandran and her mother, Jayanthi, illustrates not just viewers' variable responses to Sita but, more important, the manner in which gendered codes of conduct were naturalized so as to seem as if they came "from within." When Jayanthi praised Sita's *pativrata dharma*, Uma responded:

> What you consider a virtue, I feel is a case of a wife simply following her husband as if she has no identity of her own.
>
> *Jayanthi:* No, there is an identity. It's inside her. If she shows it all the time, it will lessen her *pativrata dharma*, its effect. We have to give our husbands our loyalty. I am educated, I work, but there are times when I don't say what's on my mind. It's my tradition [*rivaaj*], it comes from within me. That's the atmosphere I've grown up in.
>
> *Uma:* It's become inbred. It's been drilled into us for so many years that that's what we believe.
>
> *Jayanthi:* But this is what I'll teach you. You will do the same for your husband.

Thus, while Sushmita admired Sita for her tolerance and patience, Uma was skeptical of what she called Sita's "lack of independence."

It is important to note that all the viewers who discussed Sita as a role model for women were Hindus. The Sikh women I interviewed never discussed her as a model of womanhood.[73] Most of the time, they watched the *Ramayan* because they enjoyed its story. Unlike Sukumaran, Aparna Dasgupta, or Jayanthi Chandran, they never claimed to seek "moral messages" from it. As Parmindar Kaur, a twenty-five-year-old schoolteacher who lived in Basti, said:

> We are Sikhs. We were not likely to ever read the *Ramayan*. But from watching it we learned a little about Hindus. The aunty [living] opposite is Hindu. When we were children she used to tell us stories. But we had forgotten most of them. When we saw the *Ramayan* we remembered some of them. Some new stories also we learned. . . . The troubles Lakshman and Sita had to face when they went into exile. We had never read it. We weren't ever likely to read it. So it was entertain-

ing for us. We used to enjoy watching it. But naturally we don't know how authentic it was. We liked the way they showed it.

As a child, Parmindar had heard tales from the *Ramayan* from Hindu friends and neighbors, and thus was familiar with them. She repeatedly claimed that Sikh viewers like herself had not read the epic and were not likely ever to read it because it was a Hindu text. At the same time, however, Parmindar found the *Ramayan* "entertaining." Explaining that some Hindu viewers had described Sita in terms of ideal Hindu woman-hood, I asked her what she thought of the serial's portrayal of Sita. She responded: "We felt they showed the way things were in the olden days. The makeup, the clothes were just like in the olden days." It is significant that unlike the Hindu viewers, who thought that Sita was an authentic reflection of *naari dharma*, Parmindar felt that the "authenticity" of Sita's portrayal lay in her physical appearance: her makeup and clothes seemed to be appropriate for women "in the olden days."

Although, like some other Sikh women I interviewed, Parmindar admired Sita's loyalty to her husband, she was very explicit in her view that Ram had been extremely unfair to her. Parmindar's mother, Satwant Kaur, entered the room at that point and joined our discussion. Parmindar criticized Ram for throwing Sita out after she had been so loyal to him:

Parmindar Kaur: Shouldn't he [Ram] have had a mind of his own? After all he was a grown man, a king. How did he believe the rumors? He shouldn't have banished her. . . . First he fights to rescue her, then he banishes her?! What kind of intelligence is that?!

Satwant Kaur: Those days people were not very intelligent [*pehle logan di buddhi moti hondi si*].

At this point Parmindar and Satwant burst out laughing. At first, I was uneasy—my Hindu identity had frequently been a source of tension between Satwant Kaur and me. Were they saying this just because I am Hindu? Were they being hostile to me? I wondered. Eventually, my ambivalence receded; I couldn't help but join in their infectious laughter.

Parmindar Kaur: And he was supposed to be a god!

Satwant Kaur: What sort of god? He did everything wrong [*sare kam ulte kitte*]!

Parmindar Kaur: If he was god, he should have known.

Satwant Kaur: He did everything wrong. Everything he did wrong! Everything! [Satwant waved her hands in a dismissive gesture.]

Parmindar Kaur: After what a washerman says about his own wife!

Satwant Kaur: What sort of god is that?

[By then we had all dissolved in uproarious laughter.]

Parmindar Kaur: There were many episodes during which she [here Parmindar pointed to her mother] fell asleep.

Satwant Kaur [speaking through her laughter]: I saw most of the *Mahabharat* episodes. But *Ramayan!* [more laughter all around].

In his work on the narrative construction of self, political theorist Sudipta Kaviraj claims that narratives are based on a "contract" between the teller of a story and his/her audience. Interpretive communities are created when certain listeners, rather than others, are addressed by the discourses of a narrative. Others are excluded by the "very real frontiers of indifference and contempt which . . . keep them out" (Kaviraj n.d.:80). Although the *Ramayan* powerfully created the Other through its demonization of cultural difference, its exclusionary discourses were sometimes received by marginalized Others with "indifference and contempt." Earlier, I said that some of the Muslim viewers I interviewed claimed to be indifferent to the *Ramayan* by insisting that it was too boring to watch or talk about. Although I can hardly claim that they represent all Sikh viewers who watched the serial, in their outspoken condemnation of Ram, Parmindar and Satwant contrasted sharply with those Hindu viewers who spoke of Ram as a god or as an ideal man (*maryada purushottam*) and of "the glorious Hindu past." Parmindar described Ram as a man who did not have a "mind of his own." Her mother claimed that in the "olden days" people were "not very intelligent," and described Ram as an illogical man who did "everything wrong": he first fought a war with Ravan to rescue Sita, and then he banished her from his kingdom because of a rumor about her lack of chastity. More than the content of their comments, the hilarious tone of the conversation expressed their irreverent dismissal of Ram.

Velcheru Narayana Rao has described folk songs sung by Telugu upper-caste and lower-caste Hindu women that subtly question Ram's integrity and chivalry and emphasize his ill-treatment of Sita (1991). It is significant that the Doordarshan *Ramayan* seemed to create *relatively* few spaces for Hindu viewers, men or women, to criticize Ram's treatment of

Sita. When I pushed them on his treatment of Sita, some Hindu viewers (like Sukumaran, whose response I describe above) replied that Ram was "caught" in a conflict between his duties to his kingdom and to his wife. In contrast, Parmindar and her mother spoke of Ram with skepticism and ridicule. Their laughter indicated their ability to negotiate the serial's glorification of an ostensibly Hindu *dharma* that endorsed cruelty toward a woman who had proved her loyalty to her husband and his clan.

The Other as Sexual Predator

In chapter 2 I discussed the importance of distinguishing the "tactics" of the marginalized from the "strategies" of historical blocs successful in influencing cultural struggles.[74] Thus, even as some Sikh and Muslim viewers were able to negotiate the exclusionary discourses of the *Ramayan* through their indifference or contemptuous laughter, the serial appears to have participated in the consolidation of a militant Hindu identity and in the creation of a conceptual space for a Hindu *rashtra*. The politics of gender, community, and nation converge most powerfully in the serial's construction of the Other as sexual predator, and reveal the *co-implication* of Hindu nationalism and discourses of sexuality.[75]

The episodes of the *Mahabharat* and the *Ramayan* depicting the sexual dishonor of Draupadi and Sita are particularly significant. In both serials, these provide the turning point of the narrative: wars are fought over the honor of women, which in turn is conflated with and subsumed by the honor of the patriarchal clan. The humiliation of women is avenged by men who interpret it as an assault on their masculinity. But, unlike Draupadi, who is "disrobed" by her own brother-in-law (that is, by a member of her husband's clan), Sita is abducted by Ravan, the embodiment of the demonized Other. As described above, in sharp contrast to the *Mahabharat*, the core narrative of the *Ramayana* is "profoundly and fundamentally a text of 'othering'" (Pollock 1993:282–283). This is clearest in its depiction of the way women's sexuality becomes a site for contests between Self and Other.

Ravan epitomizes the lustful Other. When he first sees Sita he can barely conceal his desire for her. The political significance of representations of demonized Others who steal or dishonor "our" women becomes clearer when we place them in the context of contemporary communal discourses on sexuality,[76] according to which women have to be protected from the Other because their sexuality is a site for contests over the honor of communities. Conversely, "true men" must protect their women and avenge any assaults on them. As Amrita Chhachhi points out, "In the communal image, a Muslim was/is a man of low morals and uncontrolled lust, who was/is ever ready to seduce, abduct, and assault Hindu women. The Hindus were seen as mild, docile and emasculated. . . . [T]he symbolism of the community gets tied up closely with a particular meaning of femininity and masculinity" (1989:575). The proliferation of images of the lustful Other in communal discourses demonstrates the potential of myth to "transform history into nature" (Barthes 1972:129). For, as several observers have pointed out, communalists constantly raise the specter of the "violation of our sisters and mothers" and exhort men to "take revenge" and prove their manhood (Chhachhi 1989:577). The pristine Hindu community constructed by Hindu communalists and nationalists is _predicated_ on discourses of the Other as sexual predator, and female sexuality is a means of policing the boundaries of the community (Sarkar and Butalia 1995).

The "Traditional" Community

Communities (especially coalitional communities) are often bases for effective political action against inequality and oppression; hence, it is not my aim to dismiss all communities, but rather to problematize uncritical and romantic celebrations of community and to underscore that the community can also be a site of violence against cultural Others and women. Thus, romantic recuperations of the traditional community both by antimodernist scholars such as Nandy and by Hindu nationalists elide inequalities within communities, including so-called traditional communities.

For instance, in his arguments against modernist secularism, Nandy's solution to the specter of communalism is "the traditional community," which, he insists, is a repository of tolerance. While the traditional community does not "keep religion separate from politics," it has developed principles of tolerance "over the centuries" that must now be brought to bear on contemporary politics (Nandy 1990:84). Nandy's attempt to propose the traditional community as an alternative to secularism is flawed for several reasons.

First, this recuperation of the traditional community is based on a fundamental contradiction. On the one hand, it is part of Nandy's larger critique of modernity. Yet, ironically, his argument draws on a binary between tradition and modernity that is itself quintessentially modernist. Second, one would be hard-put to find communities that are impermeable to modernity. As proposed by Veena Das, "the community, in contemporary contexts, is defined as much by the structures of modernity, including bureaucratic law, as by a customary innate law" (1995:51). I would add that not only are communities shaped by bureaucratic law but, as evident from the foregoing analysis of the *Ramayan,* in the era of mass media and electronic capitalism the very imagination of community is mediated by modernity.

Further, as my analysis of the imagined Hindu community invoked by the *Ramayan* demonstrates, hierarchies, inequalities, and violence sometimes form the bases for communities.[77] As Kumkum Sangari has pointed out, "a defence of the idea of religious community reinforces the structural relations between religions and patriarchies, and sharpens the emerging relations between religion and communalism" (1995:3291).[78] A feminist analysis of community, gender, and nation in the *Ramayan* foregrounds not just the "impact" of communalism on discourses of gender and sexuality but also, and more important, the ways gender and sexuality were centrally implicated in the consolidation of Hindu nationalist ideologies (see also Jeffery and Basu 1998, Sangari 1995, Sarkar and Butalia 1995).

Veena Das also points out that the "nostalgic rendering of the community" elides the role of violence in defining community and "provides a rather sanitized picture of tradition and community" (1995:51). Feminist critique is particularly useful in tracing the strategies of violence, effacement, and exclusion underlying the construction of the traditional community represented in the *Ramayan* and articulated in Hindu nationalist discourses. Such a critique forecloses the romantic recuperation of "community" as a utopian space of "tolerance."

THE MEDIATION OF MODERNITIES

Myth is speech stolen and restored. (Barthes 1972:125)

In recent years, the Ram Rajya invoked by the *Ramayan* has had terrifyingly destructive effects on minorities in India. Hindu nationalists have appropriated Ram Rajya as part of their narrative of an "ancient Indian past" that has to be recuperated from the alleged suppression of "India" during "Islamic invasions" and British colonial rule. The "nation's pretense to antiquity" (Kaviraj 1989) has thus acquired a violent tone: the menace underlying the invocations of the "glorious" Hindu/Indian past surfaced in the death chants of the Hindu mobs that ravaged northern India between December 1990 and 1993, in which Muslims were represented as descendants of the Moghul emperor Babar (*Babar ki santaan*) and as foreigners who had to be exterminated in order for India to attain a pristine state of nationhood. As pointed out by anticommunal activist Dilip Simeon, Hindu nationalism was thus able "to lay a viable claim to the mantle of the 'Nation'" (1994:234). My primary objective in this chapter has been to apply feminist analysis to the exclusionary discourses of tradition, community, and nation constructed in the *Ramayan*.

Further, I have examined the positions feminist cultural critics can take in order to intervene in ongoing debates about secularism, community, modernity, and antimodernity. In his critique of orthodox secularist discourse, Purushottam Agrawal argues that there has been "little attempt to analyze the cultural substance and political project of communalism, and even less of an attempt to address the cultural semiotics of communalism and the core symbols of its political iconography" (1994:248). I have described how some Hindus' devotional viewing of the serial indicates a compelling need to broaden prevailing cultural studies perspectives on mass media by taking seriously the role of faith and everyday religiosity in viewers' engagement with television.[79] As noted above, in my plea for an acknowledgment of the power of faith, I am not arguing that faith is or can be "innocent" of politics: my argument about the inclusion of faith in our understanding of the relationship between mass media and subjectivities is based on my belief that everyday religiosity and faith are not "things" to be discarded as we march toward modernity, but rather are part of the multiple genealogies of modernity. In my efforts to expand our notion of popular culture so as to analyze the evocation and construction of faith through mass media, I build a dialogue with cultural critics such as Bharucha and Agrawal, who have reconstructed discourses of secularism so as to formulate effective critiques of Hindu nationalism. My attempt to reconceptualize the relationship between mass media, community, and religiosity has been enabled by their efforts to redefine a secularism that is based on "nothing less than a complete openness to leading questions about the nature of Indian religiosity, the importance of symbolic identities, the political functions of language and 'culture,' the historical roots of communal projects, and the limits of patriotism" (Simeon 1994:237). I have argued that, as modernist discourses par excellence, orthodox secularist perspectives on culture, politics, and identity have not allowed for an understanding of the role of everyday religiosity and faith in (some) Hindu viewers' engagement with mass-mediated texts such as the *Ramayan*. Thus, while I agree with some of the critics who alleged that the *Ramayan* participated in the creation of exclusionary discourses of identity and belonging, I believe that most of their analyses drew from orthodox secularist understandings of the public sphere, popular culture, and the relationship between religion, culture, and politics. For these reasons, most of these critiques were unable to identify the processes through which the *Ramayan* was able to construct hegemonic discourses of identity.

Some scholars (e.g., Chatterjee 1993) attempt to evoke community as a space outside of, and resistant to, capitalism. While most of these scholars are unlikely to endorse Ram Rajya, or, for that matter, Hindu nationalist aspirations and discourses, their nostalgic conceptualization of community is belied by the imbrication of the *Ramayan*'s imagined Hindu community with consumer capitalism. Arvind Rajagopal (1994) argues that the reception of the serial has to be situated in the broader context of the liberalization of the Indian economy. As discussed in chapter 2, television played a crucial role in the unprecedented rise in consumerism that followed liberalization. Rajagopal points out that discourses of liberalization and consumerism and "Hinduisation" both clashed and reinforced each other: "The euphoria over liberalisation, the growing assertiveness of its beneficiary classes, and the spread of a consumerist ethos that accompanied these phenomena, created, in fact, new spaces into which communal discourse inserted itself, to the great advantage of the latter" (1994:1659). Rajagopal posits that the "overlap" between Hindu nationalism and the rhetoric of advertising was "necessarily partial"; at the same time, however, this overlap made possible a "swift slide" from a consumerist celebration of a rejuvenated and militant identity to a "libidinal collective identity which requires violence against a satanic 'other' as its chief form of expression" (1994:1660). Rajagopal argues that televisual discourses of Hindu nationalism were framed by incitements to consume and were (partially) reinforced by them. Thus, as part of a larger consumer culture, the imagined Hindu community invoked by the *Ramayan* was hardly un-linked with capitalism and was, in fact, intrinsically modernist.

When the very notions of culture, nation, and womanhood are politi-cally fraught, the task of feminist analyses of mass media acquires a com-pelling urgency. For feminist analysts there is no Archimedean, "outside" position whence we can mediate modernity. Further, while we may con-ceptualize modernities in the plural, it is important that we do not regard them as pluralistic: although modernities are indeed heterogeneous, they are hierarchically ordered. It is thus essential that we construct a nuanced formulation of modernity that enables us to steer clear of the traps of an uncritical celebration of modernity or a simplistic resistance against it. Instead, it is crucial that we engage in a careful examination of the kinds of political action hierarchical modernities may engender for subjects un-equally positioned along axes of gender, class, and ethnicity. Feminist analyses of texts such as the *Ramayan* that invoke a utopian Hindu com-munity foreclose an uncritical celebration of "the traditional community" and compel us to acknowledge that communities are sometimes based on practices of violence and exclusion toward women and cultural Others.

Hence, I am especially concerned with how feminist cultural critics might position ourselves vis-à-vis forms of modernity that produce exclu-sionary discourses of identity. Following Veena Das, I point to the "double articulation" of tradition and modernity (1995:53). Far from reifying the distinction between tradition and modernity, this double articulation "makes institutions such as caste or the religious community into new, original entities; this is not a matter of aggregation by which new features are added to old ones" (Das 1995:53). This double articulation problema-tizes both teleological notions of progress, according to which societies move from "traditional" to "modern," and nostalgic attempts to recu-perate "the traditional community" that can somehow resist modernity (1995:53). Indeed, the community constructed by the television *Ramayan* does not manifest a displaced temporality that is somehow antimodern but is, in fact, an instantiation of the multiple temporalities of modernity.

Finally, my focus on televisual mediations of modernity in India is part of my larger project of destabilizing the predominantly Eurocentric per-spectives on mass media in cultural studies. But, in so doing, it is not my intention to exceptionalize television in India. On the contrary, my aim is to explore what the televisation of a religious epic at a specific socio-historical moment and in a particular cultural context can teach analysts about the role of mass media in the construction of gender, community, everyday religiosity, national identity, and, as in the case of some viewers, religious nationalism. My analysis of the televised *Ramayan*'s role in the reconfiguration of discourses of identity, community, and nation interrogates the relationship between popular culture, mass culture, and culture. Stuart Hall has argued against a conception of popular culture as a site of "spontaneous" resistance against dominant cultural forms (1981). The complex ways in which viewers of the *Ramayan* engaged with its texts show us the fallacies of constructing binaries between domination and resistance: there is no autonomous, authentic popular culture that lies outside the field of cultural power and domination. The *Ramayan*'s reception also problematized dominant conceptions of a monolithic mass culture. Viewers' interpretations of what they watched were mediated by their class, gender, generation, and ethnicity. These modes of engagement contradict representations of mass culture as totalizing or intrinsically manipulative, and that of consumers of mass culture as homogeneous or passive. In addition, through its participation in the culture wars of late twentieth-century India, the *Ramayan* played a crucial role in the *production* of culture, thus problematizing the binary between mass culture and dominant anthropological conceptions of culture as an authentic and organic system of shared meanings.

Chapter 5 *Television Tales, National Narratives,*
and a Woman's Rage: Multiple Interpretations of
Draupadi's "Disrobing"

The *Mahabharata* is an "ancient tale" told anew by Indian television.[1]
Like all tales, its meanings acquire new valence with every telling. Serialized on Doordarshan from September 1988 to July 1990, it was watched
by more than 200 million viewers throughout India.[2] For the purposes
of this analysis I will focus on one particular episode: the story of the
"disrobing" (*vastraharan*) of one of the epic's most important female characters, Draupadi, the wife of the five Pandava brothers. In this chapter, I
examine how the creators and Hindu viewers of Doordarshan's *Mahabha-*
rat participated, through their divergent readings, in the reconstitution of
Draupadi as a symbol of Indian Womanhood.[3]

The creators of the televised *Mahabharat* saw Draupadi as an index
of the position of "Woman" in Indian society and, more fundamentally,
as a marker of (Hindu) Indian "civilization."[4] For both the presenters of
the disrobing as well as its viewers, however, Draupadi also embodied
"Woman's rage," in particular, the rage of a woman wronged. A genealogical analysis of Draupadi-as-sign reveals how this aspect of her personality
has been appropriated in nationalist ideologies and practices both during
anticolonial struggles and, with different referents, in the postcolonial
conjuncture.[5] In this chapter we will see how both the producers and the
Hindu viewers of this scene were interpellated by particular discourses
of nationhood—how, in their retelling of the tale, Draupadi came to embody the reconfiguration of discourses not just of Hindu womanhood,
but of Indian Womanhood, thereby conflating "Hindu" with "Indian" and
community with nation.

Viewers, especially women, also perceived Draupadi as an icon of
women's vulnerability. The imaginative connections viewers made between Draupadi's experiences and their own show us that she was *more*
than just a symbol of Indian Womanhood. While producers' and viewers'
perceptions overlapped in their construction of Draupadi as a palimp-

sest for ideologies of gender and nationhood, the lack of closure in women viewers' interpretations is inescapable. For even as women accepted Draupadi as a symbol of Indian Womanhood, they used her disrobing to critique their own lives and to theorize gender relations in the worlds they inhabited. These moments of rupture, indeed of epiphany, reveal how their affective interaction with what they watched opened spaces and possibilities for social critique. The coexistence of these multiple interpretations also illustrates how viewers/consumers of mass media may sometimes appropriate hegemonic discourses to critique existing systems of power.

One objective of this chapter is to demonstrate that interpretation does not entail an "endless" process of semiosis; instead, semiosis is itself grounded in social, material, and historical relationships, conditions, and contexts. At the same time that I highlight interpretive processes, I emphasize that texts are hardly open-ended and that viewers/readers are rarely, if ever, in a position to "choose" the meanings they want to "produce." Hence, in this chapter, I attend to relationships between viewers and their specific location in sociohistorical conjunctures, and between texts and interdiscursive contexts.

In insisting on the fundamentally "incomplete" nature of hegemonic discourses underscored by moments of rupture, I have a second, somewhat urgent, objective driven by my desire for reflexive, accountable, and strategic positioning as a feminist critic of the Indian nation-state. I hope to create possibilities for counternarratives that can potentially subvert discourses of Hindu nationalism.[6] Thus, although I interviewed viewers from different religious communities, I have chosen to highlight the slippages and ruptures in the interpretations of Hindu women. At the end of the twentieth century, as the Indian nation-state is becoming increasingly repressive and religious identities are being forged through terror and bloodshed, I believe that those of us committed to feminist and secularist praxis need to foreground, seize on, and consolidate our critiques precisely in such moments of rupture.

TELEVISED EPICS AND THE POLITICS OF NATIONALISM

The serialization of the *Mahabharat* followed and overlapped with the televisation of the *Ramayan*. Both serials were telecast at a time of exclusionary discourses of community, growing Hindu nationalism, and escalating tension between Hindus versus Sikhs and Muslims. Chapter 4 described how Doordarshan's version of the *Ramayan* was unequivocal in its attempt to depict the "glorious Hindu past" often invoked by Hindu revivalists. Journalists and scholars have frequently pointed to the ways the serial may have helped to consolidate Hindu nationalism (see Philipose 1990, Thapar 1990). In serving to promote a Hindu consciousness nationwide, the *Ramayan* extravaganza was only the most recent variant on a historical theme: the *Ramayana* has long served as an ideological vehicle for articulating a theocratic polity in which "outsiders" are marginalized, even demonized. Although the *Mahabharat* did not foreground the *Ramayan's* ideological vision of a homogeneous and exclusionary polity, it is against this communalized interpretive context that we must examine its reception.[7]

Although the televisation of the *Mahabharat* probably reinforced prevailing currents of Hindu nationalism, it was also "heard" by a more inclusive audience. The Hindu, Muslim, and Sikh viewers I worked with engaged with it in more complex ways than they did with the *Ramayan*. Many viewers felt that watching the *Ramayan* was comparable to participating in a Hindu religious ritual. For instance, Hindu viewers Sukumaran and Bina Vaswani told me that some members of their families would make it a point to bathe before the serial came on and would watch it with their hands folded, with the same reverence they would show if participating in religious ceremonies. By contrast, the *Mahabharat's* tales of blood and gore, romance and family politics, conspiracy and deception made for a multitextual viewing experience (B. Chandra 1991, Dethe and Sharma 1990, Padgaonkar 1990, R. G. K. 1990, Sherif 1991).[8] One viewer compared the *Mahabharat* with the *Ramayan* in the following manner: "The *Ramayan* story is straight, like a palm tree. The *Mahabharat* story is like a banyan tree with spreading stems full of rich sub-plots and vivid characters" (quoted in Kala 1990). Several Hindu viewers I interviewed—for instance, Sukumaran and Aparna Dasgupta—seemed to disapprove of the manner in which Doordarshan's *Mahabharat* had "diluted" the epic's "Hindu message."[9] Significantly, some Hindu right-wing commentators were upset that Lord Krishna was portrayed as a Machiavelli who believed that the ends always justified the means, and felt that television's *Mahabharat* presented a distorted picture of Hinduism. The controversy spilled into op-ed pages and letters to the editor in several national dailies (see, for example, an article written by Damodar Agrawal [1990], and the response it elicited from Tabish Khair and Gyanendra Nath [1990] and from several readers who participated in these debates in their letters to the newspapers [e.g., Hoskote 1990, K. Kumar 1990, Parthasarathy 1990]).

Finally, the aporia of the *Mahabharat*'s narrative lay in its insistence that the lust for power permeates all aspects of life—from state politics to family politics—and leads always to tragedy (symbolized by the fratricidal conflicts that culminate in the apocalyptic war of Kurukshetra). Director B. R. Chopra claimed that while the *Ramayan* was about the ideal manhood of Lord Ram (*maryada purushottam*), the *Mahabharat* was about the pervasiveness of politics in "every aspect of life." According to this version of the *Mahabharat*, the pursuit of power is intrinsically corrupt: the tragedy of the battle of Kurukshetra that results in the destruction of both clans is, in researcher Satish Bhatnagar's words, indicative of "both the inevitability and futility of war." Viewers frequently appropriated the *Mahabharat*'s discourses to comment on political corruption. For instance, while discussing a major scandal that eventually ousted Prime Minister Rajiv Gandhi from power,[10] Sukumaran quoted a character in the *Mahabharat* who said that a country whose leader is corrupt can never progress. An opening episode that depicted the struggles between two aspirants to the throne in terms of the conflict between lineage and qualifications (described by scriptwriter Raza as "the conflict between *janma* [birth] and *karma* [action]") became controversial because it seemed to articulate public skepticism about Rajiv Gandhi's ability to succeed his mother, Indira Gandhi, as India's prime minister.[11]

Although the Muslim and Sikh viewers I interviewed saw the *Mahabharat* as a Hindu epic (rather than an Indian one), they felt that it was less of a transgression, less intrusive, than the *Ramayan*.[12] Muslim and Sikh women, along with their Hindu counterparts, were extremely moved by Draupadi's disrobing: temporarily abstracting this episode from the rest of the televisual text, they saw it as yet another gripping tale of the injustices (*zulm*) perpetrated on women.[13] A moment of suture was created when Draupadi stared into the camera to confront audiences and to question a husband's right to "do what he wants with his wife." This moment moved the Muslim and Sikh women I worked with to see in her disrobing a reflection of their own vulnerabilities as women living in a "man's world." Rather than engage in comparisons of the interpretations of viewers of different religions, however, my purpose here is to foreground slippages and ruptures within majority discourses; hence, in this chapter I focus on the responses of Hindu women.

I begin by narrating the episode in which Draupadi is publicly disrobed. Next, I study the discursive framework in which this scene was conceived and produced for television by examining the views of the director, the script writer, and the research director of the serial. This is followed by an analysis of how women viewers in particular sociocultural contexts interpreted Draupadi's disrobing. I then situate both the viewers and the creators of the scene in the broader discursive contexts of constructions of Indian Womanhood through a genealogical analysis of the varying appropriations of Draupadi in colonial and postcolonial nationalist ideologies. Finally, I discuss the implications of the multiple interpretations of Draupadi's disrobing for conceptualizing the relationship between texts and lives, and for developing a feminist critique that can strategically clear a space for discourses to counter the hegemonic ideologies of Hindu nationalism.

DRAUPADI'S DISROBING

The *Mahabharat* was produced for Doordarshan by one of the most successful filmmakers of the Bombay film industry, B. R. Chopra. One of the reasons the serial held the attention of viewers from different communities and drew ratings unsurpassed in Doordarshan's history was its deployment of a combination of techniques drawn from various sources: the modes of address and performative traditions of Hindi film melodrama, the use of background music and song, the narrative rhythms of U.S. soap operas, and the iconography of religious calendar art.[14] Some of these techniques, along with a summary of the episode of Draupadi's disrobing, are described below.

The *Mahabharat* story has several subplots, but the core narrative of television's version focused on the relations between two branches of the Kuru dynasty: the five Pandava brothers, their wife, Draupadi, and their mother, on the one hand; and the Kaurava clan, consisting of the blind King Dhritarashtra and his family on the other. The main story up to this point has consisted of the attempts of Duryodhana, King Dhritarashtra's son, and the Pandavas' cousin to destroy the Pandavas. The disrobing of Draupadi in the presence of her five husbands, her in-laws, and the Kaurava court forms a turning point in the narrative.

Like all the episodes, this one begins with an introduction by a commentator (*sutradhaar*), in this case Kaal, who is none other than Time himself. In a booming, disembodied voice, Kaal announces that this episode is about "appropriate conduct" (*maryada*). In a flashback from a previous episode we see Yudhishtra, the eldest Pandava brother, gambling with Duryodhana in the presence of King Dhritarashtra and the Kaurava elders. Through visual metaphors drawn from popular iconography the Pandava brothers are resplendent in white, the color of purity; Duryodhana's wicked uncle Shakuni, the instigator of all evil, wears black and red, the colors of anger and envy.

After losing his kingdom and his wealth to Duryodhana, Yudhishtra gambles and loses each of his brothers. The emotional tension inherent in this situation is heightened by conventions borrowed from Hindi film melodrama (for example, the use of close-ups and loud music) and histrionic traditions typical of some forms of north Indian folk theater (such as the stylized, exaggeratedly raucous laughter of "villains," in this case Duryodhana and his cronies). When Yudhishtra tries to stop the game by saying that he has lost everything, Duryodhana's friend Karna suggests that Yudhishtra stake his wife, "the proud, doe-eyed Draupadi." Yudhishtra's brothers (they all "share" Draupadi in a polyandrous marriage) look up in horror and despair. The shocked silence that envelops the court is broken when the prime minister, also the cousins' uncle, begs the king to intervene and prevent "the name of the daughter-in-law of the clan" from being taken in disrespect. The king, however, is silent. The same thing recurs when the court guru and Bheeshma, the venerable Kaurava elder, urge him to intervene: all appeals to the king are in vain. Encouraged, Duryodhana taunts Yudhistra into staking Draupadi. Yudhishtra does so and loses her, to the loud, derisive laughter of his opponents.

Duryodhana then sends a sentry to bring Draupadi to the gaming house. Draupadi is in seclusion because she is menstruating: her long hair loose, she is clad in the vestments of isolation. She sends the sentry back to the court with a question for Yudhistra: did he stake her before or after he lost himself?

Duryodhana is furious when the sentry returns without Draupadi. He

Figures 15 and 16
Draupadi is dragged by
her hair to the court.
Figure 16 courtesy of
B. R. Films.

commands: "Tell that women with five husbands to come here immediately!" Draupadi, rendered nameless, becomes the "woman with five husbands," a woman with a deviant sexuality.

Draupadi once again refuses to accompany the sentry; this time she
says she will come only at the behest of her elders. Duryodhana is further
enraged by her defiance. He now asks his younger brother Dushasana to
bring "that woman with five husbands" to the court. When Dushasana
contemptuously orders Draupadi to accompany him, she admonishes
him for speaking disrespectfully to a woman. As he grasps her hair and
starts to drag her to the court, she screams: "You are dragging the honor
of the clan by the hair![15] The Pandavas will never forgive you for this. And
even if they wish to forgive you, I will never let them do so" (figs. 15, 16).

After giving us an aerial view of Draupadi being dragged down the
steps of the court, the camera swings to provide us with close-ups of the
men: the leering faces of Duryodhana and his accomplices; the impotent

fury of her husbands, who sit with their heads bowed, their backs to her as she is dragged in; the distress and shock of the Kaurava elders.

Draupadi manages to break away from Dushasana's clutches and runs toward the king. The camera follows her gaze to the faces of her elders. Unable to meet her eyes, they bow their heads in impotence and shame. But she is relentless and tells them that they cannot solve the problem by lowering their eyes; because they did not prevent this *"adharma"* (in this context, misconduct) from occurring, they are responsible for it. "Is a wife her husband's property?" she demands. "Is she an object that can be gambled? And if she is, then what right did Yudhishtra have to stake me once he lost all he owned?" She insists on an answer. This question, she says, is being asked not merely by her but by all of womankind, by the earth, the mother of all human beings; this question is being raised "by the future of this country."

The Kaurava elder Bheeshma replies that although it was "improper" for Yudhishtra to use Draupadi as a stake, "the fact is that a man has the right to do what he wants with his wife." Draupadi whirls around to confront Bheeshma. She stares directly into the camera and addresses the audience, thus creating a moment of suture with viewers. "How is this 'right' to be interpreted?" she demands, "What are its limits? Isn't it a man's foremost duty to protect his wife?"

But instead of Bheeshma it is Duryodhana's friend Karna who responds, saying that since none of her five husbands could protect her, she should sit on Duryodhana's lap. Speechless, Draupadi snarls at him in rage. Karna continues: "You are already the wife of five husbands. So what harm is there in holding the hand of a sixth? A woman who lives with five husbands is not a wife but a whore. What honor can a whore have? If Draupadi had been brought here naked, it would not have been inappropriate." In a manner reminiscent of Hindi film villains, Duryodhana sneers: "My friend is telling the truth. What is honor or dishonor for a whore?" He asks Dushasana to disrobe her so he can see what the woman he has won looks like.

Dushasana lunges toward her and pulls at her sari. The camera lingers voyeuristically on her trembling, perspiring body. She struggles, then pauses with her sari between her teeth and, with her hands folded, starts to pray to Lord Krishna (figs. 17, 18). Dushasana, to the loud, contemptuous laughter of Duryodhana and his supporters, continues to pull her sari. But the sounds of their laughter are soon drowned by the ringing of

Figure 17 The disrobing of Draupadi. Courtesy of B. R. Films.

temple bells and the blowing of conches.[16] Lord Krishna has intervened: we see his face in the upper left corner of the frame. He smiles down at Draupadi beatifically, reassuringly; saris begin to flow from his palm, which he raises in blessing. As Dushasana pulls off one sari, another drapes Draupadi's body (fig. 19). All we hear for a while is Draupadi's voice praying to Krishna and the music of temple bells, conches, and drums (*tablas*). The conches become increasingly martial and the beat of the drums picks up. These are the sounds of war. The disrobing of Draupadi has started a chain of events that will culminate in war, the war of Kurukshetra that her men will fight to avenge the dishonor done to *them*.[17]

The camera swings rhythmically between the figure of Draupadi, her perspiring body the battlefield for forces of good (*dharma*, represented by the righteousness of Krishna) and evil (*adharma*, signified by the envy and lust of Duryodhana and his accomplices), and the faces of the men as they realize that Draupadi cannot be disrobed. We are provided with close-ups of their faces, and we see their expressions change: Duryodhana's, Dushasana's, and Karna's from lust and glee to incomprehension; those of the Pandava brothers from pain and defeat to relief; those of the Kaurava elders from helplessness and frustration to awe, to recognition that they are in the presence of a supernatural force. The attempted disrobing has thus become a site for divine intervention. Suddenly the music turns upbeat. The drums, temple bells, and conches reach a crescendo: still martial sounding, they now express the music of victory. And above all these sounds, we hear the strains of a flute, perhaps Lord Krishna's own.[18]

Exhausted from his efforts to strip Draupadi, Dushasana falls to the floor. Draupadi also collapses, and the background music comes to a halt. The ensuing silence is shattered by her husband Bhima's vow that he will not rest until he has drunk Dushasana's blood on the battlefield. Draupadi then stands to face the court again (fig. 20). We are made fully aware of her power as we see her standing before the men, her tense body upright and trembling with fury, her waist-length hair loose and disheveled, her eyes blazing—perhaps to some in the audience the image is reminiscent of Kali,[19] the incarnation of woman's rage. For the men assembled in the court (and, I might add, for members of the audience) the semiotics of pathos has cast its spell: a woman's tears—especially those of an angry, victimized woman—can evoke awe and fear in the hearts of all who behold her.[20]

As Draupadi begins to put a curse on the "shameless and cowardly"

Figure 18 Draupadi prays to Lord Krishna to save her honor.

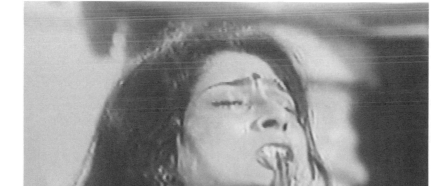

Figure 19 An endless flow of saris prevents Draupadi's disrobing. Courtesy of B. R. Films.

Figure 20 Draupadi confronts the court. Courtesy of B. R. Films.

assembly she is interrupted in mid-sentence by Gandhari, Duryodhana's mother, who pleads with her to stop. The episode ends here with a freeze-frame of Gandhari begging Draupadi to stop, a "cliff-hanger" typical of soap opera (will Gandhari succeed in preventing Draupadi from cursing her men?). We hear the strains of a song informing us that "he who insults womankind / will be destroyed by god." In the following episode we learn that although Draupadi has been prevented from putting a curse on the men of the court, she is unmoved by Gandhari's appeals to forgive Duryodhana, Karna, and Dushasana. Draupadi tells her husbands that she will leave her hair loose until she has washed it with the blood of Duryodhana and Dushasana brought from the battlefield.

THE INTERPRETATIONS OF THE CREATORS OF THE *MAHABHARAT*

My purpose in analyzing the interpretations of the serial's creators is not to privilege authorial intention but to illuminate the discursive framework within which Draupadi's disrobing was conceived. When I arrived at director B. R. Chopra's studio in Bombay, also present were researcher Satish Bhatnagar and script writer Rahi Masoom Raza, a Muslim and a renowned leftist intellectual. While their individual interpretations of the disrobing varied, they seemed to agree that Draupadi indexed the position of Woman in Indian society and hence the degree to which Indian society is "civilized." Further, while they believed that Draupadi's rage reflects the power of Woman, they were unequivocal in their insistence that this power must be contained in the interests of the integrity of the family and, more important, the unity of the nation.

Draupadi as an Index of Indian Womanhood

When Draupadi questions her husband's right to use her as a stake in his game of dice, she claims that her question is being asked not merely by her but by all Indian women, by the earth, the mother of all human beings; this question is being raised "by the future of this country." She describes herself as representing all Indian women. Thus Draupadi, the woman who was dragged to the Kaurava court by her hair, the woman who is to be publicly disrobed, is displaced by an ideological construct: she symbolizes nothing less than Indian Womanhood itself.

It hence came as no surprise to me that Chopra, Raza, and their colleagues viewed the status of women, as exemplified by Draupadi's disrobing, as the most revealing index of how "enlightened" a particular society is. As Chopra pointed out, "If you want to judge a society, judge the place of the woman in the society. We tried to underline that." He and his colleagues agreed that "Woman's position" is a marker of "civilization and culture." They pointed out that instead of being respected as "mother earth," Draupadi was humiliated. They saw Draupadi's disrobing as symptomatic of a "sick society" that had "to come to an end." Her disrobing thus indexed what Chopra described as "the extent to which the rot has seeped into her society."

Chopra and his colleagues claimed that Draupadi's disrobing indexed not just the "sickness" of her society but also that of contemporary Indian society. When I asked them to explain what they meant, Raza responded: "In spite of women's lib, woman is losing her place in society. Woman [has to] get her rightful place in society. Not in the household—to tell her 'you are the queen of the household' is just a ruse to confine her—but in society. Woman is the focal point of evolution. We should remember that. The earth is more important than the seed."

These comments contain a host of interrelated and contradictory discourses on feminism, women's sexuality, and "woman's place" in the household and in "society." According to Raza, feminism (stereotyped as "women's lib") has been ineffective and "woman" is losing her "place." But how is woman's "rightful place" in society conceptualized? At first Raza's response appears to construct a discourse of woman's agency that extends beyond the household: he claims that emphasizing the power of women within the family is deceptive and only reinforces their confinement within the home. But the vocabulary Raza falls back on to describe "woman's power" stems from a discourse of procreation in which Woman is the earth and Man the seed that impregnates the soil.[21] Woman's place in society is hence described in terms of her procreative power: it is this that marks her agency as the "focal point of evolution."

Raza and his colleagues conceived of Draupadi as an index not just of the "state of Indian society" but, more fundamentally, of ideal typical Indian Womanhood. And instead of critically analyzing gender relations in particular historical conjunctures, by speaking of "Woman" as "mother earth" and the "focal point of evolution" Chopra and his colleagues conceived of Indian Womanhood in terms of essentialist categories. For Raza, Woman must be conceived of in terms of power (*shakti*), as "mother earth," as the "focal point of evolution": only then can we give "due respect" to her. Further, as pointed out by Bhatnagar, Woman is not just mother earth but also fire (*agni*) and energy.[22] The specific location of Draupadi, or indeed that of the multitude of Indian women in particular sociohistorical contexts, is thus displaced by an ahistorical representation of Draupadi as an index of the position of "Woman" not just in "Hindu culture" but also in "Indian culture."

"Woman's Power" and the Unity of the Nation

In the discourses of the creators of the disrobing episode Draupadi is vulnerable, but she is also resilient as the earth. Her anger, her refusal to be passive, reveals the fire in her. She is the personification of power and energy. However, Chopra and his colleagues insisted that Woman's agency must be contained within the parameters of family and nation.[23]

More significant, Chopra and Raza made explicit connections between the family and the nation by insisting that the family is the "cornerstone" of a "civilized" society and a strong nation. This crucial link between the unity of the family and the unity of the nation was particularly clear when Raza said that "it [the *Mahabharat*] is about how the family is rooted in society. How the rot in the family spreads to the society to the country to the political system"; and Chopra added: "Compare it to the change in government these days. . . . [The *Mahabharat* is] about internecine conflict in the family and in the political system." Internecine conflict in the family is analogous to and symptomatic of internecine conflict in the nation. For Chopra and Raza, the "contemporary relevance" of the *Mahabharat* lay precisely in the fact that it revealed the importance of the unity of the family to the territorial integrity of the nation. Further, according to Chopra, one of the "perpetual truths inherent in the epic," what made the *Mahabharat* particularly pertinent to contemporary times, was that it spoke so forcefully about the importance of national integration, that it emphasized that the unity and integrity of the nation must be protected "at all costs."

This came up several times in our discussion but was most overt when I asked the director and the scriptwriter why their *Mahabharat* ended at an earlier point than other versions. Unlike other renditions that describe the aftermath of the war of Kurukshetra, Chopra's *Mahabharat* ended with the death of Bheeshma, the venerable Kaurava elder, on the battlefield of Kurukshetra. In this version, Bheeshma gives a long speech on patriotism, the importance of fighting against the division of one's country (significantly, Bheeshma uses the term *vibhajan,* a Hindi word frequently used for the partition of the subcontinent into India and Pakistan). Watching this scene in the context of the separatist movements currently threatening the territorial unity of the Indian nation, I had found Bheeshma's speech particularly significant. When I first brought it up, Chopra claimed that they ended the serial at that point because they had conceived of Bheeshma as the hero of their story and felt that the climax of the story came with his death. But the political undertones of Bheeshma's speech had been so plain to me that I pursued my line of questioning. Raza responded that the last scene did indeed have "contemporary relevance" because it was about how the country must never be divided: the *Mahabharat,* he said, showed how attempts to divide the kingdom led to destruction on a massive scale in the battle of Kurukshetra. The everyday discourse of many Hindus uses the war of Kurukshetra as a metaphor for apocalyptic destruction. However, Raza claimed that the *Mahabharat* was "about when to go to Kurukshetra," that is, about when to go to war, whatever the costs, to defend the unity of the nation. In his discourse, Kurukshetra symbolizes the war between patriotism and the forces threatening to divide the country.

Chopra intervened to comment that Vyasa, the poet to whom the dominant version of the *Mahabharat* is attributed, had a "different" concept of national integration because "there was a different nation then." In this discourse, all that is conceded is that the nation was of a "different" sort: as in narratives of the past constructed by Hindu nationalists, the antiquity of the nation is not in question. I thus pushed Chopra to compare the contemporary Indian nation with that supposedly envisioned by Vyasa. He replied that in "those days" the nation did not consist of heterogeneous communities and so national integration simply consisted of keeping the "center" (that is, the state) strong. The contemporary Indian nation, by contrast, consists of different communities. As a consequence, national integration today must consist of the "welding" of these communities into one national community. Echoing themes pervasive in popular liberal discourses of national integration, he added that today it is important to focus on the "unity" underlying the "diversity" of Indian culture. However, he claimed, even though the contemporary nation is qualitatively "different" from that of Vyasa's time, this notion of "unity" is in keeping with Vyasa's idea of national integration: "The country must remain united. The country, the motherland, must come first. That is what I think Vyasa wanted to emphasize."

The primacy Chopra and his colleagues gave to national integration and their views on women's location in the nation were even more forcefully evident in their description of Draupadi's desire for vengeance. According to Chopra, when Draupadi complains to Lord Krishna he first listens to her sympathetically. But when she persists in venting her anger, he "snubs Draupadi: 'What is this all the time, with your hair loose. Your personal hurt cannot engulf the political divide. The state is more important than your personal hurt. Your personal problems should not be allowed to overshadow the national problem.'" Chopra's interpretation echoes themes found in fascist discourses of nationalism. Not only is the nation conflated with the state, but it is patently clear that the "personal problems" of Indian women, iconicized by Draupadi, cannot be permitted to overshadow the "national problem": the protests of women to change the conditions of their lives must hence be kept within the parameters of national unity.

This, then, is the discursive framework in which Draupadi's disrobing was conceived. For the creators of this episode, Draupadi indexed the place of Woman not just in Hindu society but in Indian society as a whole: at the same time that she is vulnerable, she also represents the creative power, resilience, fire, and energy of Indian Womanhood. Further, articulated at a historical moment when the Indian nation-state was becoming increasingly fascist, this insistence that Draupadi's rage, though justified, must be contained and that the family and, more important, the nation must remain unscathed and "supreme," even at the cost of an apocalyptic war of Kurukshetra, is particularly significant.

VIEWERS' INTERPRETATIONS

The confluence of ideologies of gender and sexuality, viewers' precarious class positions, and their locations in the politics of their families account for some of the differences between viewers' responses and those of the *Mahabharat*'s producers. Viewers' interpretations of other serials seldom varied solely according to gender; the disrobing episode, however, seemed to have polarized men and women. In their conversations about the *Mahabharat*, men would talk about the war of Kurukshetra, family and state politics, and political corruption; their discussion of Draupadi's disrobing was almost invariably in terms of how it unleashed a sequence of events that culminated in the war of Kurukshetra. While women touched on other aspects of the narrative, it was the disrobing episode that they talked about at length. Some reverted to it in several conversations, and these discussions often provided a point of entry into narratives about their own lives. In fact, I found that Draupadi's disrobing enabled some of these viewers to confront and critique their own positions in their family, community, and class.[24] I focus on women viewers because they, more than men, seemed profoundly moved by the disrobing and could narrate the episode and their responses to it in vivid detail and with astonishing emotional intensity for months after it was telecast. Even the most reserved and recalcitrant women would become passionate and eloquent on the subject.

While the producers claimed that the climax of their story was the death of the Kaurava elder Bheeshma, the women I worked with unequivocally believed that the disrobing was the climax. Predictably, their ethnic background, age, household position, and life experiences inflected their interpretations of what they saw. But even as their responses were embedded in their own life narratives, some common themes emerged in their interpretations of what they had seen. All the women I spoke with saw Draupadi as an icon of women's vulnerability; for many she evoked the power of women's rage, and for some, an intimate engagement with her disrobing enabled them to rupture hegemonic constructions of Hindu/Indian Womanhood.

Draupadi as an Icon of Women's Vulnerability

Unlike the *Mahabharat* crew, who spoke of Draupadi in terms of abstract conceptions of gender and nationhood, women viewers *intimately* identified with Draupadi and saw in her disrobing a reflection of their own struggles to negotiate an environment that they considered hostile to their dignity. Threats to their physical safety in the public spaces of New Delhi; sexual harassment at work; economic, sexual, and emotional exploitation in the family: these were the daily realities faced by the women I describe here. Watching Draupadi's disrobing compelled them to confront and theorize their own emotional, financial, and sexual vulnerabilities. The disrobing episode seemed to affect young, unmarried women particularly profoundly. What struck them most was the fact that Draupadi was disrobed by her brother-in-law, at the behest of her husband's kinsmen, in her in-laws' court, in front of the elders of her clan and her husbands.

In chapter 2 I described Sushmita Dasgupta, who lived with her large family in Vikas Nagar. She and her father were the family's primary breadwinners; her father was about to retire. Sushmita seemed to be the financial and emotional mainstay of her family, a fact that often overwhelmed her. She frequently spoke to me of her loneliness. Her cousin informed me that Sushmita desperately wanted to escape the claustrophobia of her family, to get married and start a life of her own, but her father and elder brother had become so dependent on her salary that every time a proposal came for her marriage, they found an excuse to turn it down. This, along with persistent financial anxiety, created considerable tension in the family. For the most part, Sushmita appeared to take her family politics in stride. But every now and then she would slip into a depression that would last for weeks, sometimes months.

Apprehensive about whether her father would ever allow her to get married, terrified that she would be mistreated if she entered her in-laws' home without a dowry, Sushmita told me on two different occasions that what shocked her most about the disrobing episode was the failure of Draupadi's elders to protect their daughter-in-law. But I did not realize how deeply shaken she had been by it until one day, more than a year after the episode was telecast and about a month after the serialization of the *Mahabharat* concluded, her mother related Sushmita's reaction:

> My daughter, when she saw [what happened], cried and cried. She cried all morning. Imagine what happened to Draupadi! And in public, in front of her in-laws! A feeling came to my daughter. what will happen to me when I get married and go to my in-laws' home?

Evidently, Sushmita profoundly identified with Draupadi and saw in Draupadi's disrobing her own vulnerability. For although she felt isolated in her parents' house, she was also extremely anxious about what would happen if she ever did get married. She was acutely conscious of the fact that her precariously lower-middle-class family did not have the resources for a dowry. How would she protect herself if her in-laws humiliated her for not bringing a dowry? All her insecurities and fears surfaced when she saw Draupadi's disrobing.

Indeed, the vulnerability of women was discussed by every single woman that I interviewed about this episode. This happened without exception—across classes, across generations, across communities. Draupadi embodied what seemed to be a crucial aspect of their understanding of what it meant to be a woman, an Indian woman, living in a man's world.

Consider, for instance, the following exchange between Uma and her mother, Jayanthi Chandran, a pair who seemed more like friends than mother and daughter. Although the Chandran family identified themselves as south Indian, Jayanthi often teased Uma that she had become a "Dilli-wali" (a person from Delhi) because she preferred north Indian food to Malayali cuisine and spoke Malayalam with a Delhi accent. Uma was very proud of being the first woman in her family to graduate from college, but, as noted in chapter 2, she was extremely insecure about her future. She was profoundly conscious of her class position (lower middle class), and she often expressed her fear that she would never be financially secure. Unlike Uma, Jayanthi was articulate and extremely self-confident. She believed that while it was tough to be a woman in search of a career in a man's world, if she were resolute in her objectives and developed a thick skin, a woman could achieve some degree of financial security. However, Jayanthi also had no doubts that in the ultimate analysis, security and happiness could only ensue from a successful marriage and a contented family life.

Several months after the televisation of the *Mahabharat* concluded, the three of us discussed Draupadi's disrobing:

> *Jayanthi:* Draupadi, [in] that scene in which her hair was pulled, showed that things have been this way since the olden times. Now of course it's this way anyway. But this shows how a man shows his "manpower." It's been going on since then.
>
> *Uma:* I didn't realize that this is not a new thing. You suddenly realize that in every situation it's the same thing that's happening—a man has the power to put a woman down simply because he has physical superiority. It's we that get stuck in the "hot water"; nothing happens to him.
>
> *Jayanthi:* No matter how many associations or institutions you have for women, there is nothing you can do about this. [Pointing to Uma] . . . see how much I have educated her? I've sent her to a co-educational school. Still, if she's a little late [getting home], I worry about her. It's natural, it comes from within [to worry].

I agreed with Jayanthi and described how, when I was a student in India, my mother would wait for me at our gate every time I was a little late coming home from Delhi University. Jayanthi added that if Uma had been a boy, she wouldn't worry as much. She said: "That's the basic difference, the natural thing, it can never change, no matter how many women's organizations you might have." Reverting to Draupadi's disrobing, she said:

If you ever have to really insult a woman, this is what you'll do. You can't do worse than this, isn't it? It should never have happened. But they [the men who tried to disrobe her] had so much lust in them.

Uma: This is a good point, *amma* [mother]. Males know that they can't go any further.

Jayanthi: This is the last, the ultimate thing they can do to a woman. They also know that. In this *zamana* [era/world] also the same things happen.

PM: So you think similar things still happen to women?

Uma: It won't be as dramatic that someone pulls a woman by the hair. But they'll find a thousand and one things. Like in buses, they'll pinch you, they'll treat you as if you have no dignity at all. You're just there as their plaything.

Jayanthi: . . . Inside all of us, there is a shard of fear. You can't see it, you can't explain it.

Uma: This is very true. It's like a reflex action. Like if someone stares at you for a long time.

Most of the women I spoke with were convinced that their vulnerability stemmed from their sexuality. Many young women told me that when they watched Draupadi's disrobing they were surprised to learn that women have been the target of sexual violence since the days of the epics (as Uma put it: "I didn't realize that this is not a new thing"). For Uma and her mother, and for many other women that I spoke with, women's sexual vulnerability is what distinguishes girls from boys, women from men: this is a fact that all the women's organizations in the world cannot erase, the source of the fear that resides "inside all of us."

Although I do not, even for a moment, wish to imply that the home is a haven where women are safe from predatory males, this exchange needs to be considered in the light of New Delhi's legendary hostility to women. For example, taking public transportation in New Delhi has always been extremely humiliating for women (myself included), who have to deal constantly with men trying to push, paw, and pinch them. I have seen (and experienced) how the memory of previous brushes with the sexual aggression of strangers is inscribed in women's bodies as they sit hunched in buses, their arms wrapped tightly across their breasts; the warning flashed in a mother's glance when her daughter's *chunni,* the shawl covering the upper body, accidentally slips off her shoulders; the knot that forms in the pit of one's stomach when, in Uma's words, a strange man "stares at you for a long time." These and other experiences reinforce women's sense of insecurity as they go about their daily lives.

But if women articulate their sense of insecurity, do they also feel *totally* helpless? Was Draupadi no more than an icon of the vulnerability of women? Was there nothing empowering in her image? I found that if Draupadi's disrobing enabled these viewers to reexperience their vulnerability, her fury at her husbands and in-laws also evoked the power of women's rage.

Draupadi and Women's Rage

Draupadi's disrobing reminded Sushmita Dasgupta of an experience at her neighborhood post office. One day when she went to buy stamps, she noticed a man who looked at her with "very bad intentions" (*bahut kharab nazar se*). At first she pretended that she didn't see him. But when she went and stood in a separate "ladies' line," he said, "Why are you going to the front [of the line]? I have been standing here for so long."[25] When she replied that she was within her rights to stand in the ladies line, he continued to argue with her in "an insulting fashion." Reexperiencing her humiliation and her sense of isolation in a post office full of men, Sushmita recollected that one person alone had had the courage to speak, "an old man, my father's age, that is why he spoke up." She added:

> If he [the "bad man"] had asked me nicely, if he had been in a hurry, I would have let him buy [what he wanted] first. But he said: "I'll buy what I want. What can you do?" I replied, "Okay, take what you want. There's no need to talk nonsense." I took what I wanted from the separate line. If this had happened at our place [*hamare udhar*—here Sushmita was referring to Calcutta] he would have been slapped. But this is Delhi. And I am a girl, alone. And his gaze had been full of bad intentions [*nazar bhi uski buri thi*]. So I cursed him a lot [*bahut shraap diya*] [saying] that the way he has looked at me, I hope someone looks the same way at his sister. Then he will know.

Sushmita became visibly upset as she recounted these events. In fact, she was much more upset than I would have expected. After all, compared with the way women were sometimes molested on the streets and in buses, her experience at the Post Office seemed fairly mild. Thus, I couldn't help feeling that her sense of outrage was fueled, and reconstituted, by seeing Draupadi's disrobing. First, as mentioned above, it was during her discussion of this episode that she seemed to remember and relive her humiliation in the post office. Second, I was struck by the language she used when she described her anger at "that bad man": "*bahut shraap diya*" (I cursed him a lot). *Shraap* is not a word frequently used in everyday conversation. It has mythological connotations and refers to the curse of supernatural beings, learned persons (*rishis* or *sadhus*), or, occasionally, to the rage of a righteous woman who has been wronged. It was the word Draupadi used when she began to put a curse on her in-laws.

When Sushmita described Draupadi's rage, her voice became shrill with emotion:

> After what happened with her, any girl would become that angry. The way she was insulted! In front of a court full of men! It is not an ordinary thing to tolerate that kind of insult. If any woman gets that angry, she can burn to ashes!
>
> PM: What do you mean she can burn to ashes?
>
> Sushmita: The anger and grief in her mind will turn her to ashes . . .
>
> PM: Draupadi also curses, doesn't she?
>
> Sushmita: Yes, in the *Ramayan* it's written that if a woman is righteous . . . her curse [*shruup*] is always effective, whether he [i.e., the man abusing her] is big or small.
>
> PM: So you think she exhibited her power [*shakti*] well?
>
> Sushmita: Yes, she showed that a woman has power too [*aurat ki bhi shakti hoti hai*] . . . we have Mother Kali [Kali *Mata*]. We see that even a mother won't tolerate sin. She too will kill the culprit.
>
> PM: So do you think Draupadi and Mother Kali are similar? What difference did you see between them?
>
> Sushmita: Draupadi was a woman. She wasn't a goddess. That is why she needed her husbands' help. Mother Kali is a goddess, she can come in any form. That day when I was insulted at the post office, I too needed someone to help me. I was so angry, so hurt. But one man did come to my aid. But still I couldn't eat lunch that day, I couldn't sleep that night. I thought, women are so weak.

"I thought, women are so weak." Time and again I heard these words from women as they discussed Draupadi's disrobing; her plight made them relive their own humiliation at the hands of men. But many also felt that the rage of a woman who has been wronged can be all-consuming. As Sushmita put it, it has the power to burn her to ashes, but the curses she heaps on her perpetrators will always be effective. Yet, although "a woman has power too," she is *not* as powerful as a goddess: Draupadi needed Lord Krishna to come to her aid; Sushmita needed an older man to help her out in the post office. Sushmita eloquently pointed to the difference between goddesses and lesser mortals, between idealizations of "Woman's power" in Hindu revivalism and the vulnerability of women like her. A goddess can, in her wrath, destroy the world. But women must keep their rage on a leash. Hence, even though in Hindu mythology women's anger has a legitimate place in restoring moral order, the rage of ordinary women, however righteous, must be contained. It cannot be permitted to overflow and threaten the family—or, as we will see shortly, the nation.

Discourses about women's rage surfaced most vividly when Draupadi was compared with one of the ideals of Hindu Womanhood, Sita of the *Ramayan*. Like Draupadi, Sita was the subject of endless discussion—in kitchens, living rooms, offices, even academic circles—throughout India. And although the fiery Draupadi was a lot more controversial than Sita, whose devotion to her husband made her a paragon of tolerance and patience, many viewers were undecided as to which of the two better represented contemporary Indian Womanhood.

Draupadi was not considered a role model for Hindu women in the same way that Sita was. In fact, all the viewers I spoke with *contrasted* Draupadi with Sita. As Sushmita pointed out, "Draupadi did not hesitate to take revenge"; unlike Sita, she "didn't bow her head." Some viewers felt that Draupadi was "too modern" or "too Westernized." For instance, Sushmita felt that Draupadi was like a "modern *naari*" (woman) because "she did not hesitate to take revenge," she "didn't bow her head" (*sir nahi jhukaya*). She "confronted things" (*aage se vaar kiya*). "She didn't tolerate what happened." However, although Draupadi iconicized the traits she associated with contemporary Indian Womanhood, Sushmita wondered if Sita made a better role model. She admired Sita's humility (as opposed to Draupadi's fire) and Sita's respect for her elders (unlike Draupadi, who did not flinch at challenging her in-laws, thus transgressing her role as a daughter-in-law).

Hence, most of these women were also ambivalent about the power of women's rage. But if Sita represented an *ideal* model of Hindu Womanhood, Draupadi was iconic of the brute *reality* of contemporary Indian Womanhood. Sushmita felt that while Sita's patience and tolerance were laudable virtues, women continued to be victims of injustice. She expressed her skepticism toward idealizations of Sita's tolerance: "Everybody says that Sita is an ideal woman. [I feel that] sometimes if you tolerate too much people try to take advantage of you. But my mother says that with tolerance a solution will always emerge. *For us, we can't tell what path we should take. Should we tolerate or not?* My mother says, 'We also went to our in-laws' home, I also tolerated your father's ways'" (emphasis added).

Sushmita seemed genuinely confused as to how far she could rebel against the injustice meted out to her by her family. Should she aspire to Sita's tolerance rather than Draupadi's rage? What was the appropriate conduct for her as a woman, as an Indian woman? Her mother insisted that tolerance, rather than anger, was a source of strength for women. But perhaps Sushmita's own life experience as a contemporary woman led her to feel that far from empowering women, tolerance made them weak because "people" could then "take advantage" of them. More important, implicit in her dilemma was a skepticism toward the valorization of Hindu Womanhood exemplified in the idealization of Sita and emphasized in the discourses of Hindu revivalists.

Despite their ambivalence toward the different models of womanhood represented by Sita and Draupadi, however, several women seemed to believe that tolerance (*sahansheelta*) was fundamental to Hindu *and* Indian Womanhood. My discussions with Poonam and her mother, Shakuntala Sharma, were helpful in tracing the place that women's interpretations of Draupadi may have occupied in the construction of their own subjectivities. Poonam was artistic and sensitive; she often expressed her thoughts in a journal. She wanted to be a poet but knew that she would soon have to get a job to support herself because her father was due to retire. This alone, she felt, would give her security. Reserved in public, Poonam was outspoken at home and often contradicted her mother. Shakuntala Sharma was soft-spoken and extremely dignified. As noted in chapter 3, she believed that women need to be stronger than men because they have to manage the household, and that the women back in her village in northern Uttar Pradesh were a lot more enterprising and courageous than the men. She felt that women's strength often lay in their silence and worried that Poonam was too blunt, too candid, to "adjust" in her in-laws' house.

When Poonam expressed her outrage at what happened to Draupadi, Shakuntala turned to me and said that she was terribly worried that Poonam was "too sharp tongued." Poonam's views on dowry terrified her even more: she frequently told her parents that she would refuse to marry anybody who asked for a dowry. And if her in-laws harassed her for a dowry after the wedding she would defy all social conventions and leave their home in anger. Shakuntala conceded that to give and take dowry was to participate in and endorse an evil that humiliated women. But if giving or taking dowry was bad, leaving the home of one's husband and in-laws in rage was worse. She said: "This is not something women in our family do; this is not something Indian women do." Most striking in her discourse is the elision from family to nation; indeed, the two become analogous, if not synonymous.

When I asked them whom they preferred, Draupadi or Sita, Shakuntala Sharma immediately said, "Sita." Poonam was undecided. She felt that although Draupadi had "modern thoughts [*naye vichar*]," they had not developed completely because she also had *"purane sanskar"* (here, traditional values; more generally, spiritual heritage). She felt that Draupadi represented an ideal type of modern Indian Womanhood; that is, she was a contemporary *Bharatiya naari*. And what made her so typically "Indian" in Poonam's eyes? The fact that, despite the humiliation caused by her husbands' passivity, she accompanied them when they went into exile. Today's woman, Poonam added, has been influenced by the West (*paschatya ka asar*); yet she remains Indian because of her "training"; she is raised to fit into a certain "mold." Shakuntala added that although it is less true than in the past, Indian women "still" have forbearance.

DRAUPADI AS A SYMBOL OF HINDU/INDIAN WOMANHOOD

At the "barest level of the plot" (to the extent that one can ever posit this level), Draupadi is the queen of Indraprastha and wife of the Pandavas, and a woman who has been gambled away by her husband Yudhishtra in a game of dice. However, when she questions the right of a man to stake his wife, she claims to speak for all women. There is yet another level at which her image assumes tremendous potency: the larger discursive context of nationalism in which the *Mahabharat* and many other programs were presented on Doordarshan. Indeed, the opening and closing images of every episode, which presented the title in different Indian languages, suggested that this epic was meant not just for Hindi-speaking or Hindu audiences but was "pan-Indian." Every episode ended with a song that may be transliterated thus:

This story of Bharat
Is an ancient one
This is the Ganga of knowledge,
The immortal words of the sages
This is a story at once old and new
This is the story of Bharat.

The first and the last lines of the song are particularly interesting in this regard. "Bharat" refers to the lineage of the Pandavas and the Kauravas, but it is also a popular (Hindu) name for India. Thus, at the same time that the *Mahabharat* advertised itself as a tale of a lineage called Bharat, it also proclaimed itself the story of the Indian nation.

In addition, Draupadi repeatedly reminded the audience that she symbolized "the woman of this country," the woman "of the present and the future." In this manner, television's rendition of the story of Draupadi became a narrative not just of Hindu womanhood, but of *Indian* Womanhood. The producers of the serial and its viewers perceived Draupadi as a more faithful representation of contemporary Indian Womanhood than Sita. According to the actress who played Draupadi: "Draupadi does not believe in suffering silently. Like a modern Indian woman, she reacts angrily."[26] Yet, as pointed out by Poonam, Draupadi, for all her rage against her husbands, follows them to the forest when they go into exile: it is clear that her place is with them. Her rage (and that of the contemporary Indian Woman) is valid only as long as it is contained within master narratives of family and nation.

The notions of Indian Womanhood posited in this book have been neither homogeneous nor monolithic: the foregoing analyses reveal how notions of appropriate behavior for women have been circumscribed by a cultural nationalism shaped, in turn, by Hindu revivalism. As in other Doordarshan discourses in which the experiences of Hindu women were constructed as normative or "typical," the reconstitution of Draupadi as a symbol of Indian Womanhood revealed a slippage between Hindu and Indian nationalism. This Hindu/Indian nationalist interpretation of the disrobing was clearly the "preferred" reading (Hall 1977), the point at which the interpretations of both the creators of this episode and those of Hindu viewers overlapped.

Further, viewers' interpretations of Draupadi reveal the power of nationalist ideologies as they percolate through popular culture into the everyday lives of ordinary women. The women described here encountered discourses of Hindu/Indian Womanhood not as an abstract construct but as a material reality that inflected everyday practice: as girls growing into womanhood, when they negotiated and participated in discourses on the family, the community, and the nation; in notions of appropriate behavior for women; most commonly, in popular texts such as the cinema and in literature of different genres; and now, in television serials. If we are to understand why these nationalist readings acquired such potency for the women described here, why certain readings more than others seemed the most "natural," the most "commonsensical" (Hall 1977), it is essential that we undertake a genealogical analysis of the production of Draupadi as a symbol of Indian Womanhood in the recent past. For like other discursive practices, semiotic processes are not synchronic: signs have lives, trajectories, and genealogies as well.

The Co-implication of Gender and Nationhood

The foregoing analysis of the interpretations of the *Mahabharat*'s creators and viewers reveals some of the gendered subject positions created by the discursive practices of nationalism. As noted in previous chapters, no singular model of Indian Womanhood has ever existed—either at different moments of the nationalist struggle or at any other moment. As I argued above, unlike other symbols of Indian Womanhood (such as Sita, who is invoked for her loyalty to her husband and his clan), the mythic figure of Draupadi is polysemic. Nor is the invocation of oppressed womanhood to symbolize the nation new to Indian nationalism. Studies of debates on sati and widow remarriage describe some of the contexts in which nationalist thought emerged and took shape. At the hands of colonialists and nationalists, the status of women in India came to symbolize the status of "Indian culture." Emblematic of tradition, women became the "ground" for discourses on sati (Mani 1989), on what constituted "authentic tradition," and on how "civilized" India was (Chakravarti 1989). The attribution of a superior morality to colonial masters, and an inferior morality to their subjects, was discussed primarily in terms of the condition of Indian women; for most male nationalists, "the nation's identity lay in the culture and more specifically in its womanhood . . . the image of womanhood was more important than the reality . . . but the image also came to be perceived as *the* reality" (Chakravarti 1989:78; emphasis added). Although these constructs were neither static, homogeneous, nor universal with regard to class and region, they constituted a material force that individual women had to contend with in their daily lives.[27]

It is significant that neither the preindependence nationalist representation of Draupadi nor the 1990 television version depicted her as passive or defeated. Draupadi's rage was first invoked by early nationalists as a call to action to Indian *men*. It is not surprising that the mythic figure of Draupadi fired the imagination of many nationalist poets. For instance, the nationalist Tamil litterateur Subramania Bharati wrote a poem on Draupadi entitled "Panchali's Vow" in which he compared her disrobing to colonial domination and chided Indian men for not avenging the insult to their country. Similarly, although it is not explicitly about Draupadi, Bankim Chandra's famous epic *Anandmath* derives its rhetorical force from the image of the nation as a humiliated mother who must be avenged.[28] Later, Gandhi and his contemporaries focused on Draupadi's agency to encourage Hindu *women* to participate in the freedom struggle.[29] Thus, it was Draupadi's anger (and it is vital that we remember that her anger is directed at the helplessness of her men) and her desire for revenge that attracted nationalists who appropriated this facet of her image to symbolize first the subjugated nation and, in the postcolonial conjuncture, the fledgling nation-state.

Although Draupadi's image acquires most potency when she assumes the positions of angry victim and vengeful heroine, her appeals to her elders to save her and her incitement to her husbands to avenge her resonate with the most common subject positions created for women by nationalist ideology: victims to be protected (as in discussions of satis and child widows in preindependence nationalist discourse, or as objects of development in postcolonial nationalism), and heroines to be glorified (as in representations of figures like Rani Lakshmibai or, in the words of Chopra et al., as mother earth and fire). These examples illustrate some of the ways in which nationalism has been consolidated as a gendered and engendering discourse. For, as the discourses of those involved in the production of the *Mahabharat* show us, women continue to be markers of tradition and nationhood: Draupadi indexes not only the degree of civilization of her society but also the place of Woman in contemporary culture. At the same time, despite considering Woman the "focal point of evolution," regardless of her power, the show's creators concurred with viewers that women continue to be vulnerable in Indian society. As the discourses of those involved in the production of the *Mahabharat* show us, at the same time that women continue to be markers of tradition and nationhood, there is also an attempt to invoke, in however essentialist a fashion, their agency and power.

As the focus of nationalism has changed from national liberation to the consolidation of the postcolonial nation-state, the uneasy relationship between discourses of womanhood and nationalism has left an enduring legacy. Some of the parallels between Doordarshan's portrayal of Draupadi's disrobing and representations of women's oppression in postcolonial nationalist discourse are inescapable. In television's narration, the real forces in combat are revealed in the camera's jerky movements between Draupadi's body and the faces of the men surrounding her. Similarly, public debates on the plight of oppressed women (the cases of Mathura, Roop Kanwar, Shahbano, and, more recently, Ameena come immediately to mind)[30] have become sites not for an inquiry into the structural conditions that make women vulnerable, but for discussions on civil society, "tradition," and nationhood.

By conflating their construct of Woman with individual women, narratives of Indian Womanhood like the one contained in Draupadi's disrobing deny women a complex subjectivity. As noted above, the conjuncture in which the *Mahabharat* was produced and received was marked by the "hijacking" of mainstream Indian nationalism by Hindu nationalism: this was a historical moment when the very notion of the nation had become contentious. It is thus especially critical that we focus on the slippage between Hindu Womanhood and Indian Womanhood at a time when exclusionary nationalist ideologies were being consolidated. As we have seen, these constructions had profound consequences for the lives of ordinary women—a testimony to the materiality of a discursive practice that engenders national subjects even as it constitutes them.

CRITICAL NEGOTIATIONS

We have seen that the producers of the *Mahabharat* as well as its viewers felt, to varying degrees, that Woman's power needs to be contained within the parameters of nation and family: the director and his colleagues viewed the family as sacrosanct because it was the cornerstone of the nation; for viewers like Shakuntala Sharma, who rebuked her daughter for being outspoken, master narratives of family and nation slid into one another ("This is not something women in my family do; this is not something Indian women do"). But if the overlaps in the interpretations analyzed above are significant, equally telling are the points at which they diverge. Thus, while Draupadi symbolized Hindu/Indian Womanhood for both the presenters of the disrobing and its viewers, it is equally evident that there were points of rupture, moments that forestalled ideological closure.

What do the foregoing interpretations of Draupadi's disrobing tell us about the relationship between contexts, texts, and lives? Many analyses of televisual texts fall into one of the following traps: they are either purely textual, with little interest in the manner in which audiences actively interpret what they watch, or, at the other extreme, they focus on individual responses and ignore the wider societal discourses that mediate viewers' interpretations. One way to avoid these positions is to ethnographically investigate the ways that communicative codes and their interpretations are mediated by broader ideological practices. Viewers' responses to spectacles like Draupadi's disrobing are refracted by the discursive contexts in which they live. Thus, although televisual signs, like many other signs, are polysemous, this polysemy cannot be equated with pluralism: the connotations of these signs are not "equal" among themselves but are mediated by hegemonic discourses. And audiences are not always in a position to choose the meanings they attribute to what they watch. Instead, preferred readings emerge from specific discursive frameworks.

According to Stuart Hall (1980), when viewers interpret a text in terms of the reference code in which it has been encoded, they operate from the "dominant position." *At first glance,* the viewers I described above seem to occupy this position when they interpret Draupadi as a symbol of Hindu/Indian Womanhood and when, like the creators of the disrobing episode, they seem to accept hegemonic discourses regarding the containment of women's energies.

However, it is very clear that this apparent convergence of interpretations in no way entails closure. Rather, these viewers seem to occupy what Hall labels the "negotiated position"—a stance that enables viewers to accept hegemonic discourses, in this case nationalism, while simultaneously formulating their own "ground rules."[31] This position accepts some dominant definitions while making a "more negotiated application to 'local conditions.'" Negotiated readings of dominant ideology are therefore "shot through" with contradictions (Hall 1980:338). Even though viewers seem to accept the hegemonic discourses pertaining to the containment of women's energies, they appropriate Draupadi's disrobing, the moment when she is at her most vulnerable, to reflect on and critique their own positions in family, community, and nation.

While mass media, by repetition and selection, can reinforce dominant, "commonsense" notions of self and identity, these representations do not affect us as if we are "blank screens"; instead "they occupy and rework the interior contradictions of feeling and perception . . . find or clear a space of recognition in those who respond to them" (Hall 1981:232). Thus, concepts such as "compliance" and "resistance" are, in and of themselves, inadequate to understand the processes by which viewers engage with television texts. "Compliance" neglects the place of interpretation on the part of heterogeneous viewers who, variably located in specific sociocultural contexts, actively interact with television texts. Similarly, as an analytical construct "resistance" is too totalizing to capture the ephemeral yet profound nature of the interactions between texts and viewers: it fails to concede the multiplicity of subject positions offered by texts and negotiated by viewers. Hence, it seems more fruitful to conceptualize the points of rupture in viewers' engagement with dominant discourses in terms of active negotiation. The moments of epiphany underlying Sushmita's tears, Poonam's outrage, and Uma's fears at watching Draupadi's disrobing suggest that compliance and resistance coexist, often sliding into one another imperceptibly. In this manner, processes of intimate engagement with the texts of television open spaces and opportunities for women to understand as well as critique their own lives and destinies.

I have attempted to show that, by focusing on women's active negotiation of dominant ideologies and foregrounding the slippages and ruptures within hegemonic discourses, feminist analyses of mass media can create spaces for political critique. Raymond Williams explains that hegemony is a "complex of experiences, relationships, and activities, with specific and changing pressures and limits," that does not "passively exist as a form of dominance. It has continually to be renewed, recreated, defended, and modified" (1977:112). Put another way, the task(s) of hegemony is never completed. The divergent interpretations I described above exemplify the overlaps and disjunctures between the formulation of hegemonic ideologies and their appropriation by viewers in positions of subalternity (see, for example, Amin's analysis of the appropriation of Gandhi's discourses by peasants in Gorakhpur [1989] and Bhabha's discussion of the rupture between the "pedagogic" and "performative" aspects of nationalist ideology [1990]). Instead of assuming that viewers unproblematically accept the subject positions created by dominant ideologies such as those of Hindu/Indian nationalism, I have tried to highlight some of the fissures intrinsic to hegemonic discourses.[32] This is especially crucial if we are to create a space for the construction of feminist and secularist praxis. Given the Indian nation-state's attempts to use Doordarshan to construct a hegemonic, pan-Indian "national culture" and the ascendancy of Hindu nationalism, this conceptualization of viewers as active subjects has significant theoretical and political implications.

As described above, the creators of this episode saw Draupadi as an index of the status of women not just in "Kaurava civilization" but in contemporary Indian society as well: as a marker of Indian culture, Draupadi represents nothing less than Indian Womanhood itself, an ideal-typical construct based on essentialist and ahistorical understandings of gender relations. In contrast, the women viewers I spoke with profoundly identified with Draupadi. The disrobing scene made them relive personal humiliations in their families, in their offices, in the public spaces of New Delhi. It powerfully brought home to them their vulnerability as women. Even as they acknowledged the power of her rage, Draupadi was, above all, an icon of their "weakness" as women. In these moments of epiphany, Draupadi's disrobing enabled women viewers to reflect on, and sometimes critique, their own positions in their family, class, and community. Thus, while Uma and Jayanthi Chandran felt that women's vulnerability stems largely from their sexuality—the biological, essential "difference" between men and women—Sushmita Dasgupta was acutely aware of her position as a lower-middle-class woman in an acquisitive, consumerist society. Fear of prospective in-laws and anxieties surrounding issues of dowry also surfaced in Poonam's and Shakuntala's responses to Draupadi's disrobing. Even when they were uncertain about the extent to which they could express their anger, Draupadi's rage encouraged women like Uma, Jayanthi, Sushmita, and Poonam to confront what they saw as the injustices perpetrated on women like themselves.

Nationalism attempts to create unified subject positions (cf. Visweswaran 1990). But the semiotic excess surrounding the figure of Draupadi as she was disrobed in front of her family, the range of emotions and memories sparked by her predicament, enabled the Hindu viewers I describe here to confront and theorize their own vulnerabilities as women. I want to close by recalling Uma's horror that sexual violence toward women is not a "modern" phenomenon but was inflicted on women even in what Hindu revivalists have called "the glorious Hindu past." Similarly, let us remember Sushmita's eloquent description of the difference between idealizations of womanhood in orthodox Hindu ideology and what she called the "reality of women's lives." I write at a time when the violence of the Indian state and rising Hindu chauvinism leave me very few spaces either for critique or for constructive intervention. Hence, Uma's and Sushmita's words are heartening. Not only do they rupture nationalist master narratives, they also counter nostalgic, right-wing Hindu invocations of "ancient Hindu civilization" as an egalitarian era when women not only had equal rights but were revered for their power. It is these counternarratives, these moments of slippage and rupture, that secular feminists need to strategically seize on and consolidate if we are ever to construct a counterhegemonic praxis.

Part III *Technologies of Violence*

Chapter 6 *"Air Force Women Don't Cry":*

Militaristic Nationalism and Representations of Gender

■ *Major Shaitaan Singh takes his wife and child to see a play. Based on a popular Rajput tale of heroism and war, the play is about a young prince of Mewar and his bride, Haarhi Rani.[1] Along with Major Singh and his wife, we the audience see the prince and his bride celebrate their love during their wedding night (suhaag raat). The next morning the prince is informed that his kingdom has been attacked. But he is so besotted by his bride that he is unable to tear himself away from her. She, on the other hand, is very concerned that their passion is causing him to neglect his duty to the motherland. She realizes that it is now up to her to make him understand that his place is on the battlefront defending his kingdom, and not with her. She attempts to coax him into going by promising him a parting gift that he will value all his life. He is waiting outside their room for her gift when a woman servant brings him a covered tray. He lifts the cover to see his bride's severed head on the tray. This is her gift to him and to their motherland: she has had herself beheaded, has dismembered the body that has tempted her husband to neglect his duty to his kingdom. The play ends with a song that tells us that the prince is so inspired by her sacrifice that he goes into battle and valiantly defends his kingdom.*

After they return home, Major Shaitaan Singh tells his wife that India has been attacked and that he has to join his regiment immediately. His wife remembers the play she has just seen. She realizes that her husband had taken her to see it so she too could be inspired by the princess's heroism. She realizes that her patriotic duty lies in her ability to let go of him and encourage him to defend the motherland. The next morning she adorns herself in her wedding clothes and valiantly bids him farewell as he leaves for the front.

This episode of *Param Veer Chakra*, a series shown on Doordarshan from July to October 1990, vividly dramatized the central problematic of the melodrama series: the construction of nationalist zeal and the depiction and naturalization of female sexuality as a threat to masculine valor.

Param Veer Chakra (*PVC*) exemplified how, in popular narrative, violence on behalf of the nation—the willingness to kill and to die—is coded as militaristic nationalism. Theorists of popular narrative have pointed out that melodramas perform a myth-making function because their characters exist as metaphors for certain existential states rather than as "autonomous individuals" (Thornburn 1976, in Ang 1985:64). In *PVC*, male soldiers personified militaristic nationalism, wives and (heterosexual) lovers embodied the lure of female sexuality, and the heroes' mothers iconicized nothing less than the nation itself. Like most melodrama, *PVC* spoke the language of heightened emotions; its myth-making functions hence rested on its ability to construct the affective bases of militaristic nationalism. I am interested in the relationship between militaristic nationalism and representations of Indian Womanhood. Most important, I am concerned with the role of discourses of gender and sexuality in the normalization (Foucault 1979) of violence in the name of the nation.

PARAM VEER CHAKRA: "REAL LIFE STORIES OF REAL HEROES"

I will frame my analysis of interpretations of *PVC* by presenting a conversation I had with one of its most loyal fans. Gurdeep Kaur, a lower-caste Sikh woman, loved *PVC* and hated to miss it. When I asked her why she liked the program so much, she replied that she appreciated the fact that the memory of the nation's martyrs was being kept alive. She was particularly moved that "after they are married suddenly they are called [to the front]. It's a 'must.' . . . This happens in every program. It's a 'must.' The army's discipline cannot be ignored. They have to fight for the country. They show that. . . . They just keep fighting, keep fighting. Then they become immortal [*amar ho jate hain*] and are given *PVC*. That's how it is. This is how it happened in real life too, isn't it? It's good they show this." Gurdeep Kaur was not the only Sikh woman I interviewed who enjoyed watching *PVC* and was moved by its tales. But her response perplexed me because I had been assuming that it was the drama inherent in the narrative (the tragic story of a husband and wife who are separated soon after they get married), rather than its depiction of nationalist zeal, that compelled her to intimately engage with its texts. After all, the army had been used to suppress dissent in Punjab, and its excesses against the (primarily Sikh) local population were well known. In fact, Gurdeep Kaur had, on several occasions, told me of relatives in Punjab who felt trapped between the brutality of the militant separatists who terrorized the local population and the violence of state agencies such as the police and the army.

I continue to be perplexed by her response and present it here to emphasize that the enunciations of people marginalized by dominant discourses are often opaque to glib interpretation.[2] I find it difficult to "explain" Gurdeep's words as an example of "false consciousness" or as the "internalization" of hegemonic nationalism. At first glance, there seems to be little to distinguish the responses of the Sikh women I interviewed from those of Hindu viewers. But might her words have illustrated the distance that she felt compelled to put between herself and her relatives in Punjab in order to survive, both emotionally and physically, in the nation's capital, in a predominantly Hindu city? Or might this response have been an expression of a loosely formulated desire for community rather than a specifically nationalist allegiance (Susan Jeffords, personal communication, July 1993)? Given that PVC's discourses aimed at constructing explicitly nationalist structures of feeling, I have interpreted Gurdeep Kaur's response to the series in terms of her feelings of *entrapment* between her subject position as an engaged viewer of PVC and her position as a Sikh at a historical moment when Sikh identity was being constructed at the margins of (and, frequently, in opposition to) Indian nationalist identity. Hence, rather than infer that her loyalty to PVC was indicative of her allegiance to the Indian nation, I have tried to indicate the contradictory subject positions occupied by Sikh women vis-à-vis Doordarshan's narratives of militaristic nationalism.

Once again, it is essential that I foreground my own location as a middle-class woman from the majority community, and the politics of ethnicity and nation that undoubtedly refracted the words of a poor, Sikh woman to me. As a woman from a minority community that had been terrorized by Hindu mobs a few short years ago, was Gurdeep Kaur telling me what she thought a Hindu woman might want to hear? If so, what was I to make of my observation that she seemed so absorbed while watching PVC? Does my desire to "interpret" her words represent a will to smooth the apparent disjuncture between her positions as a fan of a nationalistic series valorizing the army and as a Sikh woman whose family had been subjected to military repression?

It seems fitting that I begin my analysis of the meanings of PVC with her response, and that the opacity of her words frames the interpretations that follow. I use her words to underscore both the fragility of my ethnographic authority and the fact that viewers' responses to narratives such as *PVC* were deeply embedded in their different, often contradictory, locations in the very "national community" that the state was attempting to create.

Although referred to as a serial by its fans and critics, *PVC* was an episodic series consisting of narratives about Indian army and air force soldiers who had been awarded the Param Veer Chakra, the highest military decoration for service in combat. Twelve of the thirteen recipients depicted in this series received the award posthumously. The opening shots of all the episodes were identical: as the titles rolled by, viewers saw scenes from the annual Republic Day parade, during which the nation's military might is exhibited. The title scenes ended with a shot of Amar Jawaan Jyoti, the site of the eternal flame commemorating the unknown soldier, in the center of New Delhi. The specific story of the hero that followed was synecdochic of the martrydom of hundreds of unknown soldiers who had died for the nation. *PVC* took viewers through the lives of each of these soldiers with the aid of a plot structure that was always the same: scenes from their youth and family life, their induction into the military, and, finally, a few scenes of combat to explain why these heroes deserved the Param Veer Chakra.

PVC was different from other episodic series in that its narratives did not revolve around the life of a single protagonist: the heroes of all its episodes personified, and allegorized, militaristic nationalism. Unlike soap operas based on melodrama, in which suspense revolves around psychological conflicts, the content and the trajectories of the emotional conflicts dramatized in *PVC* were predictable: heroes were torn between their love for their family and love for the nation; sexual passion was pitted against passion for the nation; and in all cases nationalist affect prevailed over the pull of other emotions. Despite its predictability and dependence on formula, many viewers I worked with claimed that *PVC* was their current favorite: indeed, their pleasure in the series derived precisely from watching the story unfold through twists and turns that were familiar to them.

PVC was shown on Sunday mornings, from 9:00 to 10:00 A.M., for a period of thirteen weeks. The Sunday morning slot was prized by advertisers and producers because it was a favorite (and convenient) time for most families to watch television: men and children would be home, breakfast would have been eaten, and some (but by no means all) women would be lucky enough to have a couple of hours of leisure before start-ing to prepare the midday meal. This time slot hence promised a large audience. Moreover, because *PVC* followed immediately on the heels of and occupied the same time slot as the *Mahabharat,* it benefited from the popularity of its predecessor and tapped into its "captive audience." This, along with its nationalist story line, brought the serial high ratings in the metropolitan centers of Bombay, Bangalore, Calcutta, and Delhi.[3]

As can be expected, the narratives of *PVC,* like those of many other war narratives, focused on the heroism of its male protagonists. Yet discourses of gender were essential to its representation of militaristic nationalism—perhaps because, as Susan Jeffords points out in her study of Vietnam War representations, war is a "construction of gendered inter-ests" (1989:xi). But while the locus of action in many war films (particu-larly those made in the West) is the male protagonist, and women exist on the margins of narrative spaces, either to titillate (heterosexual) male viewers or as justifications for fighting, this was not the case with *PVC.* Not only were women characters extremely visible in that they occu-pied more than half the discursive space, but a good part of the enigma revolved around the feelings, decisions, and actions of women.[4] The nar-rative tone of *PVC* was set by melodrama rather than the "action" of war; indeed, its action, or its narrative movement, ensued less from the com-bat scenes than from the emotional drama that preceded them.

PVC was produced and directed by Chetan Anand, a Hindi film di-rector who has dedicated his career to what he described to me as his two main interests: "love and war."[5] Anand seemed to be motivated by nationalist and practical impulses in equal measure. He claimed that the emotional and political climate in India was conducive to a film on war heroes: with secessionist movements in the Punjab and Kashmir threat-ening to tear the nation asunder, and with acute political instability in the government (the government had changed three times in the past twelve months), "the country was ripe for something like this." He added that his aim was to show that "in the present context when India is going through such a period of political uncertainty and turbulence, there are national forces beyond party politics." If audiences seemed ready to hear tales of nationalism, he expected that the government would be even more receptive, an important consideration in the extremely competitive world of TV entertainment. Besides, as described in chapter 2, the slump in the Hindi film industry and the successes of *Buniyaad, Mahabharat,* and *Ramayan* (all of which had been made by Hindi film producers) had encouraged many film people to turn to television as an outlet for their work. Anand said that when he saw how successful the *Mahabharat* was, he thought, "Why not do something on today's Mahabharats?" Anand was alluding to the unprecedented success of the *Mahabharat* but also to the fact that, in popular discourse, that epic is described as a narrative of the war between good and evil. In Anand's view, then, militaristic nationalism was coded in moral terms, with "good" signifying the passion that enables men to martyr themselves for the nation, and "evil" the forces that threaten the nation's integrity. It was in this discursive context that Anand wished to portray the winners of the Param Veer Chakra—"real life stories of real war heroes."

Like many other Doordarshan narratives, *PVC* trafficked in emotions; to misquote Stuart Hall (1981), emotions were the "site" and "stake" of its discourses. In its use of melodrama as a narrative technique, in the highly emotional content and tone of its dialogue, its focus on relationships within the family, and its use of music (which, to viewers schooled in the reception of Hindi film music, was coded to induce a mood of compassion and heroic grief), *PVC* attempted to produce and evoke the range of sentiments surrounding nationalistic zeal.[6] The series's plot structure repeated the same orchestration of affect in every episode: beginning with scenes depicting the youth and family life of the hero, the emotional tempo of the narrative rose as we saw him struggle to leave his family, undergo military training, battle the enemy on the front, and (in all cases except one) achieve martyrdom fighting for his country. Almost every episode ended with an identical scene: as the title music reached a crescendo, the mother (sometimes accompanied by the father) or the wife received the Param Veer Chakra on behalf of the martyred hero with dry-eyed, stoic dignity.

Indeed, the title music provided the aural cues. A song anthropomorphizing the nation and describing the heroic and tragic death of the soldier was sung at the beginning and repeated at the end of every episode:

May your grandeur never be diminished
My country, oh, my country.
May your dignity never decrease
My country, oh, my country.

We will sing songs of love to you
Even as we die.
May your light never be diminished
And so we give our blood for you.
The sky will bow to you
My country, oh, my country.

In the neighborhoods where I did my research, television sets were turned on every Sunday morning, as soon as the family awoke. For the most part, people went about their morning routines with the sound-track forming a background to their activities. But the title music of *PVC* functioned as a call to viewers to come and watch. Older members of the family, children, and men of all ages would stream in as soon as the open-ing notes of the song flowed through their home. Typically, many women would watch as they continued their household chores, but in their case as well, the signature tune would induce a heightened attention toward the sounds and images they would try to snatch as they went about their work. As with many signature tunes, the title music of *PVC* functioned both to remind viewers that the episode was about to begin and to emo-tionally prepare them for its narratives. As far as I could tell, on hearing the title song at the beginning of the episode, viewers would relive the pathos of the closing scenes of the previous episode and slip into a mood of tragic expectancy as they sat down to watch that morning's show.

When I mentioned to Anand how moved viewers were by the title music, he replied that the producers had been extremely conscious of its affective importance when they were making the series. They "worked hard on it" for three months "until they got it just right." They had to be careful to not let the tune get "too melodramatic" because that would "put people off." His aim was to "underplay the emotions, yet make the drama effective." That they were successful became clear to me when Sukumaran, who was otherwise critical of the "shoddy" manner in which *PVC* was produced, said: "No matter how they've shown it, to be very frank at the end I always have tears in my eyes. I feel . . . I *always* have tears in my eyes. In spite of it being so shoddy. But the point is that somebody has really sacrificed himself for our country."

OF MARTYRS AND MEN

Although the episodic and formulaic structure of *PVC*'s weekly narratives did not allow for an in-depth development of any of the characters, their plots portrayed men in an even less complex fashion than women. Despite the fact that men were depicted as torn between their love for their families and their love for the nation, the only subject position ultimately available to them was that of masculine nationalism. Men, more than women, were denied a complex subjectivity and emerged as "flat" characters: all we learned about them was that they were steadfast in their love for the nation. But it was the fact that they epitomized and embodied nationalism and discipline that made the series and its characters so appealing to viewers.

Many of the men I spoke with were very moved by the soldiers' discipline and sacrifice of their lives and their futures to defend the country. But if they were moved by the soldiers' emotional courage (*himmat*) in leaving their families and by their physical valor on the battlefront, they were equally impressed by their self-discipline, in particular their capacity to obey orders and fight despite debilitating pain and injury.

For instance, I was once watching a combat scene with Sarojini, Sukumaran, and their daughter, Lata. After being shot in the stomach the hero ordered his junior officer to move him behind a rock and put a gun in his hand so he could continue to fight the enemy. When the junior officer hesitated to leave him in such a condition, the hero reminded him that that was an order. When the junior officer eventually complied, Sarojini expressed her bewilderment at his obedience, "Oh, so he leaves him?! He's been shot in the stomach!" Her husband, Sukumaran, replied, "An order is an order. Of course he has to leave him." He shook his head from side to side as if to emphasize his point. "This is the discipline of the army," he continued, still shaking his head. He seemed very moved, very impressed by the hero's valor and, more important, by his self-discipline.

Some of this admiration for discipline needs to be interpreted in the light of middle-class discourses about the alleged lack of discipline of the "Indian masses."[7] Discipline was associated with order, which all middle-class and lower-middle-class Indians I spoke with deemed essential for the nation to modernize and progress. Further, many people I spoke with were extremely anxious about what they perceived as the political and social chaos around them. Thus, viewers' admiration for the order and discipline portrayed in *PVC* emerged from and was compounded by their profound disenchantment with contemporary political culture (as one viewer put it, the army is "not like our government, which gives holidays whenever people ask").

Unlike many other masculinist narratives of militaristic nationalism (Jeffords 1989), in *PVC* masculinity and femininity were not "consistently opposed." Nor was femininity associated with emotions and masculinity with action; thus, "emotional" women were not posed against "unemotional" men. In fact, even though women provided the "emotional thread" that gave the stories coherence (see below), the affective force of *PVC*'s narratives derived not just from the military battles fought by men but from their internal conflicts as they struggled between love for family and love for the nation. Thus men, as much as women, were driven by emotions: their decision to fight for their country stemmed from their devotion to the motherland rather than from a "professional" obligation to join their regiments. Conversely, because the battleground was an emotional terrain as well as a military one, women, as much as men, were the locus of *PVC*'s action: women's decisions, however overdetermined, to "let go" of their men *enabled* men to fight valiantly. Men were not the only agents of militaristic nationalism, and therefore of the violence committed in the name of the nation; by endorsing and encouraging "their men" to go into battle, women also participated in the defense of the nation. Hence, devotion to the nation was not the exclusive preserve of males: as we will soon see, the stoic, desexualized mother and the wife/lover whose sexuality was contained were also capable of heroic nationalism. It was active (female) sexuality, rather than femininity per se, that was presented as a threat to militaristic nationalism.

MILITARISTIC NATIONALISM AND WOMEN

I was so struck by the centrality of women to the narratives of *PVC* that my first question to Anand related to the kind of roles he had envisioned for women. What were his reasons for giving women so much space in what could have been tales exclusively about the heroism of men? Anand replied that women provided the "emotional thread" that held the stories together. Unlike "Western" audiences of war narratives, he said, audiences in India need an "emotional thread," and this was provided by giving the personal background of soldiers and including "their" women and families.[8] Further, even though he depicted men's emotional lives and struggles in considerable detail, his experience as a filmmaker had taught him that women provided the emotional energy so necessary for gripping the attention of Indian audiences.

Thus, even though men were spurred to martyrdom by their nationalist passion, it was women who provided emotional energy to the narratives of *PVC*. Further, while underscoring the intimate relationship between discourses of gender and nationhood, *PVC*'s tales revealed polarizations *within* discourses of Indian Womanhood: between sexual women and those whose sexuality was erased; between "cowardly" women and those who had the courage to surrender their men for the defense of the nation; and between women who "clung to their men's feet" and those who actively inspired and enabled men to fight for the nation. These conceptions of womanhood were interwoven. Rather than try to unravel each strand, I will discuss their *co*-implication in *PVC*'s portrayals of sexually active women and those whose sexuality was contained, of the tension between family and nation, and of the spaces occupied by the mother/motherland in the construction of militaristic nationalism.

The Sexual Woman

PVC normalized heterosexual passion through its depictions of conjugality and its enshrinement of motherhood. Andrew Parker et al. (1992) point to the importance of the bonds of homosociality, and an attendant policing of homoeroticism, as the basis of national identity. *PVC*'s narratives similarly illustrated the policing of desire in the interest of the nation. These disciplinary mechanisms were manifest in the normalization of the heterosexual family and the exclusion of nonreproductive sexuality.[9] As noted above, *PVC*'s discourses did not revolve around a purported opposition between masculinity and femininity; instead, a dichotomy existed between sexual women such as wives or lovers and those whose sexuality was contained, such as mothers.[10] Even as *PVC* naturalized and reestablished sexual passion in terms of normative heterosexuality, wives and lovers were depicted as potentially dangerous: their cowardly clinging and, more important, their active sexuality would tempt men to neglect their nationalist duties.[11]

Part of viewers' pleasures in the text arose from the depiction of the discipline of military life, a sharp contrast with what they saw as the chaos around them. However, *PVC* also suggested that order and discipline are fragile: both men and women need to struggle to guard it. More significant, a closer scrutiny of the discourses of *PVC* and those of its viewers reveals that in order to maintain "discipline"—that imposed by the army or, by extension, the patriarchal state—female sexuality has to be contained. Love for the nation is predicated on disciplining other attachments: hence, women must contain their sexuality, and men must fight their passions for women in order to defend their country. As Haarhi Rani, the Rajput princess described at the beginning of this chapter, realized, the attractions of women's bodies prevent men from leaving them to fight for the country. Only by beheading herself was she able to demonstrate to her husband, the prince of Mewar, his duty (*dharma*) as a Rajput.

Through the soldier's eventual rejection of female sexuality, male sexuality is policed and contained as well. But it is women's sexuality that constitutes the greater threat to militaristic nationalism, and more specifically, to men's love for the nation. In this sense, the sexuality of women is active, and the sexuality of men is reactive. Let me illustrate with a couple of examples from the series. The hero of one episode, Jadunath Singh, vows to become celibate so as to devote himself to his guru and, later, the nation.[12] The greatest threat to his vows is a village girl who, dressed in the skimpy attire typical of the "village belles" of Hindi film, is in hot pursuit of him. In a crucial scene, Jadunath Singh is shown bathing in a river. Standing bare-chested in the waist-deep water, he is praying to the god Hanuman, venerated for his physical prowess and celibacy, when he is confronted by none other than his seductive temptress. As the camera follows his gaze to linger on her wet body, it becomes increasingly clear that he is attracted to her. But suddenly he breaks away from his voyeuristic reverie and sees, with a shock, the temptations embodied in this woman. He leaps out of the water, runs to the Hanuman temple nearby, and prays for the strength to keep his vows. This encounter reinforces his commitment to celibacy and he is now determined to channel his energies to the service and defense of the nation.

In another episode, a soldier is called to the front soon after his marriage. His wife weeps and begs him not to leave her. Despite his passionate love for her, he realizes that his love for the nation must come first. Eventually, it is she who "allows" him to go: only then can he resist the temptation to stay with her. After he has joined his regiment, he misses his wife and expresses his longing for her in a heartrending song describing his struggle between his passion for his wife and his duties to his country. As Uma Chandran commented, "He is caught between his wife and his country. He wants to go to war, but he loves his wife too."

I discussed this scene with several viewers. Some, like Poonam Sharma, felt that the emphasis on the soldier's "inner conflict" was irrelevant to the main story, which, she insisted, was about his steadfast love for the nation: "The theme is [why the soldier deserved the] Param Veer Chakra, so what's the point of showing all this romantic stuff? What was the need for them to expand it? . . . [T]hey're getting confused" (*bhatak rahe hain*). It was clear to me that Poonam thought that the creators of *PVC* were getting sidetracked by dwelling on the love between the soldier and his wife. Of course, Poonam, like many other viewers I discussed the episode with, was moved to tears by the end of the song; yet, as far as she was concerned, the main purpose of the story was to describe the protagonist's heroism. The "romantic stuff" was a diversion: just as it distracted the soldier from his duty to the nation, romance diverted viewers from attending to the "real point of the story."

For most viewers, however, the "romantic stuff" heightened the pathos of the soldier's tragic separation from his wife and his subsequent death in the battlefield. Several episodes show wedding night (*suhaag raat*) scenes, another technique borrowed from Hindi films, to accentuate the sexual attachment between soldiers and their wives. The *suhaag raat* ritual, as encoded in the lexicon of popular Hindi cinema, is as follows. In a typical *suhaag raat* scene, the soldier and his bride sit on a bed bedecked with flowers. The bridegroom lifts his bride's veil and she bashfully raises her eyes to meet his. The camera then swings to the lamp at their side as it flickers and glows: the flame symbolizes the passion between the bride and the groom. Long accustomed to the codes of Hindi films (and the rules of censors who frowned on any explicit depiction of sexuality), this was all that most viewers needed to know that the hero and heroine's passion had been consummated.

Even when soldiers were called to the front several years after their wedding night, the passion and romance of that night were recaptured either through flashbacks or, in one case, by a wife who re-created it by wearing her wedding clothes and decorating their bed with flowers. Many of the women I spoke with felt shy and uncomfortable watching these romantic scenes with the rest of their families. As Paramjeet

Kaur, a young bride who lived with her in-laws and undoubtedly watched television in their presence, said: "They shouldn't make it so romantic because children and old people sit together to watch." It was evident that she experienced even such covert representations of sexual passion as embarrassing and invasive: given that, in most extended families, public demonstrations of conjugal love were frowned on, it is not surprising that such depictions of intimacy made her extremely uncomfortable.[13]

But it was evident to me that such scenes moved viewers, heightening their sense of pathos at the anguish suffered by both the soldier and his wife when they sacrificed their passion for the love of the nation. When I discussed these scenes with Jayanthi Chandran this is what I learned:

> *PM:* I noticed a change—they have tried to make the last two episodes more romantic. Did you notice that?
>
> *Jayanthi:* Yes, the last one was a little too romantic.
>
> *PM:* They showed a *suhaag raat* [wedding night] scene in both.
>
> *Jayanthi:* But what I understood was that there is so much affection between them, despite so much affection. . . . The two hearts might be interlinked, but even then they have to be apart. . . . After so much affection, the next day, how difficult it must be to separate. Didn't you note that? . . . So that's why they make it so romantic. The husband-wife are so close, they become as close as two people can be, still the next day they have to be separated. After that if she becomes pregnant, he will not know. Everyone knows that he has left, he will become a martyr [*shaheed*] for his country.

While romance functioned to heighten the pathos of the soldier's martyrdom, the relationship between sexuality and nationalism was complicated. This became clearer in my discussions with Selapan and his wife, Padmini. The Selapans had a troubled relationship. He often distressed me by making rude comments about his wife in her presence. Yet, I knew that he spent days and nights nursing her when she was sick (which was quite often). She was usually silent when her husband held forth. But when she and I were alone together, she unhesitatingly contradicted and sometimes belittled him.

One day we watched an episode that depicted the life and heroism of Abdul Hamid, one of the recipients of the Param Veer Chakra. This episode contained a significant (although temporary) shift from other *PVC* narratives: the newly wed wife, instead of clinging to her husband and

Figure 21 Abdul Hamid resolves to rejoin his regiment

begging him to not leave her, encouraged her husband to join the army (fig. 21). However, later in the story when Hamid came home on leave, his wife, who had been longing for him in his absence, begged him to not rejoin his regiment. A war was now on and she was terrified of what might happen to him. Eventually, she submitted to his will and he left, torn between his passion for her and his love for the nation.

Soon after the episode ended, I asked Selapan what he thought of the way Hamid's wife persuaded her reluctant husband to go to the front the morning after their wedding night. He had been impressed by her courage. "But," he went on to say, "all Indian women are not like that. If all women were like that no one would be able to look disrespectfully at India" (*koi bhi aankh utha kar dekh nahi payega*). His response contains two interlinked discourses: on the one hand, in the sexual metaphor he used—that of a predatory male assaulting a woman with his sexually aggressive gaze—India is feminized and made the object of protectionist discourse; at the same time, he seemed to imply that if only women were more courageous and steadfast in their roles as nationalist wives and mothers, men would be better able to defend the honor of the country. It was women's responsibility to actively encourage their men to defend the nation: hence, women's agency was directed toward enabling men's passionate desire to fight for the nation.

How did these notions affect Selapan's behavior toward his wife? I found that he seemed to apply similarly exacting standards to her. In the same episode, the hero's mother had persuaded his father to get their son married by saying, "Put a ring through the bull's nose. That will prevent him from roaming around." I was deeply offended by this metaphor and said as much while the episode was still on. After it concluded, I asked both Selapan and Padmini (who was sitting quietly after serving us all tea) what they thought of it. Selapan replied that he agreed with Hamid's mother: "Women these days cling to their husband's feet and don't allow them to go anywhere. My wife even stops me from going by bus these days, let alone allow me to go into a war."[14] Implicit in this image of the woman clinging to the man's feet like a parasitical vine is the anxiety that the attachment between the two is what deters men from fulfilling their obligations to the nation. I silently turned to Padmini, willing her to reply. She didn't contradict her husband directly. Instead she pointed out that Hamid's wife, despite all her fears, had run after him to bid him farewell. "When he was so keen to go, what could she do. She had to submit to his wishes," she replied, her voice heavy with resignation.

Clearly, both Hamid's mother and Selapan saw wives as sources of constraint. While Hamid's mother had implied that a wife's sexuality would help to rein in the restlessness of a young man, Selapan seemed to feel that men had to curb their "courageous" impulses because of the temptations embodied in women, who trapped their husbands with their sexual wiles; moreover, women made their men curb their "courageous" impulses because of their cowardly fears for their safety. In both cases, sexual women were conceived as obstacles to masculine heroism.

Selapan hoped that *PVC* would have a beneficial effect on women by making them "brave" (*bahadur*) enough to encourage their husbands to sacrifice their lives for the country. "Don't you think there are many women who are brave, women who themselves do brave things?" I persisted. He replied that such women were very rare. He gave an example of a soldier's wife in South Arcot whose husband had died in Operation

Bluestar, the Indian government's 1984 raid on the Golden Temple, the holiest of Sikh temples, in Punjab. It did not surprise me to hear Selapan, a nationalist and a Hindu, describe the soldier who died during Operation Bluestar as a martyr who fought to defend the integrity of the nation from its enemies (*dushman*). But his words were chilling in their appropriation of *PVC*'s discourses of "the enemy without" (usually Pakistan or China) to conceptualize the "enemy within," that is, the separatists who, according to him, were threatening the unity of the Indian nation.

Selapan added that when the government organized a function in South Arcot to honor the soldier and presented his widow with a check, she returned it, saying that the glory her husband had earned defending his country was compensation enough for her. And what's more, he continued, she insisted on wearing her *mangalsutra* (the necklace worn by some Hindu women that signifies their married, as opposed to single or widowed, status). According to Selapan, she said, "My husband is not dead, he is a martyr [*shaheed*]." He was so moved by this that he repeated the sentence at least three times. Then, after keeping quiet for a few seconds, he shook his head and said in a low voice, "Indian women are great."

Many viewers, men and women, believed that wives would have to be exceptional in order to successfully fight their fears and overcome their "natural" cowardice—unless, of course, they were Rajput or Sikh, ethnic groups stereotyped as "martial races" with a "tradition" of brave women, in which case valor would come "naturally" to them. After watching the Haarhi Rani episode, Jayanthi claimed that, unlike other women who clung to their husbands, Rajput wives sent their husbands to war "happily," that is, they encouraged their men to fight for their country. She felt that this "tradition" existed only in some communities, the Rajputs and the Sikhs: "That's their tradition. Among us, we would hold the husband's feet and say don't go, don't go. That's the difference. But it's different for the Rajasthanis, it's also different for the Punjabis, for the Sikhs."

In addition to echoing the image of the wife clinging to the soldier's feet found in many episodes, Jayanthi's comments reveal the manner in which representations of "martial races" such as Rajputs and Sikhs are transposed onto discourses of gender.[15] These stereotypes underscore the exceptionality of "brave" women who prove the rule: not only are women naturally cowardly, their active sexuality traps men and makes them cowardly as well.

Thus it came as no surprise to me when, on asking a viewer about

Hamid's wife's patriotism, I was told: "They didn't show her patriotism at all. They show her as an ordinary woman." In other words, it takes an extraordinary wife to be brave. But, as we will see shortly, courage seems to come more easily to mothers.

Nation and Family: Divided Loyalties?

Given this negative depiction of wives—indeed, of the conjugal unit—how is the family located vis-à-vis the nation? After all, most of the soldiers depicted in *PVC* lived in extended families: along with wives, they also "left behind" parents, siblings, and children when they went to the front. In advocating that soldiers put their love of the nation above their attachment to their families, was *PVC* rejecting the family in preference for the nation? Many studies of nationalism speak of how the trope of the family represents the nation; in fact, the family and nation often stand in a metonymic relation to each other (see chapters 2 and 3).[16] But in some episodes of *PVC*, it almost seemed as if the family stood in opposition to the nation: the soldier was torn between his attachment to his family and his love for his nation, a conflict that was always resolved in favor of the latter. I was anxious to learn whether viewers felt that the family sometimes seemed to be pitted against the nation. In particular, I was interested in whether they felt that the soldier was fulfilling his obligations as a husband, son, and father (fig. 22).

Somewhat uncertain about the response I would get (*PVC*, after all, had resolved this conflict unequivocally), I asked several viewers what they felt about the soldiers' commitment to their families. Jayanthi Chandran's response exemplifies the perspective of many of the women I spoke with: "Of course he doesn't take care of all his responsibilities toward his family! You are asking the right question. He's got married, he got himself entertained [here Jayanthi is referring to the episode in which the soldier is called to the front soon after his wedding night], then went off. But—the point is, where the question of the country comes up, there the family has to take a backseat [*peeche hatna padta hai*]. If it was me, [even] being a woman, if something happens to the country I also won't worry about my family."

So Jayanthi felt that the soldier had been remiss in his responsibilities to his family. Her sardonic description of his relationship with his wife ("he's got married, he got himself entertained, then went off") is particu-

Figure 22 A soldier, Major Somnath Sharma, with his loving mother and sisters

larly telling. But she felt that the soldier's apparently cavalier attitude to his loved ones was the result of a conscious choice he made between his love for his family and his devotion to the nation. When it came to the defense of the country, even she, a woman, would make the same choice: it was inevitable—indeed, it was the "normal" thing for a nationalistic woman to do.

PVC also depicted the fears of aging parents who did not want their soldier sons to leave for the front. Viewers often speculated about what would happen to parents in their old age if their son had to be away for long periods. And who would take care of them if he died? But viewers also felt that rather than focus on parents' fears, *PVC* emphasized their pride. As Sukumaran explained, this enabled *PVC* to "inspire [other] family members to send their sons to the army." Significantly, in *PVC*'s discourses and those of viewers, soldiers' attachments to their parents (as opposed to their passion for their wives) did not present a threat to militaristic nationalism. Indeed, by allowing their sons to go into the military and by encouraging them to fight for the nation, parents (and other family members) *enabled* the soldiers' nationalistic zeal.

Even though at first glance the family seemed to be rejected in preference to the nation, *PVC* actually held the two in tension with one another. At times nation and family seemed to coincide (as Lata, referring to the soldiers' martyrdom, pointed out: "They're doing all this for us"). At other times they seemed to be held in opposition (as when the soldier chose to give precedence to his love of the nation). Hence, the family is not rejected in *PVC*'s narratives; rather, the family/nation metonym is problematized, pulled apart for scrutiny, and reconstituted such that the family is put to the service of the nation. This move is accomplished in part through the role of the stoic, asexual mother, who becomes an icon for the motherland.

"It's Because of the Mother That India Is Getting Such a Child"

As mentioned above, *PVC* depicted Indian Womanhood not just in terms of (potentially destructive) sexual energy but also in terms of motherhood. Courageous mothers who encourage their sons to join the military, who stoically bid them farewell as they leave for the front, are shown to be as nationalistic as the soldiers. The sexuality of mothers is directed toward the production of sons who can (potentially) defend the nation. Their sexuality contained, they contrast with wives and other sexual women in that their courage seems to come easily, if not "naturally," to them.[17] For instance, in the first episode, the hero and his mother are extremely close. The attachment between mother and son is depicted by the physical demonstration of their love for each other (the long embrace that follows when the hero tells his mother that he has to go to the front) and also by the fact that he dies with a photograph of his mother and a copy of the Gita (a Hindu religious text that deals with the importance of doing one's duty) in his pocket. In another episode, a mother sells her jewelry to enable her son to go to a military school for officers: it is her determination that enables him to join the military. The love between mothers and sons is passionate and intense, and provides much of the emotional energy underlying *PVC*'s narratives.[18] During our conversation, director Chetan Anand pointed to the "hallowed space" mothers occupy in Indian nationalism. Although he insisted that he didn't want to "deify" women, he felt that "mothers played an important role," and thus he was very conscious of deploying the trope of the mother to his rhetorical ends.

If wives embody passion, mothers epitomize stoicism. This stoicism, however, signifies not detachment but emotional conflict. Mothers are stoic precisely because they are in the grip of very powerful emotions: their attachment to their sons, which then yields to their love for the nation. They differ from wives and lovers because the cultural framework of *PVC*'s discourses, and the moral economy of its narrative, insists on the asexual character of their love: the implication is that because their love is asexual, mothers can see the needs of the nation far more clearly and defer to it more "easily." [19]

Despite their feeling that the death of a soldier was a greater loss to his mother than to his wife, many viewers felt that it was incumbent on mothers to be stoic and "courageous." One morning, provoked by Selapan's derisive comments about "cowardly women," I asked if it was surprising that women worried about "sending" their husbands and sons into the military. Would he send his twelve-year-old son, Rajan, into the army? I asked, somewhat defiantly. He replied: "Of course! I have told him that if he does well in school I will put him in the IMA (Indian Military Academy) so that he can become an officer." I turned to Padmini and asked her what she thought of sending her son into the army. She smiled ruefully, put Rajan's head against her chest (he was sitting between his parents on the bed), and quietly stroked his hair. Her eloquent gestures made her silence all the more poignant. Then, after a pause, she turned to me and said: "He is my only child. How can I put him in the army?" Selapan laughed out loud. "See!" he exclaimed genially. "How cowardly [*buzdil*] she is! If all mothers start being scared like this, who will protect the country?" I never forgave myself for exposing Padmini to her husband's derision.

Almost all the men and women with whom I discussed *PVC* commented on the ability of mothers, as opposed to wives and other family members, to sacrifice their sons to the nation. I was so struck by the fact that the narratives seemed to downplay the roles of other family members, especially those of fathers, in the production of patriotic sons that I mentioned this to Jayanthi and her daughter, Uma. Uma explained that in "Indian families the mother's role is very special." Jayanthi added that this was how *PVC* showed women's role in defending the country: "The thing is, it's because of the mother that India is getting such a child. . . . Father is not the same, he has given the child education, but there won't be as much affection. But separation from the mother is something else. But if the situation demands it, the mother can sacrifice too. That's the thing. *More than the wife it's the mother*" (my emphasis).

By claiming that *PVC*'s narratives simply reflected the place of mothers in "Indian families," Uma both naturalized the role of mothers and essentialized Indian families. Jayanthi also seemed to take it for granted that "there won't be as much affection" between fathers and sons, and, like Uma, naturalized the attachment between mother and son. But she also claimed that in encouraging the soldier to fight for the nation, the mother made a greater "sacrifice" than a wife would have done. I pushed her a little on why she thought the wife—who was just as dependent (if not more) on the soldier—made less of a sacrifice than the mother. Uma seemed to agree with me. "The house belongs to the mother. The wife doesn't have her own house. She has left her own home and family and come to a stranger's house," she said. In response to the two of us, Jayanthi said that she agreed that wives are perhaps as dependent on husbands as mothers are on sons, "but still the woman has kept the child in her stomach for nine months, has fed him her milk, has raised him, *then sent him for the country* . . . the son was like her life [*praan tha*]" (my emphasis).

Evidently, mothers play a crucial role in nationalism not just because of their function in the biological reproduction of sons, but also in the emotional production of valiant nationalists. Mothers must raise their sons to be ardent nationalists and, despite the fact that they are as precious to them as their own lives, be prepared to sacrifice them for the defense of the nation. Most significant of all, Jayanthi's words emphasize the mother's purported agency in "sending" the son to fight for the country: after keeping the child in her womb and raising him to adulthood, she proves her courage and nationalism by surrendering him to the nation.

The Mother as Icon for the Motherland

The centrality of mothers to *PVC*'s discourses of nationalism was dramatized by the closing scene of each episode (that viewers wept despite the fact that *every* episode ended identically testified to its affective power), in which the mother, sometimes accompanied by the father, who almost invariably stood behind her, received the Param Veer Chakra on behalf of the dead soldier. In this image of the mother—stoic, dignified in her grief, the embodiment of somber pride—providing narrative closure to every episode, there is an imperceptible slippage from the mother to the motherland. The mother now allegorizes nothing less than the motherland itself, the dead soldier's love for his mother is thus displaced onto his devotion to his motherland.

This iconic representation of the motherland through the figure of the

mother existed not only in *PVC*'s narratives but also in the discourses
of its viewers. If the slippage from mother to motherland was evident in
Jayanthi's words ("it's because of the mother that India is getting such
a child"), its rhetorical force was underscored in Selapan's explanation
for why *PVC* was his favorite program. It showed the "real" stories of
men who die for the country, he said, and viewers could now see what
"real" nationalism and sacrifice was all about: "Young people who see
this program can know that instead of frittering their energies wastefully,
they can do things that will show they are worthy of the wombs of their
mothers."

According to Selapan, the heroism of the soldiers brought glory to the
mother/motherland. Obviously women play more than a supportive role
in the defense of the nation: it falls to them to inspire and, if necessary,
incite their men to fight for the motherland. And women alone have the
strength (the *shakti*) to do so.[20] Indeed, this is why only heroic sons can
be "worthy of the wombs" of their mother/motherland.

Similarly, Jayanthi referred to India as "the other mother" in several
conversations. I once pushed her on what she meant:

> *Jayanthi:* India too is like a mother [*Bharat bhi mother ke barabar hai*].
> *PM:* What do you mean?
> *Jayanthi:* To save the honor [*izzat*] of one mother, another mother has
> to sacrifice her son.
> *PM:* Meaning . . . ?
> *Jayanthi:* Meaning . . . that's true. Our India is also considered as
> mother [*mother ke barabar hi to gina jaata hai*].

Then, turning to me as if to call on my nationalism, she said that no
matter how long I lived abroad, I would always love India because "your
roots are with your mother and motherland." For instance, she explained,
no matter how much I might quarrel with my mother, I would hate it if
someone else criticized her. Similarly, she continued, startling me with
her perspicacity, no matter how I felt about India, if someone else criticized India I wouldn't be able to "bear it." She concluded: "So that's why
the country is like your mother," leaving me speechless with her insight
into my own troubled nationalism.

Jayanthi's and Selapan's responses have to be seen in the light of the
"mythicizing" of motherhood in nationalist ideologies. Its continuing
potency is evident in the ubiquity in popular discourse of the notion of

Bharat Mata (Mother India). In anticolonial nationalist discourses, the trope of Bharat Mata, with its roots in the Hindu concept of the mother-goddess, opened up a space for notions of women's energy as active and heroic (Bagchi 1990:69). Politicized by Hindu nationalists such as Bankim Chandra Chattopadhyaya, who thus created one of the most powerful icons of nationalist struggle, this concept was later appropriated by mainstream nationalist ideology.[21] During colonial rule, nationalists spoke of how the mother(land) had been ravished by the British, and the sexual imagery implicit in this trope was central to the way in which "emasculated" Indian men were inspired to militant nationalism (Chakravarti 1989). In postcolonial nationalist discourses, the trope of the mother/land threatened by hostile neighbors (and, in the late 1980s and early 1990s, by the "enemy within") was used to inspire Indian men to prove their masculinity by protecting the integrity of the nation. Thus, it did not surprise me to see that Jayanthi, Selapan, and many other viewers I talked with appeared to have picked up a major theme of *PVC*, that of the mother(land) threatened by hostile neighbors.

THE STATE, GENDER, AND THE POLICING OF AFFECT

The centrality of mothers to *PVC*'s discourses of militaristic nationalism became clearer when I learned of the state's attempts to directly influence the portrayal of women in the program. These efforts were part of a more general attempt to police the emotional effects of *PVC*'s melodrama. It is tempting to speak of the state's intervention in terms of a panoptical mode of surveillance reaching into the spaces of the everyday lives of viewers and invading the supposedly "private" realms of their emotions. But how successful was the state in its attempts to normalize nationalistic sentiments? Let us examine the complex negotiations between the state and *PVC*'s producer and director, Chetan Anand, as they jostled for the power to shape the narrative's discourses. We will see that even in instances when the state is successful in shaping cultural production (and I would like to emphasize the state's *struggles* to gain ascendancy), the reception of its discourses was far more difficult to predict. For even when the state directly intervened, viewers were sometimes able to interrupt its hegemonic discourses.

As mentioned above, Chetan Anand had made *PVC* for television because he felt that the political and emotional climate in the country was "ripe" for the tales of heroes who had martyred themselves in defense of the nation. He was thus unprepared for the hurdles he had to overcome in order to get his series accepted. As a filmmaker who had made war films all his professional life, he had known that he would have to get a green light from the Defense Ministry before he could embark on his project. And, like all producers of television programs, he was aware that he would have to please the Ministry for Information and Broadcasting and the Doordarshan Directorate, and get his pilot approved by the Screening Committee, before he could proceed with the series. But what dismayed him was that *every* episode had to be approved by the Defense Ministry and by representatives of the branch of the military featured in that particular story. No episode could be aired without final clearance from them.

Anand frequently ran into trouble with representatives of the military. Anxious that their wing of the military be portrayed "accurately," they often raised apparently "technical" objections about details that Anand had "misrepresented" in his series. The final episode, portraying the life and martyrdom of Nirmaljeet Singh Sekhon, an air force pilot who received the Param Veer Chakra posthumously, was the last straw for Anand. My interview with him took place when he came to Delhi to negotiate the episode's clearance with the top brass of the air force. After agreeing to several compromises, he was finally permitted to air the episode. But he was furious and swore never to make another television program.

The air force's first objection was to a "factual inaccuracy." Sekhon died because his parachute failed to open after he had leapt from his burning aircraft, and Anand had shown a close-up of him as he fell from the plane. The air force objected that it is impossible to see the face of a person as he falls from a plane. Anand replied that it would seem too impersonal if they showed Sekhon from a distance; he wanted a close-up to "reinforce the emotional effect." But perhaps the "emotional effect" aroused by the face of a soldier whose parachute fails him at the last minute was precisely what the representatives of the air force wanted to guard against: after all, wouldn't viewers' admiration for the hero be overshadowed by their sorrow at his death? Wouldn't the personification of militaristic nationalism, the soldier, seem all too human when seen in a close-up?

Anand got his way on this issue and Sekhon's close-up was retained. But the air force was a lot more intractable with regard to their second objection. The original episode depicted Sekhon's mother's fears: after first encouraging him to join the air force, she suddenly changed her mind. From his interview with the "real" Mrs. Sekhon, Anand had learned that she had once seen a photograph of a plane crash and could not bear the thought of what might happen to her son. The air force objected to this depiction of Sekhon's mother because it showed her in a "weak light." Anand responded that he had emphasized Sekhon's insistence on joining the air force despite his mother's fears and had shown that he had, in fact, prevailed over his mother because his desire to fight for his country was so great. But the representatives of the air force dug in their heels and refused to let him show the episode until he agreed to change his portrayal of the mother's fears for her son.

They also objected to Anand showing Sekhon's young wife crying when he left for the front. Here Anand stuck to his guns. He claims to have said to them: "She is a new bride, she has been married for just a few months. How can she not cry?" In contrast to the military's intractable position on his depiction of Sekhon's mother, Anand got his way on this particular issue.

But it was the fourth and final objection that best reveals what was at stake for the military and, through their complicity, for the other representatives of the government. After his parachute failed to unfurl and Sekhon fell to the ground, he was found, still alive, by a Kashmiri woman who took him to a hospital. After Sekhon died, his mother found out about it and tracked this woman down. Anand wanted to show the two women weeping and embracing each other when they met. The air force representatives objected to this portrayal of Sekhon's mother because they felt that her tears would rob her of dignity. Anand insisted that he did show her in a "dignified" light: "She is dignified when she receives the award." But the representatives of the air force were not impressed. According to Anand, they replied that the episode was unacceptable because "air force women don't cry." Even though they were willing to allow Anand to dwell on Sekhon's wife's grief, they refused to let him show Sekhon's mother weeping.

The episode's last scene shows the weeping figures of the soldier's widow, his father, and his brother. But his mother stands dry-eyed, a picture of grim dignity. The air force won that round against Anand. Air force women, airforcewomen, don't cry.

A CONCLUSION

Throughout the 1980s the Indian nation-state was confronted with a proliferation of secessionist movements. The state responded by attempting to protect and consolidate its power through the deployment of different technologies of violence. Political uncertainty and social turbulence did not just represent the context in which Doordarshan narratives were received; they refracted the narratives' very conceptualization and production. Compared with other examples of the increasing brutality of the state, the use of Doordarshan narratives such as *PVC* to promote national integration was a relatively benign strategy. Yet, *PVC*'s attempts to construct militaristic passion were enabled by particularly oppressive discourses of sexuality and gender. As illustrated by the interactions between Selapan and Padmini, the emotional and symbolic violence of these discourses seeped into the ways in which ordinary men and women negotiated their relationships with each other.

In making *PVC*, director Chetan Anand attempted to consolidate national integration by producing and appealing to viewers' nationalistic feelings and passions. He was concerned that feelings of patriotism and militaristic nationalism "shouldn't be allowed to dry up." His aim was to produce nationalism as a structure of feeling. In particular, he wanted to "encourage" emotions that would "bind" his viewers in sentiments of national unity. The feedback he received about the impact of his series satisfied him. He added that although he was too exhausted to continue, if people do not continue to make such programs "there is a danger of it [nationalist affect] drying up."

As described above, *PVC* used the structure and techniques of melodrama to produce and normalize militaristic nationalism, and thereby to endorse the use of violence in the name of the nation. In contrast to "real life," where we are "rarely called upon to feel so intensely, and never in such neatly escalating sequences" (Thornburn 1976:83, in Ang 1985:68), melodrama builds its affect by the heightened emotions expressed by its characters. *PVC* attempted to construct a heroic-tragic structure of feeling,[22] a delicate balance between admiration and pride at the soldier's ability to sacrifice his life for the nation and sorrow at his tragic death.

Lila Abu-Lughod and Catherine Lutz point out that in much social science discourse, emotions continue to be "tied to tropes of interiority" as the least socially constructed, or as "things" that social institutions then "act upon" or regulate (1990:1, 3). Hence, they insist, it is essential that we examine emotions as sociocultural phenomena. *PVC*'s impact lay in its ability to construct and evoke a range of emotions surrounding the production of militaristic nationalism: desire to protect the motherland from "enemies"; admiration for the sacrifices of the soldier and his family; sorrow at his death; and, above all, pride in his martyrdom. In so doing, however, *PVC* attempted to police some kinds of affect at the expense of others. Its narratives seemed to imply that sexual passion must be contained so as to never exceed love for the nation; wives must fight their "natural" fears for the lives of their husbands and encourage them to go to the front; men must discipline themselves in order to resist being trapped by female sexuality, which can only distract them from their devotion to the nation; families must be put to the service of the nation; mothers must embody stoic dignity as they sacrifice their sons to the motherland; and men must set aside their attachment to their families and remain steadfast in their loyalty to the nation.

Specific semiotic skills were required for viewers to derive pleasure from *PVC*'s melodrama and to interpret its codes. The viewers with whom I worked had developed these skills through a lifetime of watching Hindi film melodrama. I have already pointed to the use of music to invoke particular sentiments (for instance, the title music provided the aural cues essential for creating a mood of tragic expectancy). Among other codes borrowed from the cinematic techniques of Hindi film were the wedding night scenes, which at once evoked the sexual passion between the soldier and his wife and their impending parting. The use of song to express inner conflicts (as with Hamid's song) or heightened emotions (through the use of background music) were similarly borrowed from Hindi cinema. Viewers' interpretations of these images and sounds occurred within a particular intertextual discursive field constituted by the culturally specific codes of melodrama in contemporary popular culture.

Although *PVC* employed the vocabulary of affect that all melodrama makes use of, this rhetorical strategy seemed to backfire with at least two viewers: in their case the program evoked emotions that it was unable to contain. The semiotic excesses of some of its melodramatic codes created contradictory subject positions that enabled viewers to engage in divergent readings, thus illustrating that, far from being positioned by a single text, viewers' responses are circumscribed by the materiality of their own life experiences, fears, and self-perceptions. By choosing to conclude this chapter with my interpretations of these responses, I end on a note that resists ideological closure, focuses on the indeterminacy of interpretations rather than the determinacy of texts, and points to possibilities for subversive readings contained in the very subject positions offered to women by militaristic nationalism.

When I reached Sukumaran and Sarojini's home one Sunday morning, the opening credits and title music of *PVC* had just started. Sukumaran was sitting on a bed opposite the TV set, and his daughter, Lata, was standing by the door. When I arrived, Sarojini was bathing. After she emerged from her bath, she announced that she did not want to watch television with us because she had work to do; then, unable to resist, she sat down. She turned to me and said under her breath, "Well, you're here so I might as well sit with you."

When we were watching the crucial battle scene in which the hero was martyred, Sarojini turned to me and murmured, "You have to be very cruel to work in the army." I wondered about this—not just because it was a response I had never heard before, but also because she spoke with a quiet vehemence. At that moment, the tragic end of the hero seemed inevitable. Lata and Sukumaran were close to tears; so, for that matter, was Sarojini. The hardness in her voice thus surprised me.

Later, when she was walking me to the bus stop, she told me that she was not "impressed" with the heroes of *PVC* because she knew what military men were really like: her father, who had been in the army, had abused her and her brother. I am not sure whether she meant that one had to be cruel to go into the army or that the army brutalized one. Like all viewers, whose interpretations of television programs are mediated by their own life experiences, Sarojini's skepticism about the heroism of the men of *PVC* emerged from her experience of a military man she knew well, her abusive father.

Lest we dismiss Sarojini's ambivalence toward militaristic nationalism as unique or idiosyncratic, let us turn to how Padmini responded to a similar scene. On a rare occasion when Padmini and I were able to watch television by ourselves (her husband was visiting a sick friend), she turned to me toward the end of the episode, when the soldier's widow received the medal on his behalf. She was weeping; I too was having a hard time holding back my tears. As at so many other moments in my "fieldwork," my engagement with Padmini as an ethnographer was inflected by the images and memories that flooded my mind as I sat with her. I remembered some of the widows I had known in my own upper-caste family: a cousin, her bereavement deemed inauspicious by the rest of the community, sitting several feet away from the sacred fire when her son got married; a distant aunt, respected and feared by all, her head shaved as a mark of her pollution, her widowed status.

My thoughts were interrupted when Padmini looked at me and said, "These men go off. But it's the women who have to suffer because they [the men] have gone to fight." It was clear that she saw the show entirely from the point of view of the wife who had been left behind. Nevertheless, I asked: "Why do you cry?" She replied: "After all, women are one, their suffering is one, isn't it? What is the life of a widow? How can a Param Veer Chakra, all the money given as compensation, make up for the husband? The woman is left alone, helpless, helpless, with no one to support her. Support not just of money but also giving a place in society. A woman has nothing left if she's a widow."

I do not recount Padmini's words to make a universalist statement about the vulnerability of women in "Indian society"; nor am I interested in claiming the "oneness" of women. Padmini's words are valuable because they articulate a fear many women lived with, the fear of being left without "a place in society." Unlike her husband, who had earlier told me about the brave widow of the soldier who had died in Operation Bluestar, Padmini seemed a lot more realistic about the plight of women who, more often than not, indeed had "nothing left" when their men died. She emotionally identified with the helplessness of the soldier's widow and grieved for her. The image of the widow contained contradictory and shifting meanings, of courage and bereavement, or nationalistic glory and tragedy, for Padmini and for many of the women I spoke with. At one level, it was an image of containment: for many women, it reinforced their sense of helplessness and disempowerment. But by thus engaging with the plight of women who were "left alone," women like Padmini were able to go beyond the neat resolution suggested by the last scene in which the stoic woman received the Param Veer Chakra on behalf of the soldier.

In his much-cited work on nationalism, Benedict Anderson wonders about the "profound emotional legitimacy" of nationalism (1983:14). What is it about nationalism that legitimizes going to war? What induces people to encourage (or at least enable) their loved ones to face certain death? And finally, what force compels people to kill each other in the name of abstractions such as "the nation"? This chapter has attempted to address some of these questions by exploring the affective bases of militaristic nationalism and by unraveling some of the mechanisms by which it interpellates subjects to endorse violence in the name of the nation.

But while nationalism often succeeds in binding subjects to national communities, these imaginings are heterogeneous along different axes (such as those of class, generation, and ethnicity). In this chapter, I have focused on the way gendered perspectives might rupture the master narrative of nationalism. If men and women appear to have different stakes in nationalism, as they did in the case of some viewers with whom I discussed *PVC,* these variations emerge not so much from *essentially* gendered modes of engagement as from the manner in which men and women are variably interpellated by militaristic nationalism. Describing women's location vis-à-vis dominant ideologies, Teresa de Lauretis suggests that "the contradictory positions women are asked to hold within ideology enable them to gain through the disruption produced by contradictions, a distance from that ideology, one that men, whose positions in relation to ideological constructions are formed with more coherence and stability, are less able to experience" (1984, in Jeffords 1989:20).

We have seen that in *PVC*'s narratives of militaristic nationalism, men, more than women, were denied a complex subjectivity. In comparison, women occupied contradictory subject positions: on the one hand, they were expected to be "brave"; yet, women viewers were also confronted with the loneliness and social vulnerability of the widows and bereaved mothers who received the Param Veer Chakra in stoic dignity. In *PVC,* all women occupied the contradictory spaces of heroism and tragedy.[23] Multiple and shifting meanings are contained in the polysemous figure of the heroic but grieving woman who gives narrative closure to its tales. Her stoicism only emphasizes her loss—a loss that most women I worked with feared intensely. The semiotic excess contained in the dignified but tragic figure of the woman who receives the posthumous award at the end of every episode is precisely what enabled some viewers to engage in subversive readings: despite the honor bestowed on her she is, as Padmini pointed out, a woman "left alone, helpless, helpless."

Chapter 7 *Popular Narrative, the Politics*
of Location, and Memory

The mob has surrounded me. The men ask me to chant the *gayatri mantra*.[1] As I start reciting it, my voice falters and my mind goes blank. The men edge closer. I try to run away. The roar of their voices and the sound of their footsteps close in on me. I awake sweating, the roar of the mob reverberating in my head. I am reliving an old nightmare. I stand against the window, my breath fogging the glass, and force myself to look at the lights of the city twinkling in the distance. I try to remind myself that I am far away from the anger and hatred of it all. That I am in California, not Lahore. That it is 1993, not 1947. But even though I am able to calm down, the images of the night stay with me for several days. North India has been ravaged by the violence of communalism since December, and 1993 feels terrifyingly close to 1947. Terror travels well across oceans, across generations.

Born fourteen years after Partition, I am a second-generation survivor of the horror that ripped across the South Asian subcontinent. My mother's family was one of thousands displaced on both sides of the border during Partition. They came to "this part" of India for a visit that angry summer of 1947, convinced that they would return to their home once the bloodshed subsided. The violence never died down. They stayed on, living in a relative's garage until they gradually found their feet again. My mother has told me very little about what happened during that period. Yet the memory of the carnage, the agony of displacement, and, most of all, the terror are a part of my own subjectivity. I have absorbed them, as if by osmosis, from her moments of silent despair, from snatches of conversations that she will permit herself about her childhood and youth. Fractured recollections of growing up in Lahore. Dreams of summers in Murree.[2] And in 1947, a long, cold winter of deprivation, grief, and hopelessness.

Many decades after Partition, my mother continues to live in a refugee camp of the mind. And sometimes, I seem to do the same. My reading of *Tamas* (Darkness), a Doordarshan serial focusing on the riots of Partition, is refracted by the memories I have inherited. My analysis is partial because it stems from the politics of my location as a Hindu, middle-class survivor of Partition: to this extent, it is more "incomplete" than other media ethnographies. It is partial also because of the political critique I hope to construct.[3]

In this chapter I analyze *Tamas* in order to understand how Doordarshan mediated memories of the violence surrounding the birth of the postcolonial Indian nation. *Tamas* was telecast in 1988, at a time when the national past was being contested. How did memories of Partition mediate the reconfiguration of identities occurring at the time? I am also concerned with how a feminist ethnography of mass media is problematized in the face of silences, evasions, and forgetting. I begin by analyzing the discursive frameworks of *Tamas*, and follow with an exploration of the reception of the serial. Finally, I will comment on the differing responses of Hindu and Sikh viewers to the program in terms of the construction of memory and the politics of location.

Tamas was a Hindi serial made for Doordarshan by Govind Nihalani, a Bombay filmmaker noted for his avant-garde films. It was based on a novel and two short stories written by Bhisham Sahni, a well-known Hindi writer. The story, serialized over three episodes, is complex. The tragedy of Partition is sketched through the experiences of a handful of people. I retell it here in terms of its central themes: its construction of discourses of communalism and nationalism, its depiction of the role of the colonial state, the contrasting portrayals of politicians and "the common people," and the reconstitution of discourses of gender and sexuality. But first I will describe the opening scenes, which introduce the principal characters, set the tone for the rest of the serial, and lay the discursive terrain of the narrative.

Composed of three sets of images, the serial's title scenes and opening images were repeated at the start of all three episodes. The first few frames consist of close-ups of the main characters and serve to introduce the actors playing them. Next we see a still photograph of women who, surrounded by billowing smoke, are walking purposefully, majestically. The following still is of a woman in orange, hazy as she stands in the gray-blue light that will pervade the rest of the serial. The titles end with her as a backdrop. A woman's voice crying, "*O Rabba!*" (the Punjabi word for "god" used by Hindus, Sikhs, and Muslims), rises like a wail; it reverberates and fills the room in which I am sitting.

Author Bhisham Sahni next appears on the screen with an introduction to the serial. Sahni is a celebrated Hindi writer and leftist stage personality whose literary creations and activism have consistently demonstrated a commitment to Marxism and secular nationalism. Sahni begins his introduction by asserting that he himself lived through that "tragic chapter in the history of our nation." He claims that his purpose in making *Tamas* was to expose the "communal forces" that caused Partition and are still active today. He adds that by reminding people of the horrors of Partition, the serial's creators aimed not to reopen old wounds, nor to point a finger at any particular community, but to recommit themselves to secularism and to the integrity of the nation. At the end of Sahni's speech the following English words appear on the screen: "Those who forget history are condemned to repeat it." The serial begins.

It is 1947, a few weeks before independence. The camera focuses on a clay lamp flickering in an alcove in a dark wall. It then pans back into a dark room filled with the grunts of an animal and a man's heavy breathing. We see Nathu, a thin, shabbily dressed man, chasing a pig about a filthy floor strewn with straw and garbage. Nathu tries to plunge a knife into the huge body of the pig but is unable to wound it. As the flame of the lamp quivers, casting eerie shadows around the room, Nathu tries to match his strength and wits against those of the pig. But the pig seems to be an invincible adversary. After chasing the animal around the room several times, Nathu leans against the wall, breathless and defeated.

There is a flashback to a scene in which we see him and a well-dressed, obviously upper-class man with a blue turban and a luxuriant mustache. The upper-class man orders Nathu to kill a pig for the town's veterinarian. At first Nathu refuses because he doesn't know how to kill pigs. But the man ordering him to do so is a labor contractor (from this point on, he is known as Thekedar [the Hindi word for "contractor"]); Nathu depends on him for his livelihood. Besides, he is an upper-class man whose arrogant demeanor will brook no opposition. Before Nathu can plead any further, Thekedar pushes five rupees into his palm, turns on his heel, and swaggers away.

Nathu, remembering all this in the dark room, curses his fate. He is obligated to kill the pig. But the pig is strong and wily. Nathu gathers his strength once again and plans his next move. After a few more futile chases around the room, just as he is about to give up all hope, he lifts a huge stone and throws it at the pig. The pig sways from side to side, then, with a huge shudder, falls to the ground in a heap, dead at last. Nathu is exhausted. He drags the pig into a jute sack and places it in the cart of a man who is waiting outside. As the man drags the cart away, Nathu leans against the wall of the hut, smokes a *bidi* (a country cigarette), and watches the light change. It is almost dawn.

Cut to another part of town. An elderly man in white *khadi* (coarse, homespun fabric) and a white Gandhi cap (the uniform of Congress Party workers) walks purposefully toward a group of similarly clad men. This is Bakshiji, the leader of the town's Congress Party. The Congress men are waiting for Bakshiji so they can go for their *prabhat-pheri*, the rounds they make through the lanes of the town, during which they herald the dawn with patriotic songs. Hearing the men converse with one another, one is struck by their vanity and by the tension among them. An old Sikh in a crumpled, dirty khaki uniform, his tunic covered with flashy medals and ribbons, marches toward them chanting: "Left, right, left, right." The waiting men welcome him; a couple of them tease him into standing on a wall and giving a nationalist speech. The old Sikh, called Jarnail (General) by his companions, seems half crazed with his passion for the nation. His speech is punctuated with admonitions and threats to expose the traitors around him. When he finishes, he leads the group around the town singing patriotic songs. The group is to go to a poorer part of town and, following Gandhi's dictum of community service, clean the sewage drains that run through the lanes.

Cut to Nathu, who is on his way home. He stumbles on a clay figurine: someone in the neighborhood has been practicing black magic. The mood of foreboding that has been clouding his mind since he killed the pig now deepens. It is inauspicious to see, much less stumble over, black magic totems so early in the morning. He worries about the child his wife is carrying in her womb (fig. 23). This is her second attempt to bear a child. He prays to *saccha badshah* (a term for "god" used by Sikhs) to protect his wife and unborn child. He walks through the lanes of the town mute, nervous; he is unable to return home. He cannot understand why he feels so apprehensive.

In the meantime, a couple of lanes away from where Nathu is standing,

Figure 23 Nathu's wife, Karmo, awaits his return

the Congress workers chant slogans to India's freedom and to the glory
of Mahatma Gandhi. They are met with counterslogans from a group of
Muslim League workers standing at the entrance to a lane, who chant,
"Pakistan zindabad" (Long live Pakistan) and *"Quaid-e-Azam zindabad"*
(Long live Jinnah). Their leader, Hayaat Saab, an elderly, distinguished-
looking gentleman in a cap and gold-rimmed glasses, tries to prevent the
Congress group from coming into the lane because this is a Muslim part
of town. Hayaat Saab alleges that the Congress Party can never represent
Muslims because it is a Hindu party; Bakshiji retorts that it represents
India, not Hindus; after all, isn't Aziz part of their party? The reference
to Aziz, a Muslim member of the Congress, enrages Hayaat Saab. "Don't
mention those traitors!" he shouts. Nathu watches the encounter between
the Congress men and the Muslim League workers from a distance.
Over the heads of these two groups he spots Thekedar, who is also watching the two groups and listening to them argue with great concentration.
Suddenly, inexplicably, Nathu's sense of foreboding turns into fear.

Hayaat Saab and his men are ultimately unable to prevent the Congress group from going into "their" lane. The Congress men begin their
task of cleaning the drains. One of them talks about the riots that have

started in Calcutta. The Congress men continue their work until they are interrupted by someone running wildly into the lane. He whispers something to a man sitting by the roadside. The two of them rush all the inhabitants of the neighborhood indoors. In seconds, the lane is empty except for the Congress men and Nathu, who is loitering aimlessly in the distance. (Watching this scene, I could sense the fear that suddenly overtakes the lane: how many times have I felt a familiar street turn strange and terrifying as a nameless tension filled the air?) The Congress men put down their brooms and look around uncertainly, nervously. An elderly Muslim whom they had greeted as he went to the neighborhood mosque to say his morning prayers walks back waving his cane in fury. He tells the Congress men to leave immediately. They look stunned: just a few minutes ago, he had returned their greeting with affectionate blessings. They are further mystified when another passerby warns them to leave. Then they learn that a pig's corpse has been thrown down at the entrance to the mosque; the mosque has been polluted.

The Congress men are terrified. Bakshiji and Jarnail drag the pig off to the side of the road. As they do, a man chases a cow into the lane. (Most South Asian viewers will understand what this means: the pollution of a mosque is often avenged by throwing a cow's carcass into a temple. This invariably unleashes a sequence of events leading to widespread bloodshed.) Bakshiji looks on in fear; he knows it is too late to make amends for the pollution of the mosque. Also watching and listening from a distance is Nathu, now numb with fear. Although he cannot see the pig clearly from his distance, he suspects it is the one that he killed. He is so paralyzed with horror that he cannot move. At long last, he starts to stumble toward his home. He will be unable to return until much later that night.

Within a few hours, flames fill the horizon. The riots have started.

It has been estimated that more than a million people lost their lives during Partition (Khosla 1989). How did *Tamas* represent those days of horror, when neighbors turned on one another and men killed "their" women to protect them from a "fate worse than death"?[4] How did it portray the relationship between the forging of national identities at the eve of independence and the reconfiguration of religious subjectivities that occurred around Partition? More broadly, what is the place of violence in the engendering of postcolonial nationhood? And how are memories of violence recast during times when the very meaning of the nation is being contested? I will now examine *Tamas* in terms of some of its principal themes.

COMMUNITY AND NATION IN *TAMAS*

Halfway through its telecast, *Tamas* was almost pulled off the air. On January 21, 1988, the Bombay High Court passed a stay order at the request of a local businessman, Javed Siddiqui, who claimed that the serial would "poison the minds of the people."[5] There was fear that *Tamas*, with its depiction of the violence of Partition, would ignite hatred between Hindus, Muslims, and Sikhs by reopening wounds that had not yet healed. Many critics were worried that the serial would incite violence between communities, in particular between Hindus and Muslims. On January 23, however, the Bombay High Court revoked the stay order and permitted the telecast to continue. Doordarshan's director-general, Bhaskar Ghosh, stood by the filmmakers, countering that, as a secular narrative, *Tamas* did not identify particular perpetrators of communal violence but blamed all communal organizations equally.

To my mind, *Tamas* was unequivocal in its condemnation of Hindu communal organizations such as the Hindu Sabha and the RSS. Viewers are first introduced to Hindu communalism in a scene depicting a meeting of the "inner circle" of the Hindu Sabha. Chairing the meeting is Guruji, an austere man who speaks of defending the community from "the enemy" (Muslims). The assembled members discuss ways in which they can prepare themselves for the impending "war." One person suggests that the temple bell in the heart of the main market be repaired and kept in readiness: during moments of danger, the bell can be used to warn community members all over the city. On hearing this, an older member murmurs that he hopes the bell will never ring again: the memory of the last time it pealed evokes sadness and fear in him. Guruji retorts that this is the problem with "us Hindus": "we" are always afraid of danger. The old man counters that he endorses Guruji's attempts to train their sons in the defense of the community; they will become truly brave (*soorma*), he adds, and this will make them real men. But, he continues, it is also important to communicate the fears of the community (the Hindu Sabha, which seems to be composed of wealthy, upper-caste Hindus and Sikhs, claims to speak on behalf of all Hindus and Sikhs) to the deputy commissioner, the local representative of the British state. At some point during the meeting, Guruji reprimands the assembled members for arguing over strategies: in an eerie echo of contemporary Hindu nationalist leaders, he claims that the problem with "us Hindus" is that "we" lack unity (*ham mein ekta ki bahut kami hai*).

Two of the most violent scenes in the serial depict the initiation and training of RSS (Rashtriya Swayamsevak Sangh, the militant Hindu organization described in earlier chapters) volunteers. Even though the RSS is never mentioned by name, its members are identified by their khaki shorts and white shirts (all over north India, a derogatory term for RSS volunteers is "khaki knickerwallas"). *Tamas* dwells on the brutalization of Ranvir, a young recruit, who is transformed from a wide-eyed, impressionable teenager to a bloodthirsty fascist. Ranvir is made to undergo a secret initiation ritual that consists of beheading a hen with a knife. At first he is terrified; when he finally beheads the hen he is so revolted that he throws up. The RSS member leading the ritual smears a *tikka* (the auspicious red mark worn on the forehead by some Hindus) on him with the beheaded hen's blood. When Ranvir raises his face so the *tikka* can be applied, his eyes are full of awe and pride. He has been initiated as a member of the RSS; his transformation is complete.

This transformation is reinforced in a later scene in which he "trains" his companions, other RSS recruits, to fight "the enemy." His newly acquired ruthlessness enables him to acquire power over a group of fellow recruits. In a long scene, we see him beat an old Hindu sweet seller who refuses to give him a *karhai* (a vessel resembling a wok). Ranvir wants the *karhai* to boil oil, which they can pour from above on Muslim mobs. The *karhai* is an important part of the armory he is putting together for "the war," and he does not hesitate to strike a defenseless old man to acquire it. His companions are so impressed with his ruthlessness that they now call him "commander" (*senapati*).

In another scene, Ranvir trains his companions in strategies for killing "the enemy." Peering through a crack in the door, they watch the deserted street for a Muslim whom they can kill as part of their "training" while Ranvir calmly and ruthlessly describes strategies for murder. A Muslim finally appears and Ranvir orders one of "his men" to kill him. When the recruit hesitates, Ranvir reprimands him for being indecisive: "Guruji says never look at an enemy's face for too long; this will only make you empathize with him and will make you waiver in your resolve." Soon they see another Muslim walk down the street. This is a friend of Ranvir's father, but he refers to him as "the *mleccha*" (a derogatory term for Muslims; sometimes used to mean "barbarian"): from being a regular visitor to Ranvir's home, he has become depersonalized as the enemy. When the boy is unable to get to him in time, a disgusted Ranvir proclaims: "Let *me* show you how to kill an enemy." After a few seconds, a third Muslim, an old beggar, walks down the street. Ranvir runs up to him, stabs him to death, and runs back to his companions. He is excited by what he has done; his companions are proud of him.

In his introductory remarks at the beginning of the serial, Sahni poses communalism against nationalism. He says that during that "tragic chapter in the nation's history," on the one hand, people were dying for the nation's freedom, while "on the other hand, the poison of communalism was being spread." As mentioned above, he claims that he made *Tamas* to expose communal organizations not just for their role in bringing about Partition but also for their destructive activities in *contemporary* India: "Forty years later we have still not been able to get rid of communal elements. Today, these communal elements are still active in our society. The purpose of *Tamas* is to understand the tactics of communal elements in our society. . . . Our effort is to expose the same communal elements that played a crucial role in Partition that are now raising their heads. [Our objective in making] *Tamas* is to recommit ourselves to secularism and the unity of the nation. Participating in this commitment are not only myself and Govind Nihalani, but thousands of people of the nation."

What were Sahni's views on the role of religious organizations in civil society and in the nation, and more specifically in communalism? I was particularly anxious to understand his position because I had been distressed by a scene in *Tamas* in which a group of Sikhs surrounded by a Muslim mob shout: "The Turks are here!" It seemed to me that the Sikhs were transported back to an earlier era when Turkish armies allegedly stormed through the subcontinent. I was disturbed by *Tamas*'s evocation of such an explosive interpretation of the past, so I asked Sahni why he had the Sikhs refer to Muslims as Turks.[6] Did it not reinscribe a communal construction of history? His response was that it was precisely this communal appropriation of the past that he wanted to expose. He was only too aware that similar statements were being made by militant Hindus trying to mobilize support for the destruction of the Babri Mosque in Ayodhya by calling Indian Muslims "children of Babar," a sixteenth-century Moghul emperor. (As described in chapter 1, by thus linking Muslims with Babar, who, they claimed, was responsible for the destruction of the "original" Ram Temple and the construction of the Babri Mosque, these organizations had been successful in whipping up hatred against Muslims.) Sahni hoped that his depiction of communal violence as "medieval" would encourage viewers to reflect on the barbarism of postcolonial communalism.

I was not quite satisfied with Sahni's explanation of postcolonial communalism as a residual, "medieval" phenomenon, so I tried another tack. I asked him what he thought about the resurgence of Hindu nationalism in the 1980s. As noted earlier, since the 1980s, discourses of Indian nationalism had been appropriated by militant Hindus claiming to be "the true nationalists." Plagued by the slippages between Indian and Hindu nationalism that I saw around me, I was curious to get Sahni's views. He clearly conceived of *Tamas* as a secular and nationalist serial. How did he articulate *his* nationalism?

Sahni asserted that his nationalism was deeply embedded in his commitment to secularism. When I asked him to comment on the trajectory followed by nationalist ideologies in contemporary India, he replied that the birth of Indian nationalism could be traced to eighteenth-century Hindu revivalism. But, he continued, it was also important to acknowledge that Indian nationalism "broadened itself under the influence of Western education, secularism, and socialist ideologies. Till Tilak we see the influence of revivalism, but then we see the influence of people with a secular outlook." He pointed to the contributions of Gandhi and Nehru, and of socialism. Hence, although "the influence of Bhakti, Vedanta, and Vivekananda on Gandhian nationalism cannot be underestimated," *Indian* nationalism is a lot more broad based and syncretic than *Hindu* nationalism. It is for this reason, he added, that Indian nationalism cannot be conflated with Hindu nationalism; instead, he said, we need to reclaim it from militant Hindus and construct it as a secular discourse.

Sahni's notion of secularism was based on a strict separation of religion from both the state and the public spheres of civil society.[7] He seemed to subscribe to a state-centered view of secularism and nationalism predicated on the capacity of a strong state that would assume the responsibility of policing civil society. He conceded that revivalist forces were resurfacing again. His diagnosis was that this happened because "the government did not strengthen secular institutions." He looked to the state to strengthen secularism and to keep communalism at bay. "Why should religion be permitted to play such an important role?" he asked. He added that although the Arya Samaj, a Hindu organization, "was in its own time a reformist movement against caste, ritual, etc., because of powerful political motivations, it is now part of Hindu revivalism."

Yet in another context, when I asked for his opinion on the serialization of religious epics such as the *Mahabharata* and *Ramayana*, he claimed that there was "no denying the centrality of religion in *our* cultural development" (my emphasis). For instance, he said, "religion as poetry is very illuminating. There's no doubt about the rich cultural heritage we have received from the past." But, he added, in addition to texts, "we have also inherited certain social institutions and distortions, for instance, the caste system and the low status of women." One of the "burdens" of the past, he asserted, was "obscurantism." He said: "We need to cherish good things—for example, philosophy—but reject things that are obscurantist and don't go with modern life."

Sahni's conception of religion was clearly modernist in that he felt that it was important to selectively retain some aspects of "our cultural development" such as poetry, *bhakti,* and philosophy and shed those aspects that lead to communalism. "Obscurantism" was to be guarded against because it was incompatible with "modern life." He insisted that "[religious] fundamentalism always feeds on obscurantism." I pushed him on what he thought of the kinds of nationalisms that were gaining ascendancy in late-1980s India, many of which I perceived as unequivocally modernist. Referring to militant Hindu nationalism, he replied that he was most concerned about the "narrow nationalism" sweeping the nation because it reminded him of the "nationalism of Hitler." He added, "We should learn from that experience and know how dangerous it can be." His interventionist goals in making *Tamas* thus became clear to me: in constructing a secular nationalist portrayal of the communal conflicts leading to Partition, his aim was to warn his viewers to be vigilant about the potentially harmful consequences of Hindu nationalism for the integrity of the nation.

THE ROLE OF THE COLONIAL STATE

Many analysts of Hindu-Muslim violence during the preindependence era and Partition are unequivocal in their condemnation of the colonial state for its part in constructing and exacerbating communalism.[8] Thus, it did not surprise me to see that *Tamas* did not pull its punches with regard to the colonial state's role in permitting the escalation of violence during Partition. The colonial administration is represented in *Tamas* by the local deputy commissioner (the DC, as he is known in the serial). The DC is a scholar of Indian history and a lover of ancient texts and art. His study is full of antiques, and he is frequently shown poring tenderly over ancient Sanskrit texts. Not surprisingly, he has nothing but contempt for Indians. When he is awakened at night with the news that the riots have started, his reaction is one of impatience and disgust. "I thought they were going to run this country by themselves," he says as he goes back to sleep. He is unaffected by the tragedy faced by the people around him. His wife, Lisa, on the other hand, is a foil to him: her concern over the suffering of the local people contrasts with his callousness. One scene is particularly revealing. The riots have temporarily subsided. He is sitting in his study, surrounded by statues of the Buddha, leafing through an old Sanskrit text with immense reverence. Lisa announces that she is going to help at the refugee camp. He tries to stop her because it is "unsafe" and "very disturbing," but she is adamant.

The DC's complicity goes beyond his indifference to the impending violence and his escape into ancient Sanskrit texts. There are indirect hints that he is well aware of the mounting tension in the city: at the very beginning we see Bakshiji walk past two sinister men standing in the shadows as he goes to join his comrades. Later in the serial, we see these men conferring with the DC (the novel makes it clear that these men work for the CID, the administration's intelligence wing). After the discovery of the pig at the entrance of the mosque, Bakshiji, Hayaat Saab, and other community leaders plead with the DC to impose a curfew on the city. He refuses outright, arguing that it is beyond his power to do so. When Bakshiji persists, the DC retorts that imposing curfew might exacerbate the tension in the city. The community representatives then try to persuade him to increase the police presence in the city. He turns down this request as well. Bakshiji pleads that if even one helicopter was seen flying over the city, the local people would be reassured: they would know that the state is vigilant and would contain the tension. But the DC refuses to budge. The community leaders are devastated at his lack of responsiveness. Bakshiji says to him: "The British government can do everything to prevent the violence if it wishes to do so. . . . Kites will now fly over the city."[9]

"THE COMMON PEOPLE"

Nationalist historiography often explains Partition as the result of the machinations of politicians and other members of the elite who, aided by the complicity of the colonial state, incited people to violence against each other (e.g., B. Chandra 1984). *Tamas* largely subscribes to this perspective in its diagnosis of the riots. The dichotomy between nationalism and communalism set up in Sahni's introduction is paralleled by a second set of contrasts: the serial's depiction of politicians, community leaders, and the wealthy diverges sharply from its portrayal of the "common people." As Sahni says in his introduction, "While on the one hand, people were dying for the nation's freedom, on the other hand, the poison of communalism was *being spread*" (my emphasis). *Tamas* holds politicians responsible for communalism, which is like a poison seeping through a society. Almost all politicians are shown as vain and self-promoting. The first time we are introduced to the Congress men in the serial, all, except for Bakshiji, are portrayed as petty, vain, and jealous of each other.[10] They are always portrayed as self-absorbed, argumentative individuals who constantly trade allegations, unable to agree on any strategy to defuse the crisis. Even though they position themselves as leaders of their communities, they are either inept at containing the violence unleashed by the riots or, as in the case of the Hindu Sabha and the RSS, are directly responsible for it. Politicians hence represent the divisive forces responsible for tearing the country apart.

The tragicomic figure of Jarnail (fig. 24), whose passionate desire to prevent the partition of the nation sets him apart, is a constant foil to the politicians: his sincerity contrasts with their vanity and selfishness, his courage exposes their cowardice. Half-crazed with patriotism, he is truly devoted to the nation. When the assembled Congress men hear for the first time that the top leadership has agreed to partition the country, they all feel betrayed. But Jarnail is particularly devastated. Heartbroken, he starts to weep disconsolately, saying: "The kites will first have to fly over

Figure 24 Jarnail Singh in the town square

my dead body; the kites will not fly over the nation." He is enraged with the Congress men, whom he accuses of being too cowardly to contain the violence that is tearing the nation apart, and decides to speak to the people directly. While giving a passionate speech in the town square, he is hit on the head by an unknown assailant. He falls to the ground dead, a martyr to the cause of the integrity of the nation. His prophecy that the nation will be divided over his dead body comes true.

Tamas portrays the role of the left in fighting communalism in terms of both its strengths and its limitations. The leader of the local Communist party organizes a meeting of the town's community leaders and tries desperately to mediate between the Congress, the Muslim League, and other political organizations. Unlike other politicians, most of whom are helpless or caught unprepared, the Communists have a clear plan for dealing with the violence overtaking the region. But, despite their best efforts, they are helpless to stem the tide of communalism.

I found one scene particularly memorable for its portrayal of the praxis of the communist activists. Jamil, a Muslim member, is disillusioned with the party and wants to leave. "Why do you blame the colonial state for everything?" he protests. "Why can't you understand that this is a conflict between Hindus and Muslims?" When the leader tries to calm him, he replies that it is essential that they acknowledge the role of "colonial and imperialist" forces in "this conspiracy." Jamil cannot be mollified. He cries: "For how long will we shut our eyes to the truth? You can never bring socialism into this society until you understand the role of religion and community. And you don't even make an effort to understand it." Adding that he is very disappointed with the party, he leaves. The rest of the group is upset by this dissent, but their leader explains that Jamil's "ideological base" is weak. Apparently satisfied with this explanation, they proceed to draw up plans for containing the violence.[11] The leader informs the group that the violence has not yet reached the poor parts of town, but it has started spreading through the villages in the countryside. Tension is mounting in one village, Sayyidpur, where Sikhs and Muslims are gathering reinforcements to fight one another. Mir Daad, a Muslim, is deputed to work with the Muslims of Sayyidpur, and Sohn Singh, a Sikh, with the Sikhs, who have reportedly assembled in the local *gurud-wara* (Sikh temple).

Unlike other politicians, the communist activists are committed to secularism and to bringing about peace between the communities, and they make every effort to develop concrete strategies to contain the violence. They try their hardest to mediate between the warring communities, often at risk to their own lives. But even as their commitment to secularism motivates them to risk their lives for peace, it also undercuts their credibility within their own communities. Mir Daad is estranged from his father and neighbors because, they allege, he continues to "side" with Hindus even when their own community is endangered. He is almost killed when he presses for peace in Sayyidpur. Similarly, Sohn Singh is almost attacked in the *gurudwara* in Sayyidpur when he argues with Sikh elders for peace. Both are accused of being traitors to their respective communities and are treated with such hostility and suspicion that they are unable to persuade people to negotiate with each other. When they finally get Sikh and Muslim leaders to meet, it is too late: the tension between the two communities has reached such overwhelming proportions that there is nothing anyone can do to stem the tide of violence that overtakes the village. Sayyidpur, as we will see shortly, is to become the site of one of the worst tragedies in the serial.

Toward the end of *Tamas*, the refugees have gathered in a relief camp and we see a bureaucrat drawing up a list of losses to life and property according to the religion of the victim. The communist leader asks him to draw up another column so that the victim's class can be noted, claiming that this will prove that in communal riots it is usually the poor who suffer the most. His words are confirmed in one of the final scenes of the serial. The town elite gather: they seem to be back to business as usual. The politicians stand around arguing with each other; businessmen discuss their losses and strike deals with one another; a real estate broker tries to sell property left behind by fleeing refugees. With the blessings of the DC, a Peace Committee is set up, and the political leaders of the town file into a bus to spread messages of peace around the town. A person sitting next to the driver of the bus shouts slogans of peace and amity into a loudspeaker: "*Hindu-Muslim bhai bhai*" (Hindus and Muslims are brothers). As the camera zooms toward him we see that he is none other than Thekedar, the man who ordered Nathu to kill the pig, the event that unleashed all the violence in the first place.

In depicting all politicians as opportunistic and manipulative, *Tamas* echoes a common theme in post-Partition historiography that posits that politicians and other members of the elite incited the "common people" against each other so as to further their own ambitions. While the role of politicians in inciting communal hatred cannot be underestimated, *Tamas*'s depiction of Partition renders the common people mere instruments. From all accounts the lives of common people were irreparably affected by Partition. But in *Tamas* they are valorized as possessing an *essential* wisdom and humanity.[12] Robbed of all agency, they become unwitting pawns in the hands of a power-hungry elite. As Sahni says in his introduction: "[This was] a time of chaos [*uthal-puthal*]; suspicion, hatred had been sown between Hindus, Muslims, and Sikhs in order to further political aims. This was the era when the intelligentsia had started talking unintelligently. On the other hand, simple people were showing exemplary common sense, courage, compassion."

Sahni repeated this to me when we met. Delineating his secular humanist objectives in writing the novel, he said that he "meant to show that while, on one level, people were incited into committing inhuman acts, the humanistic [*sic*] level also emerged." He tried to show that many people, in fact, "came forward to help their neighbors and protect them," and he wanted to emphasize the "compassion" of the "common people": if it didn't foreground the "humanistic values" of the common people, *Tamas* would become "sensational . . . a pointless, gruesome thing." He wanted to show that "the common people of India cherish the tradition of live and let live."

Nathu epitomizes the innocence (and mute helplessness) of the common man. I described in detail the opening scene in which he kills the pig because it serves as a metaphor for the narrative that is to follow. It is an ugly scene, unpleasant and difficult to watch. By introducing a mood of foreboding, it sets the tone for the rest of the serial. The killing of the pig and its discovery at the entrance of the mosque lead to widespread violence; the killing of the pig also symbolizes the bestiality that is to overtake the region. But, as I see it, it serves a more important function. The scene portrays the way in which "common people" like Nathu are pawns in the hands of the rich and powerful. By killing the pig, he *unwittingly* becomes the instrument that unleashes the violence. Filled with foreboding, he cannot even articulate his fears until much later. Nathu thus represents the complete lack of agency subscribed to the subaltern in the nationalist historiography of Partition: he is outside history, a victim rather than a subject of his destiny.

Communal violence in India is often interpreted either in terms of conspiracy theory (as in the postcolonial state's obsession with "foreign subversion") or with economistic explanations such as conflicts over resources and markets. As historian Gyanendra Pandey points out, "The mass of 'the people' appear to count for very little in our analyses of 'riot' situations" (1992:41). At first glance, *Tamas* seems exceptional in its focus on the experiences of ordinary people: the story is told, ostensibly, from the perspective of ordinary people such as Nathu and Karmo, and Harnam Singh and Banto. It is only when we realize that they too are depicted as scapegoats in the hands of the elite that we see that *Tamas* is yet another nationalist representation of Partition in which all agency is located in "economic factors" and the manipulations of an opportunistic elite. The implication is that left to themselves, the "common people" would have lived in perfect harmony. There are several scenes showing "ordinary" Muslims, Hindus, and Sikhs living and working together in blissful amity: they seem untouched by the tension the politicians and elite are so obsessed with. As Sahni said to me, all they want to do is to "live and let live"; this is their "tradition." Even as *Tamas* valorizes them, it marginalizes the actions of the common people, who are thus robbed of their subjecthood. They appear as helpless onlookers, victims who are reduced to spectators of the great drama of Partition and independence.

Figure 25 Nathu, Karmo, and Nathu's mother flee their home

Such discourses represent common people in monolithic terms and divest them of all agency. Worse, such valorizing representations forestall an understanding of some of the most terrifying aspects of collective violence by eliding the complex ways in which "ordinary people" perpetrate indescribable atrocities on each other.

At the same time, *Tamas* does powerfully portray the agony of displacement experienced by thousands of people during Partition. When Nathu witnesses Jarnail's murder, he realizes that his family has no option but to leave their home. He and his pregnant wife, who is due to deliver her baby in a few days, throw their meager belongings into a bundle. Nathu carries his old mother on his back and they start their long walk to safety on the other side of the border that will divide India and Pakistan (fig. 25). The old woman dies of fatigue the first night on the road. (Watching her die, I remember what I have heard about that long, arduous walk to safety: "So many people died during the journey! When old people sat down to rest, their families simply walked on. They couldn't stop for anyone, not even for their own old ones.")

Tamas vividly depicts how homes, neighborhoods, bazaars, places of worship, and other familiar spaces are transformed into sites of danger and horror when violence is unleashed in the name of community and nation. A Muslim scholar of Sanskrit reassures his family that even though they live in a Hindu majority area, nobody will touch them because he has lived there all his life. When the cries of the Hindu rioters draw closer he can scarcely believe that they will turn on him. Shouting "*Har har Mahadev,*" the battle-cry of Hindu rioters, the mob breaks into his house and burns his books. In another scene, Harnam Singh and Banto, a gentle, elderly Sikh couple, watch their home and tea shop being burned by a mob of Muslim rioters (fig. 26). Harnam Singh recognizes the people looting and burning his home. Up until this moment he has resisted the idea of fleeing his village, but he now realizes that he has no choice. His tragedy is made more poignant because, despite all he has seen, he still clings to the hope that he will return to his village when the violence dies down. (Years ago, I was told: "We did not expect to stay on in India, we planned to go back. It was our home.") Harnam Singh's plight represents that of many Partition refugees: the tragedy that occurs in the loss of faith in the ability (or will?) of neighbors, people one grew up with, to protect each other when the familiar spaces of home and neighborhood turn menacing—truly, the loss of one's home.

Figure 26 Harnam Singh and Banto watch as their home is looted

The desperation of the people who had to leave their homes and move to safety is powerfully brought out in images of people walking across the countryside carrying their belongings on their heads, their elderly relatives on their shoulders, their children in their arms. Their desperation and fatigue make them walk like robots. They seem not to know where they are headed; all they know is that they have to keep walking in order to survive. Harnam Singh says to his exhausted wife when she wants to rest for the day, "Don't talk of rest, Banto" (*Parhe rahne ki baat mat kar, Banto*). Words from my childhood come back to me: "The caravans of refugees crossing the border from both sides seemed endless; so many people died on their way over. Sometimes caravans from opposite sides would meet and all hell [*qayamat*] would break loose. The things that happened, the things that happened." A familiar ache rises to my teeth; I weep every time I see this scene.

Unlike narratives that represent Partition violence as a "breakdown of signification" or a "loss of humanity" (Das and Nandy 1986), *Tamas* aims to foreground the "humanity" of the common people. At the same time, however, it also essentializes them as victims. While it is true that hundreds of thousands of people were either killed or displaced, in *Tamas* the common people are represented either as nameless, faceless mobs; as valorized subalterns who are exploited but still retain their "essential humanity"; or as desperate refugees walking to safety. Paragons of "basic wisdom" and "innate humanity," they appear either as puppets or as helpless scapegoats in the hands of the all-powerful elite.

Indeed, the subjectivities of most of the characters are displaced by the serial's focus on the "larger historical drama" taking place: Indian independence and the "accompanying" partition of the subcontinent. Unlike some other Doordarshan serials, the characters of *Tamas* are not well developed; they appear either as symbols of specific historical predicaments or, at the very most, as embodiments of particular emotional states. As noted above, even though we are shown Nathu's anguish after he kills the pig, he allegorizes the mute helplessness of the working class, pawns in the hands of the "real forces" that engineered the riots (that is, the colonial state, religious fanatics, and capitalists—symbolized by the district commissioner, Ranvir, and Thekedar, respectively). The only possible exception to this flattening out of the subjectivities of the common people is Nathu's wife, Karmo, who understands the significance of the killing of the pig even before the riots start and is torn between her fear for her safety and her desire to comfort Nathu. But in the end, even Karmo is represented as the bearer of a child whose birth symbolizes the future of the nation.

As a result, despite its powerful depiction of the suffering and displacement of ordinary people, *Tamas* remains primarily a narrative of the birth of the nation. As pointed out by Pandey, *Tamas* "marks a return to a less subtle nationalist statement in which agent-provocateurs and mysterious evil folk pulling the strings from behind the scenes mislead an innocent and bewildered but brave people. Partition is represented here, moreover, in the likeness of a natural disaster in which human actions play little part, far removed from the run of daily life. . . . [T]his is also the line that respectable, academic nationalist historiography has followed" (1992:32).

These representations of ordinary people reveal that the true subject of the narrative of *Tamas* is the nation: the nation is assumed as a pregiven entity waiting to be "born" with the departure of the British. Partition becomes something that "accompanies" the birth of the postcolonial nation; to repeat Sahni's words, it is a "tragic chapter in our nation's history." In the end, the violence of Partition is represented as a temporary (although horrifying) obstacle in India's teleological trajectory toward predestined nationhood.

VIOLENT SEXUALITIES

Rape is a dominant image in popular narratives not just of Partition but of all communal conflicts in India. What place do representations of sexual violence hold in the construction of discourses of gender, community, and nation? The fictional literature on Partition is full of stories of abductions, of women's breasts being chopped off, of gang rapes. In *Tamas*, we see that the control of women's sexuality is a crucial way in which the boundaries of communities are policed and contested: further, women's sexuality is metonymic of the honor of communities. We see parents agonize about the fate of their young daughters; very often it is the fear of the rape of daughters that compels people to flee. One middle-aged father cries, "Where in my home can I hide my young daughter?" (*Jawaan beti ko ghar mein kahan rakhun?*) Women of the "enemy community," both com-

munities, are "claimed" by being abducted, raped, and, very often, mutilated. Women's sexuality becomes the property of men who then take it
upon themselves to protect and avenge the honor of communities.[13]

Tamas shows us that all women, irrespective of age, class, or community, are vulnerable during communal riots as they become victims of
violent contests over community and identity. Often, men who felt they
would be unable to protect "their" women killed them before they fell
into the hands of "the enemy." When Harnam Singh and Banto leave
their village, he says to her: "If they come to kill me, I will first kill you,
then kill myself." Banto looks back at him with love, respect, and complete understanding in her eyes. He repeats later in the narrative: "As
long as I am alive, I won't let you come in anyone's hands."

Tamas also considers the many young women who were disowned by
their families after they had been raped or abducted during Partition. In
one of the closing scenes of the serial we see an old couple resolve to not
look for their missing daughter because, they say, there is no point in
bringing her back. First, they can barely feed themselves, how would they
ever support her? Second, she has probably been "defiled" by the enemy:
what is the point in looking for her?

The vulnerability of women and the place of sexuality in discourses of
community and honor are further revealed in one of *Tamas*'s most horrifying scenes. Harnam Singh and Banto go to a *gurudwara* in Sayyidpur
where their daughter Jasbir has sought refuge along with other Sikhs of
the area. The scene opens with a Sikh hymn. After the singing is over,
the congregation is led by an elderly Sikh, Teja Singh, a man of great
presence and dignity. Teja Singh gives a speech in which he says that the
moment of sacrifice has arrived. When they finish their prayers, a roar
goes up outside the *gurudwara*: the battle cry of Muslim rioters fills the
air. Teja Singh and the assembled Sikhs strategize about how best to protect themselves. They are outnumbered, and their spies have informed
them that the rioters are waiting for reinforcements from surrounding
areas. The sun sets across the countryside; the tension inside the *gurudwara* mounts; the night drags slowly by.

The next morning, the rioters seem to have edged closer to the *gurudwara*. Their chants and the drums with which they announce themselves
become louder. Inside the *gurudwara*, the Sikhs retaliate with their battle
cry. The sentries guarding the *gurudwara* cry: "The Turks are coming! The
rioters are coming!" Jasbir's hand goes to the *kirpan*, the small ceremo-

nial sword slung across her body.[14] The drums draw nearer. Next we see that Sohn Singh and Mir Daad (the two communist activists deputed to Sayyidpur to negotiate for peace) have got the community leaders to talk about compromise. A sum of Rs 200,000 (Rs 2 lakh) is mentioned. Teja Singh and the older men of the community haggle: they want to propose Rs 100,000. When they send their emissary back to the rioters, Nathu is chosen to accompany him. As they watch from the *gurudwara*'s roof they see their emissary and Nathu surrounded and attacked by the rioters. The men charge out to defend the *gurudwara*, shouting that this is an opportunity for them to sacrifice themselves: "*Yeh mauka hai apna balidaan dene ka.*" We hear the shouts of the two armies confronting each other.

Their roar is drowned by the sound of cymbals clashing rhythmically. Sitting in front of the Granth Sahib (the Holy Book of the Sikhs), Jasbir begins to sing another hymn of courage and martyrdom: "*Jo larhe deen ke het soora sohi . . .*" (Those who fight for the faith are the truly brave . . .). All the women gather in front of the Granth Sahib and begin singing in a frenzy, their voices rising like shrieks. At the end of the hymn, Jasbir asks them to rise: she tells them that the Turks have come; their command has come: "*Guru ki singhnion, turk aa gaye. Hamara hukam naama aa gaya.*" Without another word, Jasbir leads the women out of the *gurudwara*; an orderly procession of women and children run silently behind her (fig. 27). Barely visible in the smoke that billows around them, they run to a well in the compound of the *gurudwara*. Jasbir stands on the wall of the well, whispers a prayer, and throws herself in. One by one all the women, some with their children in their arms, jump silently into the well. Later, the stillness of the compound is punctuated by the wind whistling in the surrounding fields. Back in the *gurudwara*, we see Jasbir's parents and Karmo, silent and dry-eyed, mourning the deaths of the women.

I continue to find this one of the most painful scenes in the serial. I also find it extremely disturbing because of the way this tragedy is conceptualized: there is something menacing about the atmosphere in the *gurudwara*, and this seems to overshadow the tragedy of the mass suicide of the women. When I asked Sahni why he had conceptualized it in this way, he replied that he had presented it as a scene marked by a "pervasive sense of hopelessness." It is this hopelessness, he claimed, that drives the women to mass suicide. He proceeded to tell me that as a worker in a refugee relief camp in 1947, he had seen a well into which women from a *gurudwara* had flung themselves, and he still remembered the sight of

Figure 27 The women in the *gurudwara* on their way to commit mass suicide

the bodies floating on top. "The village had been surrounded and there seemed no hope," he said, in a matter-of-fact tone. "In that situation, the men often preferred to kill the women themselves to avert the tragedy of letting their women be dishonored." Without commenting on why the men should have "preferred" to kill their women rather than "let" them be "dishonored," he proceeded to say something that continues to disturb me. Describing the mental state of the women in *Tamas* who committed mass suicide as "a trance of religious ecstasy," he claimed that these women "link themselves with the past but it's not a rational linking."

Even though Sahni intended to use this scene to describe their hopelessness, the portrayal of the women in a near-hysterical state highlights their religious frenzy rather than the tragedy that befell them. The religious emotions that overtake the women as they sing the hymn are depicted as menacing. I was upset by this depiction and asked Sahni what he thought of Jasbir's ability to lead the women to mass suicide. He replied that her actions were "not the result of a conscious choice but of early influences of childhood, religious influences. So you don't rationalize. She's been told Muslims are your enemies, so she follows her training."

He described it in terms of following one's *samskaras* (the Hindu notion of karma in which our deeds, both in this life and previous ones, lead us to act in particular ways). He said that even though he is an atheist, he was brought up in an Arya Samaj family, and the Arya Samaj hymns evoke in him a "strange sort of nostalgia." What disturbed me was the dichotomy he constructed between religion and rationality: he seemed to imply that religion made people do "irrational" things. He suggested that all of us, even atheists like himself, are trapped in our *samskaras* and, during moments of crisis, simply follow our training.

But what was it about the training of women like Jasbir that made them commit suicide? What discourses of community and sexuality compelled Harnam Singh, one of the gentlest characters in the serial, to tell his wife repeatedly that he would kill her and then kill himself before anyone would have a chance to touch her? And what was it that made Banto gaze back at him with such love and respect every time he said it?

A few days before I met Sahni, an upper-caste Hindu friend had described the scene at the well as *"jauhar,"* a form of sati supposedly committed by Rajput women when their kingdoms were attacked by Turkic armies in the twelfth century. I mentioned this to Sahni and said that this interpretation had bothered me a great deal because of its evocation of anti-Muslim and patriarchal discourses. His response was that he had conceptualized this scene to prove that "behind communal frenzy there's always a medieval outlook." He simply reiterated what he had already said: "They [the women in the *gurudwara*] link themselves with the past . . . fundamentalism feeds on the past." I was struck by the fact that he conceptualized their actions in terms of "medieval outlook" and "communal frenzy" rather than the desperation and fear of women who have been surrounded by a hostile mob.

For me, the tragedy of this scene lies in the vulnerability of the women and the fact that they felt *compelled* to commit suicide.[15] The coimplication of discourses of community, sexuality, and purity that compelled men to kill the women they loved, and women to kill themselves at the sound of the approaching mobs, is what makes this scene so distressing for me. Moreover, the women were shown in a frenzy that seemed almost menacing. This portrayal of the women at a particular historical moment, when Sikhs all over India had to contend with being stereotyped as gun-toting extremists or religious fanatics, made me question the (ostensibly) secular polemics of the serial.

Urvashi Butalia (1994) and Veena Das (1995) have noted that stories of women's suicides proliferate in survivors' recollections of Partition,[16] and these stories stress the valor of the women, not their helplessness. It is important to remember that the "defilement" of women's bodies was often accompanied by the "defilement" of their souls through conversion. According to Butalia and Das, oral narratives of Partition emphasize women's agency, their "choice" in sacrificing themselves to protect the purity of their religion, and therefore the honor of their communities. Compared with the oral histories described by Butalia and Das, *Tamas*'s representation of the women's mass drowning seems more ambivalent: at the same time that it portrays them as heroines who have the courage to take their own lives, it depicts them as driven by an "irrational" religious frenzy. The serial thus raises troubling questions about representations of women's agency in narratives of violence, in particular, narratives of violence perpetrated in the name of the community and the nation. It is to these questions that I turn next.

VICTIMS AND HEROINES: NATIONALIZING WOMEN'S AGENCY

Because I have analyzed *Tamas* as a popular historical narrative, my critique of its discourses of gender must be located with respect to the rich tradition of feminist historiography in India.[17] Revisionist feminist histories of social movements have been particularly helpful in thinking through issues of representation: for instance, the Stree Shakti Sanghatana's outstanding collection of oral narratives of women who participated in the Telangana movement attempts to represent women as *making* history rather than simply contributing to it (1989:19–33).

It is important to note that unspeakable horrors were visited on women during Partition: in one city alone, between 400 and 500 women were abducted (Butalia 1994:41). According to G. D. Khosla, close to 100,000 women were raped and abducted (cited in Das 1995:59). Seventy-five percent of these abducted women were still being sold as late as 1949 (Kidwai 1990, in Butalia 1994:41). However, *Tamas* seems to follow the pattern set by patriarchal histories in its depiction of women *primarily* as either helpless observers/victims or courageous heroines, thereby eliding disturbing questions about women's complicity, if not active participation, in the violence that accompanied the birth of the nation. The serial lacks a more complex analysis of women's agency that would have disrupted the heroine/victim binary.[18] The Stree Shakti Sanghatana anthology critiques patriarchal historiography because it "not only marginalizes women but mythologizes them in the terms of a male-centred world" (1989:19). I would like to extend their critique and argue that popular historical narratives such as *Tamas* marginalize women *by* mythologizing them as victims or heroines.

Colonial discourses on sati also represented women as either victims or heroines (Mani 1989). Although discourses of gender are constantly reconfigured in terms of the contingencies of the present, it is perhaps not surprising that colonial representations of women in terms of this dichotomy have found their way into postcolonial nationalist discourse. As political fields, mythologies naturalize the structural inequalities that position women as victims of contests over masculine honor, or as emblems of courage and sacrifice; as Barthes pointed out in another context, "myths transform history into nature" (1972:129). By mythologizing women as victims or heroines, *Tamas,* a secular nationalist narrative of the birth of the Indian nation, leaves unexamined the construction of women's subjectivities during Partition.

What sorts of gender discourses does *Tamas* construct? At the same time that it represents women as vulnerable, it also essentializes their "inherent" humanity, courage, and nobility. A woman television critic told Sahni that she thought all the women characters in *Tamas* were "positively drawn," and that they were "not communal—with the exception of one." I had also been struck by the fact that the women who are not victims are portrayed as extremely courageous, wise, and full of compassion. For instance, early in the serial we see an older Sikh woman physically defend a Muslim schoolteacher who lives in her neighborhood. In another scene, when Ranvir's father, a rich businessman, wants to leave his mentally disabled servant behind to "protect the house" while he and his family flee to a safer part of town, his wife tries to prevent him from doing so. In addition to having more compassion than he does, she is also more perceptive. The father is proud of his rss son's "community service," but she recognizes the relationship between this "community service" and the violence around them.

Of the women characters, Sahni's favorite was Akran, a Muslim woman who fights the rest of her family to give shelter to Harnam Singh and Banto. Akran physically struggles with her son to prevent him from killing the old couple; her moral strength prevails as he inexplicably stops himself from striking Harnam Singh. Sahni also found Karmo, Nathu's pregnant wife, "very memorable." He felt that Karmo had a "more bal-

Figure 28 The pregnant Karmo identifies her husband's body

anced mind, a wider perspective," than Nathu. She is portrayed as an intelligent and perceptive woman: when Nathu tells her what he has done, she immediately realizes that he has become an unwitting instrument of Thekedar's nefarious designs. Sahni insisted that she illustrated the best of Indian Womanhood. Essentializing both "Indianness" and womanhood, he said: "The human trait among Indian women is very strong. Among us in India, women are very sensitive to other people's pain, particularly where their own dear ones are concerned." In Sahni's discourse, Karmo becomes emblematic of ideal Indian Womanhood.

As I noted above, the pregnant Karmo also embodies the future of the nation. In one of the closing scenes, Karmo identifies her husband's body from a long line of corpses brought to the refugee camp (fig. 28). She faints and is taken into a nearby tent, where she immediately goes into labor. As Harnam Singh and Banto wait outside, we hear the cry of a newborn baby. Harnam Singh and Banto smile at each other and pray their thanks. But at that very moment, cries of *"Allaho akbar"* (God is great) and *"Har har Mahadev"* (Glory to Shiva) fill the air. Harnam and Banto recognize these as the war cries of rampaging Muslim and Hindu mobs and realize that the violence is far from over. They look at each other in consternation and fear. The serial ends with a freeze-frame of the two of them looking uncertainly, nervously, at each other. The birth of the child symbolizes the bloody birth of the nation.[19]

TELEVISUAL TERRORS: REPRESENTATIONS AND RESPONSES

When *Tamas* was telecast, many viewers complained about the brutality of its images. Newspapers were full of protests against the violence depicted in the serial:

> The camera lingers excessively on the images of violence and inhumanity.

> From the very first episode *Tamas* presents a dementia. I don't know what educative value that can have.

> It is an overwhelming projection of violence. Sure there are scenes of humane intervention (by people of one community to save an individual from the other) but the images that linger in your mind are the ones dealing with violence.[20]

These complaints are striking because a close analysis of the serial reveals relatively few images of explicit bloodshed:[21] in contrast, the weekend Hindi films typically shown on Doordarshan, with their gory depictions of fights and rapes, had much more violence. Yet, *Tamas* was extraordinarily difficult to watch. As I will describe shortly, for some of the viewers I interviewed and for myself, *Tamas* was terrifying precisely because it evoked nightmares that all survivors of Partition, some more vividly than others, must continue to live with.

Tamas portrays the horrors of Partition through a series of semiotic codes. Violence is often signified by fire; for instance, Nathu realizes that the riots have started when he looks out of his hut and sees flames filling the horizon. The violence of the riots is also represented through smoke, the roar of mobs, and silhouettes of people running through dark streets. There are several scenes of mobs surrounding homes and attempting to break in. But there are few scenes of murder, and none of people being raped, burned alive, castrated, or mutilated in any way—all of which became commonplace during the riots and are described in brutal detail in some of the fictional literature of the period. There is one particularly graphic scene of Hindu mobs breaking into a Muslim scholar's home and setting fire to his books, and another terrifying scene of a man being chased through the streets like a rat, but given the brutality of the violence that marked Partition riots, there are few explicit depictions in *Tamas*. Instead, the terror of the times is expressed through darkness. Most of the action takes place in scenes pervaded with darkness: either in dark rooms, in the smoke-filled countryside, or in the recesses of streets and buildings.[22]

In addition to the semiotic codes described above (fires lighting up the horizon, smoke billowing through vast spaces, the roar of mobs), *Tamas* powerfully communicates the terror of the times by focusing on the internal state, the fear, despair, and grief of victims. The vulnerability of women is indicated by depicting parents' fears for their daughters and the mass suicide of desperate women rather than by showing rapes; the desolation of a riot-torn town is suggested by the howling of dogs in empty streets; the despair and dehumanization of some of the refugees is revealed by showing a young man seeking his wife's corpse in order to retrieve her gold bangles and chain.

As mentioned earlier, the telecast of *Tamas* was temporarily halted when a private citizen sued to have it banned. When the High Court revoked the stay order, the controversy increased. *Tamas* had clearly stirred the emotions of a number of people all over India. Protests in Bombay, Delhi, and Hyderabad turned explosive when the police fired on demonstrators who wanted the ban reimposed. Newspapers of the time reveal that there was a great deal of public debate—in public meetings; in columns and letters to newspapers; in homes, offices, and buses—over whether the ban should have been lifted. Some commentators, nervous about the fragility of the nation-state, were worried that the serial would plunge India into communal frenzy. Others asserted that Partition had inflicted a trauma on not just the Indian nation but on the entire subcontinent and that *Tamas* brought it all back. Yet others spoke of *Tamas* as "revisiting the scene of the subcontinent's greatest collective shame" (Singh and Rahman 1988:73).

These receptions of *Tamas* are significant in what they reveal about discourses of nationalism, communalism and community identity, civil society, and the role of the state. Immediately after the ban was revoked, the Shiv Sena, a powerful right-wing Hindu organization, launched a wave of protests. Siddiqui, the plaintiff who had sued for the ban, claimed that he would appeal to the Supreme Court. Ironically, but not surprisingly, Hindu and Muslim right-wing organizations with diametrically opposed perspectives on the way in which the serial had depicted Partition (each felt it was biased in favor of the other) agreed that the ban should be reimposed. Right-wing Hindu organizations such as the BJP, Shiv Sena, and the RSS were the most vocal in their protests. Shiv Sena leader Pramod Nawalkar alleged that *Tamas* showed Muslims in a favorable light. And BJP president L. K. Advani complained that *Tamas* was "a distortion of history" because it depicted the RSS and Arya Samaj as "beastly fanatics" while Muslim League members were dismissed as "mere ruffians" and Congress men as "anaemic nincompoops." He claimed that while he was not pushing for a ban, he objected to government media being used to propagate "this kind of view of the Partition holocaust."[23]

If communal organizations led the fight against *Tamas*, proponents of secularism staunchly defended it. At a large public meeting in Bombay, film and theater professionals collaborated with social activists in taking to the streets and symbolically joining hands in a show of support for its continued telecast. Many of those who argued in favor of *Tamas* claimed that the serial exposed all communal organizations equally and vindicated the need for a commitment to secularism.

The High Court judges who ruled in its favor agreed that the serial attacked all fundamentalists equally: "The message is loud and clear, directed as it is against the sickness of communalism. . . . The extremists . . . stand exposed . . . when realization dawns on both communities who ultimately unite as brothers" (from Tripathi 1988:23). As in many nationalist discourses on communal strife, the judges' statement was based on notions of community and nation that were in turn predicated on a faith in the supposedly natural inclination of people to "unite as brothers" until "extremists" spread the "sickness" of communalism among them.

Clearly, such a vision of the "sickness" of communalism was based on an implicit faith in national integration. This naturalization of national integration was echoed in metropolitan newspapers and newsmagazines. *India Today*, a popular English newsmagazine, pointed out that all the protests against *Tamas* had been launched by "vigilantes, usually representing a minority in their own community," who were increasingly able to "impose" their orthodox views on the majority. "Most often, they themselves have not viewed the play or film under controversy. In addition, they usually challenge what has been vetted, approved and censored by the appropriate legal authority" (Tripathi 1988:23). This statement reveals some of the struggles over the control of civil society. Who decides whether a particular representation of religious conflict is valid: the state or self-appointed leaders of "communities"? Does the state have the right to insist on a particular interpretation of an event that continues to traumatize so many people, a past that is so bloodily contested?

And once again, "vigilantes" are represented as extremists who gain control of communities and are able to "impose" their view on others. By constructing discourses of communities that are homogeneous except for the presence of extremists and vigilantes, such assumptions render static the temporal and contingent nature of the ways that moments of crisis bring people of varying structural positions together on a single platform. This view leaves no space for examining the role of hegemonic discourses in enabling (or compelling) diverse people to find common cause with one another. It is silent on what makes people with multiple subjectivities re-cognize their identities during moments of collective danger. Such a view is predicated on the assumption that people have a natural inclination to live in harmony: "A very private yearning for communal amity must still exist in the hearts of common people who used to stop Delhi actor Virendra Saxena on the roads to ask whether Jarnail Singh— the fiery, hyper-emotional nationalist played by Saxena in *Tamas*—would make a reappearance in the final episode. . . . 'Most viewers identify and empathise with the character of Jarnail,' says Saxena" (Singh and Rahman 1988:74).

In their discussions of *Tamas*'s potential for political intervention in favor of secularism, its supporters echoed the state's discourses on the deployment of television for national integration. Journalists Ramindar Singh and M. Rahman compared the potential of serials like *Tamas* to U.S. television's role in making the American public aware of the tragedy of the Vietnam War: "Just as the daily dose of gore on TV screens helped convince the '60s generation in the US of the futility of Vietnam, *Tamas* may have a similar impact on a generation of Indians who were born after the communal convulsions of 1947. If that happens it would have succeeded in its mission" (Singh and Rahman 1988:74).

Nietzsche points out that we "explain the past only by what is most powerful in the present" (1949:40). The director of *Tamas*, Govind Nihalani, commented on its potential for changing public consciousness in the 1980s: "We are becoming polarised as a society and strong consciousness is needed among people so that the saner elements in each community see this pattern" (Tripathi 1988:23). His objective in making the serial was to emphasize the importance of national integration in light of communal conflicts in contemporary India. For Nihalani and Sahni, *Tamas* was not just a commentary on Partition; it represented their personal intervention in contemporary politics. Nihalani claimed that although he was not a "social reformer," he felt compelled to make a film on Partition because the "communal elements" that had "created the holocaust" of 1947 were becoming increasingly active. In his view, "Partition provided a good historical backdrop"; his main objective, however, was to expose the role of these communal forces so as to prevent the violence and tragedy of Partition from being repeated.[24]

The controversy around *Tamas* was uppermost in my mind when I met Sahni. I was curious as to how he had positioned himself when it first erupted and what he made of it in retrospect, two years after it was telecast. Sahni said that the controversy was at its "hottest during the first two episodes. It later died down because people's curiosity [about the serial] got the better of them." According to Sahni, although it reached its peak by the second episode, the controversy actually began before *Tamas* was telecast. He said that Doordarshan officials were nervous about how the serial would be received and asked him to introduce it with explanatory comments.

I had just read the novel on which the serial was based when I met Sahni. I had noticed that in the novel, Thekedar is called Murad Ali, a name that immediately identifies him as Muslim. In the serial, however, he is not given any name. He is referred to simply as Thekedar; his religious identity is left ambiguous. Nihalani and Doordarshan officials had deemed it safer to not specify his community. Speaking to journalists at the time of the controversy, Sahni said: "Thekedar is an agent provocateur of the kind that can be found in any community. The link between the thekedar and the British is obvious, as also the implication that the British started the riots, let things get out of control and then stepped in as peacemakers. Thekedar's religion is utterly irrelevant. The question is not whether he is a Hindu or a Muslim, for such a person has no religion" (from Singh and Rahman 1988:74).

As in much nationalist discourse on communal conflict, the potency of religious identity, the role of politics within and between communities, and the power of religion as a worldview and a cosmology are here rendered epiphenomenal. While making Thekedar's religious identity ambiguous was essential given the volatile relationship between Hindus and Muslims in the 1980s, in Sahni's reckoning Thekedar is simply an "agent provocateur." Further, as suggested above, Partition is represented as yet another example of the British policy of "divide and rule": as one of the colonial state's most diabolical projects, Partition becomes the story of the (attempted) subversion of India's independence.

In his work on the historiography of communalism, Pandey comments that the history of sectarian strife is narrated as a "secondary story" against the "main drama" of India's struggle for independence (1992:30). In the final analysis, *Tamas* narrates the violence of Partition in terms of the tragic division of the nation. As noted above, Partition is represented as a painful chapter, an episode in the nation's history: however horrifying the narrative, it remains a single (and singular) interruption in the inevitable birth of the Indian nation.

Between Memory and Silence

Sahni asserted that *Tamas* was aimed at viewers from all communities. He claimed that viewers realized that "the communal elements on both sides had been depicted as inciting people to violence and that the British were very complicit in all of this." He added that *Tamas* was "very well received by people in general" and that he received congratulatory phone calls from people in different parts of the country saying that "such things should not happen again." In fact, he recollected that he was sent a newspaper report about how the *maulvi* (Muslim religious leader) of a remote town had prevented communal riots from occurring after the discovery of a slaughtered pig on the steps of the local mosque: the *maulvi* had seen *Tamas* and hence suspected foul play. The newspaper report was headlined: "*Tamas* has prevented *tamas* [darkness] from happening." According to press reports on the effects of its telecast, *Tamas* generated very strong reactions in its viewers: one man reported that his son vomited and developed a fever after seeing the third episode; an army officer wrote to a Delhi newspaper complaining that he was unable to sleep after watching it (Singh and Rahman 1988:72). I close my analysis of *Tamas* by describing the ways the people I worked with responded to it.

Although I was in the United States when *Tamas* was shown on Doordarshan, I was able to follow some of the controversy it generated. I arrived in "the field" two years later, determined to interview viewers on what they had thought of it. As I noted in chapter 1, I began my fieldwork in Vikas Nagar, a predominantly Hindu neighborhood. Every time I met a viewer for the first time, I would ask him or her to tell me what serials they had watched in the past. Because I was anxious to find at least one person who would be willing to talk about *Tamas,* I always specifically asked about it. I was soon frustrated by the lack of response I got to that question. Sarojini and Sukumaran told me that they had not watched it because it was too gory and they had not wanted their daughter, Lata, to get nightmares. When I pointed out that the average Hindi film had even more gory representations of rape and murder, Sarojini shrugged her shoulders and pointedly changed the subject. Aparna and Sushmita Dasgupta insisted that though they had seen it, they had "forgotten" the story—this made me very impatient because they were able to talk in some detail about serials shown much earlier, but despite my best efforts, I seemed unable to jog their memory of *Tamas.* Selapan and Padmini claimed that they had not seen the serial because they had not owned a television set when it was telecast.

Every now and then, however, one of them would say something to indicate that he or she might, in fact, have seen *Tamas.* For instance, Shakuntala Sharma told me that they had not been able to watch the serial because they did not own a television set when it was telecast. I found that strange because she discussed *Rajani,* a serial shown three years before *Tamas,* with great enthusiasm. I had no doubt that she had owned a TV set for many years before *Tamas* was shown. My suspicions were confirmed when one day, in the middle of a conversation about another serial, her daughter, Poonam, let slip something about the horrifying images of *Tamas* ("*Tamas* used to make my hair stand on end"). I knew that she could not have watched it at a neighbor's house because she was not allowed to socialize with any of them.

When I tried to follow up on "discrepancies" of this sort, I was met by silence. I knew that many refugees of Partition had, in fact, not watched it because it brought back memories they were unable to confront. But none of the people described above were refugees; nor had they been directly affected by Partition. Most were either from south India and had no family history of Partition, or had been living in parts of north India that had been relatively unaffected by it. My bewilderment at their resistance to talking about *Tamas* soon turned to frustrated resignation. I felt there was nothing I could do about their silence.

When I started fieldwork in a predominantly Sikh section of Basti, I was reluctant to raise the subject of *Tamas*. Most of the people I knew in Basti had experienced Partition, and it pained me to remind them about their experiences not just in 1947 but in the more recent 1984 anti-Sikh violence. Nevertheless, when I met Bibi Satwant Kaur, an elderly Sikh woman whom everybody called Bibiji in deference to her somewhat formidable presence, I mumbled: "Did you see *Tamas*?"

"No!" she said, spitting out her response.

I was a little taken aback at her vehemence. But I knew that unlike the "common people" of *Tamas*, who seemed to live together in blissful amity, the lives of the residents of Basti had been irrevocably marred by the anti-Sikh violence. On October 31, 1984, Prime Minister Indira Gandhi was assassinated by her Sikh bodyguards. This led to three days of violence against Sikhs all over north India. New Delhi, the capital of the nation, became the site of unabated violence. More than two thousand Sikhs were killed.[25] Truckloads of rioters descended on neighborhoods all over the city to single out Sikh men, many of whom were pulled out of buses and trains and were beaten or burned to death.

Bibiji's daughter Parmindar Kaur had told me that before 1984 it was customary for the residents of their lane, most of whom had known each other all their lives, to pull their beds into the streets and sleep under the stars during the simmering summer nights when their tiny flats became unbearably hot. But after the events of November 1984 they had stopped doing that because they didn't feel safe. Thus, although they maintained superficially friendly relationships with their Hindu neighbors, they no longer felt secure in their own neighborhood.

All my conversations with Bibiji were mediated by her memory of the 1984 anti-Sikh violence: she was always cool and reserved toward me because, I sensed, she saw me as a representative of a community that had betrayed Sikhs like herself. As described in chapter 1, it had taken all of Parmindar Kaur's persistence to get Bibiji to thaw toward me. Despite the fact that she was now less suspicious of me, I knew better than to force Bibiji to talk about *Tamas*. I had grown up with the silence imposed around the subject of Partition; I was acutely aware of the nightmares unleashed when this silence was broken. I had to respect Bibiji's refusal to talk.

Several months later, I arrived at Bibiji's home one bright November morning. I had made an appointment with her and was looking forward to discussing *Yugantar,* a serial on social reform movements in the nineteenth century. Bibiji was standing at her gate waiting for me. Wearing a sparkling white salwar-kameez, her hair neatly oiled and braided, she looked magnificent. It was obvious that she was dressed to go out. There was an *akhand path* (a Sikh religious ceremony) going on about three houses down the street. The gentle music of the hymns and the fragrance of *karha prashad* (the sweet distributed at the end of the prayers) filled the air. I assumed that Bibiji was on her way to the *akhand path.* She apologized for not being able to see me that morning. When I said that I would visit Harbhajan Kaur, another woman in the neighborhood, instead, she offered to walk me over. I was touched and not a little surprised when she insisted on doing so; we had finally become comfortable with each other, but she always treated me with the distant formality with which older matriarchs treat young women like myself. I told myself that she had condescended to walk with me because she was feeling guilty about missing our appointment.

As we made our way to Harbhajan Kaur's, Bibiji confirmed that she was going to the *akhand path* in her neighbor's house and proceeded to tell me about him. "He is from our village," she said. "Every year, on this very day, he holds an *akhand path* in memory of his wife and two daughters. You know, in 1947, when the rioters came, he took out his sword and killed them." Without waiting for my response, Bibiji continued: "You know that scene in *Tamas?* In which the women jump into the well? It was like that. What choice did people have in those days? What could he have done? When he saw there was nothing he could do, he killed them [his wife and daughters]." I could barely absorb what she had said. As I stood there, suddenly cold in the sunlight, she continued: "In '84 when the mobs came, we thought, do we have to go through that again?" She left me and made her way to the *akhand path.* Her words rang in my ears for days; I thought a great deal about the meanings of silence.

At one level, the silence of Hindu viewers on *Tamas* seems to parallel the silence surrounding Partition in general. Some novelists and poets have tried to represent the violence of Partition in their novels and poetry, but until very recently, social scientists seemed unable to articulate the displacement and terror of those times.[26] Urvashi Butalia asks: "Why had the history of Partition been so incomplete, so silent on the experiences of the thousands of people it affected? Was this just historiographical neglect or something deeper: a fear, on the part of some historians, of reopening a trauma so profound, so riven with both pain and guilt, that they were reluctant to approach it?" (1993:12).

Perhaps the modernist language of social science and its myth of detached objectivity render the horrors of Partition difficult to analyze. If so, it is not surprising that, in my efforts to understand the (differently constructed) silences of Hindu and Sikh women, I should turn to a work of fiction about the power of the imagination. In *The Shadow Lines*, a novel on memory and postcolonial identity, anthropologist-novelist Amitav Ghosh attempts to describe the silence surrounding communal violence in terms of the fear it evokes in the minds of people who have, however indirectly, experienced it. He compares it to the fear of victims of an earthquake, "of people who have lost faith in the stillness of the earth" (1990:200). Yet, he claims, it is a fear without analogy—it comes from the knowledge that "normalcy" is "utterly contingent"; "it is the special quality of loneliness that grows out of the fear of the war between oneself and one's image in the mirror" (1990:200). The protagonist of *The Shadow Lines* "remembers" the communal violence that killed his cousin when, during his doctoral research on another topic, he accidentally comes across a reference to it. Writing about it, however, is another matter: "Every word I write about those events of 1964 is the product of a struggle with silence. It is a struggle I am destined to lose. . . . All I know of it is what it is not. It is not, for example, the silence of an imperfect memory. Nor is it a silence enforced by a ruthless state—nothing like that: no barbed wire, no check-points to tell me where its boundaries lie. I know nothing of this silence except that it lies outside the reach of my intelligence, beyond words" (1990:214).

It is difficult for me to watch *Tamas* in New Delhi without thinking about other eruptions of communal violence there in the recent past: the 1984 anti-Sikh violence, for example, and the periodic outbursts of Hindu-Muslim violence in different parts of the city. The "contrived collapse" of the state to prevent the violence against innocent Sikhs in 1984 was accompanied by media representations that projected the violence as "natural and inevitable" (Chakravarti and Haksar 1987:24). On the second or third day of unabated violence, in a brief appearance on Door-darshan, heir-apparent Rajiv Gandhi made a cursory reference to the violence: when a huge tree falls, he said, the ground will shake. I remember feeling shocked at the callous and matter-of-fact manner in which he naturalized the violence against an innocent minority.

Some activist organizations protested the complicity of the state in allowing the anti-Sikh violence of November 1984 to take place,[27] but for the most part the city lapsed into silence within a few months after the violence subsided. It is not my intention, following *Tamas*'s depiction of "common people," to construct Bibi Satwant Kaur as a repository of essential wisdom or humanity, or to valorize her as an oracle of anti-hegemonic resistance. However, my conversation with her underscored for me other erasures in the discourses of the Hindu viewers I worked with. The Sikhs I interviewed spoke frequently of their experiences dur-ing the 1984 violence. They would go into painstaking detail about what happened during those three days of terror: the way they hid in their homes, how they worried about their friends and relatives in neighbor-hoods in which Sikhs were in a minority, the truckloads of "outsiders" who terrorized neighborhoods, the way the police turned a blind eye to what was happening, the smell of the smoke that filled their neighbor-hood for days after the violence subsided, the nightmares their children continued to have. I had been struck by the numerous ways they incorpo-rated the memories of November 1984 into their everyday discourse on a variety of apparently unconnected topics. Since the assault on the Golden Temple in June 1984 they had felt particularly marked and alien in New Delhi. But in November 1984 their marginalized position in the nation was brought home to them, figuratively and literally, when angry mobs dragged them into the streets to beat them to death or pour kerosene on them and burn them alive.

By contrast, in all the conversations that I had with Hindu viewers, not once was there a single reference to the anti-Sikh violence. Although Vikas Nagar was not directly affected, *all* of the neighborhoods around it had experienced incidents of terror. From my own recollection of the vio-lence, I knew that for days afterward the city was full of tales of Sikh men pulled out of their homes and beaten or burned to death, with women and children forced to watch. But the Hindu viewers I interviewed never mentioned any of this in any of our conversations. It was as if November 1984 had never happened. The silence of the Hindus I worked with began to haunt me because it revealed the erasure of antiminority violence from hegemonic nationalist discourses. Their resistance to talking about *Tamas* indexed the complicity of the majority community that permitted genocides such as the 1984 massacre of Sikhs.

Feminist Ethnography: Location and Identity

In her theorization of feminist ethnography, Kamala Visweswaran argues that feminist anthropologists "stand to learn not only from women's speech, but women's silences as well" (1994:31). In much feminist analysis, speech is frequently deemed the site of women's agency, even their resistance (cf. Spivak 1988). Like Visweswaran, I believe that we must pay careful attention to women's silences as well as to their voices. Far from assuming the "willingness of women to talk," it is important to trace when and why women talk, and when and why they keep silent. Indeed, a feminist ethnography "can take the silences among women as the central site for the analysis of power between them. We can begin to shape a notion of agency that, while it privileges speaking, is not reducible to it" (Visweswaran 1994:51).

Although the foregoing chapters also examine women's practices, their nonverbal expressions, and their negotiation of space, they focus primarily on the place of narrative in the construction of subjectivity. It seems fitting that I close my book on women's interpretations of television serials with a reflection on how women's silences, their recalcitrant evasions, and their acts of forgetting might complicate the project(s) of feminist ethnography. My experience with Bibiji and with Hindu viewers of *Tamas* taught me that in addition to recording women's testimonies, feminist analysts also have to learn to "listen carefully to grasp and appreciate" the silences, the waverings of women as they formulate their narratives (Stree Shakti Sanghatana 1989:27). Further, the *construction* of silences, as much as their interruption, illustrates some of the ways we remember and actively forget the past. Far from indicating a breakdown in signification, the silences of the Hindu and Sikh viewers I worked with seethed with signification. If the silence of the majority community encoded their complicity and shame, Bibi Satwant Kaur's silence revealed her *will* to first withhold and then narrate her own story of the past: a story constructed in the margins of hegemonic discourses of nation, community, and sexuality. Living in a city that had ignored her pain, she decided to break her silence to tell me of her memories of 1947 and 1984.

Furthermore, Bibiji's silence, and the manner in which she staged its puncturing, also bring my own position as a middle-class Hindu who was raised to be a nationalist to the fore. My encounters with Bibiji and with the Hindu viewers who resisted talking about *Tamas* forced me to question my own investment in my nation. They also made me think about the coimplication of my memory with Bibiji's, the ways my history and hers are hierarchically related. I had absorbed from my nationalist father the hope that the departure of the British would give "us" a chance to build a future in which "we" would be treated with respect. I remember that many years ago, when Hindu-Muslim riots broke out in a neighboring town, my father turned to me and said that he felt like his body was being dismembered. As an atheist and ardent secularist, he could never understand how communalism could pit neighbor against neighbor, how communal affiliation could ever rival passion for the nation. When anti-Muslim riots broke out in December 1992, without realizing how closely I echoed his anguish, I cried that I felt like someone was tearing my body apart. So deeply was the nation embedded in our subjectivities that threats of the disintegration of India were experienced in terms of dismemberment, as threats to our very existence.

And from my mother I inherited the hope that a united India would be a sanctuary where I would be "safe." But on what exclusions, repressions, and erasures are these hopes of respect and security built? What discourses of Self and Other underlie these obsessions with safety? There are many for whom the Indian nation is anything but a sanctuary. As a member of the majority community, what is my investment in holding on to a dream of a united, peaceful India? Feminists who have relentlessly examined their own privilege have described the dangers and complicities underlying a "pursuit of safe places" that relies on "unexamined notions of home, family and nation, and severely limits the scope of feminist inquiry and struggle" (Martin and Mohanty 1986:191–192, Pratt 1984). I continue to fear the risks involved in abandoning my nationalism and its "safe places":[28] it is perhaps no coincidence that in the months following the last round of riots, the mobs in my nightmares were Hindu; it is no accident that they were so clearly male. As a feminist, I must persist in my struggles with my own nationalism and its complicity with the repression of the memories of those who feel insecure in India.

POPULAR NARRATIVE, MEMORY, AND FORGETTING

Forgetting and even the historical error are an essential factor of the formation of a nation. (Renan 1882, quoted in van der Veer 1994:193)

In this chapter I have examined how popular narratives like *Tamas* may have participated in the recasting of the past at a time when the meaning of the nation was being violently contested. By comparing my memory of Partition with Bibi Satwant Kaur's, I have tried to trace how memories of the past are constructed differently according to one's sociohistorical location. Feminist activists Uma Chakravarti and Nandita Haksar, who worked among the survivors of the 1984 anti-Sikh violence, outline the importance of oral testimony for understanding the construction of individual and collective memory: "The experience of narration, even if it is of a single event, is not an isolated act of reconstructing just that specific moment in time but an evocation of feelings and perceptions about everything that has gone into placing that event within the totality of the experience of the narrator. When that moment is not an ordinary humdrum event but represents a crisis, both for the individual and the community, there is an immediate link with other crisis moments in the life of the narrator and the life of the nation" (1987:16–17). Bibi Satwant Kaur had insisted on walking me to my next appointment and, by telling me the story of her neighbor and his wife and daughters, had broken her silence to inform me about the terrors faced by women in her community in 1984. She had spoken when she had deemed it appropriate to do so, and *Tamas* had given her a mode of representing what had happened. In this manner, both her silence and her speech had challenged majority discourses of nation and community.[29]

My encounters with Bibiji and with Hindu viewers of *Tamas* revealed to me the power of popular narrative in the construction of memory for people differently located in the "national community" that Doordarshan was attempting to forge. The silence of the Hindus I interviewed indexed the ways in which they had actively forgotten not just *Tamas* but also the antiminority riots that had swept through their city. For the most part, the majority community had quietly, passively, watched the events of November 1984; in silence, it had now forgotten what had happened. This silence was indicative of a strategic forgetting that underscored the majority community's complicity in the violence of 1984.

As a feminist ethnographer I have tried to pay respectful attention to women's acts of subterfuge, their active forgetting and remembering. Debbora Battaglia points out that, in most analyses of memory, forgetting "is treated either as forgetfulness, an unintended 'social amnesia' . . . or as a coercive weapon, implying forced compliance with official versions of the truth. While the issues it raises must be acknowledged and examined, this approach effectively excludes consideration of *forgetting as a willed transformation of memory*" (1992:14; emphasis in original). Both memory and forgetting thus have to be analyzed as social and political phenomena in which historical subjects recast the past in their efforts to negotiate and make sense of their world. I have tried to "read" women's testimonies as well as their silences against the grain so as to trace their acts of remembering and forgetting. My purpose here is not to construct a dichotomy between communities in terms of oppressors (Hindus) and victims (Sikhs), but to delineate the importance of location in the construction of memory. While I can forget my nightmares in the noisy bustle of daily life, Bibiji must confront hers as she negotiates the silences of a city that has forgotten her terror. She must continue to live with her nightmare. Walter Benjamin has pointed out that to "articulate the past historically does not mean to recognize it 'the way it really was.' . . . It means to seize hold of a memory as it flashes up at a moment of danger" (1968:255). As indices of forgetting, the silences of the Hindu viewers I describe here were imposed by official histories; Bibi Satwant Kaur's silence was constructed in willed opposition to them. Remembering and forgetting are thus neither spontaneous nor innocent of politics.[30] I have tried to understand the construction of social and personal memory by listening for and attending to acts of forgetting.

I remember that the air was thick with hatred for days after the 1984 events. The memory of the screams of mobs and the cries of their victims is still fresh in my mind. The violence of that time reinforced for me some of the tragic consequences of forgetting the "birth of our nation." In popular nationalist narratives such as *Tamas*, the widespread and horrific violence wrought by Partition becomes a tragic *backdrop* to "the real story" of the birth of the nation. As Pandey points out, the place of Partition in the collective memory of the people of South Asia is comparable in magnitude with that of World War II in Japan or France. But, although World War II is commemorated in major national monuments in France and Japan, "there is, not surprisingly, no equivalent for Partition in India" (1992:31). Indeed, except for fictional literature and some recent academic work on Partition, there appears to have been a public repression of its memory. Some philosophers of history advocate the importance of an "ethics of forgetting" (Nietzsche 1949) to the construction of individual and collective destinies. For those of us committed to feminist and secularist praxis, however, perhaps the time has come to use our revisionist histories to interrogate (nationalist) History. Hence, instead of trying to exist without memory (after all, as Nietzsche has pointed out, only beasts and the dead can do that [1949:5]), we need to confront contending narratives of the past in order to analyze the configurations of power that led to the violence surrounding Partition and continue to result in the violence ravaging the postcolonial polity.

My purpose here has been to analyze *Tamas* as a televisual representation of the role of violence in engendering postcolonial nationhood. In so doing, I have focused on some of the exclusions, repressions, and silences underlying representations of the birth of the Indian nation. How does television problematize distinctions between history, mythology, and narrative as it shapes collective memory through its tales? The "meaning" of mythologies, according to Barthes, is "already complete, it postulates a kind of knowledge, a past, a memory, a comparative order of facts, ideas, decisions" (1972:117). By blaming the violence between communities almost exclusively on the colonial state and the machinations of ruling elites, by reducing the "ordinary people" implicated in the riots to pawns or mute spectators of the great drama of the birth of the nation, *Tamas* enacted one of the most powerful nationalist myths constructed about Partition. And, by valorizing "ordinary people" as repositories of essential humanity, *Tamas* forestalled an examination of what makes ordinary people commit horrifying acts of violence against one another.

Historical consciousness "streams" on subjects from "sources that are inexhaustible, strange incoherences come together, memory opens all its gates and yet is never open wide enough" (Nietzsche 1949:23). The words and the silences of the Sikh and Hindu viewers of *Tamas* reveal how myth and memory, history and biography overlap in the construction of historical consciousness in contexts where identity, community, and nationhood are sites of violent, often bloody, battles. In presenting a feminist analysis of the role of television in the constitution of memory, I have tried to historicize and politically locate my own memories of Partition as they surface in my reading of *Tamas:* I have tried to locate my positionality as a Hindu, with particular privileges of perspective and voice, as I recall the imbrication of my own history with the "national past."

I have attempted, at the same time, to outline the relationship between my memory and the "alternative, resistant spaces occupied by oppositional histories and memories" (Mohanty 1987:41). By emphasizing the way in which nationalist memories are predicated on repressions and erasures of the memories of the Other, I have tried to touch on the myriad ways in which contending historical consciousnesses are constructed during ferocious conflicts over the past. According to Sudipta Kaviraj, given the linearity of historical time, "distances cannot be reduced by an imaginative conceptual technique. The present time is equally calendrically distanced from past times" (n.d.:109). But in Bibi Satwant Kaur's interpretation of *Tamas*, Partition collapsed into the present as a reality that Sikhs in New Delhi must continue to live with in spaces familiar to them, now become sinister. Muslims and Sikhs all over India cannot afford the luxury of "distance" from events such as Partition.

Tamas's power lay in its ability to evoke the fears of violence that lay very close to the surface for many Indian viewers in the late 1980s. I have tried to understand, through the silences and voices of some Hindu and Sikh women, what happens when history is configured as the memory of a people, "a discourse in which a people retell to itself its own past" (Kaviraj n.d.:48). My encounters with Sikh viewers such as Bibi Satwant Kaur and with Hindu viewers who claimed to have forgotten *Tamas* reinforced for me the materiality of memory as it is forged through silence, erasure, and violence.

Epilogue *Sky Wars*

It is December 1997 and I have returned to New Delhi to do follow-up fieldwork for this project. This is my third trip to India since I concluded my last fieldwork in summer 1992. This trip is different; this has been a harsh winter. The smog has not lifted in weeks. Smoke from factory chimneys hovers close to the ground. Emissions from the thousands of scooters, trucks, buses, and cars that ply the streets swirl around me. On crowded street corners, in bare homes, in slums, poor people sit around charcoal stoves, huddling close to the heat. The smoke from the stoves rises, then lingers, blending with the winter fog and the smoke from the factories and the emissions from motor vehicles. The city lurches toward the twenty-first century. Roughly fifty years after India's independence, modernity, the telos of the Indian nation, seems just a little less elusive.

I have been able to stay in touch with many of the people with whom I did fieldwork in Vikas Nagar and Basti, but not all. A few, like the Das-guptas, retired and returned to their villages. Others, like the Sharmas, live with their adult children and grandchildren in other parts of the city where housing is cheaper. In Vikas Nagar, some families have inched up the socioeconomic ladder and now live in slightly more upscale neighbor-hoods all the way across town. Basti is unrecognizable. Rehana and her family moved to Moradabad after her husband suddenly died in 1992. A shabby office building now stands where her house once was. In 1995, I learned that many of the families I worked with in Basti had been evicted by their landlords, who demolished their quarters to make way for tall, multistory apartments. To my sorrow I learned that Bibi Satwant Kaur, Parminder Kaur and the rest of their family, and Harbhajan Kaur and her children had left. Nobody knew for sure where they were. There were rumors that Harbhajan Kaur and her children now lived with her brother in the outskirts of the city. I inquired about Bibi Satwant Kaur's family at a shop where they used to buy their groceries. The shop owner put down his glass of tea and wiped his mustache with the back of his sleeve. He turned to me, shrugged his shoulders, and replied: "They've probably gone back to Punjab. They never really liked it here." *Back* to Punjab? This had been their home; they had lived in New Delhi since 1947.

Half a century has passed since the bloody birth of the nation in 1947. India's independence was characterized by cataclysmic violence and the erasure of the experiences of those at the margins of the national imaginary. What kinds of narratives can be constructed of the present moment? The fiftieth year of independence has been marked by much introspection on the part of scholars, journalists, and activists about the state of the nation, economic progress, social justice, and national sovereignty. In the 1980s and early 1990s, a unified national culture was deemed a prophylactic against secessionist movements and burgeoning subnationalisms. But after 1991, national sovereignty was perceived to be under threat from a new, although not unexpected, source: transnational satellite television.[1] During the Gulf War in early 1991, cNN began to beam its news programs into India via satellite. Middle-class and upper-class households, who watched cNN through cable, were thus introduced to transnational satellite television.

The Indian state, which until that moment had exerted monopolistic control over television production, was caught napping. It was not until after 1992, after other transnational satellite networks such as Star (Satellite Television for the Asian Region), Zee TV, and BBC had been introduced, that the Indian state realized that its hold on middle-class viewers was slipping. As late as March 1992, Saroj Malik, a senior official in Doordarshan's audience research unit, told me in an interview that the new networks would never "catch on" with Indian viewers. "The programs are too foreign . . . they are alien to our culture. Why would the masses want to watch *Santa Barbara?* What would it mean to them? And anyway, nobody has the . . . reach [of] Doordarshan."

In 1997, five years after that interview, transnational satellite networks still did not have the reach of Doordarshan. These networks had, however, become extremely popular with the urban, middle-class core of Doordarshan's target audience. By that point, Doordarshan was engaged in a serious battle with Zee, Star, and the Sony Entertainment Network. At stake once again was culture: the identities, aspirations, and fantasies of Indian viewers; the consumer practices of the ever-expanding middle classes; discursive practices of masculinity, femininity, and sexuality; constructions of personal and collective memory.

Fears about "cultural invasion" had always been an important factor in India's television policies.[2] But the response of the Indian state to transnational satellite television suggested that it was not just India's territorial borders that had to be protected but also its airwaves. There were fears that transnational satellite television would undermine the project of nationhood by inaugurating a new era of cultural infiltration.[3] The culture wars of the 1990s would be fought in the skies.

The greatest fear of critics of transnational television was that Indian culture would be "homogenized" or, more specifically, "Americanized." But the plethora of channels, ranging from CNN to the BBC World Service, Star, Zee, and the regional channels targeted at India's diverse linguistic groups, pointed to a more complex scenario.[4] In some ways it seemed as if cultural production had been deterritorialized as a result of transnational satellite television (Gupta and Ferguson 1997b; Morley and Robins 1995). At the same time, as illustrated by their increasing dependence on Indian films, transnational television networks such as Star started to draw on "local" cultural productions in their effort to cater to local tastes and markets. These apparently local productions and markets, however, were always permeated by transnational styles, aesthetics, and desires.

David Morley and Kevin Robins's description of the reconfiguration of space in 1990s Europe resonates with what was happening in India:

> We are seeing the restructuring of information and image spaces and the production of a new communications geography, characterized by global networks and an international space of information flows; by an increasing crisis of the national sphere; and by new forms of regional and local activity. Our senses of space and place are all being significantly reconfigured. . . . Increasingly we must think in terms of communications and transport networks and of the symbolic boundaries of language and culture—the "spaces of transmission" defined by satellite footprints or radio signals—as providing the crucial, and permeable, boundaries of our age (1995:1).

How does transnational satellite television participate in the remapping of cultural spaces in an era of globalization? Globalization has often been conceived in terms of a relentless "penetration" of capitalism into all areas of social life. A persuasive counterargument to this model of globalization is provided by Lisa Lowe and David Lloyd, who argue that "transnational or neocolonial capitalism, like colonialist capitalism before it, continues to produce sites of contradiction that are effects of its always uneven expansion but that cannot be subsumed by the logic of commodification" (1997:1).[5] What kinds of sites of contradiction were created when cultural production articulated with the global capital represented by transnational satellite television? What sorts of cultural spaces were produced for the reimagination of community (Gupta and Ferguson 1997b; Morley and Robins 1995)?

In this epilogue I outline some of the developments surrounding the expansion of transnational satellite networks in India. Following Lowe and Lloyd, I understand the transnational to denote a historically specific stage of advanced capitalism marked by "a differentiated mode of production that relies on flexible accumulation and mixed production" (1997:1).[6] How has "Indian culture" been redefined in conjunction with transnational satellite television? As in the rest of this book, I argue that culture continues to be a crucial battleground and an object of struggles over identity and political control. The consequences of transnational capital and media for the reconfiguration of gender identity are worthy of a separate investigation. Nevertheless, in the last section of this epilogue I point to directions for the further research on the implications of transnational satellite television for the reconstitution of notions of Indian Womanhood in late twentieth-century India.

BATTLES IN THE SKIES

Soon after Star TV was launched in 1991, it captured the loyalties of the urban upper and middle classes who watched it via cable. A four-city survey conducted in October 1991 revealed that the highest "penetration" of Star TV was in Bombay (23.4 percent), followed by Madras with 7.2 percent, Delhi with 6.5 percent, and Calcutta with 3.2 percent (MARG, cited in S. Ninan 1995:157). However, when I concluded my fieldwork in summer 1992, and even as late as December 1995, the lower-middle-class and working-class families I knew in Vikas Nagar and Basti were not yet part of this audience. Transnational satellite television was still the preserve of upper-middle-class and upper-class households who could afford to subscribe to cable services that would give them access to Star and Zee TV. Yet, I knew that things were changing: I heard reports of low-income neighborhoods in other parts of New Delhi and in Bombay where households pooled their resources to obtain cable subscriptions. By November 1992, an estimated 1.28 million Indians (most of them middle and upper class) watched Star TV. These figures represented an increase of over 200 percent since the beginning of 1992. At the end of 1994, in addition to Star TV's four channels, Zee TV, CNN, and the BBC, there were five other networks beaming into India: Jain TV, Sun TV, El TV (a subsidiary of Zee TV), Asianet, and ATN. By 1996, there were seventy-six channels, churning out a total of 1,800 hours of programming daily (Sahgal 1997:30).

When I visited New Delhi in December 1997, many households in Vikas Nagar and Basti had finally obtained access to transnational satellite television. A few families had also invested in new television sets that would enable them to watch the new channels. Most families, however, had to be content with their old TV sets and thus watched fewer channels than their more affluent neighbors: they could barely afford the monthly subscription fees charged by their local cable operators; buying a new television set was out of the question.[7] Nonetheless, they had more options in terms of what they could watch. Doordarshan no longer had a monopoly on their attention.

Network owners depended largely on advertisers for their revenue (the "free to air" system), as opposed to pay television, and thus had to be extremely vigilant about viewers' loyalties. Predictably, not all the new networks were equally popular with urban, middle-class audiences. From my conversations with friends, relatives, and people in my own upper-middle-class neighborhood, I knew that the loyalties of Doordarshan's upper-class viewers had shifted to Star. For instance, one upper-class woman characterized Zee TV as a "lightweight" and "escapist" network devoted to Hindi films and film-based programs. She claimed that while she did not herself watch Zee, she turned it on between 3:00 and 4:00 P.M., when the rest of her household retired for their afternoon naps, so that her servants could enjoy it for a few hours. Viewership of the different networks could be further segmented according to viewers' class positions: Doordarshan and Zee TV occupied the more "downmarket" segments of the market, while Star TV, with its imported serials and English-language news shows, was deemed more "upmarket."

Zee TV represented itself as a South Asian channel aimed at viewers in India, the rest of the subcontinent, and the Middle East. Overall, Zee seemed to have captured a larger share of the audience than Star, which represented itself as a pan-Asian channel. In 1993, an Indian Marketing Research Bureau survey of about 250 Indian households revealed that 58 percent watched Zee, while 16 percent watched Star Plus. Not content with being one of the most watched satellite networks, Zee tried to expand the class base of its audience by producing more upmarket programs that would attract viewers with larger disposable incomes and bring in higher advertising revenues. Among these were programs such as *Sajan Sajani,* which portrayed the trials of married couples in contemporary India; "women-oriented" talk shows such as *Shakti;* and programs such as *Tol Mol Ke Bol,* modeled after the U.S. game show *The Price Is Right,* in which members of the studio audience guessed at the prices of expensive commodities. In addition, Zee commissioned small-budget serials and made-for-television films, or telefilms, such as Sridhar Kshirsagar's *Gulmohar West* and Bollywood producer Mahesh Bhatt's *Phir Teri Kahani Yaad Aayee.* The producers of these films and serials were relieved to work with a network that did not present the same bureaucratic obstacles as Doordarshan. Some, like Bhatt, were reported to be excited about expanding their access to a transnational South Asian audience: "I like the idea of being watched in Lahore and Dhaka" (A. Agarwal 1993:93).

By 1993, the number of satellites—and therefore, the choice of channels—had multiplied.[8] Insat 2B had eight transponders (transmitters that enabled satellites to receive and rebroadcast channels back to earth), of which five were used by the Indian government. Revenues from advertisements shown on satellite television soared from a mere Rs 15 crore (approximately $3.75 million) in 1992 to Rs 115 crore (approximately $28.75 million) in 1993 (Mitra 1995:112).

In response to the growing popularity of the transnational networks, Doordarshan launched the Metro Channel, originally conceived as a forum for programs produced in the four metropolitan centers—Bombay, Delhi, Calcutta, and Madras—which would be terrestrially linked, thereby drawing in viewers from all over the nation. By 1994, of the 8 million or so households that received cable television, the Metro Channel reached more than 6.3 million in the four metros alone, as compared with the estimated 1.6 million households reached by Zee (V. Kohli 1994:111).

By 1995, 10 million Indian households watched transnational satellite television via cable (Indian Market Research Bureau study, cited in S. Ninan 1995:189–190). By mid-1996, representatives of the transnational satellite television industry were estimating that, between 1996 and 2000, the number of homes in India with televisions would increase from 45 million to 65 million, and the number of satellite TV homes would rise from 12 million to 25 million. These estimates were based on sales of television sets: 4 million TV sets were being sold in India annually. Advertising revenue was expected to grow from Rs 1,000 crore (approximately $250 million) in 1995 to Rs 3,000 crore (approximately $750 million) by the year 2000. The transnational networks also hoped that Doordarshan's market share, which had dropped from 80 percent in 1993 to 70 percent in 1995, would decline to between 55 and 60 percent by the end of the decade, leaving potential revenues of between Rs 1,200 and 1,350 crore (approximately $300–347 million) for them. Media analysts believed that 50 percent of this revenue was likely to go to the Zee platform, with other transnational networks such as Sony, Home TV, and Star procuring approximately 10 percent each. They predicted that the remaining 20 percent would be split among the regional channels (A. Agarwal 1996:99).

Zee TV led the way in terms of advertising revenues. Yet, because Doordarshan continued to reach the maximum number of homes throughout the nation, producers continued to line up outside Doordarshan headquarters in New Delhi, hoping to get contracts for the National Network and the Metro Channel. However, the question was not just of the *number* of households "covered" but of the *kinds* of viewers that could now be reached: as pointed out by journalist Sara Adhikari, "it is not the growing viewership which is drawing television companies to India. . . . More importantly, it is the purchasing power of the middle class Indian, rated by the IMF to be higher than countries like Italy and Britain, which has created the current buzz" (1994:8).

Questions about national sovereignty came to the fore several times in state and public discourses about transnational satellite television. In November 1993, fears about Pakistani propaganda led to the banning of Pakistan Television (PTV2) in Bombay. Viewers had been watching PTV2 via Asiasat (the same satellite that beamed Star TV), and the city administrators feared that these programs would exacerbate tensions between Hindus and Muslims. This became a particularly sensitive issue after the Bombay blasts in March 1993: the administration was getting increasingly nervous about PTV2's allegations that Islam was under attack in India. By 1995, Doordarshan was using the Zee transponder for its external service, which was aimed primarily to counter Pakistani television's negative representations of India. The Indian government was concerned about the impact of these representations on viewers not just in India, but also elsewhere in the subcontinent and in the Middle East. As a result of the state's efforts to obtain higher visibility, viewers in the Middle East and Southeast Asia started to see more Indian programs than ever before.

THE RETERRITORIALIZATION OF CULTURE

Significant as regional politics were, national sovereignty was more deeply imbricated with multinational and transnational regimes of capital than with the geopolitical agendas of states. Akhil Gupta and James Ferguson point out that changes in a global political economy that is based on increasingly intense movements of information, commodities, capital, and peoples have contributed to "the invention of new forms of cultural difference and new forms of imagining community. Something like a transnational public sphere has certainly rendered any strictly bounded sense of community or locality obsolete" (1992:9). They add that the current transnational public sphere(s) may have engendered "forms of solidarity and identity that do not rest on an appropriation of space where contiguity and face-to-face contact are paramount" (1992:9).

How did transnational satellite television participate in the reterritorialization of culture occurring in late twentieth-century India? I now outline the implications of transnational satellite television for our understanding of the relationship between cultural production, the state, and global capital in late twentieth-century India. How do transnational cultural productions compel us to redefine what is meant by culture and, in particular, national culture?

Transnational Television and the Nation-State

With the introduction of commercial sponsorship in the mid-1980s, the Indian state's commitment to development communication had already been replaced with the objective of producing entertainment programs. Some media critics alleged that the state's agenda was further transformed by transnational television conglomerates (e.g., S. Ninan 1995:17). What do the changing agendas of the Indian government reveal about the fate of the nation-state in an era of transnational capital? The Indian state's first response to the success of transnational satellite television was to deregulate its operations and launch the Metro Channel. The state also tried to restrict the commercial success of transnational networks by limiting the amount of foreign exchange available to Indian companies that wished to advertise on Zee and Star.

A landmark judgment of the Indian Supreme Court in 1995 foregrounded issues of national sovereignty and the question of national borders. In 1994, the Cricket Association of Bengal (CAB) and the Board of Control for Cricket in India (BCCI) filed a suit against the Indian government challenging the government's refusal to grant them and their foreign partners permission to uplink a satellite and directly telecast two cricket matches, the Hero Cup in 1993 and the India–West Indies series in 1994. The CAB and the BCCI had sold the rights of the two events to two international companies, Trans-World International (TWI) and Entertainment and Sports Network (ESPN), but Doordarshan had insisted that, as the state-owned network, only it could sell the rights. The Supreme Court decreed that airwaves were public property and ought to be regulated by an independent public authority. The court also held that all Indian citizens had the fundamental right to impart as well as receive information, and that to exercise this fundamental right, all citizens had to have access to broadcasting.[9] The Supreme Court judgment revealed just how complex the position of the Indian state, which had been compelled to adapt to reconfigurations of territoriality and culture introduced by transnational television, had become.

In February 1997, the ruling United Front government tried to pass the Broadcast Bill, aimed at private broadcasters, in an attempt to rein in transnational satellite networks. The bill would have required all companies telecasting commercial programs within India to uplink from within the nation (here the bill was making a distinction between public service networks such as Discovery and BBC World, and corporations such as Star, Zee, and Sony, which depended on advertising). In order to uplink from within India, however, companies would have to get a license from the government, which would be issued by a newly constituted Broadcasting Authority. Further, and more important, companies owned by foreigners, Indian companies in which foreign equity exceeded 49 percent, and companies that ran a direct-to-home service would be dis-qualified from applying for a license.[10] As a consequence, transnational networks such as Star, Zee, and Sony would automatically be barred from obtaining licenses and, consequently, from telecasting into India. (As it happened, the Broadcast Bill was never implemented because the government fell before the bill could be passed in Parliament.)

As part of its efforts to make Doordarshan autonomous and, more im-portantly, to enable it to compete with the transnational networks, the government also resurrected the Prasar Bharati Act (which had first been drafted in 1990). The Prasar Bharati Board was nominated in November 1997, and S. S. Gill, the former bureaucrat responsible for the expansion of Doordarshan in the mid-1980s and for the introduction of serials such as *Hum Log*, was appointed CEO of the Prasar Bharati Corporation. Gill announced that he would ban from Doordarshan all advertisements that objectified women, mythological serials that caricatured religious figures, and teleshopping channels. However, neither he nor the board lasted very long. In March 1998, a new BJP-led government and its allies vowed to "take a fresh look" at the Prasar Bharati Act. Their intention was to make the act "accountable to Parliament" by having a parliamentary commit-tee oversee Prasar Bharati. This statement generated concerns that the operation of Prasar Bharati would become subject to interference from politicians, thereby subverting the original objective of making Doordar-shan autonomous.[11] When the Prasar Bharati Board was formed in 1997, the Hindu nationalist BJP claimed that it was "packed" with leftists with "political bias." A year later, the BJP-led government announced that it would reconstitute the Prasar Bharati committee. At the time of the writ-ing of this epilogue, it seems likely that the BJP government will allow the act to lapse without ratification. Prasar Bharati will thus lose its legality and the current government will be free to create a new body. Once again, the state's unwillingness to relinquish control of Doordarshan indicates the significance of broadcasting to national politics.

Theorists of transnational media argue that the expansion of transna-tional capital requires a strong state that can provide "safe investment environments," create markets, and provide patent and trademark pro-tection (e.g., Hamelink 1993:386). The struggles waged by the Indian state to safeguard its ability to shape cultural production are of consider-able theoretical and political significance and indicate the continuing re-silience of the nation-state vis-à-vis transnational capital. Thus, instead of debating whether the nation-state has been made obsolete by transnational media, it seems more pertinent to investigate how transnational regimes of capital and information have participated in the reterritorialization of culture and the reimagining of the national community occurring in late twentieth-century India.

The Re-production of the Local?

The dominant view of globalization is that it results in the creation of giant media conglomerates and greater standardization and homogenization of production, and that it detaches "media cultures from the particularities of place and context" (Morley and Robins 1995:17). Herbert Schiller defines globalization as "transnational corporate cultural domination, a world in which private giant economic enterprises pursue—sometimes competitively, sometimes co-operatively—historical capitalist objectives of profit making and capital accumulation, in continuously changing market and geopolitical conditions" (Schiller 1991:20–21, in Morley and Robins 1995:12–13). To what extent does this description of globalization resonate with what was happening in India in the late-1990s?

What was the role of transnational capital in the re-production of the local? The new transnational networks were not just "new conduits of distribution" (Morley and Robins 1995:36); they also created new sites of cultural production. The site of the local (whether conceptualized as the local television program, the local television studio, or the local network) was reconfigured, if not produced, by the takeovers, mergers, and strategic collaborations engaged in by transnational satellite conglomerates.[12] In July 1993, the Australian media baron Rupert Murdoch bought a controlling share of Star TV. Subsequently, in 1994, Murdoch purchased a 49.9 percent stake in the broadcaster of Zee TV, Asia Today, Limited (ATL). Star TV had been running into losses in its South Asia sector because it had failed to click with a majority of viewers, many of whom had shown a preference for Zee. Ostensibly, one of Murdoch's objectives in buying Zee was to draw on Zee's knowledge of India's markets, and hence "piggyback" on its successes in India. Zee was to aid Star in planning its programming, and, in exchange for helping Star in program concepts, production, acquisition, and marketing, Zee was to retain full editorial and managerial control of its own programming. Zee would also gain access to the expertise of Murdoch's media organization News Corp and, more important, to the international markets and channels controlled by Murdoch in the United Kingdom, Europe, and North America.

The consolidation of Star's presence in India was only partially accomplished by buying Zee stock and capitalizing on Zee's knowledge and access to Indian audiences. Star also planned to produce Hindi news programs and films, and to launch channels in regional languages. It had become clear to Murdoch that if Star was to succeed in India, it would have to "Indianize" its programming.[13] Such efforts by transnational television networks to Indianize their programming created sites for the reterritorialization of (Indian) culture. Satellite television programming in the mid and late 1990s was marked by an apparent paradox. At the same time that television production was deeply imbricated in the transnational movements of capital, commodities, and desires, there seemed to be a turn to local and localized production. It seemed that transnational television networks would have to cater to locally segmented markets if they were to become profitable.

Market segmentation, or niche marketing, is hardly a novel idea for marketing professionals: indeed, as Morley and Robins point out, the emergence of the local in the form of niche markets exemplifies the inherent logic of globalization (1995). In an age of multinational and transnational capital, the meaning of the local—indeed, the production of the local—has been recast by global conglomerates such as NBC and Sony that are acutely aware that the local-global nexus is crucial (Morley and Robins 1995:116). Thus, for example, Sony (a key player among the transnational networks in India) describes its strategy as "global localization"; and NBC vice president J. B. Holston is reported to be "resolutely 'for localism'" because he "recognizes that globalization is 'not just about putting factories into countries, it's being part of that culture too'" (Brown 1989, in Morley and Robins 1995:117).

But did the reterritorialized local revise or re-produce hegemonic constructions of the national? As part of its efforts to Indianize its programming, Star introduced Hindi talk shows and programs, and screened an increasing number of Hindi films and film-based shows. By now, Star had changed its earlier objective of producing pan-Asian programming and had decided to segment its channels along region-specific and, in the case of India, nation-specific lines. Nation-specific programming was enabled by splitting Star's channels into two beams, with the northern one targeting China and Taiwan and the southern one covering India.

In October 1996, Star hired former Doordarshan director-general Rati-kant Basu as its CEO and entrusted him with the task of leading the Indianization of the Star TV network. He began by starting a daily Hindi band (from 7:00 to 9:00 P.M.) on Star Plus, on which he showed such serials as *Imtihaan, Chandrakanta,* and *Alif Laila,* which had been big hits on Doordarshan. Star's new marketing strategies brought it into direct competition with Zee, which countered by consolidating its program-ming. It introduced a Hindi news bulletin against Star's at 7:00 P.M. and expanded the middle-class orientation of its soaps to appeal to a broader range of viewers.

Star TV launched a new music channel, Channel V, modeled on MTV. But while MTV had adamantly refused to Indianize its programming, Channel V had a nine-hour daily window that consisted of up to 50 per-cent local programming specifically targeted at Indian viewers. With its combination of Hindi, English, and (with the inclusion of Daler Mehendi) Punjabi pop, and veejays such as Quick Gun Murugan, Javed Jaffrey, and Ruby Bhatia, who became cultural icons of a generation of young viewers in cities and small towns, Channel V's success demonstrated the enor-mous possibilities of the Indianization of music programs.[14]

All the networks, including Doordarshan, now had to struggle to main-tain their hold on viewers' attentions and loyalties and, if possible, expand their audience base. It was at this juncture that Doordarshan, Zee, Sony, and Star turned to a tried-and-tested source for programs that would attract viewers and ensure their loyalties: the Indian film industry.[15] In re-sorting to the Indian film industry as a means of procuring viewership, transnational networks were especially encouraged by the success of film-based programs on Doordarshan's Metro Channel.[16] Producers, directors, and script writers in the film industry who had turned to television in the mid-1980s once again found it profitable to produce programs for the small screen. Television offered them yet another means of reaching a mass market; more important, the financial risks entailed in produc-ing television shows, serials, and film-based programs were substantially lower than those incurred in making films for the box office. Telefilms with "nonformula" storylines and nonstar costs became a permanent part of Doordarshan and transnational satellite programming. The telefilm trend was launched in August 1993 by Zee's *Phir Teri Kahani Yaad Ayee,* which was a huge marketing success, bringing in Rs 1.25 crore in reve-nue (Katiyar 1995:146–147).

Programs based on film music were another staple of television.[17] Doordarshan's film music programs *Chitrahaar* and *Chayageet* had always been enormously successful, often capturing larger and more loyal audiences than some of the serials. But the film music programs now shown on television were markedly different from *Chitrahaar* and *Chayageet,* which seemed stodgy and old-fashioned in comparison. A new film-based program, *Superhit Muqabla,* which was telecast in the 9:00–10:00 P.M. slot on Doordarshan's Metro Channel, became phenomenally popular.

Superhit Muqabla was followed by *BPL Oye!,* which was shown on Channel V, and *Phillips Top Ten* on Zee TV. *BPL Oye!* sparked a new trend in programs that combined Hindi and English pop, song, and dance sequences from Hindi films with MTV-style presentation formats and veejays. These new programs were based on the MTV format and were explicitly aimed at younger viewers. By 1994, Doordarshan's national network was telecasting three film music shows, the Metro Channel had two film music programs, and Zee TV had five film music–based shows. *Close-Up Antakshiri* was the second-highest-rated show on Zee (after the popular serial *Tara*). Star TV introduced two extremely popular programs, *Winner Mangta Hai,* which combined Hindi and English pop, and the *Great Indian Manovaigyanik Show,* which represented itself as a lifestyle *cum* music show.

The rearticulation of the national with the transnational is illustrated in Doordarshan's alliance with CNN in June 1995. Given Doordarshan's earlier claims to telecast exclusively "indigenous programming," this collaboration was ironic. Doordarshan stood to gain financially from the deal with CNN; more important, it sought to gain strategically by turning a potential competitor into a collaborator. Further, the tie-in with CNN offered India an opportunity to retaliate against PTV2's alleged propaganda against India: Pakistani viewers would now receive Doordarshan news on a regular window on CNN (S. Ninan 1995:40). Doordarshan's alliance with CNN was emblematic of the constraints and changing agendas of the Indian nation-state and the ways the very meaning of nationhood was being transformed in response to global capitalism.

Another factor in the rearticulation of the national and the transnational was the mobility of non–resident Indian (NRI) capital and its importance to the production of transnational satellite television. The growth of Zee TV as a major player in the transnational arena was the result of a fortuitous combination of Indian entrepreneurship and NRI capital. In

1992, Li Ka-Shing and Richard Li, then owners of Star TV, offered Indian businessman Subhash Chandra a satellite channel for $5 million. Chandra bought the channel with the help of his Hong Kong–based NRI associate. When it was first launched, Zee marketed itself as a South Asian network. By 1995, it was explicitly targeting the South Asian diaspora in Africa and the Middle East. Advertisements for Zee TV elaborated themes of homesickness and nostalgia for India and promised diasporic viewers a means to "keep in touch with Indian culture." In 1995, Zee bought out TV-Asia, a pay channel beaming to Britain and Europe that was owned by NRIS in Dubai and Britain. Zee TV, with its entertainment channel beamed on the Star platform, was already a major presence in Southeast Asia, and the takeover of TV-Asia was but the first step in Zee's strategy to target South Asians in three other sectors: Europe, North America, and South Africa. The centrality of NRI capital to the marketing of "India" via transnational television crucially mediated the production and reterritorialization of Indian culture.[18]

The reterritorialization of culture thus drew (apparently) local sites of cultural production into increasingly complex relationships with each other and with global circuits of capital. The "choices" of viewers and the pleasures they derived from these texts were themselves shaped by transnational regimes of capital, information, and desire.[19] At the same time, the mobility of transnational capital was *refracted through* these local sites of production because of the creation of active audiences.

It is important to note that even as the national was reappearing in the guise of the local, the meanings attributed to the nation—to what it meant to be Indian—were themselves undergoing rapid transformation as a result of the transnational circulation of cultures, capital, and commodities. Discourses of national culture have never been stable in India: as I have argued elsewhere in this book, the politics of identity and transnational discourses of modernity and progress have always played a central role in the formation and contestation of hegemonic notions of national culture. However, while the politics of identity continued to destabilize hegemonic discourses of national culture in the postsatellite era, transnational television appears to have mediated the continuous reconstitution of "India" and "Indian culture." It is therefore necessary to interrogate notions of cultural imperialism that "presume the existence of pure, internally homogeneous and authentic cultures, which are then seen to be, belatedly, subverted or corrupted by foreign influences"

(Morley 1992, in Morley and Robins 1995:7). From all indications, the Indianization of transnational television programs was occurring at the same time that "Indian culture" was itself being reconstructed.

DIRECTIONS FOR FUTURE RESEARCH

This book has explored the cultural and political significance of television by investigating Doordarshan's role in the reconstitution of gender and nation during the late 1980s and early 1990s, a crucial period in postcolonial India. Not only is that history important in its own right, it also critically sets the stage for the cultural developments introduced by transnational satellite television. In what follows, my objective will be to raise questions for future research. What does the Indianization of transnational satellite production imply when the meanings, symbols, and discursive practices relating to nationhood, national subjectivity, and national culture are themselves undergoing rapid transformation in conjunction with global capitalism? Whose experiences gain center stage in these new cultural productions? "Culture" continues to be an important political weapon as the culture wars within India persist, religious and regional identities are sharpened, and inequalities of caste and class are exacerbated. Can the cultural changes brought about by transnational satellite television be disentangled from those introduced by Doordarshan more than a decade ago?

What spaces do transnational texts create for resistance, subversion, or appropriation through the production of desire, fantasy, and imagination?[20] How do viewers' interpretations of these texts articulate with their social relationships? These questions have important consequences not just for cultural critique and politics, but also for the formulation of communications policy and for interventions by NGOs and citizens' groups concerned with the role of mass media in social and political life. Further investigation of the cultural consequences of transnational television production may, therefore, be pursued in terms of the following: the impact of regional channels on the reimagination of the national audience, changing aspirations of the middle classes, implications for the formation of religious identities, new forms of political discourse, and the reconstitution of Indian Womanhood.

The Launch of "Regional" Networks

As I argue elsewhere in this book, the prime-time programs shown on Doordarshan's National Programme tended to have a north Indian bias in that they built on north Indian perspectives on sociality, community, and nation. This was particularly true of narrative serials, all of which were in Hindi. Similarly, news programs were produced entirely from a "Delhi-centric" framework, and the "national audience" was conceived from a (middle-class and upper-caste) north Indian perspective.

The mid-1990s, however, witnessed a proliferation of vernacular and regional channels, some of which were telecast on privately owned networks and beamed via satellite to viewers in different parts of the country and overseas. Doordarshan launched ten vernacular channels in 1994, thus demonstrating a shift from Hindi-dominated programming. Subsequently, Asianet started to telecast Malayalam programs targeted at viewers not just in Kerala but also in the rest of India and in the Gulf states, where there was a high concentration of Malayali migrant laborers. In 1994, Zee TV introduced Bengali telecasts and Jain TV started to show films in south Indian languages on a regular basis.

Not only did some of the new channels broadcast in vernacular languages, they also focused on regional issues and politics. For instance, Tamil Sun TV, owned by Kalanidhi Maran and shown on Star's platform, telecast a number of Tamil films and film-based programs, although its popularity rested on its many programs covering Tamil politics. These programs were avidly viewed by Tamils within the state of Tamil Nadu as well as elsewhere in India and overseas. Networks such as Sun TV enabled viewers all over India and overseas to keep in touch with political developments in their home states.

In considering the cultural and political implications of satellite television, it is important to explore the extent to which regional channels may (potentially) interrogate hegemonic notions of a monolithic national audience. Unlike Doordarshan's National Programme, these programs explicitly recognize linguistic communities spread across different regions of India as well as in the diaspora: to this extent, their audiences are both more "local" than the National Programme and less "local" in that they include (reterritorialized) transnational communities. What consequences do these regional cultural productions have for the reimagination of the "national community"?

*Transnational Television and the Expansion of
the Indian Middle Classes*

At least since the mid-1980s, when commercial sponsorship enabled the
production of narrative serials, discourses of Indian culture have been
mediated by a consumer culture targeted at the middle classes. The cultural constitution of the Indian middle classes was central to the project of
redefining nationhood and national identity. What, then, is the relationship between recent transnational cultural productions and the cultural
constitution of the rapidly expanding middle classes? What has been the
impact of the desires engendered by transnational cultural texts on the
identities and aspirations of the new middle classes?

As indicated by the ubiquity of the combination of Hindi and English
(termed Hinglish by some middle-class Indians) in programs on Zee TV
and the mix of English and Hindi pop on Channel V and MTV, the new
middle classes no longer consist exclusively of the English-speaking professional classes living "Westernized lives" in metropolitan centers. The
presence of the new middle classes, who speak in the vernacular and live
in small towns all over the nation, is also indexed by the new home shopping channels that display phone numbers of their retail outlets in small
towns like Roorkee, Vijaywada, and Nasik.

While the role of commodities in the imagination of modernity seems
to have expanded, we need to carefully investigate the implications of
modern *lifestyles* for modernist *subjectivities*. Many of the viewers I worked
with could not afford to buy the products advertised on television. Yet,
they derived great pleasure from watching the advertisements, from gazing at the products, and, perhaps, from imagining what their lives would
be like if they could afford them. While it is likely that gazing on these
objects, or more specifically, their advertisements, led to frustration, perhaps even to an envy of people who could afford them (Steedman 1986),
it was evident to me that longing for these objects and fantasizing about
them produced their own forms of pleasure.[21] My observations about the
fantasies and longings engendered by advertisements are corroborated
by Sevanti Ninan, who alludes to the "yearning" they produce (1995:141).
What kinds of practices, behaviors, and actions do these yearnings lead
to? What is the role of these longings and fantasies in the continuing constitution of middle-class subjectivity?

As I argued earlier in this book, television's role in the expansion and cultural constitution of the Indian middle classes was unprecedented: in many ways, transnational television may have only built on and accelerated the changes brought about by Doordarshan. Nonetheless, the imagination and experience of modernity and cosmopolitanism have been altered as a result of transnational television.

Religious Identities

Earlier, I argued against the notion that capital "enters" communities from the outside and suggested instead that capital participates in the production of localities and communities.[22] In so doing, capital creates sites of difference within and across social formations, and to this extent is productive of subjectivities and identities.[23] This production of cultural difference, however, does not necessarily entail a tolerance of difference. It is similarly problematic to assume the emancipatory potential of these sites of difference. To what extent, then, are the differences created by transnational capital hierarchically constructed? In a cultural and historical context in which difference is frequently articulated in terms of religion, what has been the role of transnational capital and transnational cultural productions in the reconfiguration of religious identities? In chapter 4 I discussed Doordarshan's role in the consolidation of Hindu nationalism. What difference have the texts of transnational satellite television made to a strengthening of communal identities?

The 1990s have witnessed the persistent popularity of TV mythologicals that are either spin-offs of older ones (e.g., the *Mahabharat Katha*) or are entirely new (e.g., *Om Namah Shivay*). In 1994, *Sri Krishna* was the most watched Doordarshan serial in New Delhi and Calcutta, with TRP (television rating points) of 64.7 and 60.1 respectively; it earned the second highest ratings in Bombay (52.5) and the third highest ratings in Madras (47.1) (Indian Market Research Bureau 1994:8).[24] Earlier, Hindu nationalism had been associated, accurately or not, with particular segments of the population, specifically, those who had a vernacular education and lived "traditional" lifestyles. In recent years, professionals, scientists, and yuppies living "modern," even Westernized, lifestyles have begun to espouse a Hindu nationalist vision of nationhood based on exclusionary representations of a pristine Hindu past. How do televised depictions of Hindu/Indian tradition articulate with transnational, seemingly contradictory, discourses of cosmopolitanism and modernity? Does the continuing polarization between communal communities represent a deepening of the trends introduced by Doordarshan in the late 1980s and early 1990s?

Changes in Political Discourse

Although the press has enjoyed relative freedom in India, this freedom has been severely restricted in the case of the state-owned broadcast media, All India Radio and Doordarshan. Most of the people I worked with in Vikas Nagar and Basti were well aware that news about domestic politics on All India Radio and Doordarshan was censored by the state. Before the advent of transnational television, they obtained information about national and international events either through newspapers, from each other, or by way of rumor. If something momentous happened, many of them would turn to the BBC World Service on their transistors to get the "true story." For instance, during the anti-Sikh violence in November 1984, Parmindar Kaur's brother kept himself informed of the spread of anti-Sikh violence to different parts of north India by listening to the news on the BBC World Service: Doordarshan news had minimized the extent of the violence. People like Sukumaran, who were relatively comfortable with English, listened to the BBC World Service news a couple of times a week because they thought it was the most reliable source of information about events not just in the rest of the world but in their own country.

The success of video newsmagazines in the mid-1980s demonstrated the demand for audiovisual news programs about domestic politics. Although video newsmagazines had to be certified by a special wing of the Film Certification Board, they were not subjected to the same forms of censorship as Doordarshan or All India Radio. Video newsmagazines became the medium of choice for those who had access to them. The most popular video newsmagazines in Vikas Nagar and Basti were the English *Newstrack* and the Hindi *Chakravyuh*. Even though most people I knew did not own VCRs, they rented them about once a month to catch up with their favorite video newsmagazines. Thus, many people learned about the anti-Mandal violence either from the press or from video newsmagazines. Similarly, they learned about the success of Hindu nationalist BJP leader L. K. Advani's journey across the country, in which he mobilized support for the demolition of the Babri Mosque, from video newsmagazines.

Doordarshan news's dubious reputation was further eroded with the advent of CNN and BBC television. (It is not surprising that CNN, which paved the way for transnational satellite television in India, was a news channel.) In the early years of transnational television in India, middle-class viewers avidly watched the BBC and CNN news. However, the popularity of these programs was not restricted to middle-class, English-speaking viewers. Even though most of the people I knew in Vikas Nagar and Basti had not been educated in English and were not comfortable speaking it, the BBC was their news of choice, particularly during national and international crises.

Star and Zee gradually established themselves as producers of news feature programs; talk shows; panel discussions consisting of politicians, journalists, and political analysts; and televised political debates. Most episodes of talk shows such as *Rubaroo, Aap Ki Adalat* (or, after it moved from Zee to Star, *Janata Ki Adalat*), *Chakravyuh,* and *The Shotgun Show* focused on politics and contemporary events and were avidly watched by viewers in Vikas Nagar and Basti. *Rubaroo* consisted of an hour-long interview with political celebrities on matters ranging from the latest political scandal to upcoming debates in Parliament. *Aap Ki Adalat* drew on the format of a court trial. A series of charges would be leveled on behalf of "the people" against a political celebrity, who would then have to defend himself. Talk shows, chat shows, and televised debates on the regional channels were especially popular because, as noted above, they enabled viewers in various parts of the country and overseas to stay informed of political developments in their home states.[25] Political analyst and television anchor Cho Ramaswamy is reported to have commented that the advantage of satellite television (as opposed to Doordarshan) was its lack of government censorship: "I do not want to come on Doordarshan because the amount of freedom that one gets in satellite channels would not be there. And many things I say would not be palatable to the regional and national parties" (Pillai 1996:27). By December 1997, there were more news programs than ever before. In January 1998, Zee TV started a channel that was exclusively dedicated to covering the upcoming national elections.

The changing role of audiovisual news in shaping public discourse on politics is an important area of investigation for academics, media critics, and media activists. To what extent do these news programs create, or participate in, *new* forms of political socialization? Do they result in greater expectations of accountability from elected officials? What do they tell us about the changing relationship between the state and civil society, and between discourses of nationalism, identity, and citizenship?

The Reconstitution of Indian Womanhood

Throughout the 1990s, narrative serials continued to be a major draw for television viewers. While, initially, imported soap operas like *The Bold and the Beautiful* and *Santa Barbara* were avidly watched by upper-class and upper-middle-class viewers, with the subsequent expansion of target audiences to middle- and lower-income viewers, the popularity of these soap operas waned, and eventually they attracted only about 1 percent of the cable television viewers in metropolitan centers (Swami 1994:83). Star TV began to invest in television serials in Hindi, and Doordarshan and Zee stepped up their production of serials.

One of the most striking aspects of serial production in the mid and late 1990s has been not just the dramatic increase in the number of serials being produced but also their changed content. Unlike the Doordarshan serials of the late 1980s and early 1990s, which were explicitly nationalist, relatively few of the new serials pretend to have a "social message." While the earlier generation of serials had themes such as the depiction of anticolonial struggles, the "uplift" of women, the social reformist efforts of patriotic men and women, and the portrayal of military heroes, most of the new serials are about adultery, the trials of single women, corporate wars, and so on (e.g., *Tara, Andaaz, Parampara, Swabhimaan*).[26] This is not to say that nationalist serials are no longer telecast (for instance, *Gaatha*, telecast on Star Plus in December 1997, was about anticolonial struggles); however, there has been a decided shift in the content of the new serials from the politics of nation and community to an explicit focus on the politics of family, sexuality, and intimacy. Does the changing content of the new serials correlate with a reconfiguration of family, gender, and sexuality in women's everyday lives?

How do viewers interpret portrayals of women in the new serials? Many of the women I interviewed said that their lives were "very different" from those depicted in the new serials: the women in these serials make choices that they had neither the ability nor, always, the desire to emulate. Who, then, are the new serials addressing, and what kinds of subjectivities are they creating? What forms of pleasure, fantasy, and desire are produced by this heightened sense of the disjuncture women perceive between their lives and those of the characters they love to watch on the television screen? And how do men respond to these representations of New Indian Womanhood?

In her work on popular culture in Japan, anthropologist Anne Allison insists that fantasy and reality are sometimes indistinguishable in the material effects they have on people's lives (1996:xiii). It is therefore especially important to investigate the relationship between fantasy and reality experienced by viewers of these new serials—not as binary opposites of each other but in terms of how reality is mediated, perhaps even constructed, as a result of the fantasies and desires introduced by transnational television. Like the Doordarshan serials of the late 1980s and early 1990s, the new serials, for all the fantasy they engender for their viewers, are not passively consumed. Indeed, the relationship between desire, fantasy, and reality is especially significant because audiences express their opinions about serials either by switching their loyalties, through market surveys conducted by networks and advertising agencies, or by writing to the networks. For instance, producer Vinta Nanda claimed that every time the protagonist of the hit serial *Tara* cried "a lot," the serial's rating went down because, according to Nanda, "She is supposed to be a fighter, and if she cries, not in public" (Jain 1994:105). While viewers' active engagements with these narratives should not be valorized as expressions of choice, resistance, or some sort of sovereign agency, it is also essential to note that producers, script writers, and advertisers keep a close watch on viewers' responses, and, very often, story lines and characters are changed accordingly.

Future research on viewers' engagements with representations of the New Indian Woman might entail close textual analysis and careful ethnographic study in order to trace how these new serials (and the advertisements that frame them) create specifically gendered subject positions for viewers. How do these subject positions differ from those analyzed earlier in this book? In their focus on relations of family, sexuality, and intimacy, have the serials opened up new domains to scrutiny and discursive production? Have they enlarged the range of possibilities for women who experience their own lives as markedly different from those they see unfold on the screen? Or have they, in fact, introduced new forms of discipline and governance into women's lives?

As I have indicated above, not all the cultural and political characteristics of transnational television are new or unprecedented; indeed, in some respects transnational television may have deepened or expanded the trends and developments introduced by Doordarshan more than a decade ago. But the new cultural texts seem to have repositioned women as subjects of a transnational order of capital and desire which, in Lowe and Lloyd's words, might create "sites of contradiction and dynamics of its own negation and critique. These contradictions produce new possibilities precisely because they have led to a breakdown and a reformulation of the categories of nation, race, class, and gender" (1997:21). Future research on television in India might trace how the very categories of gender, family, and community through which women make sense of their experiences have been reconfigured through these intersections of texts and lives.

Notes

Chapter 1 *Culture Wars*

1   After independence, the Indian Constitution set aside quotas in government
     jobs and educational institutions for the lowest castes and tribal communities,
     termed the Scheduled Castes and Scheduled Tribes, respectively. The Man-
     dal Commission Bill proposed the expansion of these quotas to include other
     lower castes, or, in bureaucratic parlance, Other Backward Castes (oBcs).

2   Gyanendra Pandey provides a pithy definition of communalism as it is used
     in the Indian context:

> "Communalism" refers to a condition of suspicion, fear and hostility be-
> tween members of different religious communities. In academic investi-
> gations, more often than not, the term is applied to organised political
> movements based on the proclaimed interests of a religious community,
> usually in response to a real or imagined threat from another religious
> community (or communities). It denotes movements that make sectional
> demands on state policy for a given share in jobs, education and legisla-
> tive positions, leading on in some instances to demands for the creation of
> new provinces and states. (1992:6)

3   I am referring, of course, to Uma Bharati and Sadhvi Rithambara, who were
     extremely effective in drawing crowds with their fiery anti-Muslim speeches.
     They were so successful in mobilizing support that local chapters of the
     Bharatiya Janata Party and its allies distributed copies of their speeches on
     audiocassettes.

4   Sara Dickey's pioneering ethnography of Tamil film (1993) and the work of
     Prabha Krishnan and Anita Dighe (1990), M. S. S. Pandian (1992), Arvind
     Rajagopal (1994; forthcoming), Patricia Uberoi (1995), and Ravi Vasudevan
     (1989, 1990, 1992) are exceptions to the general neglect of the role of mass
     media in contemporary politics in South Asia.

5   My use of quotation marks is intended to highlight the position of the "non-
     West" in opposition to "the West," which I see as a discursive, geopolitical,
     and historically produced space, and a hegemonic site of knowledge produc-
     tion (cf. Hall 1996).

6   I analyze the relationship between the formulation of television policy and the state's agenda for nation building in greater detail in chapter 2.

7   By pointing to Doordarshan's centrality in the redeployment of culture I am not implying that notions of culture were static or uncontested before the advent of television. Instead, my purpose is to foreground the political and cultural spaces occupied by Doordarshan in culture wars at a particular historical moment when battles over the meaning of nationhood, community, and identity were particularly explosive.

8   From *Advertising and Marketing*, October 1991, pp. 59–95.

9   Regretfully, my analysis of Doordarshan programs is restricted to its "fictional" narratives, that is, to entertainment serials and series. It should be clear, however, that this does not imply a dichotomy between entertainment and information (embodied, for instance, in news programs), nor does it stem from reified distinctions between fiction versus reality or pleasure versus politics. On the contrary, the following analyses will demonstrate precisely the fragility of these distinctions.

10 With the exception of two episodic series, *Param Veer Chakra* and *Rajni*, all the narratives I will analyze in this book are serials. Regardless of their genre, all prime-time narratives, including episodic series, were called serials, or *seeriyals*, by the viewers I met in the course of my research.

11 See Mukherjee 1985 on the unresolved tension between "indigenous" concepts of personhood and notions of the individual in modern Indian fiction.

12 For instance, according to Punwani (1989:224), the serial *Hum Log* aroused such "intense viewer identification" that producers regularly received mail advising them on how the story should develop.

13 This conception of audiences acquires particular significance in light of the fact that audiences do not exist a priori but are constructed by discursive and marketing practices. For excellent discussions on this aspect of audience formation, see Ang 1990, 1996, and Radway 1988. The reconstitution of the family as audience through television viewing practices is further analyzed in chapter 2.

14 This positioning of viewers as subjects is based on the premise that "ideologies do not operate through single ideas; they operate, in discursive chains, in clusters, in semantic fields, in discursive formations" (Hall 1985:104; see also Althusser 1971:121–173).

15 For my North American readers: notions of Indian Womanhood have as much currency and are as central to discourses of cultural nationalism as the ideology of the American Dream in the United States.

16 The demographic expansion of the middle classes in the 1980s (to be described in more detail in the next chapter) led to a proliferation of groups, including bureaucrats, professionals, small businessmen and entrepreneurs, and upwardly mobile working classes, all of whom had differential access to

economic security and political power. Only some of them owned property or had control over the means of production, and in this sense cannot be categorized as the bourgeoisie. Furthermore, the expansion of the urban middle classes was accompanied by the growth of the middle classes in some rural areas of India. In this book, I concentrate on the primary target audience for television in the late 1980s and early 1990s: the lower-middle classes and upwardly mobile working classes who lived in urban areas.

17 The implications of the demographic expansion and political consolidation of the middle classes for the formulation of television policy will be examined in more detail in chapter 2.

18 The consolidation of the middle classes as a historical bloc cannot be posited a priori, nor can we assume that the conglomeration of historical forces represented by the nationalist elite had a unity of interests and strategies or a homogeneous vision of the nation. The notion of social formation is helpful in understanding the societal bases of the struggles around identity taking place in India in the 1980s. According to Althusser and Balibar (1970), the term *social formation* refers to societies as "complexly structured totalities, with different levels of articulation (the economic, the political, the ideological instances) in different combinations; each combination giving rise to a different configuration of social forces and hence to a different type of social development" (from Hall 1986:112). Thus, instead of analyzing the politics of popular culture in terms of the dominance of a single class or in terms of modes of production, I conceptualize the consolidation of the historical forces representing the Hindu, upper-caste, upper- and middle-class nationalist elites as constituting a social formation.

19 Again, I would like to caution against the assumption that battles over culture were unprecedented. Partha Chatterjee, for instance, has analyzed the significance of notions of culture during encounters between colonial administrators and indigenous elites (1989). See Mani 1989 for a discussion of representations of tradition and gender in colonial discourse in the late nineteenth century, and Tharu and Lalita 1993a and b, for an analysis of the relationship between gender and national culture in colonial and postcolonial India.

20 Following Ang, it is important to note that viewers' active interpretations are a point of entry into understanding the *contradictions* underlying cultural production and do not automatically "guarantee any critical purchase, let alone resistance or subversion" (1996:14).

21 Cf. Ang 1996:23.

22 I will return to my use of the trope of the setting later in this chapter. I have used pseudonyms to protect the privacy of the people with whom I worked.

23 See also the work of Dorinne Kondo on the crafting of selves in Japan (1990).

24 Cf. Behar and Gordon 1995 for a discussion of how the work of radical feminists of color has "forced anthropology to come home" (1995:6).

25 My use of quotes is intended to problematize this ethnographic strategy: the politics of feminist ethnography with television viewers will be discussed in further detail later.

26 In chapter 2, I demonstrate that viewers' modes of viewing television offered a lens through which to examine power dynamics within the family.

27 Here I draw on Foucault's critique of hermeneutics. According to Dreyfus and Rabinow, Foucault's aim was to show that "the world is not a play which simply masks a truer reality that exists behind the scenes" (1982:109); instead of looking for hidden meanings, Foucault turned his analytical gaze to the effects of everyday practices.

28 Cf. Abu-Lughod 1993, Mankekar 1993b, Mohanty 1984.

29 I include the original Hindustani words where English translations fail to capture their polyvalence.

30 The *bhaav* with which Hindu viewers related to the televisation of Hindu epics will be discussed in greater detail in chapter 4.

31 The responses of Hindu women to Draupadi will be analyzed in detail in chapter 5.

32 The *rasasutra* refers to the "aesthetic organization" of a state of being or emotion (*bhaav*) found in classical Sanskrit literature (Gerow 1974:216). The *rasasutra* singles out the following emotions for aesthetic exegesis: love, mirth, grief, energy, terror, disgust, anger, wonder, and peace. Works of art "transmute" each of these into a corresponding mood (*rasa*)—for instance, grief inspires the mood of compassion—and *rasas* "render the personal and the incommunicable generalizable and communicable" (Ramanujan 1974:118). Effective realization of a *rasa* depends not only on whether or not a particular performance or other work of art is "suited" to its construction, but also on the capacity of the viewer or reader to apprehend and therefore affirm the prevailing *rasa* (Gerow 1974:221). Hence *rasa* refers at once to an aesthetic tradition and a philosophical state of being. Perhaps the *rasasutra* provided a vocabulary, if not a conceptual apparatus, to viewers like Aparna, who often spoke of the street plays and musical performances she had watched in her village during her childhood. Attempting to identify "indigenous traditions" of spectatorship is tricky, however, because it can sometimes lead one to overemphasize continuity and underestimate change and borrowing: this danger is particularly acute in the case of popular culture, which necessarily operates in a world of increasingly transnational cultural flows. Therefore, we need to pay particular attention to the sociopolitical contexts in which these interpretive processes occur.

33 Pendakur reported a similar experience when he did fieldwork in a small town: lower-middle-class children demonstrated an astonishing knowledge of production techniques, such as freeze shots and instant replay (1989a:178).

34 Surjeet Kaur's opinion is interesting in the light of Modleski's attempt to link

the lack of narrative closure on American soaps with the subject positions of women in suburban U.S. culture (1983).

35 Their suspicion of the state came as no surprise to me: when I was growing up in India, strangers in trains, buses, and other public spaces frequently treated me to long, often vitriolic, discourses on the government's inefficiency, corruption, and so on.

36 The political effects of such a discourse, in the context of the global hegemony of the West in the production and circulation of ideas, are particularly significant (Mohanty 1984).

37 For an excellent discussion of "the setting" trope, see Kondo 1990:7–9.

38 Cf. Visweswaran 1994 on fieldwork and "homework." See, also, Behar and Gordon 1995 and John 1996.

39 For a subtle and nuanced critique of "reflexive" ethnography, see Daniel 1985.

40 See also Fox 1991. Although Fox mistakenly equates reflexive anthropologists with postmodern anthropologists, his critique of the valorization of anthropologists as "artisan workers" and "independent craftsmen" (1991:7–8) is well taken. Like Clifford and Marcus, however, whom he roundly criticizes for being postmodern anthropologists, Fox ignores the contributions of feminist ethnographers to textual innovation and to discussions of positionality that are firmly grounded in the institutional and political contexts within which we do our research and writing.

41 See also Probyn 1993:27.

42 In chapter 3 I elaborate more fully the question of feminist vantage points.

43 I borrow the term *denaturalize* from Yanagisako and Delaney 1995. Cf. Behar and Gordon 1995, John 1996, and Visweswaran 1994.

44 Cf. hooks 1990.

45 Cf. Rouse 1991 on cultural bifocality.

46 Cf. also Behar and Gordon 1995 and Ong 1995 for critiques of binaries of Subject/Object, Self/Other, and the West and the Rest.

47 Cf. Abu-Lughod 1995.

48 I am indebted to Janaki Bakhle (personal communication, March 1995) for encouraging me to think through some of these aspects of my positionality.

49 By arguing against the project of "discovering" Otherness, I am not erasing differences among women. Instead, I intend to point to *shifting* registers of affinity and difference. I thank Saba Mahmood and Donald Moore for their help in clarifying some of the ideas expressed in these pages.

50 See chapter 7 for a fuller account of my relationship with Bibi Satwant Kaur.

51 A sensitive exploration of the limits of feminist ethnography may be seen in essays by Judith Stacey (1988) and Lila Abu-Lughod (1990a). For a powerful investigation of feminist assumptions about sisterhood and community, see Visweswaran's analysis of "feminist betrayal" (1994).

52 While I agree with Modleski's concerns about the empiricism, sociological re-

ductionism, and celebratory tone of some audience ethnographies, I hope to demonstrate that, if deployed reflexively and strategically, audience ethnographies can enable us to trace the *unpredictable* outcomes of the contestation and negotiation of hegemonic discourses. See also Ang's refutations of Modeleski's argument (1996:100).

53 Chapter 3 contains a detailed examination of my negotiation of pleasure and power in constructing a feminist critique of popular narratives.

54 This chapter is a slightly modified version of Mankekar 1993a.

Chapter 2 *National Television and the "Viewing Family"*

1 Rayna Rapp (1992) and Sylvia Yanagisako (1984) take contrasting positions vis-à-vis analytical distinctions between household and family. Rapp argues that family, an ideological and normative construct, must be distinguished from household, which she defines as "empirically measurable units within which people pool resources and perform certain tasks" (1992:50). As a residential unit, then, households are different from families, which, she suggests, are "a bit more slippery" because they entail ideological and affective relationships. Yanagisako, on the other hand, argues that, like the family, the household must be analyzed in terms of cultural meanings because there is "no such thing as a unified household strategy," and members of a household do not "share a collective motive and will" (1984:331). She adds that "labeling such sets of people households does not describe accurately the activities they share or the structure of their relations" (1984:331). Engaging this debate is outside the scope of this paper. Hence, I have chosen to focus on the family as a normative ideal metonymically linked with the "national community" invoked by the state, and as a web of affects, duties, and negotiations engaged by subjects as they were constituted into viewing audiences by television and advertising discourses.

2 I put the term *local* in quotation marks in order to problematize it; having thus flagged it, I will no longer use quotation marks with it in the rest of this chapter.

3 My use of the term *desire* builds on and extends psychoanalytic conceptions. According to Lacan, desire marks the entry of the subject into the symbolic (the world of language, and of rules and customs) (1977). But, rather than locate the production of desire entirely in a primal oedipal moment, I extend it to include the experience of lack or a profound dissatisfaction in the everyday; as Anne Allison insightfully points out, "desire is both of and beyond the everyday" (1996:xiii). Cf. Silverman 1983 for an excellent explication of the place of desire in the semiotic constitution of subjectivity. For a persuasive application of Lacanian semiotics to the everyday life of a Tamil family, see Trawick 1990.

4 For an excellent interdisciplinary feminist critique of local versus translocal binaries, see Grewal and Kaplan 1994.

5 As elsewhere in this book, I am also interested in how Doordarshan was able to recruit and interpellate subjects as viewers through specific televisual modes of address, narrative techniques, and forms of pleasure.

6 Not all forms of modernity were *desired* by viewers. Some forms of modernity introduced by television also unleashed anxieties and terrors for many men and women, who saw modernity as the harbinger of cultural disorder and moral chaos. Modernity was constructed in opposition to "tradition," which was perceived as eternal, authentic, and pure. See chapter 4 for an analysis of how television may have participated in the creation of a "traditional" Hindu community; ironically, this traditional community was, in fact, quintessentially modernist.

7 Cf. Spiegel and Mann 1992.

8 Cf. Spiegel's discussion of the "home as a space of exhibition" in the United States in the 1950s (1992).

9 I analyze the metonymy of family and nation in Mankekar 1993a, 1993b, and in the next chapter.

10 To explain Sushmita's powerlessness at this stage in her life would take us into an examination of her interpellation by discourses of womanhood and familial duty, and her position along axes of generation, class, and gender — an analysis beyond the scope of this analysis.

11 Cf. Ang 1990, 1996.

12 Interview with Iqbal Masud, December 15, 1990.

13 Singhal and Rogers 1989:67.

14 Chatterji 1991:135.

15 Modernization refers to socioeconomic changes for which certain alterations in attitude and behavior were required (e.g., Daniel Lerner's [1958] evolutionary schema in which traditional societies evolved into modernized societies). Modernity refers to the epistemological, cultural, and political characteristics of the discursive formations following the Enlightenment and, in the case of India, colonialism.

16 This linearity was also reflected in the KAP (knowledge, attitude, and practice) models used for evaluating development-communication programs.

17 Cf. Chakrabarty 1992a, 1992b on citizenship and colonial discourses. The implications of postcolonial nationalist discourses of citizenship for television's representations of gender and the family are further analyzed in chapter 3.

18 Interview with S. S. Gill, January 23, 1992.

19 Interview with Iqbal Masud, December 15, 1990.

20 "Central government" refers to the national government operating out of New Delhi.

21   I thank Lata Mani for emphasizing the role of realpolitik in the expansion of the National Programme (personal communication, October 1992).

22   The data cited in this section are from Chatterji 1991:151–152.

23   A particularly blatant example was the coverage of the communal carnage at Nellie in distant Assam in 1982, a major national tragedy that left seven thousand dead. It was barely mentioned on Doordarshan largely because, for television officials and politicians based in New Delhi, it seemed so remote. The tragedy of Nellie was eclipsed by the excitement of the Asian Games, the great image-building exercise of the Indian state (Chatterji 1991:101–102).

24   Cf. Morley 1992 and Scannell 1988 for analyses of similar functions performed by the BBC in Britain. See Anderson 1983 for a discussion of simultaneity in the construction of national communities.

25   I was able to understand the causes of her ambivalence on another occasion, when she spoke of the abuse she and her brother had undergone at the hands of her soldier father. See chapter 6 for an extended discussion.

26   While most of the programs introduced in the mid-1980s were narrative serials, there were also some episodic series. As noted in chapter 1, regardless of their formal structure, they were all called serials by policy makers, Doordarshan officials, media critics, and viewers. For the sake of simplicity, I will use the term *serial* in all general discussions about Doordarshan; when discussing particular narratives, I will use the appropriate generic term.

27   See Lopez 1995 and Martín-Barbero 1995 for analyses of Latin American telenovelas.

28   Interview with S. S. Gill, January 23, 1992.

29   See Bandura 1977, on social learning theory. The terms *pro-development* and *pro-social* are from Singhal and Rogers 1989.

30   Singhal and Rogers 1989:90.

31   Sabido recommended that "positive messages" would have to be reinforced at least three times a week in order to have any impact on people. But according to Gill, Doordarshan did not have the resources to produce and telecast that many episodes and instead decided to broadcast twice a week. Interviews with S. S. Gill (January 23, 1992) and Kunwar Sinha (April 13, 1992).

32   Interview with S. S. Gill, January 23, 1992.

33   *Hum Log* will be analyzed in detail in chapter 3.

34   Predictably, because of its north Indian bias, *Hum Log* was received much more enthusiastically in north India than in south India. According to Singhal and Rogers, it received 65–90 percent ratings in north India as compared with 20–45 percent ratings in south India (1989:101).

35   The relationship between "mainstream" Bombay (or Bollywood) films and Doordarshan serials was particularly ambivalent during the 1980s and early 1990s. Doordarshan policy makers and producers perceived Bollywood not just as its major competitor but also as an important resource of capital, per-

sonnel, scripts, and narrative techniques. At the same time, Doordarshan tried to define itself as different from Bollywood: in contrast to Bollywood, which allegedly offered "mindless entertainment," Doordarshan aimed to merge entertainment with "socially oriented" programming. In addition, since the 1980s "alternative" and New Wave films were no longer commercially viable, Doordarshan offered a forum for these filmmakers and for other media activists (e.g., Kavita Choudhry, who produced *Udaan* [chapter 3]) and alternative filmmakers such as Shyam Benegal, Govind Nihalani, and Saeed Mirza to launch "socially oriented" serials and telefilms that were self-consciously different from Bollywood films. Thus, even though many genres of Bombay film had strong nationalist themes, Doordarshan serials were much more assertive in their efforts to wed socially relevant themes to entertainment. Moreover, some Doordarshan serials (e.g., *Param Veer Chakra* [chapter 5]) drew more centrally on the narrative techniques of Bombay film than others (e.g., *Hum Log* and *Humraahi*), which strove to create their own hybrid modes of address by borrowing from transnational, self-consciously Third World genres of "development-oriented" soap opera (e.g., *Simplemente Maria*), television plays, and Bombay films. Clearly, the relationship between Bombay film and Doordarshan is complex and warrants a separate investigation.

36 Singhal and Rogers 1989:83.

37 From Sethi and Mitra 1985:79.

38 Jain 1985:25, in Singhal and Rogers 1989:111.

39 Interview with Akshay Kumar Jain, October 6, 1992.

40 As noted earlier, my understanding of the cultural constitution of the middle classes in India draws on, as well as departs from, Marxist theories of relations of production and Weberian concepts of status and political power. The Indian middle classes were a heterogeneous historical bloc with differential access to relations of production, status, and political power. As I will demonstrate in this book, discourses of gender, domesticity, and sexuality were central to the cultural constitution of middle-class subjectivity. Further, what constituted them as middle class was their (sometimes self-conscious) differentiation from the working classes and upper classes and, most pertinent to this chapter, their aspirations to upward mobility and modernity through consumerism. Several scholars have pointed to the difficulties of delineating the sociological boundaries of middle classes (see, e.g., Lev 1990a, 1990b; Tanter and Young 1990). As specified in the previous chapter, the sliver of the urban population that I focused on, the lower middle class and upwardly mobile working class, was caught in the interstices between working-class and middle-class positions.

41 Although it was a less widespread phenomenon than in urban areas, the 1980s also witnessed the expansion of the rural middle classes. In this book, I focus specifically on the cultural constitution of the *urban* middle classes.

42 As the director of a major market research company put it, "This is one population bulge Indians can truly be proud of" (Kartik Kumar, in Kulkarni 1992:44).

43 National Council for Applied Economic Research, cited in Kulkarni 1993:45.

44 Kulkarni 1992:45.

45 Cf. Hall 1985, Morley 1992, and Poulantzas 1971 on the nonmonolithic character of class identities. Even though some sections of the middle classes lobbied for economic changes, others (e.g., bureaucrats) initially resisted the reforms (A. Kohli 1987).

46 As stated in chapter 1, this survey drew from 290 towns and villages throughout India.

47 *A & M*, October 1991, p. 63.

48 R. Srinivasan, *Times of India*, October 17, 1990, p. 11.

49 However, despite its focus on the lives of working-class people, *Nukkad* was criticized for subscribing to middle-class values. For instance, Krishan and Dighe claim that "the values endorsed of individual upward mobility were those of the middle class. The inhabitants of the street corner did not organise to fight the exploitative conditions under which they lived" (1990:84).

50 From Sethi and Mitra 1985:81.

51 Cf. Spiegel 1992 for a similar discussion of television and sociality in the United States.

52 While advertising per se was not novel to Doordarshan or to economic liberalization, the introduction of private sponsorship of serials in 1982 was clearly linked with a shift in national economic policy from capital goods to consumer goods investment. Thus, although advertisements were a part of public culture before the 1980s (in the form of billboards, print ads, and radio jingles), they became ubiquitous after Doordarshan inaugurated its sponsorship programs. This resulted in a dramatic increase in the advertising budgets of companies in the mid-1980s, a major proportion of which was devoted to television sponsorship and commercials.

53 The information contained in this paragraph is from Singhal and Rogers 1989, and from my interview with S. S. Gill on January 23, 1992.

54 Mitra 1985:104, 105.

55 Interview with R. Srinivasan, January 17, 1992.

56 Sethi and Mitra 1985:78, 80.

57 Sethi and Mitra 1985:78, 80.

58 From A. Chatterjee, *Economic Times*, January 30, 1991.

59 Sethi and Mitra 1985:83.

60 From Kulkarni 1992:45.

61 *A & M*, October 1991:103.

62 Mike Khanna, the chief of Hindustan Thompson and Associates, a subsidiary of the multinational J. Walter Thompson, quoted in Mitra 1985:104–105.

63 A. Chatterjee, *Economic Times*, January 30, 1991:4.

64 Unani and ayurvedic medicines are two of the most popular "indigenous" systems of medicine.

65 A *dupatta* (also called a *chunni*) is an intrinsic part of the north Indian salwar kameez; it refers to the shawl that covers the top part of the body.

66 As Susan Hayward points out, "fantasy is the mise-en-scène of desire" (1996: 96).

67 From Singhal and Rogers 1989:81.

68 *Economic Times*, January 30, 1991:12.

69 Cf. Raymond Williams's notion of "flow" in television narrative (1974).

70 The contradictory messages of *Swayamsiddha* and the advertisements that framed it are briefly discussed in Krishnan and Dighe 1990:113.

71 See Doane 1989 on the fetishization of the female body in U.S. television advertisements.

72 From *A & M*, April 1992, p. 74.

73 I analyze "women-oriented" serials in more detail in the next chapter.

74 From *A & M*, April 1992, p. 87.

75 Until the advent of commercials on television, ads for Vicco Turmeric Creme had mainly appeared in the press, on billboards, and on the radio (the radio ad, which had an extremely catchy jingle, was the most popular). The Doordarshan ad, however, was remarkable because it *televisually* represented the convergence of discourses of femininity and "Indian culture."

76 In her study of working-class childhood, Carolyn Steedman talks of the politics of envy that underlie working-class desires to acquire objects (1986). Steedman's goal is to forestall a romanticization of working-class subjectivity. My attempts to bring to the foreground the anxieties and aspirations of people like Selapan are intended to highlight the complex concerns of upwardly mobile lower-middle class subjects. Furthermore, Selapan's near-poverty illustrates the poignant contradiction faced by many lower-middle-class people who expressed their aspirations to middle-class status even as they struggled to make ends meet.

77 At the same time, as suggested by my discussion of Razia, Jayanthi, and Sarojini, advertisements did not have monolithic effects on all women consumers. While Razia responded to advertisements by engaging in fantasies about financial security and upward mobility, Jayanthi and Sarojini attempted to use their ability to buy consumer goods to negotiate their positions in their families.

78 I borrow the term *family subjects* from Visweswaran 1990.

79 See Ang 1990, Curran 1990, Morley 1992, and Morris 1990 for critiques of such work.

80 Cf. d'Acci 1992 for a similar discussion of U.S. television.

81   For critiques of anthropology's construction of "the field," community, and culture, see Appadurai 1986b and Gupta and Ferguson 1992, 1997a.

82   Some mass media scholars, such as Meyrowitz, have discussed how electronic media have "undermined the traditional relationship between physical setting and social situation" (1985, from Morley 1991:7). Although it is true that communication technologies, among other features of late capitalism, have accelerated people's contact with translocal fields of power, and to this extent have configured what "community" means for many people, perhaps Meyrowitz goes too far in eliding local relations of power.

Chapter 3   *"Women-Oriented" Narratives and the New Indian Woman*

1   Significantly, *darshan* also connotes worship.

2   Here I am drawing on Keya Ganguly's eloquent discussion of the politics of representation in feminist analysis, in which she extends Gayatri Spivak's distinction between *Vertretung*, or "speaking for," and *Darstellung*, or "making present" (Ganguly 1992, Spivak 1988).

3   As discussed in chapter 2, it is necessary to underscore the influence of advertisers and sponsors in the formulation of Doordarshan's programs. Since women were subjects as well as objects of consumption (that is, because their desires to purchase commodities were constructed by television), advertisers and producers perceived them as an important target audience.

4   Interviewed on November 1, 1990. Again, I would like to caution against conceptualizing the state as a monolithic or unitary agency, and emphasize its conjunctural constitution as a *historical* bloc. In fact, I am pointing to the ways in which some potentially oppositional agencies (such as feminists and other grassroots activists) were incorporated into the state. See Gupta 1995 for an argument about the "blurred boundaries" of state and civil society.

5   According to Balasubrahmanyam, sᴇᴡᴀ has the image of an organization that takes up "developmental" rather than "ideologically feminist" issues (1988:63).

6   I owe some of the ideas expressed in this paragraph to discussions with Sujata Patel.

7   Before the advent of women-oriented serials, several Doordarshan plays focused on the family and the status of women. During the days of black-and-white television, noted Hindi playwright and poet Kamleshwar (then Doordarshan's director-general) produced a magazine program called *Parikrama*, many episodes of which dealt with relationships and conflicts within the middle-class family. A precursor to feminist activist Nalini Singh's *Hullo Zindagi*, a 1992 magazine program that also focused on relationships within the middle-class family, *Parikrama* was one of the first "nonfictional" programs that attempted to analyze relationships within the family.

8   Interviewed on December 15, 1990.

9   The New Indian Woman of postcolonial nationalism reveals some traces of early nationalist representations of Indian Womanhood. For instance, in the nineteenth century, the New Woman was constructed by the "new patriarchies" of nascent nationalism partially in opposition to stereotypes of the coarse, sexually promiscuous, disorderly, working-class woman who was a victim of the brutality of men (cf. Chatterjee 1989:244–245). See also Bannerjee 1989 for an excellent analysis of the relationship between the "cleansing" of women's popular culture in nineteenth-century Bengal and the middle-class and upper-caste constitution of the *bhadramahila* (respectable woman).

10 There were two notable exceptions to Doordarshan's focus on the middle classes. *Nukkad* (Street corner) was unique in its portrayal of the lives of the inhabitants of a slum and was hailed as the *Hum Log* of the poor; however, its middle-class bias surfaced in its depiction of a middle-class teacher who mediates the conflicts among street people. *Basunti* was the tale of how a poor girl who lives in a slum fends for herself. Not surprisingly, despite their high production values, these serials received very low viewership ratings (Punwani 1989:229).

11 Cf. Carolyn Steedman's insightful and moving exposition of the role of discourses of gender and class in mediating her relationship with her mother (1986).

12 On the "paradoxical" significance of women's sexuality in dominant Hindu traditions, see Wadley 1980.

13 Many of these representations drew on the discourse of *kanyadan*, according to which the father "gifts" his virgin daughter to her husband's family, in Hindu kinship traditions. For analyses of the practice of *kanyadan* in north India, see Inden and Nicholas 1977; for *kanyadan* in south India, see Gough 1956, Trautmann 1981, and Trawick 1990. Dube 1988, Raheja and Gold 1994, Jacobson 1977, and Vatuk 1975, and Dube 1988a and b have complicated dominant analyses of *kanyadan* by focusing on the fluidity of women's ties to their natal homes.

14 Cf. V. Das 1988 and Dube 1988a.

15 I will return to the effacement of Kalyani's sexuality later in this essay.

16 Cf. Raheja and Gold's discussion of the complicated positions occupied by daughters in families in Pahansu: little girls are described as "little birds destined to fly away . . . this departure is mourned rather than welcomed" (1994:xxxi–xxxii). At the same time, the authors note a strong correlation in rural India between poverty and increased female suffering, and also that little girls were much more vulnerable to poverty and malnourishment than were little boys (1994:xxxi–xxxii). For an analysis of the place of daughters in patrilineal families in Tamil Nadu, see Trawick 1990:158, 169.

17 Cf. Dube's discussion of the "training" of young daughters for "feminine tasks" (1988a:179).

18 For an analysis of the socialization of daughters in north Indian families and its implications for their mobility, see Dube 1988a:176–177, 174–175.

19 The Sharmas were not atypical in their favoritism toward their son; discrimination against daughters is not uncommon among Hindu families in north India. These were some of the attitudes that serials such as *Hum Log* and *Udaan* were trying to counter through their emphasis on the education of daughters. Cf. Karlekar 1988 on the implications of notions of femininity for women's access to education in Bengal, and Chanana 1988a on gender-differentiated school enrollment for boys and girls in India.

20 I should point out that college and university education were relatively inexpensive in New Delhi. Thus, Poonam's tuition was not likely to have strained her family's finances a great deal.

21 Cf. Raheja and Gold 1994, M. Roy 1992, and Trawick 1990 for discussions of the place of daughters-in-law in the extended family in rural north India, Bengal, and Tamil Nadu, respectively.

22 Cf. Ghadially and Kumar 1988 for an excellent discussion of dowry and "bride burning." For an analysis of the practice of dowry (in particular its implications for the positions of unmarried daughters) in rural north India and Tamil Nadu, see Raheja and Gold 1994, and Trawick 1990:108, respectively.

23 This was also a major concern of the Joshi Committee on Software (1985).

24 Some organizations working to eliminate dowry at the time of telecast were Karmika, Saheli, All India Women's Conference, and Jagori (New Delhi); Naari Atyachar Virodhi Manch, and Stri Aadhar Kendra (Bombay); and Vimochana (Bangalore).

25 Raheja and Gold point to the permeability and multivalent meanings of *purdah,* or the veil: "Coverings are not opaque; wraps can also unwrap; from the women's perspective, poses of sexual modesty and reticence can readily flow into allurement, involvement and manipulation" (1994:52). For an analysis of the deployment of *purdah* through the eyes, garments, and voice, and as a mode of resistance, see Raheja and Gold 1994:168.

26 In this regard, my observations contrast with those of Raheja and Gold, who interpret the songs of women in rural north India as frank and often irreverent expressions of sensuality (1994). Raheja and Gold also point to a disjuncture between women's silence about sexuality and their songs, which present evidence of an "exuberant sexuality, a positive valuation of sexual pleasures, and a conjoining of eroticism and birthgiving that undermine and resist that split between sexuality and fertility posited in the dominant ideology" (1994:27).

27 The sexuality of young wives (and its consequences for their positions in their husbands' homes) is analyzed in Bennet 1983 and Raheja and Gold 1994.

28 Cf. Raheja and Gold's analysis of how women's perspectives on kinship shift in accordance with their own constitution as "sisters, wives and mothers within these relations" (1994:147). Cf. also Mohanty's critique of the construction of Woman as a monolithic category existing "prior to" kinship relations (1984).

29 It was difficult for me to assess exactly what she meant by "highly educated." I gathered that she felt it was essential for women to have a college education; however, she seemed to think that women pursuing doctoral degrees or other equally demanding programs of study were clearly indifferent to the welfare of their families.

30 When I discuss their discourses of gender in more general terms, I will refer to these serials as *Udaan.*

31 Interviewed on April 17, 1992.

32 Cf. Kobena Mercer's formulation of ambivalence as a critical position (1991).

33 See Balasubrahmanyam 1988:81–83 for a discussion of dilemmas expressed by media women.

34 *Independent,* February 2, 1992.

35 *Indian Express,* April 5, 1992, p. 8.

36 Interviewed on April 15, 1992.

37 My sense is that Uma's response to this scene was shaped by her own feelings of inadequacy as a lower-middle-class woman (see chapter 2). Out of deference to her feelings, I was disinclined to prod her further about how she viewed this scene: the ethnographer decided to back off and leave her to her thoughts.

38 From *Dainik Jagaran,* December 20, 1991. Interview by Shivji Gupta.

39 *Pukaar,* shown in the summer of 1991, was a bit of an exception. An episodic series, it consisted of cameos of women who fought the injustice they faced in the workplace, family, and community. Again, however, the few episodes that depicted women's efforts to organize as a collectivity were superficial and simplistic. Perhaps part of the problem stemmed from the episodic series format, which did not permit the writers to present women's struggles in any depth. But an important reason for the superficial treatment given to women's collective struggles for empowerment was that the institutional structures in which serials were produced and telecast, that of a state-controlled entertainment medium, did not permit a serious engagement with the cultural and socioeconomic factors underlying women's oppression.

40 While Shakuntala's narrative of how she was inspired by Rajani was extraordinarily eloquent, it was by no means idiosyncratic or exceptional. Many women in Vikas Nagar and Basti spoke of being inspired after watching *Rajani.* Similar reactions were reported in the press. See, for instance, the report on *Rajani*'s reception in cities across India in the metropolitan newsmagazine *India Today,* August 21, 1985.

41 My discomfort with Shakuntala's refusal or inability to reflect on her position within her family does not pertain to her wish to serve her family. My unease stems from my observation that for her, and for many of the women I spoke with, service to the family (and nation) was the only legitimate site for women's agency, and, more importantly, discourses of service to the family often elided abuses of power within the family.

42 In her work on Mzeina allegories of Bedouin identity under Israeli and Egyptian rule, Smadar Lavie writes of how allegories can temporarily "transform" the speaker (1990:330–333).

43 Cf. Charlotte Brunsdon's warnings about the binaries constructed by feminist researchers between "ordinary" women and themselves (1991).

44 Several scholars have commented on the complicated place of class and class consciousness in the development of feminist praxis in India. See, for example, John 1996 and R. Kumar 1993.

45 Indeed, the scenario of middle-class women "saving" poor and working-class women from the men who brutalize them was a feature of several women-oriented programs. In their stereotyping of poor and working class women as victims, these narratives were similar to nineteenth-century discourses on middle-class Indian Womanhood (Bannerjee 1989, Chatterjee 1993).

46 The metropolitan newsmagazine *India Today* described Rajani thus: "The idea was to create a wholly Indian character not merely coping with routinely Indian problems but fighting them and somehow resolving them" (August 31, 1985).

47 Interviewed on December 4, 1990.

48 Cf. Balasubrahmanyam 1988:69.

49 The metonymy between family and nation is also discussed in Visweswaran 1990.

50 A senior bureaucrat in the Ministry of Information and Broadcasting informed me that, after the "Shahbano fiasco," Doordarshan officials were ordered to steer clear of stories advocating the "uplift" of Muslim women. See Pathak and Sunder Rajan 1989 for a feminist analysis of the "Shahbano case."

51 *Tikka* refers to the vermilion mark worn on the forehead, and *mangalsutra* is a black necklace worn by some Hindu women. The *mangalsutra*, and in some communities the *tikka*, signify married status.

Chapter 4 *Mediating Modernities: The* Ramayan *and the Creation of Community and Nation*

1 I will refer to the larger narrative traditions of the epic as the *Ramayana*; in keeping with its Hindustani title, I will refer to the television serial as the *Ramayan*.

2 It is estimated that between 80 and 100 million viewers watched the *Ramayan*.

Its success can also be gauged from the advertising revenues it generated. A few months after the commencement of its telecast, advertisers were lining up to pay up to Rs 40,000 per ten-second slot. In the next nine months, the *Ramayan* outgrossed all other serials, yielding an estimated weekly income of Rs 2,800,000–3,000,000 ($2.8–3 million) for the network (Lutgendorf 1990:136).

Doordarshan's initial contract with the serial's producer and director, Ramanand Sagar, was for only a year. When the year drew to a close, Doordarshan planned to bring the serial to a halt without telecasting the seventh book of the *Ramayan*, the *Uttarkand*, allegedly written by the lower-cast poet Valmiki. Viewers all over India protested. The loudest and most forceful protests came from the lower-caste community of Balmiks, who claim descent from Valmiki. Balmiks constituted the bulk of the sanitation workers in north India, and they protested the impending termination of the serial by going on strike in Delhi and in cities in Punjab, Uttar Pradesh, and Madhya Pradesh. The fear of cholera epidemics, combined with the prospect of continuing to collect the huge revenues that the serial was yielding for Doordarshan, forced the government's hand. Sagar was finally given an extension that enabled him to telecast the *Uttarkand*, or *Uttar Ramayan* (*India Today*, August 31, 1988, cited in Lutgendorf 1990:136).

3 Cf. Sarkar and Butalia 1995 and van der Veer 1994 for analyses of the events that led to the destruction of the Babri Mosque.

4 It is important to note that Hindu nationalism within India is part of larger, transnational processes. Hindu nationalism "operates transnationally in its attempts to create a 'world Hinduism,' which reveals an interesting dialectic between nationalism and transnationalism" (van der Veer 1994:108). See Rai 1995 for a fascinating discussion of the transnational construction of Hindu nationalism via the Internet.

5 The overlaps between Hindu and Indian nationalism have been pointed out by several scholars, most recently Peter van der Veer (1994) and Dilip Simeon (1994). Simeon notes that during its initial decades Indian nationalism was predicated on the mobilization of community identity. Communalism was constructed as the "antinomy of nationalism" only after the Kanpur riots in 1931 (Simeon 1994:230).

6 This was by no means the first time that mass media were used for the narration of religious or mythological stories in India. Indian film history reveals a rich tradition of the genre of the mythological film. The pioneering filmmaker Dadasaheb Phalke was inspired by a film on the life of Jesus to make the first Indian feature film, *Raja Harishchandra* (1912), thereby inaugurating the genre of the mythological film. *Raja Harishchandra* was followed by *Lanka Dahan* (1917), which was based on the story of the burning of Lanka in the *Ramayana*, and *Krishna Janma* (The birth of Krishna, 1919). Mythological

films continue to be popular with film viewers. In 1975, the film *Jai Santoshi Maa,* about a little-known goddess, was released and became an enormous box-office success.

7 The deployment of Ram Rajya as political discourse was not unprecedented. I will point to some of the transformations in the meaning of Ram Rajya later in the chapter.

8 In an important essay on television criticism, Charlotte Brunsdon makes a similar argument against the "ethnography of particular practices" (1990:65–66).

9 Since I conducted my fieldwork in 1990–1992, two years after the *Ramayan* had concluded, I was unable to facilitate or participate in viewers' discussions during the time the serial was being telecast. However, most viewers were able to vividly recount scenes and dialogues from the serial. The interpretations that I present in this chapter are therefore based on viewers' recollections of the serial.

10 It is important to note that all the Sikh and Muslim viewers I spoke with knew the *Ramayana*'s plot. A. K. Ramanujan has argued that "in India and in Southeast Asia, no one ever reads the *Ramayana* or the *Mahabharata* for the first time. The stories are there, 'always already'" (1991:46). Thus, although these Sikh and Muslim viewers were unlikely to have read the *Ramayana,* several were quite familiar with it.

11 Ramanujan points out that the "cultural area in which Ramayanas are endemic has a pool of signifiers (like a gene pool), signifiers that include plots, characters, names, geography, incidents, and relationships. Oral, written, and performance traditions, phrases, proverbs, and even sneers carry allusions to the Rama story" (1991:46).

12 Ramanujan argues that, far from there being a single "Ur-text" of the *Ramayana,* there are "hundreds of tellings"; he therefore prefers "tellings" over "versions or variants because the latter terms can and typically do imply that there is an invariant or original or Ur-text—usually Valmiki's Sanskrit *Ramayana*" (1991:24–25). Ramanujan adds that Valmiki's narrative was not always "carried from one language to another" (1991:25). Further, as pointed out by Paula Richman, "the story" of the *Ramayana* is "inseparable from the different forms it takes, forms which reflect differences in religious affiliation, linguistic allegiance, and social location" (1991a:5). Nonetheless, I am providing a "skeletal" version of the Rama story for readers unfamiliar with it. I follow the pronunciation used in the serial and use the colloquial Hindi spelling for the names of the *Ramayan*'s characters.

13 Although the Valmiki *Ramayana* does not contain the same sort of aporias as the *Mahabharata,* it contains, or to use Lutgendorf's term, "enacts," several irresolvable paradoxes (1991:342).

14 See Richman 1991a and Thapar 1989. Lutgendorf contests allegations about

the "homogenization" of the Ramayana tradition by pointing out that other performative forms coexisted with the television version (1990:166), adding that "local" performative traditions are also "bound up in local networks of power and hegemony" (1990:168–169). While I agree with Lutgendorf that the Sagar *Ramayan* did not eradicate other performative forms and that "local" forms are also likely to be embedded in relations of power and hegemony, I believe that the television version attempted to make available a "master text" *on a mass scale.* Like Thapar (1989), I am particularly concerned that this hegemonic master narrative was shown on state-controlled television at a historical moment when religious tensions were high and Hindu nationalism was on the rise.

15   Lutgendorf argues that even though it occasionally draws on Valmiki and Kampan, Sagar's narrative chiefly follows Tulsidas's *Ramcharitamanas* (1990: 147).

16   Ramasami's exegesis of the *Ramayana,* distributed mainly in the form of inexpensive pamphlets and booklets, aimed not only at critiquing "the respect with which Tamilians have traditionally viewed the *Ramayana,* arguing that the story is both an account of and a continuing vehicle for northern cultural domination," but also at persuading his readers to forgo their "superstitious" beliefs and adopt a "desacralized view of the world" (Richman 1991b:181).

17   In 1956, in a controversial and crucial symbolic move, Ramasami led his followers in burning pictures of Rama on Marina Beach in Madras. This action represented a reversal of north Indian performances of the *Ramayana,* in which effigies of Ravana are burned in public ceremonies to celebrate Rama's defeat of Ravana (Richman 1991b:175). Richman points out that the burning of Rama's pictures was the "centerpiece" of Ramasami's "campaign against brahmanical Hindus, conducted in the context of his assertion of Dravidian, that is, South Indian identity" (1991b:175).

18   See chapter 2 for a more detailed discussion of the implications of the National Programme for regional struggles over the definition of "national culture."

19   I describe their relationship in greater detail in chapter 6.

20   Padmini's interpretation seems to resonate with David Shulman's 1991 analysis of Kampan's Sita. Cf. also Kathleen Erndl's comparison of the Valmiki *Ramayana* and the Kampan *Ramayana* (1991).

21   Linda Hess points out that the Sagar *Ramayan* had the "same core narrative" as the Kampan *Ramayana,* and was "similarly soaked in *bhakti.*" She adds that the two texts are indeed quite similar in terms of their depiction of the conflicts of *dharma;* therefore, "it is not surprising that Tamilians recognized the Sagar *Ramayan* as theirs" (comments on MS, January 1997). David Shulman has also argued that for Kampan, Rama is "God in visible and earthly form . . . though . . . its implications for the hero's own consciousness are rather different than in the case of Valmiki's representation of the avatar. The Tamil

Ramayana is a devotional *kavya,* replete with the poses and values of Tamil *bhakti* religion" (1991:90).

22   The *Dharmasastras,* the normative texts of brahmanism, concede the coexistence of a broad range of communities shaped by caste, occupation, and the worship of specific deities, rather than bound by a common religious identity (Thapar 1989:220). As a consequence, identities were segmented and determined by multiply overlapping contexts. Several Hindu sects coexisted but were never integrated or assimilated into a unified whole. Further, struggles for political legitimation revolved around the mobilization of sects rather than a single religious identity.

23   Linda Hess points out that in the Sagar *Ramayan* Taaraka was played by a man (comments on MS, January 1997).

24   Cf. Pandey 1990 for an examination of the colonial construction of communalism. For the difference between Hindu nationalism and fundamentalism, see Basu 1998, especially pp. 169–171.

25   I use the term *history* to denote not just an evocation of a past but a specifically *historical* past. Cf. Hayden White's 1973 work on the development of historical consciousness in nineteenth-century Europe.

26   While I agree with scholars such as van der Veer that religious identities are constituted by religious discourse and practice and are not "ideological smoke screens that hide the real clash of material interests and social classes" (1994:ix), I believe that we need to make a distinction between religious identities and religious nationalisms, and, furthermore, that we must engage the role of political economy in the construction of religious nationalisms.

27   Cf. Fox 1990 for a detailed analysis of the class bases of Hindu nationalism.

28   Cf. V. Das 1995 for a critique of counterarguments that use historical and archaeological evidence to buttress their claims.

29   See Bagchi 1990 for a detailed analysis of the centrality of the mother goddess to discourses about Mother India.

30   Leaders of the Vishwa Hindu Parishad, however, continue to be highly critical of Gandhi.

31   Cf. van der Veer's discussion of a parallel tendency in anthropological writings on Indian Islam (1994:196).

32   The Muslims viewers I interviewed found the *Mahabharat* story much more complex than the *Ramayan.* They could engage it at several levels, and constructed very interesting interpretations. For instance, I was struck by how many of them made it a point to talk about a sati that occurred early in the *Mahabharat* and how many mentioned that Krishna had been depicted as something of a philanderer. None of this was *ever* mentioned by Hindu viewers. I believe that what Muslim viewers chose to say to me about the *Mahabharat* was shaped by my identity as a Hindu woman, as well as by the

politics of their position as a minority community derided by the majority community for its alleged "mistreatment" of women.

33 This response has also been reported by van der Veer (1994:177).

34 I discuss the place of subterfuge, elisions, and silences in ethnography in chapter 7.

35 However, it has been reported that, initially, Sagar's proposal for the televisation of the *Ramayan* was rejected by Doordarshan because of a concern that "the airing of such a serial would arouse communal sentiments" (Mazumdar 1988, in Lutgendorf 1990:134).

36 Van der Veer argues that Hindu nationalist discourses about foreign rule extend back into the nineteenth century (1994:65). Further, while contemporary Hindu nationalists may well be drawing on a Hindu belief that the contemporary age is marked by a decline of moral values (*kaliyuga*), Hindu nationalist organizations such as the vhp insist that Hindu/Indian society can be redeemed through religious reform and the establishment of Hindutva (van der Veer 1994:65).

37 According to the *Mahabharata*, Eklavya was a lower caste boy who wanted to learn archery from the great master Drona. Drona refused to teach him because of his caste status: he claimed that only upper castes deserved to learn archery from him. Eklavya practiced in front of a clay statue of Drona and mastered the art of archery. When Drona learned of this, he asked for Eklavya's right thumb, the part of his hand most important for using the bow and arrow, as his fee (*dakshina*). Contemporary lower-caste movements against upper-caste political and cultural hegemony (such as the Dalit movement) have appropriated the story of Eklavya as a symbol of upper-caste oppression to mobilize support for themselves.

38 The exact meaning of *dharma* is elusive (see O'Flaherty and Derrett 1978, cited in Lutgendorf 1991:352). Nonetheless, the Sagar *Ramayan*'s idealization of Ram draws on the dominant versions of the Ram story in Valmiki and Tulsi (Linda Hess, comments on MS, January 1997).

39 Cf. Kishwar 1990.

40 For a discussion of the performative conventions of *ramlila* and *katha*, see Kapur 1990; Lutgendorf 1990, 1991; and Schechner and Hess 1997. See Smith 1995 for a fascinating analysis of "god posters." The iconography of the television *Ramayan* both influenced and was inspired by the god posters. As Smith points out, scenes from the serial became a popular subject for god posters (1995:28).

41 As argued by Susan Hayward (1996), close-ups perform the ideological function of imposing a "preferred" reading on viewers: "A shot lends itself to a greater or lesser readability dependent on its type or length. As the camera moves further away from the main subject (whether person or object) the

visual field lends itself to an increasingly more complex reading . . . there is more for the spectator's eye to read or decode. This means that the closer up the shot the more the spectator's eye is directed to a specified reading" (1996:319). The close-ups of Ram were designed to induce a devotional mode of engagement from Hindu viewers. However, as I demonstrate in my discussion of some Sikh, Muslim, and skeptical Hindu viewers, not all viewers automatically assumed the subject positions created by these strategies of representation.

42 *Nautanki* is a performative tradition popular in small towns and rural communities in north India.

43 See Pritchett 1995 for a discussion of the *Amar Chitra Katha* comic books' iconography and their popularity among urban, middle-class children in India and the diaspora.

44 I discuss the discourses of realism employed by viewers and producers elsewhere (Mankekar n.d.).

45 I would like to caution against reading the different opinions of mother and daughter as indicative of a generational split: as suggested in my earlier discussion of Renuka Sengupta's responses to the *Ramayan,* young people were as likely as adults to subscribe to the Hindu nationalist constructions of Self and Other.

46 As noted in chapter 2, a primary objective of the postcolonial state has been to build a modern nation. In newly independent India, modernity was to be achieved in (at least) two ways: through the construction of modern infrastructure such as dams, bridges, and heavy industry; and through the careful construction of an "integrated" national culture that was "rational" and scientific. As pointed out by van der Veer, postcolonial nationalism depends on a discourse of modernity, which in turn constitutes the "traditional" as its "antithesis and interprets difference as backwardness. A crucial element of the discourse of modernity is the opposition of the 'religious' to the 'secular'" (1994:x). In postcolonial nationalism, religious passions, religious identities, and questions of faith were to be relegated to the so-called private sphere. See Madan 1995:394 for a brief analysis of the history of secularization in Europe. Cf. van der Veer's discussion (1994:13–16) of the secularist assumptions of scholars of nationalism like Anderson 1991 and Gellner 1983.

47 See Bharucha for a discussion of two important streams in nationalist secularism: *dharma nirpekshata,* which claimed that the state was to be impartial to religion, and *sarva dharma samabhava,* according to which all religions were equal (1998:15).

48 Unfortunately, some of this questioning of secularism has been appropriated, in ingenious and terrifying ways, by Hindu nationalists who condemn all prevailing secularist discourses as "pseudo secularism" in order to claim that they are the "true" secularists. Therefore, I wish to emphatically distinguish

between the positions of Hindu nationalists and the critiques of secularism that follow.

49 T. N. Madan has been another vocal advocate of rethinking secularism and putting it "in its place" (1995). Like Nandy, Madan believes that secularism is "impotent as a blueprint for the future because, by its very nature, it is incapable of countering religious fundamentalism and fanaticism" (1995:395).

50 Madan (1995) has launched a similar critique of state secularism. I remain unconvinced by his critique because, at the same time that the postcolonial state claims that its objective is to "lead" India toward modernity, it frequently appropriates Hindu religious traditions in its efforts to shape Indian nationalism. Tracing the apparent contradictions of the trajectories taken by the postcolonial state is beyond the scope of this book; nonetheless, I would like to stress that these trajectories are not paradoxical but are, in fact, intrinsic to the multiple and contradictory paths created by discourses of modernity. Cf. also van der Veer's critique of Madan (1994:12–13).

51 For a powerful argument for the *separation* of religion from governance, see Bhargava 1994.

52 Madan makes an almost identical argument: "it is the marginalization of religious faith, which is what secularization is, that permits the perversion of religion. There are no fundamentalists or revivalists in traditional society" (1995:396). While I cannot go into the pitfalls of the Durkheimian notion of society implicit in this claim, I will problematize this romanticization of "traditional society" as a site for tolerance shortly.

53 John Hawley notes that "anyone familiar with Indian religion knows the potency that Hindus sense in the experience of sight (*darsan*). Much of Hindu *bhakti* is specifically iconic" (1981:42).

54 This response to the *Ramayan* was not unprecedented. Lutgendorf points out that the devotional behavior of viewers was a "response with long, indigenous pedigree, rooted in the ritualized but complete identification of actor with deity that is central to Hindu folk performance" (1990:129).

55 Cf. also Lutgendorf 1990 and Richman 1991a.

56 See, for instance, Hawley 1981, Ishwaran 1981, Kinsley 1981, Lele 1981, Lutgendorf 1991, and Raheja and Gold 1994 for discussions of *bhakti*. Raheja and Gold provide a pithy definition of *bhakti*: "*Bhakti* is regularly translated as 'devotion' and occasionally as 'love,' with the qualification that it is a worshipful love that flows up. If *bhakti* as religious practice teaches humans to adore superior deities, *bhakti* in society is associated with antihierarchical ideas and movements. These include the understanding that priestcraft is unnecessary to mediate between the true devotee and divinity; and that with love any human, regardless of caste or sex, can touch God and receive a bountiful grace" (1994:169). For a study of the political consequences of *bhakti*, see Gokhale-Turner 1981; for analyses of the "antihierarchical" and gender impli-

cations of the *bhakti* of Mira, a celebrated woman saint from Rajasthan, see Harlan 1995, Kishwar and Vanita 1989, and Sangari 1990.

57 Purushottam Agrawal contends that in dominant contemporary readings, from "the Hindu cultural variety, the Hindu Nationalist type, left-liberal in orientation or even of the subaltern school of historians," *bhakti* is depicted as a "unilinear continuum that goes back to the days of the Gupta empire and before. In these readings, the medieval *Bhakti* poetic sensibility is nothing but an emotional restatement of scriptural religiosity. . . . *Bhakti* poetry in all its diversity is nurtured by a cultural and poetic content much larger than this correlation allows for, and in fact has an extremely uneasy relationship with scriptural religiosity. . . . The poetic *Bhakti* conception thus signified an arena of unresolved conflicts, a sensibility that is constantly struggling to evolve into a full-fledged world-view" (1994:258). He alleges that in modernist analytical discourse (here Agrawal seems to be pointing to orthodox secularist discourses in particular) *bhakti* is "reduced to a finished product which has already resolved these conflicts in favour of the dominant classes and their hegemonistic cultures" (1994:258).

58 Linda Hess points out that *bhakti* toward Krishna was greatly enhanced by the director of the television *Mahabharat*, B. R. Chopra, probably in response to the *Ramayan*'s success (comments on MS, January 1997).

59 V. T. Rajshekhar 1988, in Richman 1991a:21.

60 As pointed out by Marie Gillespie in her study of a devotional viewing of the *Mahabharat* among Hindu viewers in Southall, U.K., religious films can provide faithful viewers with "comfort and solace from life's everyday anxieties" (1995:363).

61 Poonam's dreams of Lord Ram correspond to Gillespie's description of devotional viewing. Gillespie claims, "Such viewing is thought to bring the gods into you and if, after watching, you can bring the gods into your dreams then it is considered to be like a divine visitation where blessings are bestowed and favors may be requested" (1995:363).

62 While everyday religiosity can be and has been mobilized by the politics of Hindu nationalism, it should not be a priori conflated with Hindu nationalism.

63 Gillespie describes similar forms of engagement. She notes that while "religious belief and a religious mode of consciousness are prerequisities to devotional viewing," viewing with piety does not "preclude the pleasures associated with entertainment" (1995:363).

64 Cf. Lutgendorf 1990:145, 164.

65 See also Bharucha's discussion of "the question of faith" (1998:3). Aiming to reformulate a secularist praxis that engages questions of faith, Bharucha reminds "secularists of the intrinsic variations within, and heterogeneity of the diverse structures of feeling and perception which constitute religious experi-

ence" (1998:3). At the same time, he also cautions against the appropriation of faith by "the anti-secularist agenda" (1998:3).

66　Sangari's criticism of naive invocations of faith is worth bearing in mind here: "In certain kinds of contemporary analysis, overly anxious to establish that religion is not false consciousness, religion is simply turned into a matter of faith or belief alone, thus eliding the issue that religion prevails as an institution more than consciousness, true or false. This formulation not only serves as a catchall but irons out the complexity of the relations between gender and religion" (1995:3293).

67　Cf. Krishnan 1990 for a different analysis of the two serials' treatment of primogeniture.

68　Chakravarti 1989:49.

69　Van der Veer goes so far as to claim that "the story of Rama's life is essentially a cautionary tale about the disruptive effects of [female] sexual desire" (1994:89).

70　The serial draws an explicit contrast between Shurpanakha's (allegedly) uncontrolled sexuality and Sita's modesty and self-restraint. Cf. also Erndl 1991: 83.

71　Cf. Erndl 1991 for a critical reading of the mutilation of Shurpanakha.

72　Since these discussions emerged when women compared Sita with Draupadi, I will present details in the next chapter. Cf. also Velcheru Narayana Rao's analysis of the songs composed by upper- and lower-caste Telugu women who draw on *Ramayana* stories in order to "say what they wish to say, as women" (1991:114). He argues that, in these songs, "minor or lowly characters" emerge as "winners," and to this extent the songs "also make a statement against the public ramayanas, the *bhakti* ramayanas, which glorify the accepted values of a male-dominated world" (1991:129). Narayana Rao is careful to not interpret these songs as feminist or even oppositional. Instead, he describes them as expressions of "muted groups" (1991:133). In the case of brahmin women, these songs are part of a larger brahminic ideology. Lower-caste women, on the other hand, seem to use the songs to express their "disaffection" with their dominant upper-caste masters rather than with men of their own caste (1991:134).

73　The responses of Sikh women to Draupadi were quite different. Although they made no bones about the fact that they considered the *Mahabharat* a Hindu epic, in some cases, Draupadi's disrobing resonated with their own experiences of sexual vulnerability and humiliation. Recall Surjeet Kaur's description of the sexual abuse she faced from her father-in-law in terms of Draupadi's disrobing in her in-laws' court (chapter 3). Like some of the Muslim women I interviewed, many Sikh women interpreted Draupadi's predicament in terms of the vulnerability of *all* women in contemporary India and often described her as emblematic of the "reality" of Indian Womanhood.

74 Cf. de Certeau 1984.

75 Cf. van der Veer's discussion of female sexuality in Muslim communalism (1994:98–104).

76 Cf. Sarkar and Butalia 1995, especially Butalia's essay "Muslims and Hindus, Men and Women: Communal Stereotypes and the Partition of India."

77 Veena Das, for example, argues that "as political actors, communities redefine themselves and are defined by others not by face-to-face relations but by (a) their right to define a collective past, a definition which homogenizes the different kinds of memories preserved in different visions of the community; (b) the right to regulate the body and sexuality by the codification of custom; and (c) the consubstantiality between acts of violence and acts of moral solidarity" (1995:15–16).

78 Sangari also points out that:

> the idea that religious communities can provide a bulwark against capitalism, popular among indigenist intellectuals, seems, at least in India, to be equally misconceived. Their positioning of "community"—as a sign of an "unhomogenised" localism or as mark of the precapitalist still resistant to capitalism and its ideologies or as a sign of autonomy vis-à-vis the nation-state—is naive and untenable. Religious communites are neither local, nor precapitalist. . . . The processes of community formation would be difficult to separate from the rationalities that accompany and legitimate capitalism, while community claims often have a political transactional character. . . . At many levels communalism and capitalism become compatible rather than opposed terms. (1995:3291)

> Cf. van der Veer's critique of Nandy's invocation of a dichotomy between culture (which is "unadulterated") and ideology (which is tainted by modernity) (1994:197). Interestingly, however, when van der Veer concludes that religious nationalisms are "combinations of the discourses of modernity with discourses of religious community" (1994:197), he seems to slip into a similar binary between modernity and community. In contrast, I have tried to trace how the *Ramayan* may have participated in the modernist construction of the imagined Hindu community.

79 Gillespie describes the devotional viewing of television among Hindus in Southall, U.K., as a culturally specific combination of pleasure and piety (1995). Gillespie's discussion focuses on the devotional viewing of the *Mahabharat*, and not the *Ramayan*.

Chapter 5 *Television Tales, National Narratives, and a Woman's Rage*

A shorter version of this chapter appears as Mankekar 1993a.

1   This representation of the *Mahabharata* as emblematic of Indian tradition rested precisely on its purported antiquity.

2   The serial was also avidly watched by Indians in the diaspora. See Gillespie 1995 for a fascinating ethnographic study of the *Mahabharat*'s reception by a Hindu family in Southall, U.K.

3   As in the previous chapter, when referring to the television serial the spelling used by the producers, *Mahabharat*, will be used; the larger narrative tradition will be referred to as the *Mahabharata*.

4   For an elegant and remarkably lucid explication of the indexicality and iconicity of signs, see Daniel 1984. According to C. S. Peirce, the construction of meaning may be analyzed in terms of icons (firstness), indices (secondness), and symbols (thirdness). In this essay, I analyze Draupadi-as-sign by partially reversing the semiotic chain in order to denaturalize her semiotic production as a symbol of "Indian Womanhood": I hence focus first on the indexicality of her disrobing (it indexes the position of women in Indian society) and then on its iconicity (her disrobing brings women located in specific sociocultural contexts into a confrontation with their own vulnerability in a patriarchal order).

5   For a detailed explication of the genealogical method, see Foucault 1982.

6   See Williams 1977 for an important discussion of the intrinsically incomplete nature of hegemony. I will touch on questions of hegemony and subjectivity later in this chapter.

7   I thank Carol Appadurai Breckenridge for her help with this paragraph.

8   Because of its depiction of family politics, many Hindus believed it inauspicious to read the *Mahabharata* in the home; in contrast, the *Ramayana* was deemed auspicious because it portrayed "ideal family conditions" (Hiltebeitel 1994:396).

9   In contrast, the Hindu viewers Gillespie worked with in Southall derived great pleasure from the *Mahabharat*'s religious meanings (1995:374).

10 I am referring to the Bofors scandal, in which Rajiv Gandhi and key members of his cabinet were accused of receiving kickbacks from an international arms manufacturer.

11 I interviewed Chopra, Bhatnagar, and Raza in Chopra's office in Bombay on November 29, 1990.

12 For reports on the *Mahabharat*'s popularity with Muslim viewers in India and Pakistan, see I. Das 1990 and Dethe and Sharma 1990.

13 In chapter 3 I describe how Surjeet Kaur, a Sikh viewer, appropriated the tale of Draupadi's disrobing to construct her own narrative of sexual abuse by her father-in-law.

14 See Thomas 1985 for an excellent analysis of the importance of the "balanced" formula (the *masala*) required for the success of popular Hindi films. Gillespie points to the intertextual narrative address of the *Mahabharat* and its dependence on popular religious iconography. She argues that when presented with another version that did not deploy similar representational strategies, Peter Brooks's *Mahabharata*, Hindu viewers in Southall were deeply disappointed and "turned off" (1995:364–365).

15 Cf. Hiltebeitel 1994 for a discussion of the symbolism of hair in the Draupadi cult in South India.

16 To many Hindus in the audience the blowing of conches would signify both the beginning of prayers (*pooja*) and the commencement of war (Krishna's *panchjanya*).

17 In Mankekar 1990 I analyze the disrobing episode in terms of its construction of heroic masculinity.

18 In devotional literature and popular iconography Lord Krishna is often depicted playing a flute.

19 Hiltebeitel points out that in the south Indian Draupadi cult, Draupadi takes on the form of Kali and Durga when she swears vengeance against the Kauravas (1994:397).

20 My thanks to Akhil Gupta for pointing this out to me.

21 There is an interesting parallel between Raza's discourse on "woman" as soil (and, implicitly, on "man" as seed) and the ideas about creation and procreation of Muslim villagers in Turkey (analyzed by Delaney 1991).

22 Cf. Hiltebeitel's discussion of the association between images of Draupadi's hair and saris and "the primary natural elements of earth, water, and fire" (1994:398).

23 These interpretations are significant in the presence of feminist interpretations of the *Mahabharata*, and of Draupadi in particular. See, for example, Irawati Karve's depiction of Draupadi in *Yuganta* (1991).

24 Gillespie notes that the *Mahabharat*'s Hindu viewers in Southall also raised "questions about traditional gender roles" (1995:372).

25 Separate "ladies' lines" are supposed to exist in post offices, at ticket counters, etc., to facilitate women's access to these services—and, I suspect, to protect them from harassment. In New Delhi, ladies' lines rarely survive.

26 Interview with Rupa Ganguli, in S. Chandra 1990.

27 For different discussions of how women nationalists negotiated the patriarchal discourses of nationalism, see Chakravarti 1989, Forbes 1981, and Visweswaran 1990.

28 Bankim exhorts men as well as women to overthrow the colonial rulers; however, his appeal to them to come to the rescue of "Mother India" is made from an essentially masculinist perspective, thus revealing that women can be sites for discourse even when conceived as actors (cf. de Lauretis 1984).

29 The dependence of Indian nationalists on figures drawn from Hindu mythology and iconography points to the elision between Hindu cultural nationalism and mainstream Indian nationalism from the outset. However, the slippages between Hindu and Indian nationalism in anticolonial discourses is beyond the scope of this book.

30 Mathura was a young tribal girl who was raped by constables in a police station; her cause was later taken up (appropriated?) by journalists and politicians. The cases of Roop Kanwar, a young widow who was burned at her husband's funeral pyre in Rajasthan; Shahbano, a Muslim woman who appealed to the Supreme Court to demand alimony from her husband; and Ameena, a minor Muslim girl from Hyderabad allegedly "sold" in marriage to a sheikh from the Middle East, met a similar fate. I should add that some Indian feminists have been extremely suspicious and critical of the role of the protectionist Indian state in these events. See Kishwar and Vanita 1988, Sunder Rajan and Pathak 1989 and Sunder Rajan 1994, and Mankekar 1997 for discussions of Roop Kanwar's sati, the Shahbano controversy, and the "Ameena case," respectively.

31 Hall also speaks of "oppositional positions," when viewers resist hegemonic discourses and interpret messages in terms of alternative frameworks of reference; for example, if a viewer reads "class interest" into every mention of "national interest" (1980). I find this hypothetical position unconvincing because it assumes that subjects can somehow stand outside the discursive formation to which they belong in order to engage in alternative readings.

32 My attempt to seek ruptures and disjunctures within dominant Hindu nationalist discourses of gender and nation complements the work of Sarkar 1991, Sarkar and Butalia 1995, and Basu 1998, which focus on how Hindu nationalism has created, appropriated, and circumscribed women's political agency.

Chapter 6 *"Air Force Women Don't Cry"*

1 For an analysis of Haathi Rani traditions in Rajasthan, see Harlan 1995.

2 Some of my discomfort about "explaining" the "speech" of marginalized subjects is in response to Gayatri Spivak's essay "Can the Subaltern Speak?" (1988). Elsewhere in this book I discuss the multiple valences of the place of speech, silence, and subterfuge in the ethnographic situation. My objective here is not to "speak for" viewers but to problematize the politics of representation.

3 The reasons for its appeal will be explored subsequently.

4 Enigma refers to the moment when the narrative's "order" is disturbed. In classical realist texts, the enigma is resolved and order reestablished by the end of the narrative.

5 Interview with Chetan Anand, November 1, 1990, New Delhi.

6   The title and background music were based on tunes that evoked what, in the *rasasutra* theory of aesthetics described in chapter 1, are known as *veer rasa* and *karun rasa* (loosely translated, "the heroic mood" and "the compassionate mood"). I sensed that even when viewers were not discursively aware of this theory, their engagement with Hindi film music, which liberally uses techniques based on the *rasasutra*, would "habituate" them to respond in particular ways.

7   See Chakrabarty 1992a for a provocative analysis of the relationship between discourses of modernity and order.

8   Although I cannot comment on the veracity of Anand's opinions, his anthropologizing of Indian audiences, as opposed to "Western" audiences, seemed to have emerged from his experience as a successful filmmaker with a record of box-office hits.

9   I am indebted to Parker et al.'s discussion of the exclusion of nonreproductive sexuality from nationalist discourses (1992:6).

10 The asexuality of mothers does not imply that they are nonsexual, but rather that their sexuality is channeled to the reproduction of valiant patriots, and to this extent is contained. Commenting on Lynn Bennett's work with upper-caste Nepali women (1983), Raheja and Gold point out that motherhood "purifies dangerous wives and makes their sexuality auspicious instead of dangerous" (1994:36). Wadley argues that, in canonical Hindu discourses, "mothers and the mother goddesses are in control of their sexuality; wives are not" (1980:34).

11 It is important to caution against a tendency to extrapolate from PVC's dichotomization of wives versus mothers to claims about a binary between sexuality and motherhood in "Hindu tradition" (much less "Indian society"). For a critique of such dualistic analyses, see Raheja and Gold 1994:30–35.

12 The relationship between celibacy and service to the nation, echoed in Gandhi's views on the relationship between sexual abstinence and the capacity for social (and national) service, may perhaps be traced to a Hindu notion of conserving one's sexual energies to achieve greater spiritual power.

13 Cf. Kakar 1988:63 and Raheja and Gold 1994 for analyses of the ambivalence toward conjugal love in north Indian discourses of family.

14 He was referring to the unrest in the streets because of the Mandal Commission riots (see chapter 1).

15 These stereotypes can be traced to colonial attempts to establish "martial" races in order to court the loyalty of certain ethnic groups, most prominently the Sikhs, Gorkhas, and Rajputs.

16 See, for example, Heng and Devan 1992, McClintock 1991. This is the central argument in Visweswaran 1990.

17 In contrast, Raheja and Gold found that mothers were portrayed as treacherous and wives as loyal in north Indian songs about sexuality.

18 This depiction of the relationship between mothers and sons would provide fertile ground for those concerned with constructing a psychoanalytic explanation for the pleasures viewers might have found in PVC's narratives.

19 See Nandy 1988:74 for an account of the primacy of mother-son relationships in north Indian discourses of family. Cf. Kakar 1988 for a psychoanalytic perspective on this relationship.

20 See Wadley 1980 for a discussion of the Hindu concept of women's *shakti*.

21 The relationship between notions of the mother goddess and Mother India reveals, among other elisions and slippages, the tension between Hindu and Indian nationalism. The consequences of hegemonic Hindu nationalism for the formulation of mainstream Indian nationalism is analyzed in greater detail in chapter 4.

22 For an explication of the notion of structures of feeling and of the role of melodrama in their production, see Williams 1977 and Ang 1985, respectively.

23 Although widows might be left "without a place in society," heroic mothers were also likely to be left destitute.

Chapter 7 *Popular Narrative, the Politics of Location, and Memory*

1 The *gayatri mantra* is a Hindu prayer. During the 1947 riots, Hindu mobs roaming the streets looking for Muslim victims would ask strangers to recite the *gayatri mantra*. All those who could not recite it were identified as Muslim and slaughtered immediately. Another way of identifying Muslim men was by making them remove their trousers: if they were circumcised, they were killed right away. Muslim rioters would identify their victims by asking them to recite verses from the Koran.

2 Lahore is one of Pakistan's most famous cities and an important cultural and financial center. Murree is a popular hill resort in Pakistan.

3 As noted in chapter 1, following Haraway 1988, I hope to use the term *partial* in all its ambiguity and richness.

4 Women were killed not only to prevent them from being forcibly converted, but also to "protect" them from being raped by men from the "enemy community." The violation of the woman's body was as feared as the conquest of her soul.

5 Tripathi 1988:23.

6 Interview with Bhisham Sahni, November 13, 1990.

7 Cf. Nandy 1992.

8 For influential and divergent perspectives on the role of the colonial state in communalism, see B. Chandra 1984 and Pandey 1990.

9 Bakshiji refers to *cheelen*, scavenging birds related to hawks.

10 In the novel, Bakshiji is as vain and power hungry as the other politicians; but in the serial, Bakshiji is the calmest and least easily provoked. The actor cast

to play this part, A. K. Hangal, has always performed the role of kind, calm old men. It is my guess that viewers were likely to associate Bakshiji with this persona. For the most part, the serial depicts Congress Party workers as self-absorbed and inept but, in general, well intentioned. I can only speculate about the reasons for the different portrayals of the Congress, which was in power when *Tamas* was aired on state-controlled television, in the serial and the novel.

11   According to television critic Iqbal Masud, who was a leftist activist at the time of Partition, this portrayal of the communist leader's insensitivity to religious matters is unfair. Masud claimed that many leftist activists of the time struggled to confront issues pertaining to religious identity and, unlike the communist leader of *Tamas*, did not dismiss it in terms of a "weak ideological base" (interviewed on December 15, 1990).

12   For a complex perspective on the experiences of "ordinary" people during Partition, see Butalia 1994.

13   Cf. Menon and Bhasin 1993; Butalia 1993, 1994, 1995; Chanana 1993; and V. Das 1995.

14   The *kirpan* is one of the five sacred symbols of the Sikh faith: the others are *kesh* (unshorn hair), *kaccha* (pants), *kanga* (comb), and *karha* (steel bangle).

15   I hasten to add that, in such contexts, it is impossible to distinguish between choice and compulsion. See Butalia 1995 and Mani 1989 for insightful discussions of women's consent and choice.

16   According to Butalia, these stories contrast with the historical and familial silence about women who were abducted during Partition (1993:63). Cf. also V. Das 1995:63.

17   This body of scholarship includes feminist critiques of colonial discourse (e.g., Chakravarti 1989, Mani 1989) and nationalist historiography (e.g., Sangari and Vaid 1989, Tharu and Lalita 1991a, and 1993b, Visweswaran 1990).

18   Butalia points out that, in our search for stories that can inspire us in our own struggle, feminists have often sought to recuperate women's agency and, "in our anxiety to reclaim powerful women, we tend to regard every kind of agency as positive" (1994:35). Except for one brief instance, when Akran's daughter-in-law resists her efforts to give sanctuary to Harnam Singh and Banto, *Tamas* is silent on the role of women in colluding with or perpetrating communal violence.

19   Sahni told me that he wanted to end the story on a note of hope. I, however, felt that the serial ended on an ambivalent if not pessimistic note, with the battle cries of rioting mobs drowning the cries of the newborn baby.

20   From Singh and Rahman 1988:73.

21   Ranvir's attempt to train his fellow recruits to kill Muslims is exceptionally violent in its portrayal of the murder of an innocent passer-by and in the

images it conjures of future violence (through, for example, his calm discussion of the uses of boiling oil).

22 In one exceptionally bright scene at the end of the serial, Karmo stands against a gaudy turqouise sky as she identifies her husband's body and goes into labor.

23 Singh and Rahman 1988:73.

24 Singh and Rahman 1988:74.

25 Chakravarti and Haksar 1987:13.

26 Prominent among these are the Punjabi poet Amrita Pritam, Urdu novelist Saadat Hasan Manto, and English novelist Khushwant Singh. In addition, G. D. Khosla, a retired civil servant, has written a memoir that powerfully "chronicles" Partition. I believe that the current efforts of scholars to study Partition were precipitated by the 1984 anti-Sikh pogroms. In a similar vein, Butalia asks: "Could it be that just as, for many people 1984 acted as a sort of catalyst, so also for many historians, the renewed experiences of communal strife brought to the surface personal and family narratives of 1947 in a new way, and thus forced many of them to come face to face with partition again, albeit in a different way? And did this new confrontation expand and stretch the definition of what we call history?" (1994:33).

27 *Manushi*, a women's magazine brought out by activists Madhu Kishwar and Ruth Vanita, provided an important forum for protests against the riots, and some activist organizations worked with communities that had suffered violence. Among the reports brought out by groups of outraged citizens, Uma Chakravarti and Nandita Haksar's *The Delhi Riots: Three Days in the Life of a Nation* (1987) remains the most comprehensive and reflective. For excellent discussions of the impact of the violence on women and children, see V. Das 1990.

28 As noted by Visweswaran, "Home once interrogated is a place we have never before been" (1994:113).

29 I thank Inderpal Grewal (personal communication, March 1993) for helping me think through some of these issues.

30 Cf. Battaglia 1992 on the politics of memory.

Epilogue

1 For distinctions between the transnational, international, and global, see Hamelink 1993:381.

2 Cf. Jesus Martin Barbero for how perceptions of national sovereignty in Latin American nations have changed as a result of "a new phase of capitalism" (1993:132).

3 For discussions of the impact of new communications technologies on national sovereignty in different parts of the world, see Nordenstreng 1993, Nordenstreng and Schiller 1993, and Schiller 1991.

4　As Appadurai has pointed out, the United States is "only one node of a complex transnational construction of imaginary landscapes" (1996:31).

5　Lowe and Lloyd add that while they draw on Marxist concepts of contradiction, they are "revising it away from the classical notions of the primary antagonism between capital and labor and the emergence of proletarian consciousness in order to reconceptualize its sites and effects" (1997:24).

6　See also David Harvey's insightful work on cultural production in an age of late capitalism, especially chapter 17 (1989).

7　Viewers had the option of buying converters that would enable them to watch more channels on their old television sets. In 1995, converters cost about Rs 2,500. In 1997, about three-fourths of the families I met in Vikas Nagar and Basti had invested in converters.

8　In 1993, Star and Star Plus, MTV, BBC, Prime Sports, Zee TV, and PTV were sharing the Asiasat satellite; Arabsat was used by CNN, and Gorizont by ATN; Rimsat was used by Sun TV; the Indian satellites Insat 1D, 2A, and 2B were being used by Doordarshan 1, the regional channels, and the Metro Channel, respectively.

9　The Supreme Court put two restrictions on these rights: they would be subject to the availability of broadcast frequencies, and to the provisions of Article 19(2) of the Constitution, according to which broadcasts could not affect the sovereignty and security of the country, disrupt public order, or "cross the limits of decency."

10　The proposal to launch direct-to-home (or DTH) services, which had been presented by Star's parent company, News Corp, was rejected by the government in April 1997.

11　The original Prasar Bharati Act had proposed such a committee, but the United Front government, which resurrected the act in October 1997, dropped the proposal for a parliamentary committee through an ordinance. At that time, both the BJP and the Congress opposed the ordinance.

12　Arjun Appadurai argues that the local, whether in terms of the local factory or site of production, is often "a fetish that disguises the globally dispersed forces that actually drive the production process" (1996:42).

13　Cf. Appadurai 1996, Feld 1988, and Ivy 1988 for discussions of similar processes of "indigenization" of transnational texts and ideas.

14　Eventually, MTV was forced to overcome its initial resistance to Indianize its programming and by 1994 was appearing in a regular two-and-a-half-hour slot on Doordarshan.

15　Most of the programs shown on these networks were drawn from Hindi films; however, regional films and film-based programs also emerged as part of a new strategy of niche marketing that targeted viewers whose first language was not Hindi.

16 When it first launched the Metro Channel, the government set up the Air Time Committee of India to set guidelines for programming. The committee advocated that the Metro Channel concentrate on developing "quality" programs. But since officials in Doordarshan and in the Ministry for Information and Broadcasting wanted a quick response to the growing popularity of foreign networks, they ignored the committee's suggestions and decided instead to turn to the film industry as a source of programming.

17 The popularity of shows based on film music also led to a renaissance of the audiocassette industry.

18 Appadurai's notion of mediascapes might be one mode of examining the processes through which culture is reterritorialized. Mediascapes refer to the production, distribution, and consumption of images produced by electronic media in different parts of the world. Appadurai argues: "What is most important about these mediascapes is that they provide (especially in their television, film, and cassette forms) large and complex repertoires of images, narratives, and ethnoscapes to viewers throughout the world. . . . What this means is that many audiences around the world experience the media themselves as a complicated and interconnected repertoire of print, celluloid, electronic screens, and billboards" (1996:35).

19 As Appadurai points out, "The consumer is consistently helped to believe that he or she is an actor, where in fact he or she is at best a chooser" (1996:42).

20 Cf. Appadurai's discussion of imagination as a social practice (1996:31).

21 As pointed out by Harvey, advertising and media images "have come to play a very much more integrative role in cultural practices and now assume a much greater importance in the growth dynamics of capitalism . . . images have, in a sense, themselves become commodities" (1989:287).

22 This seems to be the implicit premise of those models of globalization that emphasize penetration, infiltration, or cultural invasion by capital: according to these perspectives, capital is deemed external to the formation of community and identity.

23 Cf. Lowe and Lloyd's discussion of "the differentiating process of advanced globalizing capitalism" (1997:2). See also Gupta and Ferguson 1992, Harvey 1989:271. For capital's role in the production and marketing of tradition, see Harvey 1989:303 and Rajagopal 1994.

24 These TRP ratings referred to viewership during a single week, January 22–29, 1994.

25 Three of the most popular nonfilm programs on Tamil Sun TV were *Cho's Panchayat*, which consisted of a panel discussion on regional politics anchored by the famous political analyst Cho Ramaswamy; *Aratai Arangam*, produced by a popular actor-scriptwriter, which interrogated the deeds and careers of Tamil politicians; and *Netru Indru Nallai*, in which the well-known writer

Sivasankari mediated Oprah Winfrey–style discussions between an invited audience and local politicians (Pillai 1996:26).

26 In August 1994, *Tara* was the most-watched television program in Delhi and Bombay, earning TRP ratings of 48.0 and 41.7, respectively (Indian Market Research Bureau 1994b:4).

Bibliography

Abu-Lughod, Lila. 1990a. The Romance of Resistance: Tracing Transformations of Power through Bedouin Women. *American Ethnologist* 17:41–55.

———. 1990b. Can There Be a Feminist Ethnography? *Women and Performance* 5(1):7–27.

———. 1991. Writing against Culture. In *Recapturing Anthropology*, ed. Richard Fox. Santa Fe, N.M.: School of American Research Press.

———. 1993. *Writing Women's World: Bedouin Stories.* Berkeley: University of California Press.

———. Finding a Place for Islam: Egyptian Television Serials and the National Interest. *Public Culture* 5(3):493–514.

———. 1995. A Tale of Two Pregnancies. In *Women Writing Culture*, ed. Ruth Behar and Deborah A. Gordon. Berkeley: University of California Press.

———. 1997. The Interpretations of Culture(s) after Television. *Representations* 59:109–134.

Abu-Lughod, Lila, and Catherine A. Lutz, eds. 1990. *Language and the Politics of Emotion.* Cambridge: Cambridge University Press.

Adhikari, Sara. 1994. Dish and That. *Times of India*, May 1, 1994.

Agarwal, Amit. 1993. Zee TV: In Search of Class. *India Today*, January 31, 1993, p. 93.

———. 1996. Channels: An Awful Lot of Hoping. *India Today*, June 15, 1996, pp. 98–100.

Agarwal, Damodar. 1990. Agenda. *Times of India*, June 20, 1990, p. 11.

Agrawal, Binod C., and S. R. Joshi. n.d. Role of Television in Projecting the Life and Problems of Self-Employed Women. Research Centre for Women's Studies. SNDT Women's University, Bombay.

Agrawal, Purushottam. 1994. Kan Kan Mein Vyape Hein Ram: The Slogan as a Metaphor of Cultural Interrogation. *Oxford Literary Review* 16:245–264.

Alarcón, Norma. 1990. The Theoretical Subject(s) of This Bridge Called My Back and Anglo-American Feminism. In *Making Face, Making Soul*, ed. G. Anzaldua, pp. 356–369. San Francisco: Aunt Lute Foundation.

Allen, Robert C. 1992. Audience-Oriented Criticism and Television (1987). In

Channels of Discourse, Reassembled, ed. Robert C. Allen, pp. 101–137. Chapel Hill: University of North Carolina Press.

Allison, Anne. 1996. *Permitted and Prohibited Desires: Mothers, Comics, and Censorship in Japan.* Boulder: Westview Press.

Althusser, Louis. 1971. Ideology and Ideological State Apparatuses (Notes towards an Investigation). In *Lenin and Philosophy and Other Essays,* pp. 121–173. New York: Monthly Review Press.

Althusser, Louis, and Etienne Balibar. 1970. *Reading: "Capital."* London: NLB.

Amin, Shahid. 1989. Gandhi as Mahatma: Gorakhpur District, Eastern UP, 1921–2. In *Subaltern Studies. Vol. 3: Writings on South Asian History and Society,* ed. Ranajit Guha, pp. 1–61. Delhi: Oxford University Press.

Anderson, Benedict. 1991. *Imagined Communities.* 1983. Reprint, London: Verso.

Anderson, Walter, and Shridhar Damle. 1987. *The Brotherhood in Saffron — The RSS and Hindu Revivalism.* New Delhi: Vistaar Publications.

Ang, Ien. 1985. *Watching* Dallas: *Soap Opera and the Melodramatic Imagination.* London: Routledge.

———. 1989. Wanted: Audiences. On the Politics of Empirical Audience Studies. In *Remote Control: Television, Audiences, and Cultural Power,* ed. Ellen Seiter, Hans Borchers, Gabriele Kreutzner, and Eva-Maria Warth, pp. 96–115. London: Routledge.

———. 1990. Culture and Communication. *European Journal of Communication* 5(2–3):239–260.

———. 1991a. *Desperately Seeking the Audience.* London: Routledge.

———. 1996. *Living Room Wars.* London: Routledge.

Ang, Ien, and David Morley. 1989. Mayonnaise Culture and Other European Follies. *Cultural Studies* 3(2):133–144.

Appadurai, Arjun. 1986a. Introduction: Commodities and the Politics of Value. In *The Social Life of Things,* ed. Arjun Appadurai, pp. 3–63. Cambridge: Cambridge University Press.

———. 1986b. Theory in Anthropology: Center and Periphery. *Comparative Studies in Society and History* 28(1):356–361.

———. 1990. Disjunctive and Difference in the Global Cultural Economy. *Public Culture* 2(2):1–24.

———. 1996. *Modernity at Large: Cultural Dimensions of Globalization.* Minneapolis: University of Minnesota Press.

Appadurai, Arjun, and Carol A. Breckenridge. 1988. Why Public Culture? *Public Culture* 1(1):5–9.

Babb, Lawrence A., and Susan S. Wadley, eds. 1995. *Media and the Transformation of Religion in South Asia.* Philadelphia: University of Pennsylvania Press.

Bagchi, Jasodhara. 1990. Representing Nationalism: Ideology of Motherhood in Colonial Bengal. *Economic and Political Weekly* 25(42–43):65–71.

Bakshi, Geeta. n.d. *Doordarshan and the Women of the Non-formal Sector.* Research Centre for Women's Studies. SNDT Women's University, Bombay.

Balasubrahmanyam, Vimal. 1988. *Mirror Image: The Media and the Women's Question.* Bombay: Centre for Education and Documentation.

Bandura, Albert. 1977. *Social Learning Theory.* Englewood Cliffs, N.J.: Prentice-Hall.

Bannerjee, Sumanta. 1989. Marginalization of Women's Popular Culture in Nineteenth Century Bengal. In *Recasting Women: Essays in Colonial History*, ed. K. Sangari and S. Vaid, pp. 127–179. New Delhi: Kali for Women.

Barnouw, Erik, and S. Krishnaswamy. 1980. *Indian Film.* New York: Oxford University Press.

Barthes, Roland. 1972. *Mythologies.* New York: Hill and Wang.

Basu, Amrita. 1998. Hindu Women's Activism in India and the Questions It Raises. In *Appropriating Gender: Women's Activism and Politicized Religion in South Asia*, eds. Patricia Jeffery and Amrita Basu, pp. 167–184. New York: Routledge.

Battaglia, Debbora. 1992. The Body in the Gift: Memory and Forgetting in Sabarl Mortuary Exchange. *American Ethnologist* 19(1):3–18.

Behar, Ruth, and Deborah A. Gordon, eds. 1995. *Women Writing Culture.* Berkeley: University of California Press.

Benjamin, Walter. 1968. Theses in the Philosophy of History. In *Illuminations*, pp. 253–264. New York. Schocken Books.

Bennett, Lynn. 1983. *Dangerous Wives and Sacred Sisters: Social and Symbolic Roles of High-Caste Women in Nepal.* New York: Columbia University Press.

Bernstein, Richard. 1994. *Dictatorship of Virtue.* New York: Knopf.

Bhabha, Homi. 1990. DissemiNation: Time, Narrative and the Margins of the Modern Nation. In *Nation and Narration*, ed. Homi Bhabha, pp. 291–322. London: Routledge.

Bharati, Subramania. 1977. Panchali's Vow. In *Poems of Subramania Bharati*, trans. Prema Nandakumar, pp. 151–184. New Delhi: Sahitya Akademi.

Bhargava, Rajeev. 1994. Giving Secularism Its Due. *Economic and Political Weekly* 29(28):1784–1791.

Bharucha, Rustom. 1998. *In the Name of the Secular: Contemporary Cultural Activism in India.* New Delhi: Oxford University Press.

Bobo, Jacqueline. 1988. The Color Purple: Black Women as Cultural Readers. In *Female Spectators*, ed. D. Pribram, pp. 90–109. New York: Verso.

Brown, C. 1989. Holston Exports. *Broadcast*, October 13, 1989.

Brunsdon, Charlotte. 1984. Crossroads: Notes on Soap Opera. *Screen* 22(3):32–37.

———. 1990. Television: Aesthetics and Audiences. In *Logics of Television: Essays in Cultural Criticism*, ed. Patricia Mellencamp, pp. 59–72. Bloomington: Indiana University Press.

———. 1991. Pedagogies of the Feminine: Feminist Teaching and Women's Genres. *Screen* 32(4):364–381.

Burke, Peter. 1978. *Popular Culture in Early Modern Europe*. New York: Harper and Row.

Butalia, Urvashi. 1993. Community, State and Gender: On Women's Agency during Partition. *Economic and Political Weekly* 28(17):12–21.

———. 1994. Community, State and Gender: Some Reflections on the Partition of India. *Oxford Literary Review* 16:31–68.

———. 1995. Muslims and Hindus, Men and Women: Communal Stereotypes and the Partition of India. In *Women and the Hindu Right: A Collection of Essays*, ed. Tanika Sarkar and Urvashi Butalia, pp. 58–81. New Delhi: Kali for Women.

Carragee, K. 1990. Interpretive Media Study and Interpretive Social Science. *Critical Studies in Mass Communication* 7(2):81–96.

Chakrabarty, Dipesh. 1992a. Of Garbage, Modernity and the Citizen's Gaze. *Economic and Political Weekly* 27(10–11):541–546.

———. 1992b. Postcoloniality and the Artifice of History: Who Speaks for "Indian" Pasts. *Representations* 37:1–26.

Chakravarti, Uma. 1986. Pativrata. *Seminar* 318:17–21.

———. 1989. Whatever Happened to the Vedic Dasi? Orientalism, Nationalism and a Script for the Past. In *Recasting Women*, ed. Kumkum Sangari and Sudesh Vaid, pp. 27–87. New Delhi: Kali for Women.

Chakravarti, Uma, and Nandita Haksar. 1987. *The Delhi Riots: Three Days in the Life of a Nation*. New Delhi: Lancer International.

Chakravarty, Sumita S. 1989. National Identity and the Realist Aesthetic: Indian Cinema of the Fifties. *Quarterly Review of Film and Video* 11(3):31–48.

Chanana, Karuna. 1988a. Introduction to *Socialisation, Education and Women: Explorations in Gender Identity*, ed. Karuna Chanana, pp. 1–34. New Delhi: Orient Longman.

———. 1988b. Social Change or Social Reform: The Education of Women in Pre-independence India. In *Socialisation, Education and Women: Explorations in Gender Identity*, pp. 96–128. New Delhi: Orient Longman.

———. 1993. Partition and Family Strategies: Gender Education Linkages among Punjabi Women in Delhi. *Economic and Political Weekly* 28(17):25–34.

Chandra, Bipan. 1984. *Communalism in Modern India*. Delhi: Vikas Books.

———. 1991. Communalism and the State: Some Issues in India. In *Communalism in India: History, Politics and Culture*, ed. K. N. Panikkar, pp. 132–141. New Delhi: Manohar.

Chandra, Sharmila. 1990. "Mahabharat: Echoing the Times." *India Today*, January 31, 1990.

Chatterjee, Adite. 1991. A Year of Mixed Fortunes for DD. *Economic Times*, January 30, 1991.

Chatterjee, Partha. 1986. *Nationalist Thought and the Colonial World: A Derivative Discourse*. Totowa, N.J.: Zed Press.

———. 1989. The Nationalist Resolution of the Women's Question. In *Recasting*

Women: Essays in Colonial History, ed. K. Sangari and S. Vaid, pp. 233–253. New Delhi: Kali for Women.

———. 1993. *The Nation and Its Fragments: Colonial and Postcolonial Histories.* Princeton: Princeton University Press.

Chatterji, P. C. 1991. *Broadcasting in India.* New Delhi: Sage.

Chhachhi, Amrita. 1989. The State, Religious Fundamentalism and Women: Trends in South Asia. *Economic and Political Weekly* 24:567–578.

Clifford, James. 1986. On Ethnographic Allegory. In *Writing Culture: The Poetics and Politics of Ethnography,* ed. James Clifford and George E. Marcus, pp. 98–121. Berkeley: University of California Press.

Clifford, James, and George E. Marcus, eds. 1986. *Writing Culture: The Poetics and Politics of Ethnography.* Berkeley: University of California Press.

Collier, Jane, Michelle Z. Rosaldo, and Sylvia Yanagisako. 1982. Is There a Family? New Anthropological View. In *Rethinking the Family: Some Feminist Questions,* ed. Barrie Thorne and Marilyn Yalom, pp. 25–39. New York: Longman.

Collier, Jane, and Sylvia Junko Yanagisako, eds. 1987. *Gender and Kinship: Essays toward a Unified Analysis.* Stanford: Stanford University Press.

Crapanzano, Vincent. 1980. *Tuhami: Portrait of a Moroccan.* Chicago: University of Chicago Press.

Curran, James. 1990. The "New Revisionism" in Mass Communications Research. *European Journal of Communication* 5(2–3):135–164.

D'acci, Julie. 1992. Defining Women: Television and the Case of *Cagney and Lacey.* In *Private Screenings: Television and the Female Consumer,* eds. Lynn Spiegel and Denise Mann, pp. 169–202. Minneapolis: University of Minnesota Press.

Dalal, Sucheta. 1994. Footprints across India. *Times of India,* May 1, 1994.

Daniel, E. Valentine. 1984. *Fluid Signs: Being a Person the Tamil Way.* Berkeley: University of California Press.

———. 1985. Review of *A Crack in the Mirror: Reflexive Perspectives in Anthropology,* ed. J. Ruby. *Urban Life* 2:247–248.

Daniel, E. Valentine, and Jeffery M. Peck, eds. 1996. *Culture/Contexture: Explorations in Anthropology and Literary Studies.* Berkeley: University of California Press.

Das, Indira. 1990. An Epic Transcends the Border. *Sunday Mail,* July 8, 1990, pp. 1–3.

Das, Veena. 1976. Masks and Faces: An Essay on Punjabi Kinship. *Contributions to Indian Sociology* 10:1–30.

———. 1988. Femininity and the Orientation to the Body. In *Socialism, Education and Women: Explorations in Gender Identity,* ed. Karuna Chanana, pp. 193–207. New Delhi: Orient Longman.

———. 1990. "Our Work to Cry: Your Work to Listen." In *Mirrors of Violence: Communities, Riots and Survivors in South Asia,* ed. Veena Das, pp. 345–398. New Delhi: Oxford University Press.

————. 1995. *Critical Events: An Anthropological Perspective on Contemporary India.* Delhi: Oxford University Press.

Das, Veena, and Ashish Nandy. 1986. Violence, Victimhood, and the Language of Silence. In *The Word and the World: Fantasy, Symbol and Record,* ed. Veena Das, pp. 177–195. New Delhi: Sage.

de Certeau, M. 1984. *The Practice of Everyday Life,* trans. S. Randall. Berkeley: University of California Press.

Delaney, Carol. 1991. *The Seed and the Soil: Gender and Cosmology in Turkish Village Society.* Berkeley: University of California Press.

de Lauretis, Teresa. 1984. *Alice Doesn't: Feminism, Semiotics, Cinema.* Bloomington: Indiana University Press.

Dethe, V. K., and L. K. Sharma. 1990. Pakistanis Love It! *Times of India,* June 17, 1990, p. 11.

Dickey, Sara. 1993. *Cinema and the Urban Poor in South India.* Cambridge: Cambridge University Press.

Doane, Mary Ann. 1989. The Economy of Desire: The Commodity Form in/of the Cinema. *Quarterly Review of Film & Video* 11:23–33.

Dreyfus, Hubert L., and Paul Rabinow. 1982. *Michel Foucault: Beyond Structuralism and Hermeneutics.* Chicago: University of Chicago Press.

Dube, Leela. 1988a. Socialisation of Hindu Girls in Patrilineal India. In *Socialisation, Education and Women: Explorations in Gender Identity,* ed. Karuna Chanana, pp. 166–192. New Delhi: Orient Longman.

————. 1988b. On the Construction of Gender: Hindu Girls in Patrilineal India. *Economic and Political Weekly* 23(18):11–19.

Dwyer, Kevin. 1982. *Moroccan Dialogues.* Baltimore: Johns Hopkins University Press.

Ebron, Paulla, and Anna Lowenhaupt Tsing. 1995. In Dialogue? Reading across Minority Discourse. In *Women Writing Culture,* ed. Ruth Behar and Deborah A. Gordon, pp. 390–411. Berkeley: University of California Press.

Eck, Diana. 1985. *Darsan: Seeing the Divine Image in India.* 1981. Reprint, Chambersberg, Pa.: Anima Books.

Enslin, Elizabeth. 1993. Beyond Writing: Feminist Practice and the Limitations of Ethnography. *Cultural Anthropology* 9(4):537–568.

Erndl, Kathleen M. 1991. The Mutilation of Surpanakha. In *Many Ramayanas: The Diversity of a Narrative Tradition in South Asia,* ed. Paula Richman, pp. 67–88. Berkeley: University of California Press.

Escobar, Arturo. 1994. *Encountering Development: The Making and Unmaking of the Third World.* Princeton: Princeton University Press.

Feld, Steven. 1988. Notes on World Beat. *Public Culture* 1(1):31–37.

Ferguson, James. 1988. Cultural Exchange: New Developments in the Anthropology of Commodities. *Cultural Anthropology* 3(4):488–513.

————. 1990. *The Anti-politics Machine: "Development," Depoliticization, and Bureaucratic Power in Lesotho.* Cambridge: Cambridge University Press.

Feuer, Jane. 1983. The Concept of Live Television: Ontology as Ideology. In *Regarding Television: Critical Approaches—An Anthology,* ed. E. A. Kaplan, pp. 12–22. Frederick, Md.: University Publications of America.

Fiske, John. 1988. *Television Culture.* London: Methuen.

————. 1992. British Cultural Studies and Television (1987). In *Channels of Discourse, Reassembled,* ed. Robert C. Allen, pp. 284–326. Chapel Hill: University of North Carolina Press.

Flitterman Lewis, Sandy. 1983. The Real Soap Operas: TV Commercials. In *Regarding Television: Critical Approaches—An Anthology,* ed. E. A. Kaplan, pp. 86–95. Frederick, Md.: University Publications of America.

Forbes, Geraldine. 1981. The Indian Women's Movement: A Struggle for Women's Rights or National Liberation. In *The Extended Family: Women and Political Participation in India and Pakistan,* ed. Gail Minault, pp. 49–82. Columbia, Mo.: South Asia Books.

Foucault, Michel. 1978. *The History of Sexuality.* Vol. 1: *An Introduction.* New York: Vintage Books.

————. 1982. Afterword: The Subject and Power. In *Michel Foucault: Beyond Structuralism and Hermeneutics,* ed. Hubert J. Dreyfus and Paul Rabinow, pp. 208–226. Chicago: University of Chicago Press.

Fox, Richard. 1990. Hindu Nationalism in the Making, or the Rise of the Hindian. In *Nationalist Ideologies and the Production of National Cultures,* ed. Richard G. Fox, pp. 63–80. Washington, D.C.: American Anthropological Association. American Ethnological Society Monograph Series 2.

————. 1991. *Recapturing Anthropology: Working in the Present.* Santa Fe, N.M.: School of American Research Press.

Frankenberg, Ruth. 1993. *White Women, Race Matters: The Social Construction of Whiteness.* Minneapolis: University of Minnesota Press.

Frankenberg, Ruth, and Lata Mani. 1993. Crosscurrents, Crosstalk: Race, "Postcoloniality," and the Politics of Location. *Cultural Studies* 7(2):292–310.

Ganguly, Keya. 1992. Accounting for Others: Feminism and Representation. In *Women Making Meaning: New Feminist Directions in Communication,* ed. Lana F. Rakow, pp. 60–79. New York: Routledge.

Gates, Henry Louis. 1992. *Loose Canons.* New York: Oxford University Press.

Geertz, Clifford. 1973. Deep Play: Notes on the Balinese Cockfight. In *The Interpretation of Cultures,* pp. 412–453. New York: Basic Books.

Gellner, Ernest. 1983. *Nations and Nationalism.* Oxford: Basil Blackwell.

Gerow, Edwin. 1974. The Rasa Theory of Abinavagupta and Its Application. In *The Literatures of India: An Introduction,* ed. E. C. Dimock Jr. et al., pp. 212–227. Chicago: University of Chicago Press.

Gerow, Edwin, and Margory D. Lang, eds. 1974. *Studies in the Language and Culture of South Asia*. Seattle: University of Washington Press.

Ghadially, Rehana, and Pramod Kumar. 1988. Bride-Burning: The Psycho-Social Dynamics of Dowry Deaths. In *Women in India: A Reader*, pp. 167–177. New Delhi: Sage.

Ghosh, Amitav. 1990. *The Shadow Lines*. 1988. Reprint, New York: Penguin Books.

Gillespie, Marie. 1989. Technology and Tradition: Audio-Visual Culture among South Asian Families in West London. *Cultural Studies* 2(2):226–239.

———. 1995. Sacred Serials, Devotional Viewing, and Domestic Worship: A Case-Study in the Interpretation of Two TV Versions of the Mahabharata in a Hindu Family in West London. In *To Be Continued . . . Soap Operas around the World*, ed. Robert C. Allen, pp. 354–380. London: Routledge.

Ginsburg, Faye. 1993. Aboriginal Media and the Australian Imaginary. *Public Culture* 5(3):557–578.

Gokhale-Turner, Jayashree B. 1981. Bhakti or Vidroha: Continuity and Change in Dalit Sahitya. In *Tradition and Modernity in Bhakti Movements*, ed. Jayant Lele, pp. 29–42. Leiden: E. J. Brill.

Gordon, Deborah A. 1995. Border Work: Feminist Ethnography and the Dissemination of Literacy. In *Women Writing Culture*, ed. Ruth Behar and Deborah A. Gordon, pp. 373–389. Berkeley: University of California Press.

Gough, Kathleen. 1956. Brahman Kinship in a Tamil Village. *American Anthropologist* 58:826–53.

Government of India. 1985. *An Indian Personality for Television: Report of the Working Group on Software for Doordarshan*. 2 vols. New Delhi: Publications Division, Ministry of Information and Broadcasting.

Gray, Ann. 1987. Reading the Audience. *Screen* 28(3):24–35.

———. 1995. I Want to Tell You a Story: The Narratives of Video Playtime. In *Feminist Cultural Theory: Process and Production*, ed. Beverley Skeggs, pp. 153–168. Manchester: Manchester University Press.

Grewal, Inderpal, and Caren Kaplan. 1994. Introduction: Transnational Feminist Practices and Questions of Postmodernity. In *Scattered Hegemonies: Postmodernity and Transnational Feminist Practices*, ed. Inderpal Grewal and Caren Kaplan, pp. 1–36. Minneapolis: University of Minnesota Press.

Grossberg, Lawrence. 1989. On the Road with Three Ethnographers. *Journal of Communication Inquiry* 13(2):23–26.

Gupta, Akhil. 1995. Blurred Boundaries: The Discourse of Corruption, the Culture of Politics, and the Imagined State. *American Ethnologist* 22(2):375–402.

———. 1998. *Post-colonial Developments: Agriculture in the Making of a Modern Nation*. Durham: Duke University Press.

Gupta, Akhil, and James Ferguson. 1992. Beyond "Culture": Space, Identity, and the Politics of Difference. *Cultural Anthropology* 7(1):6–23.

———. 1997a. *Anthropological Locations: Boundaries and Grounds of a Field Science.* Berkeley: University of California Press.

———. 1997b. *Culture, Power, Place: Excavations in Critical Anthropology.* Durham: Duke University Press.

Hall, Stuart. 1977. Culture, the Media and the Ideological Effect. In *Culture, Society and the Media,* ed. Michael Gurevitch et al., pp. 315–348. London: Methuen.

———. 1980. Encoding/Decoding. In *Culture, Media, Language,* ed. Stuart Hall, Dorothy Hobson, Andrew Lowe, and Paul Willis, pp. 128–138. Birmingham: Centre for Contemporary Cultural Studies.

———. 1981. Notes on Deconstructing "the Popular." In *People's History and Socialist Theory,* ed. R. Samuel, pp. 227–240. London: Routledge and Kegan Paul.

———. 1985. Signification, Representation, Ideology: Althusser and the Post-structuralist Debates. *Critical Studies in Mass Communication* 2(2):91–114.

———. 1986. Gramsci's Relevance for the Study of Race and Ethnicity. *Journal of Communication Inquiry* 10(2):5–27.

———. 1996. When Was 'the Post-Colonial'? Thinking of the Limit. In *The Post-Colonial Question,* ed. Iain Chambers and Lidia Curti. London: Routledge.

Hamelink, Cees J. 1993. Globalism and National Sovereignty. In *Beyond National Sovereignty: International Communication in the 1990s,* ed. Kaarle Nordenstreng and Herbert I. Schiller, pp. 371–393. Norwood, N.J.: Ablex.

Hannerz, Ulf. 1996. *Transnational Connections.* London: Routledge.

Haraway, Donna. 1988. Situated Knowledges: The Science Question in Feminism and the Privilege of Partial Perspective. *Feminist Studies* 14(3):575–599.

Harlan, Lindsey. 1995. Abandoning Shame: Mira and the Margins of Marriage. In *From the Margins of Hindu Marriage,* ed. Lindsey Harlan and Paul B. Courtright, pp. 204–227. New York: Oxford University Press.

Harrison, Faye V. 1995. Writing against the Grain: Cultural Politics of Difference in the Work of Alice Walker. In *Women Writing Culture,* ed. Ruth Behar and Deborah A. Gordon, pp. 233–248. Berkeley: University of California Press.

Hartley, John. 1984. Encouraging Signs: TV and the Power of Dirt, Speech, and Scandalous Categories. In *Interpreting Television: Current Research Perspectives,* ed. W. Rowland and B. Watkins, pp. 119–141. Beverly Hills: Sage.

Harvey, David. 1989. *The Condition of Postmodernity.* Oxford: Basil Blackwell.

Hawley, John Stratton. 1981. Krishna in Black and White: Darsan in the Butter Thief Poems of the Early Sur Sagar. In *Tradition and Modernity in Bhakti Movements,* ed. Jayant Lele, pp. 43–58. Leiden: E. J. Brill.

———. 1995. The Saints Subdued: Domestic Virtue and National Integration in Amar Chitra Katha. In *Media and the Transformation of Religion in South Asia,* ed. Lawrence A. Babb and Susan S. Wadley, pp. 24–50. Philadelphia: University of Pennsylvania Press.

Hayward, Susan. 1996. *Key Concepts in Cinema Studies.* London: Routledge.

Hebdige, Dick. 1979. *Subculture: The Meaning of Style*. London: Methuen.

Held, David. 1980. *Introduction to Critical Theory: Horkheimer to Habermas*. Berkeley: University of California Press.

Heng, Geraldine, and Janadas Devan. 1992. State Fatherhood: The Politics of Nationalism, Sexuality and Race in Singapore. In *Nationalisms and Sexualities*, ed. Andrew Parker, Mary Russo, Doris Sommer, and Patricia Yaeger, pp. 343–364. London: Routledge.

Hiltebeitel, Alf. 1994. The Folklore of Draupadi: Saris and Hair. In *Gender, Genre, and Power in South Asian Expressive Traditions*, ed. Arjun Appadurai, Frank J. Korom, and Margaret A. Mills, pp. 395–427. Delhi: Motilal Banarsidass.

Hobson, Dorothy. 1980. Housewives and the Mass Media. In *Culture, Media, Language*, ed. Stuart Hall, Dorothy Hobson, Andrew Lowe, and Paul Willis, pp. 105–114. Birmingham: Centre for Contemporary Cultural Studies.

hooks, bell. 1990. Homeplace: A Site of Resistance. In *Yearning: Race, Gender, and Cultural Practice*, pp. 41–49. Boston: South End Press.

Horkheimer, Max, and Theodore Adorno. 1969. The Culture Industry: Enlightenment as Mass Deception (1944). In *Dialectic of Enlightenment*, trans. J. Cumming, pp. 120–167. New York: Continuum.

Hoskote, Ranjit. 1990. Vyasa's Krishna. Letter to the editor. *Times of India*, July 27, 1990, p. 7.

Huyssen, Andreas. 1986. *After the Great Divide: Modernism, Mass Culture, Postmodernism*. Bloomington: Indiana University Press.

Inden, Ronald, and Ralph Nicholas. 1977. *Kinship in Bengali Culture*. Chicago: University of Chicago Press.

Indian Market Research Bureau. 1994a. The Best on the Box. *Economic Times*, February 23, 1994, p. 8.

———. 1994b. The Best on the Box. *Economic Times*, August 3, 1994, p. 4.

Irigaray, Luce. 1985. *This Sex Which Is Not One*. Ithaca: Cornell University Press.

Ishwaran, K. 1981. Bhakti Tradition and Modernization: The Case of Lingayatism. In *Tradition and Modernity in Bhakti Movements*, ed. Jayant Lele, pp. 72–82. Leiden: E. J. Brill.

Ivy, Marilyn. 1988. Tradition and Difference in the Japanese Mass Media. *Public Culture* 1(1):21–30.

———. 1995. *Discourses of the Vanishing: Modernity, Phantasm, Japan*. Chicago: University of Chicago Press.

Jacobson, Doranne. 1977. Flexibility in North Indian Kinship and Residence. In *The New Wind: Changing Identities in South Asia*, ed. Kenneth David, pp. 163–183. The Hague: Mouton.

Jain, Devaki. 1986. Gandhian Contributions towards a Theory of Feminist Ethics. In *Speaking of Faith: Cross-Cultural Perspectives on Women, Religion and Social Change*. London: Women's Press.

Jain, Madhu. 1985. Be Indian, See Indian. *Sunday*, April 14, 1985.

————. 1995. Beaming in a Revolution. *India Today,* December 31, 1995, pp. 104–107.

Jeffery, Patricia, and Amrita Basu, eds. 1998. *Appropriating Gender: Women's Activism and Politicized Religion in South Asia.* New York: Routledge.

Jeffords, Susan. 1989. *The Remasculinization of America: Gender and the Vietnam War.* Bloomington: Indiana University Press.

John, Mary E. 1996. *Discrepant Dislocations.* Berkeley: University of California Press.

Johnson, Richard. 1986. What Is Cultural Studies Anyway? *Social Text* 6(1):38–80.

Kakar, Sudhir. 1988. Feminine Identity in India. In *Women in Indian Society: A Reader,* ed. Rehana Ghadially, pp. 44–68. New Delhi: Sage.

Kala, Arvind. 1990. Mahabharata: The Mad Rush. *Sunday Mail,* July 1, 1990, pp. 15–16.

Kaplan, Caren. 1994. The Politics of Location as Transnational Feminist Practice. In *Scattered Hegemonies: Postmodernity and Transnational Feminist Practices,* ed. Inderpal Grewal and Caren Kaplan, pp. 127–152. Minneapolis: University of Minnesota Press.

Kapur, Anuradha. 1990. *Actors, Pilgrims, Kings, and Gods: The Ramlila of Ramnagar.* Calcutta: Seagull Books.

Karlekar, Malavika. 1988. Women's Nature and the Access to Education. In *Socialisation, Education and Women: Explorations in Gender Identity,* pp. 129–165. New Delhi: Orient Longman.

Karve, Irawati. 1991. *Yuganta.* 1974. Reprint, New Delhi: Disha.

Katiyar, Arun. 1995. A New Vision. *India Today,* January 31, 1995, pp. 146–147.

Kaviraj, Sudipta. 1989. On the Construction of Colonial Power: Structure, Discourse, Hegemony. Paper presented at the Conference on Foundations of Imperial Hegemony: Western Education, Public Health and Police in India and Anglophone Africa, 1859 until Independence. Berlin, June 1–3, 1989, organized by the German Historical Institute, London.

————. n.d. The Imaginary Institution of India. Unpublished manuscript.

Khair, Tabish, and Gyanendra Nath. 1990. Mahabharata's Krishna: A Machiavelli or a God? *Times of India,* July 10, 1990, p. 11.

Khare, R. S. 1982. From Kanya to Mata: Aspects of the Cultural Language of Kinship in Northern India. In *Concepts of Person: Kinship, Caste, and Marriage in India,* ed. Akos Ostor, Lina Fruzetti, and Steve Barnett, pp. 143–171. Cambridge: Harvard University Press.

Khosla, G. D. 1989. *Stern Reckoning.* Delhi: Oxford University Press.

Kinsley, David. 1981. Devotion as an Alternative to Marriage in the Lives of Some Hindu Women Devotees. In *Tradition and Modernity in Bhakti Movements,* ed. Jayant Lele, pp. 83–93. Leiden: E. J. Brill.

Kishwar, Madhu. 1985. Gandhi on Women. *Economic and Political Weekly* 20(40–41):1691–1702, 1753–1758.

————. 1990. Learning to Take People Seriously. *Manushi* 56:2–10.

Kishwar, Madhu, and Ruth Vanita. 1988. The Burning of Roop Kanwar. *Race and Class* 30(1):59–67.

———. 1989. Modern Versions of Mira. *Manushi* 50–52:100–101.

Kohli, Vanita. 1994. Treasure Hunt. *Advertising and Marketing*, March 1994, pp. 111–113.

Kondo, Dorinne. 1986. Dissolution and Reconstitution of Self: Implications for Anthropological Epistemology. *Cultural Anthropology* 1(1):74–88.

———. 1990. *Crafting Selves: Power, Gender, and Discourses of Identity in a Japanese Workplace.* Chicago: University of Chicago Press.

Krishnan, Prabha. 1990. In the Idiom of Loss: Ideology of Motherhood in Television Serials. *Economic and Political Weekly* 25(42–43):103–116.

———. n.d. Visibility of Working Women under the Poverty Line in Television Programs. Research Centre for Women's Studies. SNDT Women's University, Bombay.

Krishnan, Prabha, and Anita Dighe. 1990. *Affirmation and Denial: Construction of Femininity on Indian Television.* New Delhi: Sage.

Kulkarni, V. G. 1992. The Middle-Class Bulge. *Far Eastern Economic Review,* January 14, 1992.

Kumar, Kanti. 1990. Vyasa's Krishna. Letter to the Editor. *Times of India,* July 27, 1990, p. 7.

Kumar, Radha. 1993. *The History of Doing: An Illustrated Account of Movements for Women's Rights and Feminism in India, 1800–1990.* New Delhi: Kali for Women.

Lacan, Jacques. 1977. *Écrits: A Selection,* trans. A. Sheridan. 1966. Reprint, New York: International.

Laclau, Ernesto. 1990. *New Reflections on the Revolution of Our Times.* London: Verso.

Lakshmi, C. S. 1988. Feminism and the Cinema of Realism. In *Women in Indian Society,* ed. R. Ghadially, pp. 217–224. New Delhi: Sage.

Lavie, Smadar. 1990. *The Poetics of Military Occupation: Mzeina Allegories of Bedouin Identity under Israeli and Egyptian Rule.* Berkeley: University of California Press.

———. 1995. Border Poets: Translating by Dialogues. In *Women Writing Culture,* ed. Ruth Behar and Deborah A. Gordon, pp. 412–428. Berkeley: University of California Press.

Lele, Jayant. 1981. The Bhakti Movement in India: A Critical Introduction. In *Tradition and Modernity in Bhakti Movements,* ed. Jayant Lele, pp. 1–15. Leiden: E. J. Brill.

Lerner, Daniel. 1958. *The Passing of Traditional Society: Modernizing the Middle East.* New York: Free Press.

Lev, Daniel S. 1990a. Intermediate Classes and Change in Indonesia: Some Initial Reflections. In *The Politics of Middle Class Indonesia,* ed. Richard Tanter and Kenneth Young, pp. 25–43. Clayton, Victoria, Australia: Monash University.

———. 1990b. Notes on the Middle Class and Change in Indonesia. In *The Politics of Middle Class Indonesia,* ed. Richard Tanter and Kenneth Young, pp. 44–48. Clayton, Victoria, Australia: Monash University.

Limón, José. 1991. Representation, Ethnicity, and the Precursory Ethnography: Notes of a Native Anthropologist. In *Recapturing Anthropology,* ed. Richard Fox, pp. 115–136. Santa Fe, N. Mex.: School of American Research Press.

Lopez, Ana. 1995. Our Welcomed Guest: Telenovelas in Latin America. In *To Be Continued . . . Soap Operas around the World,* ed. Robert C. Allen, pp. 256–275. London: Routledge.

Lorde, Audre. 1984. *Sister Outsider.* Freedom, Calif.: Crossing Press.

Lowe, Lisa and David Lloyd. 1997. Introduction. In *The Politics of Culture in the Shadow of Capital,* ed. Lisa Lowe and David Lloyd, pp. 1–32. Durham, N.C.: Duke University Press.

Lutgendorf, Philip. 1990. Ramayan: The Video. *Drama Review* 34(2):127–176.

———. 1991. *The Life of a Text.* Berkeley: University of California Press.

Madan, T. N. 1995. Secularism in Its Place. In *Religion in India,* ed. T. N. Madan, pp. 394–409. Delhi: Oxford University Press.

Malkki, Liisa. 1992. National Geographic: The Rooting of Peoples and the Territorialization of National Identity among Scholars and Refugees. *Cultural Anthropology* 7(1):24–44.

Mani, Lata. 1989. Contentious Traditions: The Debate on Sati in Colonial India. In *Recasting Women: Essays in Colonial History,* ed. Kumkum Sangari and Sudesh Vaid, pp. 88–126. New Delhi: Kali for Women.

Mankekar, Purnima. 1988. Television and the Constitution of Women as Subjects. Research competency paper, Department of Anthropology, University of Washington.

———. 1990. "Our Men Are Heroes, Our Women Are Chaste": A Nationalist Reading of the "Disrobing" of Draupadi. Paper presented at the Annual Meeting of the American Ethnological Society, April 26–29, 1990.

———. 1993a. National Texts and Gendered Lives: An Ethnography of Television Viewers in a North Indian City. *American Ethnologist* 20(3):543–563.

———. 1993b. Reconstituting Indian Womanhood: An Ethnography of Television Viewers in a North Indian City. Ph.D. diss., University of Washington.

———. 1993c. Television Tales and a Woman's Rage: A Nationalist Recasting of Draupadi's "Disrobing." *Public Culture* 11:469–492.

———. 1994. Reflections on Diasporic Identities: A Prolegomenon to an Analysis of Political Bifocality. *Diaspora* 3(3):349–371.

———. 1997. "To whom does Ameena belong?" Childhood, Gender, and Nation in Contemporary India. *Feminist Review* 56:26–60.

Martin, Biddy, and Chandra Talpade Mohanty. 1986. Feminist Politics: What's Home Got to Do with It? In *Feminist Studies, Critical Studies,* ed. Teresa de Lauretis, pp. 191–212. Bloomington: Indiana University Press.

Martín Barbero, Jesús. 1993. Modernity, Nationalism, and Communication in Latin America. In *Beyond National Sovereignty: International Communication in the 1990s*, ed. Kaarle Nordenstreng and Herbert I. Schiller, pp. 132–147. Norwood, N.J.: Ablex.

———. 1995. Memory and Form in the Latin American Soap Opera. In *To Be Continued . . . Soap Operas around the World*, ed. Robert C. Allen, pp. 276–284. London: Routledge.

Mascia Lees, Frances E., Patricia Sharpe, and Colleen Ballerino Cohen. 1989. The Postmodernist Turn in Anthropology: Cautions from A Feminist Perspective. *Signs* 15(1):7–33.

Mazumdar, Debu. 1988. Mandi House Had Rejected Ramayan. *Indian Express*, August 1, 1988, p. 2.

Mazumdar, Vina. 1976. The Social Reform Movement in India: From Ranade to Nehru. In *Indian Women: From Purdah to Modernity*, ed. B. R. Nanda, pp. 41–66. Delhi: Vikas.

McClintock, Ann. 1991. No Longer in a Future Heaven: Women and Nationalism in South Africa. *Transition* 51:120.

McRobbie, Angela. 1982. The Politics of Feminist Research: Between Talk, Text and Action. *Feminist Review* 12:46–59.

Menon, Ritu, and Kamla Bhasin. 1993. Recovery, Rupture, Resistance: Indian State and Abduction of Women during Partition. *Economic and Political Weekly* 28(17):2–11.

Mercer, Kobena. 1991. Skin Head Sex Thing: Racial Difference and the Homoerotic Imaginary. In *How Do I Look?* Ed. Bad Object Choices. pp. 169–210. Seattle: Bay Press.

Meyrowitz, Joshua. 1985. *No Sense of Place*. Oxford: Oxford University Press.

Miller, Daniel. 1987. *Material Culture and Mass Consumption*. Oxford: Basil Blackwell.

———. 1988. Appropriating the State on the Council Estate. *Man* 23:353–72.

———. 1995a. Consumption as the Vanguard of History: A Polemic by Way of an Introduction. In *Acknowledging Consumption*, ed. Daniel Miller, pp. 1–57. London: Routledge.

———. 1995b. Consumption Studies as the Transformation of Anthropology. In *Acknowledging Consumption*, ed. Daniel Miller, pp. 264–295. London: Routledge.

Mitra, Sumit. 1995. Television: The Spreading Screen. *India Today*, December 31, 1995.

Modleski, Tania. 1979. The Search for Tomorrow in Today's Soap Operas. *Film Quarterly* 32(1):266–278.

———. 1983. The Rhythms of Reception: Daytime Television and Women's Work. In *Regarding Television: Critical Approaches—An Anthology*, ed. E. Ann Kaplan, pp. 67–75. American Film Institute Monograph Series. Los Angeles: American Film Institute.

————. 1986. Introduction. In *Studies in Entertainment: Critical Approaches to Mass Culture*, ed. Tania Modleski, pp. ix–xix. Bloomington: Indiana University Press.

Mohanty, Chandra Talpade. 1984. Under Western Eyes: Feminist Scholarship and Colonial Discourses. *Boundary 2* 13(1):333–358.

————. 1987. Feminist Encounters: Locating the Politics of Experience. *Copyright* 1:30–44.

————. 1991. Under Western Eyes: Feminist Scholarship and Colonial Discourses. In *Third World Women and the Politics of Feminism*, ed. Chandra Mohanty, Ann Russo, and Lourdes Torres, pp. 51–80. Bloomington: Indiana University Press.

Morley, David. 1980. *Everyday Television: "Nationwide."* British Film Institute Monograph. London: British Film Institute.

————. 1991. Where the Global Meets the Local: Notes from the Sitting Room. *Screen* 32:1–15.

————. 1992. *Television, Audiences and Cultural Studies*. London: Routledge.

Morley, David, and Kevin Robins. 1995. *Spaces of Identity: Global Media, Electronic Landscapes, and Cultural Boundaries*. London: Routledge.

Morris, Meaghan. 1990. Banality in Cultural Studies. In *Logics of Television: Essays in Cultural Criticism*, ed. Patricia Mellencamp, pp. 14–43. Bloomington: Indiana University Press.

Mukherjee, Meenakshi. 1985. *Realism and Reality: The Novel and Society in India*. Delhi: Oxford University Press.

Mulvey, Laura. 1989. Visual Pleasure and Narrative Cinema (1975). In *Visual and Other Pleasures*, pp. 14–28. Bloomington: Indiana University Press.

————. 1981. Afterthoughts on "Visual Pleasure and Narrative Cinema" Inspired by *Duel in the Sun*. *Framework* 6(15–17):12–15.

Nandy, Ashish. 1988. Woman versus Womanliness: An Essay in Social and Political Psychology. In *Women in Indian Society: A Reader*, ed. Rehana Ghadially, pp. 69–80. New Delhi: Sage.

————. 1990. The Politics of Secularism and the Recovery of Religious Tolerance. In *Mirrors of Violence: Communities, Riots and Survivors in South Asia*, ed. Veena Das, pp. 69–93. New Delhi: Oxford University Press.

Narayan, Kirin. 1993. How Native Is a Native Anthropologist? *American Anthropologist* 95:671–686.

Newcomb, H., and P. Hirsch. 1984. Television as a Cultural Forum. In *Interpreting Television*, ed. W. Rowland and B. Watkins, pp. 58–73. Newbury Park: Sage.

Nietzsche, Friedrich. 1949. *The Use and Abuse of History*. Indianapolis: Bobbs-Merrill.

Ninan, Sevanti. 1995. *Through the Magic Window*. New Delhi: Penguin Books.

Ninan, T. N. 1985. Rise of the Middle Class. *India Today*, December 31, 1985.

Niranjana, Tejaswini, P. Sudhir, and Vivek Dhareshwar, eds. 1993. *Interrogating Modernity: Culture and Colonialism in India*. Calcutta: Seagull Books.

Nordenstreng, Kaarle. 1993. Sovereignty and Beyond. In *Beyond National Sovereignty: International Communication in the 1990s*, ed. Kaarle Nordenstreng and Herbert I. Schiller, pp. 461–463. Norwood, N.J.: Ablex.

Nordenstreng, Kaarle, and Herbert Schiller, eds. 1993. *Beyond National Sovereignty: International Communication in the 1990s*. Norwood, N.J.: Ablex.

Ong, Aihwa. 1995. Women out of China: Traveling Tales and Traveling Theories in Postcolonial Feminism. In *Women Writing Culture*, ed. Ruth Behar and Deborah A. Gordon, pp. 350–372. Berkeley: University of California Press.

Padgaonkar, Dilip. 1990. A "Republican" Epic. *Times of India*, June 17, 1990, p. 11.

Pande, Mrinal. 1991. *The Subject Is Woman*. New Delhi: Sanchar Publications.

Pandey, Gyanendra. 1990. *The Construction of Communalism in Colonial North India*. Delhi: Oxford University Press.

———. 1992. In Defense of the Fragment: Writing about Hindu-Muslim Riots in India Today. *Representations* 37:27–55.

Pandian, M. S. S. 1992. *The Image Trap: MG Ramachandran in Film and Politics*. New Delhi: Sage.

Parker, Andrew, Mary Russo, Doris Sommer, and Patricia Yaeger, eds. 1992. *Nationalisms and Sexualities*. London: Routledge.

Parthasarathy, R. J. 1990. Vyasa's Krishna. Letter to the editor. *Times of India*, July 27, 1990, p. 7.

Patel, Sujata. 1988. Construction and Reconstruction of Woman in Gandhi. *Economic and Political Weekly* 23(6):377–387.

Pathak, Zakia, and Rajeswari Sunder Rajan. 1989. Shahbano. *Signs* 14(3):558–583.

Pendakur, Manjunath. 1989. Indian Television Comes of Age: Liberalization and the Rise of Consumer Culture. *Communication* 11:177–197.

Penley, Constance. 1988. Introduction—The Lady Doesn't Vanish: Feminism and Film Theory. In *Feminism and Film Theory*, ed. Constance Penley, pp. 1–24. New York: Routledge.

Philipose, Pamela. 1990. An Epic Mistake? *Observer*, November 1990, p. 13.

Pillai, Sreedhar. 1996. Changing Taste. *Sunday*, January 14, 1996, pp. 26–27.

Plath, David W. 1980. *Long Engagements, Maturity in Modern Japan*. Stanford: Stanford University Press.

Pollock, Sheldon. 1993. Ramayana and Political Imagination in India. *Journal of Asian Studies* 52(2):261–297.

Poulantzas, N. 1971. *Political Power and Social Classes*. London: New Left Books.

Pratt, Mary Louise. 1989. *Women, Culture, and Politics in Latin America*. Berkeley: University of California Press.

Pratt, Minnie Bruce. 1984. Identity: Skin Blood Heart. In *Yours in Struggle: Three Feminist Perspectives on Anti-Semitism and Racism*, ed. Elly Bulkin, Minnie Bruce Pratt, and Barbara Smith, pp. 11–63. New York: Long Haul Press.

Pritchett, Frances W. 1995. The World of Amar Chitra Katha. In *Media and the*

Transformation of Religion in South Asia, ed. Lawrence A. Babb and Susan S. Wadley, pp. 76–106. Philadelphia: University of Pennsylvania Press.

Probyn, Elspeth. 1993. *Sexing the Self: Gendered Positions in Cultural Studies.* London: Routledge.

Punwani, Jyoti. 1989. The Portrayal of Women on Indian Television. In *Women in Indian Society,* ed. R. Ghadially, pp. 224–232. New Delhi: Sage.

R. G. K. 1990. The Nowness of the Mahabharata. *Times of India,* June 24, 1990, pp. 1, 3.

Radway, Janice. 1984. *Reading the Romance: Women, Patriarchy, and Popular Literature.* Chapel Hill: University of North Carolina Press.

———. 1988. Reception Study: Ethnography and the Problems of Dispersed Audiences and Nomadic Subjects. *Cultural Studies* 2(3):359–376.

Raheja, Gloria, and Ann Grodzins Gold. 1994. *Listen to the Heron's Words: Reimagining Gender and Kinship in North India.* Berkeley: University of California Press.

Rai, Amit S. 1995. India On-line: Electronic Bulletin Boards and the Construction of a Diasporic Hindu Identity. *Diaspora.* Spring 1995: 31–57.

Rajadyaksha, Ashish. 1990. Beaming Messages to the Nation. *Journal of Arts and Ideas* 19:21–32.

Rajagopal, Arvind. 1994. Ram Janmabhoomi, Consumer Identity and Image-Based Politics. *Economic and Political Weekly,* July 2, 1994, pp. 1659–1668.

———. Forthcoming. *Politics After Television: Religious Nationalism and the Retailing of "Hinduness."* Cambridge, U.K.: Cambridge University Press.

Rajan, Rajeshwari Sunder Rajan. 1994. Ameena: Gender, Crisis, and National Identity. *Oxford Literary Review* 16:147–176.

Ramanujan, A. K. 1974. Indian Poetics: An Overview. In *The Literatures of India: An Introduction,* ed. E. C. Dimock Jr. et al., pp. 115–118. Chicago: University of Chicago Press.

———. 1991. Three Hundred Ramayanas: Five Examples and Three Thoughts on Translation. In *Many Ramayanas: The Diversity of a Narrative Tradition in South Asia,* ed. Paula Richman, pp. 22–49. Berkeley: University of California Press.

Rao, Velcheru Narayana. 1991. A Ramayana of Their Own: Women's Oral Tradition in Telugu. In *Many Ramayanas: The Diversity of a Narrative Tradition in South Asia,* ed. Paula Richman, pp. 114–136. Berkeley: University of California Press.

Rapp, Rayna. 1992. Family and Class in Contemporary America: Notes toward an Understanding of Ideology (1978). In *Rethinking the Family: Some Feminist Questions,* ed. Barbie Thorne and Marilyn Yalom, pp. 49–70. Boston: Northeastern University Press.

Rich, Adrienne. 1986. Notes towards a Politics of Location. In *Blood, Bread, and Poetry.* New York: W. W. Norton.

Richman, Paula. 1991a. Introduction: The Diversity of the Ramayana Tradition. In *Many Ramayanas: The Diversity of a Narrative Tradition in South Asia,* ed. Paula Richman, pp. 3–21. Berkeley: University of California Press.

————. 1991b. E. V. Ramasami's Reading of the *Ramayana*. In *Many Ramayanas: The Diversity of a Narrative Tradition in South Asia*, ed. Paula Richman, pp. 175–201. Berkeley: University of California Press.

Rosaldo, Michelle Z. 1984. Towards an Anthropology of Self and Feeling. In *Culture Theory: Essays on Mind, Self, and Emotion*, ed. R. Shweder and R. LeVine, pp. 137–157. Cambridge: Cambridge University Press.

Rosaldo, Renato. 1989. *Culture and Truth: The Remaking of Social Analysis*. Boston: Beacon Press.

————. 1994. Whose Cultural Studies? *American Anthropologist* 96(3):524–529.

Rouse, Roger. 1991. Mexican Migration and the Social Space of Postmodernism. *Diaspora* 1(1):8–23.

Roy, Debal. 1992. *Women in Peasant Movements: Tebhaga, Naxalite, and After*. New Delhi: Manohar Publications.

Roy, Manisha. 1992. *Bengali Women*. 1972. Reprint, Chicago: University of Chicago Press.

Russell, John. 1991. Race and Reflexivity: The Black Other in Contemporary Japanese Mass Culture. *Cultural Anthropology* 6:3–25.

Sahgal, Priya. 1997. Teleblues. *Sunday*, February 23, 1997, pp. 30–31.

Said, Edward. 1978. *Orientalism*. New York: Pantheon Books.

Sandoval, Chela. 1990. Feminism and Racism: A Report on the 1981 National Woman's Studies Association Conference. In *Making Face, Making Soul*. San Francisco: Aunt Lute Foundation Books.

Sangari, Kumkum. 1990. Mirabai and the Spiritual Economy of Bhakti. *Economic and Political Weekly* 25:1465.

————. 1995. Politics of Diversity: Religious Communities and Multiple Patriarchies. *Economic and Political Weekly* 30(51–52):3287–3310, 3381–3389.

Sangari, Kumkum, and Sudesh Vaid. 1989. Recasting Women: An Introduction. In *Recasting Women: Essays in Colonial History*, ed. Kumkum Sangari and Sudesh Vaid, pp. 1–26. New Delhi: Kali for Women.

Sarkar, Sumit. 1997. *Writing Social History*. Delhi: Oxford University Press.

Sarkar, Tanika. 1989. Politics and Women in Bengal—the Conditions and Meaning of Participation. In *Women in Colonial India: Essays on Survival, Work and the State*, ed. J. Krishnamurty, pp. 231–241. Delhi: Oxford University Press.

Sarkar, Tanika, and Urvashi Butalia, eds. 1995. *Women and the Hindu Right: A Collection of Essays*. New Delhi: Kali for Women.

Scannell, Paddy. 1988. Radio Times: The Temporal Arrangement of Broadcasting in the Modern World. In *Television and Its Audience*, ed. P. Drummond and R. Paterson, pp. 15–31. London: British Film Institute.

Schechner, Richard, and Linda Hess. 1977. The Ramlila of Ramnagar. *Drama Review* 21(3):51–82.

Schiller, Herbert I. 1991. Not Yet the Post-imperialist Era. *Critical Studies in Mass Communication* 8:13–28.

Seiter, Ellen, Hans Borchers, Gabriele Kreutzner, and Eva-Maria Warth, eds. 1989. *Remote Control: Television, Audiences, and Cultural Power.* London: Routledge.

Sethi, Sunil. 1985. The Rajani Phenomenon. *India Today,* August 31, 1985, pp. 32–35.

Sethi, Sunil, and Sumit Mitra. 1985. Television Serials: Soap Opera Success. *India Today,* July 15, 1985.

Sen, Ilina, ed. 1990. *A Space within the Struggle.* New Delhi: Kali for Women.

Sherif, Shameem Akhtar. 1991. Krishna: To Chant or Not. *Times of India,* September 15, 1991, p. 18.

Shostak, Marjorie. 1981. *Nisa: The Life and Words of a !Kung Woman.* Cambridge: Harvard University Press.

Shulman, David. 1991. Fire and Flood: The Testing of Sita in Kampan's Iramavataram. In *Many Ramayanas: The Diversity of a Narrative Tradition in South Asia,* ed. Paula Richman, pp. 89–113. Berkeley: University of California Press.

Silverman, Kaja. 1983. *The Subject of Semiotics.* New York: Oxford University Press.

Simeon, Dilip. 1994. Tremors of Intent: Perceptions of the Nation and Community in Contemporary India. *Oxford Literary Review* 16:225–244.

Singh, Ramindar, and M. Rahman. 1988. Tamas: Communal Controversy. *India Today,* February 29, 1988, pp. 72–73.

Singhal, Arvind, and Everett M. Rogers. 1989. *India's Information Revolution.* New Delhi: Sage.

Skeggs, Beverley, ed. 1995. *Feminist Cultural Theory: Process and Production.* Manchester: Manchester University Press.

Smith, H. Daniel. 1995. Impact of "God Posters" on Hindus and Their Devotional Traditions. In *Media and the Transformation of Religion in South Asia,* ed. Lawrence A. Babb and Susan S. Wadley, pp. 24–50. Philadelphia: University of Pennsylvania Press.

Spiegel, Lynn. 1992. Installing the Television Set: Popular Discourses on Television and Domestic Space. In *Private Screenings: Television and the Female Consumer,* ed. Lynn Spiegel and Denise Mann, pp. 3–38. Minneapolis: University of Minnesota Press.

Spiegel, Lynn, and Denise Mann, eds. 1992. *Private Screenings: Television and the Female Consumer.* Minneapolis: University of Minnesota Press.

Spivak, Gayatri C. 1988. Can the Subaltern Speak? In *Marxism and the Interpretation of Culture,* ed. Cary Nelson and Lawrence Grossberg, pp. 271–313. Urbana: University of Illinois Press.

———. 1989. The Political Economy of Women as Seen by a Literary Critic. In *Coming to Terms,* ed. Elizabeth Weed, pp. 218–229. New York: Routledge.

Srinivasan, R. 1990. TV Leads Media March. *Times of India,* October 17, 1990.

Stacey, Judith. 1988. Can There Be a Feminist Ethnography? *Women's Studies International Forum* 11(1):21–27.

Steedman, Carolyn Kay. 1986. *Landscape for a Good Woman: A Story of Two Lives.* New Brunswick: Rutgers University Press.

Strathern, Marilyn. 1987a. Out of Context: The Persuasive Fictions of Anthropology. *Current Anthropology* 28(3):251–270.

———. 1987b. An Awkward Relationship: The Case of Feminism and Anthropology. *Signs* 12(2):276–92.

Stree Shakti Sanghatana. 1989. *"We Were Making History . . .": Life Stories of Women in the Telangana People's Struggle*. New Delhi: Kali.

Sunder Rajan, Rajeshwari, and Zakia Pathak. 1989. "Shahbano": The Social Text. *Signs* 14(3):558–582.

Swami, Praveen. 1994. Beating a Retreat: Why Doordarshan's New Channels Failed. *Frontline*, January 14, 1994, pp. 81–85.

Talwar, Veer Bharat. 1989. Feminist Consciousness in Women's Journals in Hindi: 1910–1920. In *Recasting Women: Essays in Colonial History*, ed. K. Sangari and S. Vaid, pp. 204–232. New Delhi: Kali for Women.

Tanter, Richard, and Kenneth Young. 1990. *The Politics of Middle Class Indonesia*. Clayton, Victoria, Australia: Monash University.

Taylor, Ella. 1989. *Prime-Time Families: Television Culture in Postwar America*. Berkeley: University of California Press.

Thapar, Romila. 1989. Imagined Religious Communities? Ancient History and the Modern Search for a Hindu Identity. *Modern Asian Studies* 23(2):209–231.

———. 1990. The Ramayana Syndrome. *India Magazine* 10:30–43.

Tharu, Susie, and K. Lalita. 1991a. Introduction to *Women Writing in India*. Vol. 1: *600 B.C. to the Early 20th Century*, pp. 1–38. Delhi: Oxford University Press.

———. 1991b. Literature of the Reform and Nationalist Movements. In *Women Writing in India*. Vol. 1: *600 B.C. to the Early 20th Century*, pp. 143–186. Delhi: Oxford University Press.

———. 1993. Introduction. In *Women Writing in India*. Vol. 2: *The Twentieth Century*, pp. 43–116. New York: Feminist Press.

Tharu, Susie, and Tejaswini Niranjana. 1996. Problems for a Contemporary Theory of Gender. In *Subaltern Studies IX*, ed. Shahid Amin and Dipesh Chakrabarty, pp. 232–260. Delhi: Oxford University Press.

Thomas, Rosie. 1985. Indian Cinema: Pleasures and Popularity. *Screen* 26(3–4):123–135.

Thornburn, D. 1976. Television Melodrama. In *Television as a Cultural Force*, ed. R. Adler and D. Cater, pp. 77–94. New York: Praeger.

Traube, Elizabeth G. 1989. Secrets of Success in Postmodern Society. *Cultural Anthropology* 4:273–300.

———. 1992. *Dreaming Identities: Class, Gender, and Generation in 1980s Hollywood Movies*. Boulder: Westview Press.

Trautmann, Thomas. 1981. *Dravidian Kinship*. Berkeley: University of California Press.

Trawick, Margaret. 1990. *Notes on Love in a Tamil Family*. Berkeley: University of California Press.

Trinh, Minh-ha. 1989. *Woman, Native, Other: Writing Postcoloniality and Feminism.* Bloomington: Indiana University Press.

Tripathi, Salil. 1988. Tamas: Fresh Target. *India Today,* February 15, 1988, p. 23.

Uberoi, Patricia. 1995. *A Suitable Romance? Trajectories of Courtship in Indian Popular Fiction.* Paper presented at the International Institute for Asian Studies, Leiden, November 6–8, 1995.

van der Veer, Peter. 1994. *Religious Nationalism: Hindus and Muslims in India.* Berkeley: University of California Press.

Vasudevan, Ravi. 1989. The Melodramatic Mode and the Commercial Hindi Cinema. *Screen* 30(3):29–50.

———. 1990. Indian Commercial Cinema. *Screen* 31(4):446–453.

———. 1991. The Cultural Space of a Film Narrative: Interpreting "Kismet" (Bombay Talkies, 1943). *Indian Economic and Social History Review* 28(2):171–185.

———. 1993. Shifting Codes, Dissolving Identities: The Hindu Social Film of the 1950's as Popular Culture. *Journal of Arts and Ideas* 23–24:51–84.

Vatuk, Sylvia. 1975. Gifts and Affines. *Contributions to Indian Sociology* 5:155–196.

Visweswaran, Kamala. 1990. Family Subjects: An Ethnography of the "Woman Question" in Indian Nationalism. Ph.D. diss., Stanford University.

———. 1994. *Fictions of Feminist Ethnography.* Minneapolis: University of Minnesota Press.

Wadley, Susan, ed. 1980. *The Powers of Tamil Women.* Syracuse: Syracuse University Press.

Weiner, Annette. 1995. Culture and Our Discontents. *American Anthropologist* 97:14–21.

West, Cornel. 1987. Minority Discourse and the Pitfalls of Canon Formation. *Yale Journal of Criticism* 1(1):193–201.

White, Hayden. 1973. *Metahistory.* Baltimore: Johns Hopkins University Press.

Williams, Raymond. 1974. *Television: Technology and Cultural Form.* New York: Schocken Books.

———. 1977. *Marxism and Literature.* Oxford: Oxford University Press.

Williamson, Judith. 1986. The Problems of Being Popular. *New Socialist,* September 1986, pp. 14–15.

Xavier, Claramma. 1992. Advertisements and Women. *Indian Express,* May 31, 1992.

Yanagisako, Sylvia Junko. 1984. Explicating Residence: A Cultural Analysis of Changing Households among Japanese-Americans. In *Households: Comparative and Historical Studies of the Domestic Group,* ed. Robert McNetting, pp. 330–352. Berkeley: University of California Press.

Yanagisako, Sylvia, and Jane Collier. 1987. Toward a Unified Analysis of Gender and Kinship. In *Gender and Kinship: Essays toward a Unified Analysis,* ed. Jane Collier and Sylvia Yanagisako, pp. 14–50. Stanford: Stanford University Press.

Yanagisako, Sylvia, and Carol Delaney, eds. 1995. *Naturalizing Power: Essays in Feminist Cultural Analysis.* New York: Routledge.

Index

Abu-Lughod, Lila, 29, 35, 284–85

Advani, L. K., 2, 179, 354

Advertising, 368 n.52; budgets, 81–82; children and, 85; consumerism and, 81–82, 90; dowry and, 87, 99–100; Indian Womanhood and, 89–90; linking of modernity to Western technology and, 85; modernity and, 85, 90, 93; multinational capital and, 80–82; objectification of female body and, 90–91; products in, 83–84; revenues from, 340–41; segmentation by class and, 92; women and, 85, 90–91, 93. *See also* Commercial sponsorship; Consumerism; Globalization: niche marketing and

Agrawal, Purushottam, 167, 171, 176, 198–99, 204, 220

Alarcón, Norma, 17

All India Radio: Doordarshan and, 55; state control of, 64–65, 354

Allison, Anne, 357, 364 n.3

Anand, Chetan, 263–65, 281–83

Anderson, Benedict, 287–88

Ang, Ien, 361 n.20, 363 n.52

Anticolonialism. *See* Colonialism

Appadurai, Arjun, 93, 392 n.12, 393 nn. 18, 19, 20

Audience. *See* Television audience

Babri Mosque: role in Hindu-Muslim conflict, 2, 179. *See also* Bharatiya Janata Party (BJP): Ram temple and; Hindu nationalism: Ayodhya temple and

Battaglia, Debbora, 331

BBC (British Broadcasting Corporation), 64–65, 336, 339, 354–55

Benjamin, Walter, 331

Bhaav (emotion), 24–26, 28, 189, 203; Rasa and, 262 n.32, 388 n.6

Bhakti (devotion). *See* Ramayan: bhakti and

Bharatiya Janata Party (BJP): *Ramayan* and, 180; Ram temple and, 2, 179. *See also* Advani, L. K., Communalism

Bharatiya Naari: colonial and anti-colonial discourses and, 8; Indian Womanhood and, 8; nationalism and, 8

Bhargava, Rajeev, 197, 199

Bharucha, Rustom, 167, 199, 220

Buniyaad: daughters-in-law and, 126, 128; female characters in, 111–13; Partition and, 112; sexuality and, 117, 128

Butalia, Urvashi, 313–14, 326, 390 nn. 15 and 18, 391 n.26

Caste: conflicts and, 1–4; intersection of class and, 2–3, 79; intersection of class and religion and, 8; lower castes and upward mobility, 2–3, 21, 95; Mandal Commission Bill and,

Caste (*continued*)
1, 37; *Ramayan* and, 178, 202, 205–7; support of Hindu nationalism and, 3; upper-caste bias of media, 2; upper-caste parents' groups, 4; upper-caste protests, 1–2, 4. *See also* Indian women: caste and

Chakravarti, Uma, 204, 330, 386 n.27

Channel V: Hindi programming on, 347. *See also* Transnational satellite television

Chatterjee, Partha, 9, 104, 108, 136, 156–57, 221, 361 n.19

Chhachhi, Amrita, 218

Chopra, B. R., 228, 235–38

Choudhry, Kavita, 153; constraints of mass media and, 138; Doordarshan and, 139; political action and, 142–43; *Udaan* and, 137–48

Citizenship: construction of, 5. *See also* Development: modern citizenship and; Indian women: citizen-mothers and

Class: consciousness through television, 46, 79; divisions, 13–14; gender and, 113; and Hindu nationalism, 78; intersection of caste and, 2–3, 79; interstitial positions and, 114; and *Ramayan*, 191, 201–3; and subjectivity, 39; upper class, 77; upward mobility and, 54, 96, 110, 113–14, 369 n.76. *See also* Consumerism: upward mobility and; Doordarshan: working-class women and; Dowry: lower middle class and; Indian nationalism: middle class and; Lower middle class; Middle class; Television: expansion and; Transnational satellite television: class and

CNN (Cable News Network), 339, 355; Gulf War and, 336. *See also* Doordarshan: alliance with CNN

Collier, Jane, 46, 101

Colonialism: and anticolonial discourse, 179–80, 185; anticolonialism and, 130. See also *Bharatiya Naari*: colonial and anticolonial discourses and; Partition: colonial state and

Color television, 46, 53, 60

Commercial sponsorship, 69, 342; consumerism and, 80–82. *See also* Advertising

Communalism, 359 n.2; nationalism and, 3, 10, 297; and Partition, 291; and secularism, 197–99, 218–19. *See also* Indian state: religion and; *Ramayan*: communalism and; Religious identity: transnational satellite television and; *Tamas*: communalism and

Consumerism: desires and, 6; and Doordarshan, 74–75; imagination and, 352; and Indian women, 89, 92–94, 370 n.3; Maggi Noodles and, 80–81, 86; and middle class, 9, 53, 98; production of meaning and, 93; upward mobility and, 49, 88, 97–99. *See also* Advertising; Commercial sponsorship; Fantasy: consumerism and; Liberalization: consumerism and; Modernity: consumerism and; Postcoloniality: consumerism and; Transnational satellite television: consumerism and

Culture: culture wars and, 11, 19, 165–66, 337, 350, 360 n.7; Hindu nationalism and, 165–66; mass culture versus, 167, 223; national culture and, 165–66; transnational media and, 336–37, 350, 353. *See also* Ethnography; Globalization: production of local and; Modernity: tradition and; *Ramayan*: demonization of cultural others and; Transnational satellite television: fears about cultural invasion and; reterritorialization of culture and

Daniel, E. Valentine, 16, 363 n.39, 385 n.4
Darshan (visual engagement with the sacred). See *Ramayan:* darshan and
Das, Veena, 219, 222, 313–14, 384 n.77
Daughters-in-law, 125–29; and Indian family, 127, 132. See also *Buniyaad:* daughters-in-law in; *Yugantar:* daughters-in-law in
Development, 5, 55; Indian women and, 58; modern citizenship and, 48, 59; postcoloniality and, 48; social justice and, 59. *See also* Doordarshan: National Programme and; Transnational circuits: discourses of development and
Doordarshan: alliance with CNN, 348; anthropological analysis of, 5; Asian Games on, 56; Bombay film industry and, 73–74, 347–48, 366 n.35; censorship and, 66, 282; consumerism and, 74–75; Doordarshan Software Committee report and, 153; education and, 54–55, 57–58; entertainment on, 6–7, 70, 360 n.9; foreign entertainment and, 70; history of, 54–56; Indian nationalism and, 5, 7, 255, 350; Metro Channel and, 340–41, 343, 347–48, 393 n.16; middle class, targeting of, 9, 77, 114, 371 n.10; national news and, 61, 66, 354; National Programme and, 5, 60–61, 66–67, 165, 173; New Indian Woman and, 107, 148–49, 152–59, 371 n.9; North Indian bias of, 62–64, 173; perpetuation of regional stereotypes on, 62–63; political and cultural significance of, 5; Star TV and, 336; state

control of, 60–61, 139, 354; Tamil programming on, 61, 351; telefilms and, 347; and transnational satellite television, 336, 339–41; "vernacular" channels and, 61, 351; violence and, 317; women viewers, targeting of, 89, 106, 114; women's programming and, 7, 58, 104; working-class women and, 77. *See also* Advertising; Commercial sponsorship; Doordarshan serials; Dowry: Doordarshan and; Gandhi, Indira: Joshi Working Group on Software and; Indian state: communication policies and; deregulation and
Doordarshan serials: *Adhikaar,* 113; *Amar Desh,* 160, family planning and, 71; *Humraahi,* 113, *Khandaan,* 77; *Pukaar,* 113; religious epics and, 165, 167, 174, 222–23, 299, 375 n.6; *Stri,* 113; *Swayamsiddha,* 143, 155; *The Sword of Tipu Sultan,* 7, 27, 66, 161; themes of, 27, 71–72, 74, 77. See *also Bharatiya Naari; Buniyaad; Hum Log; Mahabharat; Param Veer Chakra; Rajani; Ramayan; Tamas; Udaan; Yugantar*
Dowry, 248; daughters and, 53–54, 100; Doordarshan and, 91, 99–100, 125–26; feminist activism and, 372 n.24; lower-middle class and, 125; middle class and, 53; murder and, 45, 372 n.22; Muslims and, 45, 87. *See also* Advertising: dowry and; Liberalization: dowry and

Ethnography, 20–21; conjunctural ethnography and, 39, 49–50, 102–3; cultural studies and, 5, 168; feminist ethnography and, 23, 30–31, 328–30; fieldwork at "home" and, 3, 30–32, 34–35, 329–30; insider/outsider bi-

Ethnography (*continued*)
nary and, 37–38; mass media and,
5, 168, 102, 253; methodology and,
38–39, 102–3, 167–68; as mode of
theorizing, 39; native anthropologists and, 32; participant observation
and, 20; positionality and, 31, 35,
333; silences and, 325, 328–30, 332;
strategic intervention of, 24, 225,
256; television viewers and, 168–69;
violence and, 330–33. *See also* Doordarshan: anthropological analysis
of

Family: audience as, 54, 74; feminist
scholarship on, 46, 101; relationship with nation, 74. *See also* Indian
family; Viewing practices: family and
Fantasy: advertisements and, 88; consumerism and, 352; desire and, 364
n.3, 369 n.66; experience and, 11;
pleasure and, 24. *See also* Transnational satellite television serials:
fantasy and
Feminist ethnography. *See* Ethnography
Ferguson, James, 47, 52, 101, 342

Gandhi, Indira: assassination of, 45,
324; economic growth of India and,
75; Independence Day Address and,
56; Joshi Working Group on Software and, 65. *See also* Television:
expansion of
Gandhi, Mahatma: anticolonial discourse of, 185; assassination of,
178; Draupadi's disrobing and, 251;
secularism and, 298; *Tamas* and,
293; on women's roles in Gandhian
nationalism, 108–9, 156, 180
Gandhi, Rajiv, 45–46, 185–86, 227, 327;
"uplift" of women and, 106. *See also*
Television: expansion of

Gender: and Hindu nationalism, 166,
359 n.3; and Indian family, 104; and
Indian nationalism, 107–9, 250–
52; and middle-classness, 113–16;
and militaristic nationalism, 267–
68, 287–88; and *Param Veer Chakra*,
260, 267, 284, 288; and popular
culture, 18; and postcoloniality, 104;
in *Ramayan*, 166, 207–10, 219; in
Tamas, 315. *See also* *Buniyaad*: female
characters in; Doordarshan: women's
programming and; *Hum Log*: female
characters in; Indian women; *Mahabharat*: Indian Womanhood and;
women's rage and; women's vulnerability and; Mass media: feminist
analysis and; *Rajani*: Indian Womanhood and; Transnational satellite
television serials; *Udaan*: Indian
Womanhood and; romance and
Ghosh, Amitav, 113–14, 326
Ghosh, Bhaskar, 295
Gill, S. S., 59–60, 71–72, 344
Gillespie, Marie, 382 n.60, 384 n.79,
385 n.3
Global political economy, 9; Doordarshan and, 49, 69, 75, 80, 82,
101; and global capital, 337–38, 342,
345, 348–49; transnational public
sphere and, 342. *See also* Advertising;
Globalization: niche marketing and;
Liberalization; Local: critiques of
Globalization: global capital and, 337–
38, 342, 345, 348–49; NBC and,
346; niche marketing and, 346, 392
n.15; production of local and, 345–
50, 392 n.12. *See also* Channel V;
Doordarshan: Metro Channel and;
"vernacular" channels and; Murdoch,
Rupert; Star TV: Hindi programming
on; Transnational satellite television:
globalization and; reterritorialization

of culture and; Transnational satellite television serials; Zee TV

Gold, Ann, 371 n.16, 372 nn. 21, 25, 26, and 27, 373 n.28, 381 n.56, 388 nn. 10, 11, and 17

Goswami, Rajiv: attempted suicide of, 1–2

Gramsci, Antonio, 19. *See also* Hegemony

Gupta, Akhil, 47–48, 52, 101, 342

Hall, Stuart, 17; negotiated reading and, 253–54; popular culture and, 29, 223; postcoloniality and, 104

Hegemony, 3, 19; containment of critique and, 107, 143, 148; counter narratives and, 256; Hindu nationalism and, 166; Indian state and, 60–61, 66, 105–07, 155, 162; inherent instability of, 19, 225, 255; interpretive agency of subjects and, 22–24, 29; national past and, 184–85; pan-Indian national narratives and, 67; resistance and, 20, 102; ruptures and fissures within, 225, 255, 281; women's issues and, 139. *See also* Indian women: Indian Womanhood and; Viewing practices: negotiated readings and

Hindi films. *See* Indian films

Hindu-Muslim conflict, 16, 220; Babri Mosque and, 2–4, 165, 179, 297–98, 354. *See also* Hindu nationalism; *Ramayan:* Hindu-Muslim conflict and; *Tamas:* Hindu-Muslim conflict and

Hindu nationalism, 375 n.4; anticolonialism and, 179–80; Ayodhya temple and, 2–4, 165, 179, 198, 297–98, 354; civil society and, 165; class and, 178; gender and, 166, 359 n.3; Hinduism and, 174–78; Indian state and, 161;

modernity and, 167; resurgence of, 165, 179–80, 298; role of "culture" in, 176–77, 179, 181, 182; secularism and, 218–21, 380 n.48; sexuality and, 166; slippage between Indian nationalism and, 161–62, 165, 174, 179–82, 184–86, 221, 247, 249; violence and, 168, 219, 256. *See also* Indian women: Hinduism and; *Mahabharat:* Hindu nationalism and; *Ramayan; Tamas:* religious identity and

Hum Log, 154–55; family and, 110; female characters in, 111; patriarchy and, 111, 118; sexuality and, 118, structure of, 72, 110; success of, 72, 366 n.34. *See also* Indian women: emancipation of

Identity. *See* Indian national identity

Indian family, 364 n.1; age and, 52; daughters and, 122–25; daughters-in-law and, 127, 132; gender and, 104; household position and, 52; marriage and, 133–35; modernity and, 49; mothers-in-law and, 132; nationalism and, 104–5, 157, 159–61, 275–77; political construction of, 101; television serial characters and, 79; and threats of Westernization, 156, 158; transnational contexts and, 101; women and, 118–19. See also *Buniyaad;* Doordarshan serials: family planning and; *Hum Log:* family and; Indian nationalism; *Rajani:* working women and; Sexuality: daughters and

Indian film: bhaav and, 25; *Chayageet,* 348; *Chitrahaar,* 59, 348; film music and, 348; *Hum Log* and, 72; mythological films, 375 n.6; representational techniques of, 189, 201, 210–11, 229, 232, 285; *Superhit*

Indian film (*continued*)
Muqabla, 348. *See also* Doordarshan:
Bombay film industry and; *Ma-
habharat:* televisual techniques of;
Ramayan: televisual techniques of;
Transnational satellite television:
Indian film and
Indian national identity: construction
of, 177; Doordarshan's role in reconstructing, 5, 7, 255, 350; national
culture and, 165–66; nationalism of
Indian women, 107, 161; relationship
of the *Mahabharat* to national integration, 237–39; role of mass media
in constructing, 222–23, 350. *See also*
Hindu nationalism; Indian nationalism; Modernity: nationalism and;
Ramayan: exclusionary narratives
and; Religious identity
Indian nationalism: Doordarshan's
role in reconstructing, 5, 7, 255, 350;
family and, 104; gender and, 107–9,
250–52; Hindu nationalism versus,
229; Indian women and, 107, 161,
315; middle class and, 9–10; motherland and, 180; national integration
and, 66, 174; national sovereignty
and, 55–56, 69–70, 336, 341–42;
postcolonialism and, 104, 156, 380
n.46; relationship of *Mahabharat* to
national integration, 237–39; and
religious identity, 174; shift from
liberation to consolidation and, 252.
See also Communalism: nationalism and; Doordarshan: New Indian
Woman and; Militaristic nationalism; *Tamas:* birth of the nation and;
national integration and; Transnational satellite television: reconstitution of Indian nationhood and;
threats to Indian nation and
Indian Space Research Organization, 55

Indian state, 370 n.4; caste and, 359
n.1; communication policies and,
65; deregulation and, 343; development of modern state, 48, 57–59;
and Doordarshan's National Programme, 5, 60–61, 66–67, 139, 165,
173, 354; and Hindu nationalism, 161;
and national integration, 66, 174;
policing of affect and, 281–83; Prasar
Bharat Act, 344, 392 n.11; religion
and, 225; repression by, 10, 65; safety
and, 329–30; secessionist movements and, 284; and secularism,
66, 298–99; violence and, 261, 284.
See also All India Radio: state control of; Hegemony: Indian state and;
Militaristic nationalism; *Param Veer
Chakra; Ramayan:* state legitimacy
and; Supreme Court of India; *Tamas;*
Transnational satellite television:
Indian state and
Indian Womanhood. *See* Indian women
Indian women: agency of, 28, 143, 148,
150–151, 153, 252; caste and, 111, 157;
as citizen-mothers, 161; citizenship
and, 146–49; consumerism and, 89,
92–94; containment of, 235, 249;
daughters-in-law, 125–29; domestic
violence and, 129, 152; Doordarshan
targeting of, 104–6, 114; duty and,
212–14; emancipation of, 154; and
the family, 118–19, 122–28; 275–77;
formal education and, 130–31, 135–
37; Hinduism and, 161, 166, 249;
Indian Womanhood and, 39, 104,
139, 156, 161–62, 214, 252, 316, 356–
58; labor of, 96, 126–27; legal rights
of, 113; marriage and, 34; media representations of, 19; mythologizing
of, 315; and National Perspective
Plan for Women, 106; national unity
and, 161; nationalism and, 107; and

Partition, 311–14, 389 n.4; and Self Employed Women's Association, 106; sexual harassment of, 144, 386 n.25; sexuality of, 117, 128, 217–18, 229, 243; tolerance and, 246–47; tradition and, 9, 132, 251; "uplift" of, 130–31; violence against, 256, 387 n.30; vulnerability of, 128–29, 144, 236, 241–44, 310; work and, 122. *See also* Advertising: objectification of female body and; women and; *Bharatiya Naari:* Indian Womanhood and; *Buniyaad;* Class: gender and; Gandhi, Mahatma: on women's roles; Gandhi, Rajiv: on "uplift" of women; *Mahabharat:* Indian Womanhood and; women's rage and; Militaristic nationalism: women; New Indian Woman; *Ramayan:* gender and; sexuality and; women's reactions to; *Tamas:* sexual violence and; Transnational satellite television; Transnational satellite television serials: new content of; *Udaan; Yugantar*
Interpellation: Althusser and, 17; discursive chains and, 360 n.14

Kakar, Sudhir, 210
Kishwar, Madhu, 109
Kondo, Dorinne, 30, 39

Laissez-faire capitalism, 8
Liberalization: consumerism and, 48, 60; dowry and, 99. *See also* Television: liberalization and
Limón, José, 30–31
Lloyd, David, 338, 358
Local: critiques of, 47; translocal and, 47, 50, 101, 103. *See also* Transnational satellite television: "local" cultural production and
Lowe, Lisa, 338, 358

Lower middle class: daughters and, 118–22; sexuality and, 118. *See also* Dowry: lower middle class and
Lutz, Catherine, 284–85

Mahabharat: compared with *Ramayan,* 185–86, 226–27; creators' interpretations of, 235–36, 252; disrobing of Draupadi and, 128, 227–35, 255–56; Hinduism and, 224; Hindu nationalism and, 224–26, 249, 256; Indian Womanhood and, 224–25, 235–36, 246, 248–52; interpretations of, 239–44, 254–56; Muslims and, 378 n.32; national integration and, 237–39; popularity of, 224; quest for power and, 227; sexuality and, 128, 229, 243; Sikhs and, 383 n.73; structure and theme of, 228–35; televisual techniques of, 228; war and, 238; women's rage and, 224, 237, 244–49, 251; women's vulnerability and, 236, 241–44. *See also* Doordarshan serials: religious epics and; Gandhi, Mahatma: Draupadi's disrobing and; Hall, Stuart: negotiated readings and; Nationalist poetry; Viewing practices: modes of viewing and; semiotics and
Mandal Commission Bill, 1–4, 36–37, 179, 359 n.1
Mani, Lata, 107
Marriage. *See* Indian women: marriage and
Martin, Biddy, 31, 37
Masculinity: Aryan Hindu past and, 205–7; in *Param Veer Chakra,* 259–60, 266–67, 284–85. *See also* Militaristic nationalism: courage and; *Ramayan:* gender and
Mass media: feminist analysis and, 222–23; national identity and, 222–

Mass media (*continued*)
23, 350; NGOs and, 350. *See also*
Ethnography: mass media and
Masud, Iqbal, 56, 59, 113, 143, 390 n.11
Memory. See *Tamas:* memory and
Middle class: children and, 124; consolidation of, 361 n.18; construction
of, 9, 367 n.40; consumerism and,
9, 53, 98; daughters and, 117–25;
Doordarshan targeting of, 9, 77, 114,
371 n.10; dowry and, 53; expansion
of, 9, 75–76, 360 n.16; gender and,
113–14; heterogeneity of, 9, 13–15, 361
n.18, 367 n.40, 368 n.45; sexuality
and, 99, 118; struggle to be, 9–10,
79, 94–97, 114, 116; tradition and,
10; urban middle classes, 6; versus
upper classes, 79; women's bodies
and, 113. *See also* Caste: lower castes
and upward mobility; Class; Consumerism: upward mobility and;
Liberalization; Transnational satellite
television: middle class and
Militaristic nationalism: Amar Jawaan
Jyoti (Flame of Unknown Soldier)
and, 262; courage and, 273–74;
family and, 275–77; homoeroticism
and, 268; motherland and, 279–81,
285, 389 n.21; Operation Bluestar
and, 273–74, 287; patriotism and,
275, 284; Republic Day Parade and,
262; women and, 267–68, 287–88.
See also Indian state: secessionist
movements and; *Param Veer Chakra*
Modernity: consumerism and, 48; desires for, 47, 365 n.6; gender and,
8; genealogies of, 220; modernization and, 46, 57, 365 n.15, 380
n.46; multiple temporalities of, 222;
nationalism and, 5, 47–48; Nehru's
vision of, 57; new forms of social

governance and, 137; and postcoloniality, 47, 48, 380 n.46; progress and,
57; and *Ramayan,* 167, 219–22; religion and, 299; science and, 57–58;
secularism and, 166–67; television
and, 60, 365 n.6; telos of, 48, 59;
tradition and, 86, 91–92, 111, 132,
167, 222; transnational discourses of,
54; transnational satellite television
and, 353. *See also* Advertising: linking
of modernity to Western technology
and; modernity and; Doordarshan:
education and; National Programme
and; New Indian Woman and; Hindu
nationalism: modernity and; Indian
women: tradition and; *Udaan:* family
and
Modernization. *See* Modernity
Modleski, Tania, 362 n.34, 363 n.52
Mohanty, Chandra, 31, 37
Morley, David, 47, 337, 345–46
Motherland. *See* Militaristic nationalism: motherland and; Postcoloniality: discourses of motherland
and
MTV, 347, 392 n.14
Murdoch, Rupert, 345–46
Music. *See* Indian film: film music
and; *Param Veer Chakra:* music and;
Ramayan: music and; Transnational
satellite television: music and
Music Television. *See* MTV

Nandy, Ashish, 197–98, 218–19, 386
n.19
Narayan, Kirin, 32, 35
National identity. *See* Indian national
identity
National integration. *See* Indian nation-
alism
Nationalism: subjectivity and, 7, 161–

62, 251–52, 266, 288. *See also* Indian national identity; Indian nationalism; Hindu nationalism

National Perspective Plan for Women. *See* Indian women

Nehru, Jawaharlal: secularism and, 298; vision of modernity and, 57

New Delhi: national city and, 12–13; Old Delhi and, 12–13; volatile atmosphere in, 16; women's vulnerability and, 243–44

New Indian Woman: Doordarshan and, 107, 148–49, 152–59, 371 n.9; post-coloniality and, 137, 152, 159, 371 n.9; *Rajani* and, 152; and *Udaan*, 118, 137–40, 142–43, 146–48. *See also* Indian women

Nietzsche, Friedrich, 320, 332

Nihalani, Govind, 290, 297, 320–21

Ninan, Sevanti, 338, 341, 343, 348, 352

Niranjana, Tejaswini, 18

Non-Government Organizations (NGOs). *See* Mass Media: NGOs and

Pandey, Gyanendra, 305, 309, 322, 359 n.2

Param Veer Chakra: discipline and, 260, 266–67; gender and, 260, 267, 284, 288; heterosexual desire and, 260, 284–85; Indian air force and, 282–83; Indian films and, 263–64, 269–70, 285; Indian womanhood and, 260; masculinity and, 266–67; melodrama and, 263–64, 284–85; militaristic nationalism and, 259–60, 266–68, 284–88; motherhood and, 277–81; music and, 264–65, 285; nationalist affect and, 260, 264, 287–88; popularity of, 260; responses to, 261–62, 270–77, 285–88; sexuality and, 268–75, 388 n.10;

Sikhs and, 261; structure and themes of, 260–65, 284; violence and, 260, 284, 288. *See also* Doordarshan: censorship and

Partition: and *Buniyaad*, 112; communalism and, 291; loss of life during, 294; nationhood and, 297; silences and, 325–26; suicide and, 311–14; and *Tamas*, 289–91, 294, 300–301, 324; violence and, 2, 389 n.1; women and, 314–15, 389 n.4. *See also* Violence: ordinary people and

Patel, Sujata, 106, 109

Popular culture, 18, 167; feminist analysis of, 168, 196, 223; gender and, 18; site of struggle, 11, 28–29. *See also* Hall, Stuart

Postcoloniality: birth of postcolonial nation and, 290; citizen-subjects and, 105, 156; consumerism and, 48; development and, 48; discourses of motherland and, 281; gender and, 104; Indian state and, 49, 380 n.46; modernity and, 47–48, 220–22, 365 n.15, 380 n.46; nationalism and, 104, 156, 380 n.46; New Indian Woman and, 137, 149, 152, 159, 371 n.9; popular narratives and, 19. *See also* Hall, Stuart: postcoloniality and; Indian women: Indian womanhood and; Transnational satellite television

Radway, Janice, 29

Raheja, Gloria, 371 n.16, 372 nn. 21, 25, 26, 27, 373 n.28, 381 n.56, 388 nn. 10, 11, and 17

Rajagopal, Arvind, 221–22, 393 n.23

Rajani, 111; Indian Womanhood and, 118, 149; New Indian Woman and, 152; working women and, 77, 119

Ramayan: bhakti (devotion) and, 168,

Ramayan: (continued)
196, 199–204, 381 n.56, 382 n.57;
class and, 191, 201–3; communalism
and, 165, 177, 220–21; critiques of,
165–66, 187; darshan (visual engagement with the sacred) and, 200, 203,
370 n.1; demonization of cultural
others and, 171, 175–77, 204, 218;
depiction of divinity in, 192–93; exclusionary narratives and, 166–69,
171, 196, 199, 217; feminist analysis
of, 167, 174, 219; gender and, 166,
207–10, 219; Hindu-Muslim conflict
and, 165; Hindu nationalism and,
165, 175–77, 186, 196, 217; Hinduism and, 172, 174–75, 186; Hindutva
and, 177–78; imagined Hindu community and, 167, 170; *Mahabharat*
and, 185–86, 226–27; modernity
and, 167, 218–22; music and, 172,
189–92; Muslims and, 169, 182–84,
216; north Indian bias and, 171–73;
popularity of, 165, 169, 171, 188–89,
374 n.2; Ram's treatment of Sita and,
170, 194, 216–17; *Ramcharitmanas*
and, 172, 190, 200; regional interpretations of, 172–74; secularism and,
196–99; sexuality and, 166, 208–
110, 211–12, 217–19; Sikh's and, 169,
214–16; south Indian responses to,
173–74; state legitimacy and, 171,
186, 205; televisual techniques of,
168, 189–93, 195; women's reactions
to, 174, 195, 210–17. *See also* Bhaav
(emotion); Bharatiya Janata Party
(BJP): *Ramayan* and; Caste: *Ramayan*
and; Doordarshan serials: religious
epics and; Masculinity: Aryan Hindu
past and
Rao, Velcheru Narayana, 216–17
Rashtriya Swayamsevak Sangh (RSS),
176, 178, 295, 296, 301, 315

Religion. *See* Religious identity
Religious identity: national integration and, 174; secularism and, 299;
television and, 174; transnational
satellite television and, 353. *See also*
Communalism; Doordarshan serials:
religious epics and
Robins, Kevin, 337, 345–46

Sahni, Bhisham, 191, 290–91, 297–99,
305, 311–13, 321–22
Sampradayikta Virodhi Andolan (SVA),
197–98
Sangari, Kumkum, 383 n.66, 384 n.78
Sarabhai, Vikram, 55
Satellite Instructional Television Experiment, 55
Satellite Television for the Asian Region. *See* Star TV
Secularism: communalism and, 197–
99, 218–19; ethics and, 199; and
Mahatma Gandhi, 298; and Hindu
nationalism, 218–21, 380 n.48,
Indian state and, 69, 298–99; and
modernity, 166–67; and Nehru, 298;
and religious identity, 299. See also
Ramayan: critiques of; secularism
and; Religious identity: secularism
and; *Tamas:* secularism and
Sexuality: daughters and, 117–22; and
Hindu nationalism, 166; of Indian
women, 117, 128, 217–18, 229, 243;
policing of desire and, 268; and violence and, 256; vulnerability of women
and, 114. See also *Buniyaad:* sexuality
and; *Hum log:* sexuality and; *Mahabharat:* sexuality and; Militaristic
nationalism: homoeroticism and;
Param Veer Chakra: heterosexual
desire and; sexuality and; *Ramayan:*
sexuality and; *Udaan:* sexuality and
Singh, V. P., prime minister of India, 27

Spectatorship. *See* Bhaav; Darshan; Ethnography: television viewers and; Hall, Stuart: negotiated readings and; *Mahabharat:* interpretations of; *Ramayan:* bahkti and; class and; critiques of; *Tamas:* protests against; support for; Television audience; Viewing practices

Spigel, Lynn, 365 n.8

Star TV: Ratikant Basu and, 347; Hindi programming on, 346–47, 356; launch of, 338–39. *See also* Doordarshan: Star TV and; Murdoch, Rupert; Zee TV: Star TV and

State. *See* Indian state

Stree Shakti Sanghatana, 314–15

Subjectivity, 5, 16–18, 22–23, 38–39; class and, 39; construction of, 17, 352; contradictory bases of, 35, 288; Indian Womanhood and, 39; non-unitary subjectivity, 39. *See also* Hegemony: interpretive agency of subjects and; Indian nationalism: national integration and; Nationalism; Religious identity: national integration and

Supreme Court of India, 319, 343, 392 n.9

Talk shows: *Aap ki Adalat*, 355; *Chakravyuh*, 355; games shows and, 340; *Janata ki Adalat*, 355; news shows and, 355; *Rubaroo*, 355; *Shakti*, 340; *The Shotgun Show*, 355

Tamas: birth of the nation and, 309, 315, 322; colonial state and, 300, 302–3, 322, 332; common people and, 304–6, 308–9, 332; communalism and, 291, 295, 313, 319, 321; contemporary politics and, 321, 333; feminist historiography and, 314; gender and, 315; Hindu-Muslim conflict and, 295–97; Indian Womanhood and, 316; memory and, 322–28, 330–33, 391 n.26; national integration and, 319–21; Partition and, 289–91, 294, 300–301, 324; protests against, 295, 317–22; recasting the past and, 330, 332–33; religion versus rationality in, 313; religious identity and, 322; secularism and, 298, 320; semiotic codes and, 317–18; sexual violence and, 309–14; Sikhs and, 292, 313, 324–25, 327; silences and, 323–26, 328; structure and themes of, 290–94, 296–97, 300–309; subject of, 323; support for, 322; women's agency and, 314–17; women's vulnerability and, 310. *See also* Ethnography: silences and; Indian women: mythologizing of; Gandhi, Mahatma. *Tamas* and; Partition; Violence: ordinary people and; sexuality and

Television: access in India, 6; dowry and, 53; expansion of, 55–60, 77, 82, 391 n.7; family and, 78–79; liberalization and, 221; modernity and, 48, 55, 57; social relations and, 78–80. *See also* Color television; Commercial sponsorship: consumerism and; Doordarshan; Religious identity: television and

Television audience: comparison with audience of U.S. soap operas, 7; ethnography of, 168–69; location in fields of power, 47, 50, 54, 360 n.13; pleasure and, 37–38, 77; and Star TV, 339–40, 347; and Zee TV, 339–40, 349. *See also* Bhaav; Hall, Stuart: negotiated readings and; *Mahabharat:* interpretations of; *Param Veer Chakra:* responses to; *Ramayan:* class and; critiques of; Subjectivity: construction of; *Tamas:* protests against;

Television audience (*continued*)
support for; Viewing practices
Television serials. *See* Doordarshan
serials; Transnational satellite television serials
Transnational circuits: cultural flows
and, 49; discourses of development
and, 70–72; fields of power and, 101;
Hindu nationalism and, 375 n.4;
information flows and, 55, 69–70.
See also Modernity: transnational
discourses of
Transnational satellite television:
changes in political discourse and,
354–55; class and, 339; consumerism and, 352–53; Doordarshan and,
336, 339–41; ESPN and, 343; expansion of, 336, 338–40; fears about
cultural invasion and, 336; globalization and, 337; Indian film and, 347;
Indian state and, 336, 342–45; Indian
Womanhood and, 356–58; Indianization of programming and, 347;
"local" cultural production and, 337;
middle class and, 352–53; modernity
and, 353; music and, 348; niche marketing and, 346; reconstitution of
Indian nationhood and, 350–51; "regional" networks and, 351; religious
identities and, 353; reterritorialization of culture and, 342, 345–51,
393 n.18; threats to Indian nation
and, 336; transnational capital and,
344, 348–49. *See also* Advertising:
revenues from; Doordarshan; Globalization; Indian state: deregulation
and; Westernization; Zee TV
Transnational satellite television serials, 340; fantasy and, 356–57; gender
and, 356–57; new content of, 356–58.
See also Consumerism: desires and;
imagination and

Udaan: activism and, 138–40, 143,
146–47; citizen-subjects in, 147–49;
family and, 140–41; feminist critique
of, 139, 141–42; Indian Womanhood
and, 118, 148–49; notions of Indian
culture and, 140; romance and, 145;
sexuality and, 120–21, 144; upbringing of daughters and, 140; working
women and, 119. *See also* Choudhry,
Kavita; Hegemony: containment of
critique and
UNESCO: social education in India and,
58

Video newsmagazines, 354
Viewing practices: discursive spaces
and, 125; family and, 50–53, 74, 101;
interpretations and, 8, 196; modes
of viewing, 223–25; narratives of, 8;
negotiated readings and, 254; pleasure and, 11, 77–79, 80, 146, 188,
262; semiotics and, 225, 285–86,
288, 318; viewers as critics and, 23,
26–29, 102, 168, 357. *See also* Hegemony: interpretive agency of subjects
and; *Mahabharat:* interpretations
of; *Ramayan:* class and; critiques of;
Spectatorship
Violence: anti-Sikh, 326–28; and communalism, 165–67, 219, 305, 326–
27; and Hindu nationalism, 168, 219,
256; and Indian women, 129, 152,
256, 387 n.30; ordinary people and,
306–9; sexuality and, 256. *See also*
Doordarshan: violence and; Ethnography: violence and; *Param Veer
Chakra:* violence and; Partition: suicide and; violence and; *Tamas:* sexual
violence and
Visweswaran, Kamala, 32, 35, 363 nn.
38, 51, 369 n.78, 374 n.49, 386 n.27,
391 n.28

West, Cornel, 32

Westernization: Indianization and, 93; threats to Indian family and, 156, 158

Williams, Raymond, 19, 254–55

Women. *See* Indian women

Yanagisako, Sylvia, 364 n.1

Yugantar: daughters-in-law and, 126, 135; education of women and, 130–37

Zee TV: advertising revenues and, 341; class and, 339; diasporic audiences and, 348–49; Indian audiences and, 339–40; news programming and, 355; South Asian channel and, 339–40; Star TV and, 349; transnational satellite television and, 336, 339. *See also* Advertising: revenues from; Transnational satellite television

Purnima Mankekar is Assistant Professor of Anthropology
at Stanford University.

Library of Congress Cataloging-in-Publication Data
Mankekar, Purnima
Screening culture, viewing politics : an ethnography of
television, womanhood, and nation in postcolonial India /
Purnima Mankekar.
p.   cm.
ISBN 0-8223-2357-5 (cloth : alk. paper). — ISBN 0-8223-2390-7
(pbk. : alk. paper)
I. Television broadcasting—Social aspects—India.   2. Television
programs—India.   3. Television in community development—
India.   4. Television and women—India.   5. Television in
politics—India.
HE8700.9.I5M36   1999
302.23'45'0954—dc21   99-21159   CIP